PATROLLING THE BORDER

EARLY
AMERICAN
PLACES

Early American Places is a collaborative project of the
University of Georgia Press, New York University Press,
Northern Illinois University Press, and the University of
Nebraska Press. The series is supported by the Andrew
W. Mellon Foundation. For more information, please visit
www.earlyamericanplaces.org.

Patrolling the Border

Theft and Violence on the Creek-Georgia Frontier, 1770–1796

JOSHUA S. HAYNES

The University of Georgia Press

ATHENS

Paperback edition, 2021
© 2018 by the University of Georgia Press
Athens, Georgia 30602
www.ugapress.org

Most University of Georgia Press titles are
available from popular e-book vendors.

Printed digitally

The Library of Congress has cataloged the
hardcover edition of this book as follows:
Names: Haynes, Joshua S., author.
Title: Patrolling the border : theft and violence on the
Creek-Georgia frontier, 1770–1796 / Joshua S. Haynes.
Description: Athens : The University of Georgia Press, 2018. |
Series: Early American places | Includes bibliographical
references and index.
Identifiers: LCCN 2017042882 | ISBN 9780820353166 (hardcover) |
ISBN 9780820353173 (ebook)
Subjects: LCSH: Creek Indians—History—18th century. |
Creek Nation—Boundaries. | Oconee River (Ga.) |
Georgia—History—Colonial period, ca. 1600–1775. |
Georgia—History—1775–1865.
Classification: LCC E99.C9 H39 2018 | DDC 975.8004/97385—dc23
LC record available at https://lccn.loc.gov/2017042882

Paperback ISBN 978-0-8203-6174-1

For Janice and Terry

Contents

     Them Away": State Control, 1793–1796   178

     Epilogue: "All the Apprehensions of Savage Ferocity"   201

     Notes   209

     Bibliography   271

     Index   287

ILLUSTRATIONS

Acknowledgments

This book would have been impossible without the mentorship, support, patience, and friendship of so many people that it would be impossible to thank them all here. First and foremost, however, I would like to thank Claudio Saunt, whose keen insights and disciplined approach to the historian's craft have helped me navigate a long and winding path. Like Claudio, Jace Weaver, John Inscoe, and Stephen Mihm each read multiple drafts of the project in its earliest stages. Several colleagues and friends generously volunteered to read subsequent versions and provided valuable feedback, including Kathi Nehls, Drew Cayton, and Kyle Zelner. I especially wish to thank Robbie Ethridge for her unflagging support since my earliest attempts at scholarship. She and a second, anonymous reader unwound the manuscript and helped me see it more clearly. Walter Biggins at the University of Georgia Press has been patient and supportive. I hope the book is worthy of the time they invested, and, of course, the errors that remain are mine alone.

Several organizations have supported the project over the years. While a struggling Ph.D. candidate, I received a Summer Doctoral Research Fellowship from the University of Georgia's Graduate School, a research grant from the UGA Department of History's Amanda and Greg Gregory Graduate Studies Enhancement Fund, and a travel grant from UGA's Institute of Native American Studies. A grant from the American Philosophical Society Phillips Fund for Native American Research funded additional research that became the bedrock of the initial chapters. As a junior faculty member at the University of Southern Mississippi, I received an Aubrey Keith Lucas and Ella Ginn Lucas Endowment for Faculty Excellence Award that supported final research and the preparation of the book's several maps.

Finally, I wish to thank my parents, Janice and Terry Haynes. Love and gratitude, always.

Patrolling the Border

Introduction

In March 1822, Creek Depredations Claims Commissioner James P. Preston wrote the following lines to Secretary of War John C. Calhoun from his office in Athens, Georgia: "The period under consideration [1786–90], undoubtedly, was one of great suffering and privation to the border settler on the frontier adjoining the territory of the Creeks, whose frequent irruptions into the white settlements, appear to have been marked with an uncommon degree of ferocity."[1] Americans broadly shared and often repeated Preston's assessment of Creek Indian relations with Georgia in the late eighteenth century. By contrast, Creek leader Alexander McGillivray described a particular violent incident in 1786 in milder terms: "Only six persons lost their lives on the part of the Georgians, and these fell victims to their own temerity." McGillivray likely captured most Creeks' perspective on Creek-Georgia relations when he wrote that "this affair, which their iniquitous proceedings had drawn upon them, has been held forth by the Georgians as the most violent unprovoked outrage that was ever committed."[2] In 1789, Secretary of War Henry Knox reported to President George Washington that "the State of Georgia is engaged in a serious war with the Creeks."[3] Matters grew more grave over the ensuing decades until one Georgia settler despaired in 1812: "May it please your Honor if we don't get some assistance we shall have to move off of this frontier or our familys will be kiled and skulpt by the Indians. We are too weak to Stand in our own defence."[4] Almost a century later, Georgians held Creeks in their historical memory as "by far the most numerous, powerful and warlike of all the Indian tribes in North America, and their name had gotten during the Revolutionary war, to strike terror around every hearthstone in Georgia."[5] In what early Georgia historians called the "Oconee War," Creeks waged "irregular, desultory . . . savage warfare" inspired by their "supreme chief," Alexander McGillivray, who was "especially animated by hatred of Georgia."[6]

In the late eighteenth century, Georgia's colonial encroachment pressured Creeks to manage their borders more actively. Creeks found that stemming the tide of Georgia settlers was a difficult task under their indigenous political system based on local autonomy and a system of leadership that privileged older, elite leaders yet encouraged younger men to achieve status through warfare. Border conflicts contributed to energetic debates among both Creeks and Anglo-Americans over what kind of government best suited the people. Creeks and Georgians alike favored local power, yet resolving border conflict required more centralized management of land and people. Georgia's expansion forced Creeks into a conversation about the very nature of political leadership that resulted in a remarkable period of innovation, compromise, and coalescence.

Creeks met the colonial threat by experimenting with several leadership strategies that infringed on local autonomy. Teams of town leaders conducted diplomacy. Skilled figurehead executives claimed centralized authority based on kinship ties and status achieved through war, diplomacy, and trade. Most importantly, common Creek men conducted nearly a thousand raids best understood as border patrols.

Despite experiments with centralized action, Creek people remained committed to the autonomy of each *talwa*, social units comprising a town and its associated villages, or *talofa*.[7] As intrusions from Georgia became more severe, the diverse people of Creek country reluctantly accepted that, to remain independent, they must restrict men's freedom to raid. They did so, however, in ways that emphasized talwa autonomy. They accommodated structural conflict between older leaders whose status derived from kinship and success in war and diplomacy, younger Creeks who aspired to high status through similar achievements, and a new generation of elites whose status rested on wealth accumulation.

White Georgians focused on the occasional violence of border patrols to craft a lasting political narrative that exaggerated Creek ferocity. This justified Georgia's overwhelming violence against Creeks and punitive land taking. Georgia's militias frequently transgressed Creek boundaries. Each intrusion provoked a response until Georgians' rhetoric about

Creek ferocity became a self-fulfilling prophecy. Georgians' actions also challenged federal authority over Indian affairs, ultimately leading to U.S. intervention.[8] For these reasons, Creek border patrols determined the course of Creek-Georgia relations and shaped fundamental debates over the structure of government in both Creek country and the United States.

Late eighteenth-century Creeks constituted a coalescent society in which independent talwas and their talofas were the core units of political, social, and spiritual life.[9] Most Creeks foregrounded local interests in their relations with Georgia. The autonomy of Creek talwas derived from the preceding two hundred years of coalescence during which people from several different cultures and language groups banded together. European contact shattered Mississippian chiefdoms in the sixteenth and seventeenth centuries with cycles of violence, epidemic disease, disruption of subsistence practices, and a devastating trade in Indian slaves. Many refugees from shattered Mississippian chiefdoms migrated to present-day central Alabama and southwest Georgia where they built towns near those of local populations. These new provinces became the heart of Creek country. Towns valued their distinctiveness and competed for standing with one another, yet they coalesced into a large, multilingual society capable of cooperating on matters of mutual concern. By the 1770s, Muskogees were the largest group in a Creek confederacy that also included Alabamas, Apalaches, Chickasaws, Choctaws, Hitchitis, Koasatis, Natchez, Shawnees, Tunicas, Yamasees, Yuchis, and others. The Muskogee language predominated, but residents of Creek country also spoke Koasati, Alabama, Yuchi, Shawnee, and several other indigenous, European, and likely African languages.[10]

Within this large, diverse Creek polity, talwa members labored to retain their distinctiveness in political processes, spiritual practices, and material culture while cooperating and competing with other towns and provinces.[11] Anthropologist John R. Swanton declared almost a century ago that each talwa should be considered "a little state."[12] Subsequent scholars have agreed that each talwa was "institutionally complete," with all the human and material resources needed to sustain itself and provide its members fulfilling lives.[13]

Creeks changed their leadership systems throughout the eighteenth century to better manage their borders, yet they drew on precontact, Mississippian concepts including the importance of warfare.[14] Late eighteenth-century Creek talwas typically possessed an all-male town council led by mature civil and diplomatic leaders known as *miccos*.

Miccos were assisted by a contingent of subordinate political, military, and religious officers. Together, they conducted internal and external affairs. Scholars have struggled to reconstruct eighteenth-century southeastern Indian leadership systems by carefully evaluating documentary evidence, the archaeological record, and the work of early twentieth-century anthropologists. In addition to miccos, they have identified several other Creek leadership titles. Many of the men who attempted to control Creek border patrols in the late eighteenth century claimed such titles. Alexander McGillivray took the title *isti atcagagi thlucco*, or great beloved man. Translators likely rendered literally the war title *tustanagee thlucco*, or great warrior, when they introduced the Head Warrior of Cussita and the Big Warrior of Cussita. The Second Man of Little Tallassee also went by Neothlocko, or *heneha thlucco*, a vice chief and peace advocate who presides over other town elders and advisors.[15] Scholars suggest a moiety system may have underpinned such leadership positions. Dual organization divided Creek towns and provinces into war/red and white/peace moieties from which people selected peace and war leaders. Such a moiety system may have been developed to integrate diverse peoples into the coalescent society in the late seventeenth century. As a social mechanism, it may have maintained a ranked check-and-balance system between older towns designated *Hathagalgi*, white, and newer towns designated *Tchilokogalgi*, red. "Tchilokogalgi" can also be translated as "speakers of a different language," and the more pejorative term "stinkard" often was used to indicate the lower status of newer, non-Muskogee speaking communities.[16] Late seventeenth-century Creek dual organization, however, is still poorly understood, and by the late eighteenth century, moieties appear to have played little if any role in southeastern Indian leadership. Men's rankings, particularly war titles, by contrast, retained their resonance.[17]

In the late eighteenth century, success in warfare remained as critical to a Creek man's identity and prospects as it had been for hereditary, pre-contact Mississippian elites. Across the Mississippian world, members of high-ranking lineages competed fiercely for control of chiefdoms, and success in warfare was crucial to continued leadership. In the postcontact period, hereditary hierarchies collapsed, but competition between older miccos and ambitious young men became a customary feature of eighteenth-century politics among Creeks and other Deep South coalescent societies. Young men needed war honors to prosper, and patrolling Creek borders provided an opportunity to secure them. With a distinguished military career, a man gained war titles, influence in town councils, and perhaps could eclipse older miccos eventually. By the end of the eighteenth century, access to Euro-American manufactured goods was another critical component of influence. Such access typically required strategic alliances with traders or colonial agents, or, for young men, success in hunting and raiding. Some scholars interpret this generational conflict and the eager pursuit of rank as evidence of enduring dual organization. Tension between youth and age perhaps mirrors that between red/war and white/peace moieties. Even so, older men typically dominated town councils, arriving at consensus among themselves and informing young men of their decisions.[18]

Town councils took precedence over individual miccos and distinguished warriors in eighteenth-century talwa government, and some talwas outranked others in the larger Creek polity. More importantly, both town councils and miccos lacked the power to enforce decisions. Archaeological evidence suggests that some Mississippian chiefdoms also had possessed councils, though their relationship to chiefly power remains unclear.[19] Also like their Mississippian forebears, eighteenth-century Creek leaders occasionally claimed the right to speak for multiple towns, especially leaders from older, Muskogee talwas. Several refugee groups joined Muskogees during the late seventeenth and early eighteenth centuries, but Swanton argued that "each talwa remained virtually self-governing" after joining the "federated body."[20] He even suggested that the word "talwa" itself "rather covers the English concept 'tribe.'"[21] In the late eighteenth century, U.S. Indian agent Benjamin Hawkins used the terms "tribe" and "town" interchangeably when describing Creeks.[22] Later arrivals in Creek country such as Yuchis and Shawnees appear to have been forced into subordinate positions. Dominant towns required newcomers to seek permission before settling and to defer to their leadership in the coalescent society's politics.[23] For most of the eighteenth century, there was no larger, national government with authority over towns and their residents, though the major provinces and the broader confederacy held multitown councils with increasing frequency.[24] In recent years, a growing chorus of scholars has called for closer attention to the independent towns, villages, and regional divisions that comprised eighteenth-century coalescent societies, rather than focusing on larger, ill-defined associations such as tribes, nations, or confederacies. This book contributes to that conversation by analyzing the ways conflict in a particular early American place influenced life in the talwas.[25]

Like political decision-making, Creek social and spiritual life also revolved around the talwa, its public square ground, and the sacred fire at its center. Even religious observances simultaneously asserted talwa autonomy and provided a site for cooperation and competition between towns. The most important event on the Creek religious calendar was the annual busk, or *poskita*, a purification and world-renewal ritual that bound talwa members together. The busk could last several days and included renewing human relationships by forgiving all transgressions short of murder and physical renewal through the purging of old possessions. The fundamental rite of spiritual, social, and material renewal was the extinguishment and rekindling of a sacred fire at the center of the square ground. Each household took embers from the sacred fire for a new hearth fire. Dominant towns occasionally invited allied towns to share in their poskita celebrations while excluding others, illustrating the capacity to build community yet assert primacy. The talwa's role as political, social, and spiritual center accounts for the remarkable durability of Creek dedication to talwa autonomy.[26]

Matrilineal clan membership was another critical element of Creek identity that occasionally motivated border patrols and complicated both internal politics and Creek-Georgia relations. Matrilineal clan membership and exogamous marriage practices helped foster a broader Creek identity that could transcend barriers between talwas, provinces, and speakers of different languages. Clan-based justice derived from Creek religious beliefs and served as the basis of domestic law. Usually referred to as the law of crying blood or blood revenge, clan-based justice required balance. If a person suffered death or injury, that person's clan kin were responsible for restoring cosmic balance by causing an equivalent death or injury, though material compensation could substitute in some cases. Clan-based justice emphasized restoring balance over punishing offenders, so the particular individual responsible for an offense need not be the target of a crying blood killing. When applied to homicides committed by non-Creeks, the larger polity demanded compensation from the offending polity, though the victim's close clan kin from his/her talwa likely led the chorus demanding satisfaction. Creeks decided at the talwa level whether to participate in taking satisfaction through violence. In the late eighteenth century, conflicts between Creeks and Georgians resulting from border raids often went unresolved because justice based on crying blood clashed with Euro-American notions of warfare, crime, and the punishment of guilty individuals.[27]

White Americans' assessments of Creek ferocity in late eighteenth-century border conflicts disregarded Creek territorial rights, as well as their motives and methods of border management. A systematic analysis

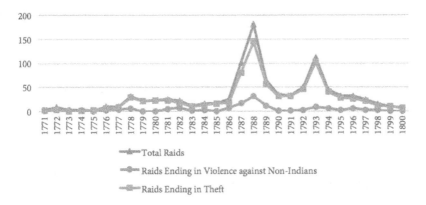

FIGURE 1. Creek Raids in Georgia, 1770–1800

of claims submitted by white Georgians reveals that late eighteenth-century Creek raiders were far more interested in divesting white settlers of their property than in depriving them of their scalps. Georgians attributed to Creeks almost a thousand raids between 1770 and 1800, yet just over 150 of them resulted in bloodshed. Brief spikes of violence followed controversial land cession treaties, especially in 1788 and 1793. In the last three decades of the century, Creeks allegedly killed at least 275 people out of a total non-Indian population of 83,000. During the same period, however, Georgians killed 108 Creeks, and probably many more not documented, out of a total Creek population of just over 17,000.[28] Proportionally, then, Creeks suffered greater loss.

While such bloodshed could be devastating for all involved, the pattern of Creek raiding reveals more than violence. Almost 75 percent of raids resulted in horse theft. Mapping Creek raids illustrates that 76 percent of them (746 of 977) took place in the Oconee strip, a long swath of land between the Oconee and Ogeechee Rivers stretching some 150 miles, roughly from present-day Athens to Vidalia, Georgia. For much of the period, the Oconee River was the contested border between Creek country and Georgia.[29] The frequency of theft, the dearth of violence, the geographical focus, and the timing of raids show that what Georgians remembered as savage warfare is much better understood as property confiscation by border patrols asserting Creek sovereignty and territoriality.

These border patrols drew on precontact ideas and a long history of experience with colonizers, yet their consequences were unpredictable.

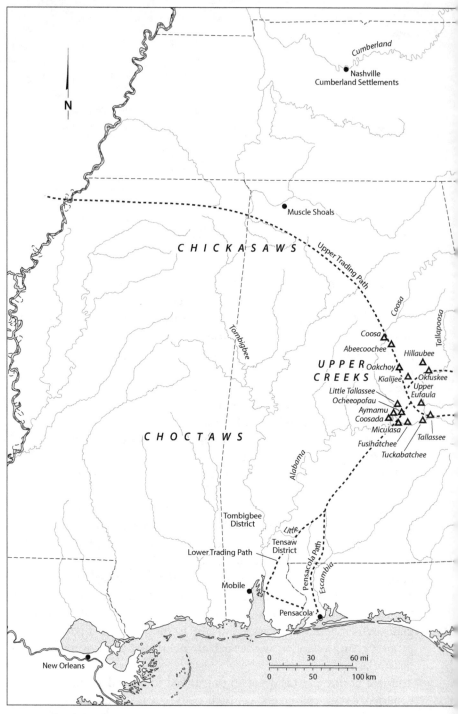

MAP 1. Creek Raids in Georgia, 1770–1800

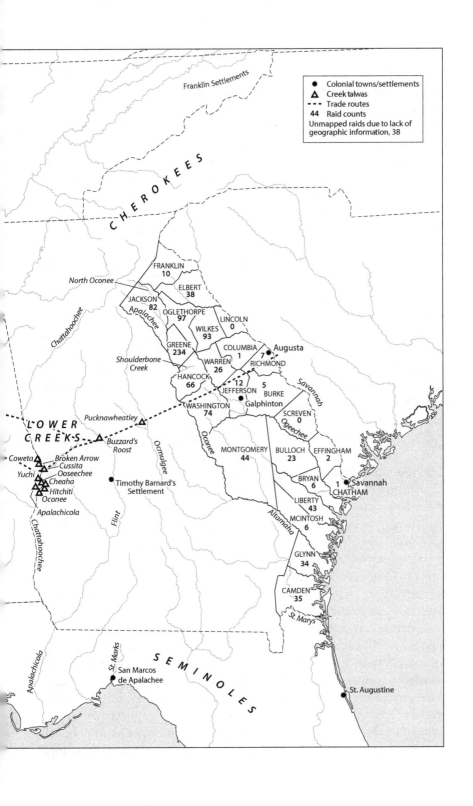

Franklin Settlements

- Colonial towns/settlements
△ Creek talwas
--- Trade routes
44 Raid counts
Unmapped raids due to lack of
geographic information, 38

CHEROKEES

FRANKLIN
10

North Oconee

ELBERT
38

JACKSON
82

Apalachee

OGLETHORPE
97

LINCOLN
0

WILKES
93

GREENE
234

Shoulderbone
Creek

COLUMBIA
1

Augusta

WARREN
26

RICHMOND

HANCOCK
66

JEFFERSON
12

5

BURKE

Savannah

Pucknawheatley

WASHINGTON
74

Galphinton

SCREVEN
0

Ogeechee

LOWER
CREEKS

Buzzard's
Roost

Ocmulgee

MONTGOMERY
44

BULLOCH
23

EFFINGHAM
2

Coweta

Broken Arrow
Cussita
Ooseechee
Cheaha
Hitchiti
Oconee

Yuchi

Timothy Barnard's
Settlement

Flint

Oconee

BRYAN
6

1

CHATHAM

Savannah

Apalachicola

LIBERTY
43

Chattahoochee

Altamaha

MCINTOSH
6

GLYNN
34

CAMDEN
35

St. Marys

SEMINOLES

St. Marks

San Marcos
de Apalachee

Apalachicola

St. Augustine

Late eighteenth-century southeastern Indians considered theft raids a substitute for warfare from which young men could gain rank by testing their spiritual power. By the end of the century, Choctaw war titles included words for horses and cattle, and during the Redstick War, Creek warriors took cow tails and painted them red, treating them in the same manner as enemy scalps.[30] When border patrols confiscated or destroyed squatters' property, their actions sometimes pushed white leaders to negotiate less onerous treaty terms and urge settlers to respect Native boundaries. Just as often, however, Creek raids provided backcountry Georgians with a political narrative they used to justify horrendous violence.[31]

Border patrols became a central political issue in late eighteenth-century Creek country. Creeks used them to assert their sovereignty within a bounded territory, yet border raiding exacerbated deep tensions in Creek society. Border patrols harnessed a popular spirit of unity in defense of sovereignty and territory, but the stress of fighting for survival sharpened internal divisions.[32] A new generation of elites who enjoyed unequal access to wealth and power attempted to control border raiding. They drew their power not from inherited status and a prestige goods economy as their Mississippian forebears had done, but from accumulated wealth, literacy, and numeracy. They envisioned a Creek Nation with a powerful, central government and an economy based on commercial ranching and slave-based agriculture. In one sense, these new elites resembled their Mississippian ancestors: they strove to institutionalize inequality and secure high status for their lineages. Indeed, several of the new, late eighteenth-century elites, most prominently Alexander McGillivray, were born into high-status, Muskogee-speaking families. Mississippian-style hereditary, chiefly power had disappeared, but a new generation appeared eager to re-create hegemonic leadership in altered form. If Creeks committed to centralized leadership could command border raiders, that control would buttress their authority and allow them to shape treaties with Georgia and the United States.[33]

Assertions of centralized leadership over a unified Creek polity threatened both talwa autonomy and the livelihoods of common hunters. An economy founded on the deerskin trade and reciprocal exchange had afforded nonelites social mobility for much of the eighteenth century. For many young men, the freedom to raid the border expressed their preference for talwa autonomy and territorial sovereignty. As a substitute for warfare, border raiding furnished opportunities to rise in political and social rank, and, importantly, improve one's economic standing.

While young men's border raiding was in keeping with customary generational tension in Creek society, it also challenged elite assertions of exclusive leadership in a unified polity.[34] By the turn of the nineteenth century, despite pressure to accept centralized leadership with monopoly control of theft and violence, most Creek people remained devoted to talwa autonomy.[35]

Paradoxically, Creek border patrols represented both deep continuity with Mississippian ideas and two and a half centuries of political innovation in a colonized space. In the late eighteenth century, Creeks used Mississippian forms of diplomacy they had adapted to colonial politics. Leading miccos managed reciprocal exchange relationships first with Spanish, British, and French colonies, and later with the State of Georgia, premised on mutual recognition of territorial boundaries. Between 1717 and 1763, Creeks honed a policy of neutrality, so-called play-off diplomacy, that kept the three competing colonial powers in the Deep South at bay. In the 1760s, autonomous talwas briefly asserted nationhood in defense of Creek borders. In the years following the Seven Years' War, Creeks sought a new foreign policy because they found themselves encircled by British colonies without the diplomatic counterweights of Spain and France. In the 1770s, they began constructing a new policy based on negotiated boundaries, border patrols, and greater coalescence.[36]

After the Treaty of Paris ended the Seven Years' War, Great Britain expanded its presence in the Deep South and tightened management of its colonies with a raft of new policies, many of which were meant to prevent conflict between Native Americans and colonials. Creeks recognized that firm borders between themselves, Georgia, and the newly British colonies of East and West Florida were critical to their independence. After 1773, Creeks understood that maintaining boundaries would require frequent diplomacy and possibly more forceful action. The Oconee River valley was the most important piece of real estate in the region. Creek country's Lower Towns, some twenty-five talwas clustered in the lower Chattahoochee River valley, asserted superior claim to the Oconee lands as vital hunting grounds. Georgians considered the region fertile farm and ranch land essential to the colony's growth. Moreover, the Lower Towns and several Upper Towns prized the trading path that crossed Oconee lands to connect them to Augusta, Georgia, and Charles Town, South Carolina, as their essential commercial artery. By 1783, some Creeks accepted the Oconee River as a sensible, natural boundary and worked to reorient trade to the Gulf Coast. Others insisted on retaining hunting rights to the Oconee's east bank. Still others rejected the Oconee boundary entirely, insisting that Georgians must confine themselves to lands behind the Ogeechee River, some thirty miles east of the Oconee. Different Creek leaders worked to create stable, majority factions—if not national consensus—on border issues. Such factions typically reflected the basic geographic distribution of the Creek population into Lower Towns on the Chattahoochee River and Upper Towns along the Coosa-Tallapoosa-Alabama Rivers. However, towns from one region occasionally allied with towns from another based on converging economic and political interests. For their part, white Georgians routinely hunted, grazed their cattle, settled, and farmed both sides of the Oconee River while denying Creek hunting rights on the east bank. In the waning decades of the eighteenth century, the conflict over the Oconee boundary became increasingly bitter between Creeks themselves, as well as between Creeks and Georgians.[37]

Creek warriors' geographical focus on the Oconee River boundary is central to characterizing their raids as an experimental vehicle for asserting sovereignty and territoriality. If late eighteenth-century raids represented only random violence or opportunistic theft by cavalier young men seeking status and profit, such raids could have focused on other settlements such as Pensacola, Mobile, the Tensaw district north of Mobile Bay, the Cumberland settlements around present-day Nashville, Tennessee, or the plantation district between the Altamaha and St. Marys Rivers on the Georgia–East Florida border. Pensacola, Mobile, and Tensaw especially were geographically closer to most Creek towns and could be reached over easier paths or by boat.[38] While some Creek warriors raided these locales, they were infrequent events compared with the hundreds of raids that struck the Oconee valley. Raids focused on the Oconee because Creeks generally agreed that Georgia posed the greatest threat to their sovereignty.

Historians have illuminated much about early American history in the Deep South, including the political transformations of southeastern Indian groups broadly and Creek-Georgia relations specifically.[39] For much of the last three decades, ethnohistorians studying early America have focused on the themes of Native American agency, negotiation, and the potentially positive outcomes of diplomatic relations between groups of people who lacked the military might to dominate one another.[40] Such scholarship on eighteenth-century relations between colonizers and Native Americans often portrays an initial period of productive negotiation and trade that inevitably degenerates into violence.

In particular, some of the best scholarship on the Creek-Georgia frontier suggests that prior to the 1750s, Creeks and colonists cocreated a land of opportunity, but by the 1780s violence defined Creek-Georgia relations, careening inexorably into the Redstick War in 1813. Creeks and Georgians certainly clashed along the border in the late eighteenth century, but such clashes represented more than the collapse of a carefully negotiated frontier exchange economy into wanton violence, and their repercussions were more than merely prelude to the Redstick War. As others have argued, border tension resulted in armed conflict along the Oconee River, a Creek-Spanish alliance influenced Creek policy, the strife exposed corrosive inequality in Creek society, and the conflict invited U.S. government intervention.[41]

A key element of this boundary dispute has been overlooked. Historians have acknowledged Creek raiding, yet they have resisted characterizing it as the deliberate policy of a coalescing, indigenous nation. Creeks could and did act in concert when their interests aligned, yet they continued to prefer local autonomy. Border raiders frequently are presented as the retainers of individual leaders, most often Alexander McGillivray, or merely as aimless youths. On the contrary, most Creek raiders acted in accord with consensus in their talwas to defend Creek country's borders. When they acted outside consensus, they risked reprisal from members of their clans, towns, and provinces. Their actions illuminate the kinds of innovative political actions that indigenous peoples contrived in their struggle to protect the larger polity's independence while pursuing local interests. Creeks need not have seen themselves as a unified nation with a centralized government and identical economic interests in order to agree that white Georgians were a threat.

Historians generally agree that colonial states pressured Native American societies to transform themselves in the late 1700s, and they have identified several factors driving Creek-Georgia relations: factionalism, generational tension, talwa autonomy, nativistic religious renewal, dependence on European manufactured goods amid a flagging deerskin trade, and the disruptive influence of Creeks devoted to property accumulation, many of whom possessed mixed ancestry.[42] Border patrols reflected and amplified these trends. They constituted a defense of Creek hunting lands—the people's most valuable political, material, and spiritual resource. They drew on long-standing practices like talwa autonomy, admiration for young men's reckless courage, the religious duty to balance deaths, and a conception of the Oconee strip's spiritual value.[43] Border patrols attracted men who shared a broad political vision of territorial integrity and political sovereignty yet agreed on little else.

While border patrols briefly harnessed a spirit of unity among Creek people to communicate sovereignty and territoriality to outsiders, the message Georgians received was quite different.[44] Georgians denied Creek rights by criminalizing resistance to white encroachment. Georgians' depicted raids as unprovoked ferocity to justify relentless, overwhelming violence and land taking. Indeed, one early historian described the Georgians' Oconee River valley settlements of the 1780s as "semi-military colonies."[45] He intended to portray them as defensive, but from the Creek perspective, they constituted an invasion. Georgians' narrative about Indian savagery and their desire to appropriate Indian lands precluded any acknowledgment of Creek rights to defend their borders.

As I examine the late eighteenth-century border conflict between Creeks and Georgia, I use the terms "Indian," "Native American," "indigenous," and "Native" interchangeably, in keeping with prevailing trends in scholarly literature and journalism. In keeping with those same trends, I use more specific national, ethnic, talwa, and clan identifiers whenever possible. I use "Muskogee" to refer to the dominant linguistic group in Creek country, but I avoid using it as a general term to refer to all Creeks. I use the terms "white" and "Indian" because, by the 1770s, both Natives and non-Natives used them frequently. I use "Anglo-American" or "British" to refer to white, English-speaking people and the broader "Euro-American" to include colonizers associated with other European nations. As always, I use more specific identifiers whenever possible. The terms "state," "nation," "confederacy," and "tribe," are of European origin, and, while scholars struggle to define, historicize, and apply them to Native polities in meaningful ways, many ethnohistorians now avoid the term "tribe" altogether. This book is in part an attempt to understand the long, messy political and social process of coalescence in Creek country that defies tidy labels.[46]

In the broadest sense, this book offers a model of relations between Natives and newcomers in the eighteenth century that avoids both romanticizing peaceful negotiation and exaggerating violence. It illuminates debates over localism versus nationalism in both Creek country and the United States. Scholarship foregrounding the roles of negotiation and violence has obscured the methods and motivations of Native warriors. Their raids constituted a measured political response to colonialism. Far from being chaotic, unprovoked warfare, border patrols functioned as a talwa-sanctioned institution founded on the principle of local autonomy. Patrollers sought to impose order by ejecting outsiders and confiscating their property. The preponderance of theft and the paucity of violence suggest that Georgians inflated the Creek threat to justify the expropriation of resources. Such rhetoric led to U.S. government intervention and Creek political innovation, yet, throughout the period, most Creeks persisted in their allegiance to talwa autonomy. Viewing border patrols as legitimate, talwa-sanctioned political action allows for a more nuanced understanding of colonial relations and political change in Native towns.

1 / "The Whole Nation in Common": Native Rights and Border Defense, 1770–1773

By 1770, the people historians refer to as Muskogees, Creeks, the Creek Confederacy, or the Creek Nation comprised a multilingual, coalescent society whose constituents had been cooperating, competing, migrating, and mixing for more than two centuries. Eighteenth-century Creeks descended from the precontact Mississippian chiefdoms of present-day Georgia, Alabama, Florida, and Tennessee. The diverse peoples of Creek country shared much owing to their common Mississippian origins, and such diversity underlain by commonality became a source of both strength and tension in the late eighteenth century.

In 1770, Creek country comprised seventeen thousand people living in sixty to eighty towns, or talwas, and their related villages. Some of the more prominent towns boasted more than a thousand residents, but most were smaller. By the early 1770s, many prominent towns were shedding population as residents separated into satellite villages to accommodate ranching and slave-based agriculture. The towns divided into five provinces, four of which clustered near present-day Montgomery, Alabama. The Coosa-Tallapoosa-Alabama River confluence region around Montgomery was home to the Tallapoosa, Alabama, Abika, and Okfuskee provinces. Over time, they became known as the Upper Creeks or Upper Towns. The fifth province, Apalachicola, clustered near present-day Columbus, Georgia, in the Chattahoochee River valley. This cluster became known as the Lower Towns or Lower Creeks. Each province emerged from a similar cycle of Mississippian chiefdom rise, collapse, migration, and coalescence over the course of the thirteenth through the seventeenth centuries.[1] Differences between the talwas and provinces endured through this long period of coalescence, and those differences help illuminate the tension between local autonomy and unity in late eighteenth-century Creek country.

The Tallapoosa province on the lower Tallapoosa River developed from the fusion of Woodland Era locals and immigrants from two Mississippian chiefdoms. In the thirteenth century, immigrants from the Moundville Chiefdom of western Alabama settled the lower Tallapoosa, and around 1400, a group from northwest Georgia's powerful Etowah Chiefdom joined them. By the mid-1500s, these groups merged into the Tallassee Chiefdom. This new chiefdom founded several towns that survived until Creek Removal in 1836, including Tallassee and Tuckabatchee. Muskogee-speaking descendants of Etowah dominated the Tallassee Chiefdom and allied it to the Coosa Paramount Chiefdom in the early 1500s. Coosa, the successor to Etowah, comprised a series of allied chiefdoms that controlled an enormous territory including parts of Alabama, Georgia, Tennessee, North Carolina, and perhaps Virginia. The people remained on the lower Tallapoosa as the Tallassee Chiefdom collapsed in the late 1500s. A Shawnee population settled near them in the late 1600s, developing close ties to Tuckabatchee.[2]

The Alabama province occupied the upper Alabama River adjacent to the Tallapoosa province. Around 1450, a Moundville Chiefdom population migrated there, and these Alabama-language speakers became the core population of the Tascalusa Chiefdom. People from the Bottle Creek Chiefdom in the Mobile-Tensaw River delta and possibly some from the Etowah Chiefdom joined them. The three populations quickly coalesced into the politically unified Tascalusa Chiefdom, though they appear to have retained some cultural distinctiveness. The Tascalusa Chiefdom's coalescence may have created the very social mechanisms that Creeks later used to incorporate additional populations.[3] European contact in the 1500s and the Indian slave trade in the 1600s triggered the collapse of both Tascalusa and many other chiefdoms. Refugees from the collapsing Alimamu Chiefdom of the Tombigbee River founded the Alabama province towns of Aymamu and Miculasa around 1650. During the late 1600s, speakers of the Koasati language, closely related to Alabama, migrated from the eastern Tennessee chiefdom of Coste, also known as Kasqui. Coste had been allied to the Coosa Paramount Chiefdom. Koasati speakers founded several Alabama province towns including Coosada, and they maintained a distinct and subordinate identity in the eighteenth-century Creek Confederacy. A Shawnee population joined the Alabama province in the late

1600s, establishing Sawanogi and Ecunhutkee, towns subordinate to Miculasa.[4] The Alabama province's three-century coalescence illustrates that, by the late 1700s, differences between talwas remained significant, yet the diverse peoples also possessed a long history of cooperation.

The Abika and Okfuskee provinces also shared origins in the Coosa Paramount Chiefdom, speaking to the deep history of Creek coalescence and local autonomy. Between 1560 and 1670, several segments of the collapsing Coosa Paramountcy migrated down the Coosa River and founded towns that anchored the Abika province, including Abika town itself and Coosa town. By the 1730s, a small Shawnee contingent lived near Coosa as a subordinate village. Refugees from the Natchez Chiefdom of the Lower Mississippi valley founded a town called Nachees in the Abika province following their war with French Louisiana in 1729. Despite such diversity, Muskogee speakers dominated the Abika province. The existence of Okfuskee as a distinct province is ambiguous, highlighting the dynamic politics of the Creek world. The Okfuskee province derived from populations migrating out of the collapsing Coosa Chiefdom in the late 1500s and early 1600s. These people established a few towns on the upper Tallapoosa River, most notably Okfuskee town. They emerged as a province separate from Abika only in the early eighteenth century by controlling trade with Charles Town.[5]

Despite their diversity, the four provinces of the Upper Creeks shared political, social, spiritual, and linguistic connections deriving from Mississippian origins. That deep commonality served as a solid foundation for cooperation in the late eighteenth century. For example, a few high-status burials at archaeological sites associated with the Coste, Moundville, Tascalusa, Tallassee, and Coosa Chiefdoms all contain distinctive Spaghetti Style shell gorgets. These gorgets attest to precontact links between peoples whose descendants became Upper Creeks. Spaghetti Style gorgets show that the chiefdoms traded with one another and shared beliefs about the relationship between humans and the spiritual world. They also may indicate political alliance secured through marriage into a leading matrilineage for which the gorgets were clan badges. Exotic prestige goods such as European medals remained important symbols of leadership for Creeks and other southeastern Indians well into the eighteenth century. By the end of the century, however, the importance of such symbols lay in demonstrating access to Euro-American trade goods rather than access to spiritual power.[6]

Approximately eighty miles east of the Coosa-Tallapoosa-Alabama confluence, the Chattahoochee River valley's Apalachicola province also coalesced from Mississippian origins. Around 1050, people from a Mississippian chiefdom in the western Tennessee River valley migrated to the central Chattahoochee valley. By 1400, they had combined with local Hitchiti speakers into several politically distinct but culturally integrated chiefdoms. Each of these polities traded with the Etowah Chiefdom, the Moundville Chiefdom, and with chiefdoms in the Florida panhandle. In the late 1500s after Spanish conquistador Hernando de Soto's entrada into the Deep South, refugees from the Coosa-Tallapoosa-Alabama River region migrated west and founded communities that ultimately became the most powerful Lower Creek Towns, Cussita and Coweta. This migration evinced in archaeology likely corresponds to the migration depicted in a Cussita origin story famously related in 1735 by Chighelly, a Coweta war leader. Cussita likely derived from the town of Casiste, noted by Soto's chroniclers in 1540. Casiste may have been a town of Muskogee speakers at the border between the Tallassee and Tascalusa Chiefdoms that was responsible for delivering Tallassee's tribute to Tascalusa.[7]

Precontact political ties testify to powerful, long-standing relations between the people whose descendants became Creeks. Despite those common origins and the coalescence of cultures over several hundred years, divisions endured in the eighteenth-century Apalachicola province. Hitchiti-speaking towns generally clustered together south of Muskogee-speaking towns. Shell-tempered pottery prevailed in Hitchiti-speaking towns whereas Muskogee-speaking towns used shell less frequently. Yuchi town was a significant yet marginalized constituent of the eighteenth-century Apalachicola province. Scholars suggest that Yuchis, speakers of a language isolate, derived from a Mississippian chiefdom in northeastern Tennessee. By the 1720s, most Yuchis had settled a town on the Chattahoochee River as subordinates of Cussita. Like the Upper Towns, the intricate, long-term dynamics of coalescence in the Lower Towns show the diverse, polyglot character of Creek country. The people shared a deep Mississippian history, they possessed social structures that allowed for frequent migration and recombination with neighboring peoples, yet they were diverse and locally distinctive.[8]

Given its complex history as a coalescent society, it is unsurprising that historians still struggle with the terminology for Creeks. Creeks as well as British and Spanish colonials used province names such as Abika and Tallapoosa inconsistently. Creeks often identified themselves by regional division using terms including "Upper Towns" and "Lower Towns" rather than talwa or province names. They used terms such as "nation" even less consistently. Indeed, leaders sometimes used "nation" to refer to one regional division. At other times, they referred to all the talwas together as the Creek nation. Eighteenth-century Creeks were a famously pluralistic society that incorporated outsiders, though most Creeks spoke mutually intelligible languages deriving from a proto-Muskogean tongue. Muskogee was the primary language, particularly in the Tallapoosa and Abika provinces. The Muskogee-speaking towns of Coweta and Cussita dominated the Apalachicola province, though most Apalachicola towns spoke Hitchiti. The Alabama and Koasati languages predominated in the Alabama province. Several marginalized ethnic groups existed throughout Creek country speaking Apalachee, Yuchi, Shawnee, Natchez, Chickasaw, and Choctaw.[9]

Owing to this long history of coalescence that accommodated difference between groups, each eighteenth-century Creek town, or talwa, constituted an autonomous polity governed by a cadre of mature men habitually challenged by younger men. Each talwa participated in the larger polity, but the seventeen thousand people of Creek country were bound more by clan membership, marriage ties, situational military alliances, and land claims than by any central, national institution. Creeks claimed, managed, and seasonally occupied millions of acres of land encompassing most of present-day Georgia, Alabama, and Florida. This territory and its resources were the foundation of the Creek economy built on the commercial deerskin trade and subsistence agriculture.[10]

The colony of Georgia, by contrast, contained fifteen thousand Euro-American people and eighteen thousand enslaved Africans and African Americans by 1775.[11] The colony remained confined to a few coastal towns, agricultural districts along the Savannah, Ogeechee, Canoochee, and Altamaha Rivers, and an inland trading hub at Augusta. Georgia's population, however, was growing far faster than that of Creeks.

Relentless colonial pressure to cede land troubled Creeks. Between 1770 and 1783, Georgians and Creeks endured tense, mutually resentful, yet mostly peaceful relations. Occasional outbursts of violence punctuated the relationship, and attempts to quell simmering tension always followed. During these years, Georgia colonists reported 180 raids committed by Creeks. Forty-one of those raids ended violently, causing the deaths of ninety-three white people, three African American slaves, and twenty-eight Creeks. By contrast, theft was far more frequent. During the same period, 151 raids ended in theft, 125 of which included horse theft.

The conflict that defined Creek-Georgia relations between 1770 and 1783 derived from disagreements over trade and land. In the years preceding the American Revolution, British traders engaged in disruptive, dishonest, and, by British law, illegal trading practices. They flooded the market with alcohol, traded for raw skins at backcountry stands outside the purview of talwa leaders, and traded without British licenses. The Revolutionary War disrupted trade further. Throughout the period, Georgians squatted on Creek lands, grazed cattle, and drove herds through the Creek heartland to markets as far away as Pensacola.

In the early 1770s, Creeks developed a foreign policy centered on limited border raiding to harass colonists and force them to observe established boundaries.[12] Disruptive trading practices led to isolated violence between Native consumers and British traders. To discourage encroachment, some Creeks deprived squatters of their property, including livestock, and destroyed their buildings. Such raiding constitutes the rise of Creek border patrols as a consciously constructed, talwa-sanctioned instrument of foreign policy. British officials, unable to control their colonists, actually encouraged Creeks to patrol and defend their borders against unauthorized settlers.[13] The success of border patrols and diplomacy generated popular support for defending the coalescent society's territory. The methods of border raiders and negotiators allowed the diverse people to pursue their local interests. The 1773 Treaty of Augusta illustrated this paradoxical combination of coalescent unity and talwa autonomy. The treaty included a large land cession that was a bitter pill for many Creeks, yet all swallowed it.

Emistisiguo, an influential leader from the Tallapoosa province town of Little Tallassee in the Upper Creeks, rose to prominence in the 1770s. He controlled the Creek relationship with John Stuart, British superintendent of Indian Affairs for the Southern Department. Emistisiguo embodied the tension between Creek unity and talwa autonomy. He presented Creeks as a nation unified by communal ownership of territory and a desire to defend it, yet Creeks sometimes disagreed on who had the authority to cede lands and organize defense—the nation, the regional divisions, the separate provinces, or each talwa.

The British West Florida Border

In the early 1770s, the British West Florida frontier concerned Creek and colonial leaders more than the Georgia frontier. The Gulf Coast was more easily accessible to most Creeks. A British officer measured the road from Upper Towns on the Tallapoosa River to Pensacola at just two hundred miles with "No River or obstruction all the way."[14] By contrast, the road from Lower Towns on the Chattahoochee to Augusta ran 270 miles and required four major river crossings.[15] Since most Creeks lived in Upper Towns, proximity and ease of travel made Pensacola a preferable trade hub for many.[16] Abika Upper Towns and most of the Lower Towns still preferred trade oriented toward Augusta, but despite these differing economic interests, evidence suggests that Creeks were increasingly united by the desire to limit Anglo-American encroachment. Some Creeks harassed trespassers from West Florida while others appealed to the colony's leaders. Problems on the West Florida border prompted Creeks to consider the relationship between talwas and the larger Creek polity.

Violence was rare on the Creek–West Florida border, yet colonists constantly expected attack. Colonial leaders described Creeks as puerile barbarians motivated by gifts and the joy of combat rather than recognizable economic and political goals. For example, West Florida lieutenant governor Elias Durnford reinforced Pensacola's defenses in July 1770 because he anticipated Indian "Barbarities" during their frequent visits.[17] The Creek–West Florida boundary also merited attention because Creeks were embroiled in a protracted war with Choctaws. Creeks were keen to prevent Choctaws from trading for guns at Mobile, and they often clashed along the river systems north of Mobile Bay. Durnford was eager to encourage the conflict without appearing to do so. He feared that "if they are not at War Amongst themselves we shall find them not only Troublesome but mischievous."[18]

Lieutenant Governor Durnford grew particularly irritated during the summer of 1770 because Creeks committed "Roberys at our Plantations." Upper Creeks had committed similar offenses throughout the late 1760s, but Durnford was convinced that Spanish agents from Havana had excited Lower Creeks to the recent "daily . . . Insolence."[19] The methods of Lower Town raiders, however, reveal motives that Durnford failed to acknowledge.

Three Lower Creek raids on plantations west of Mobile Bay in July 1770 employed tactics that came to define border patrols.[20] Warriors "forced" inhabitants near Dauphin Island to abandon their plantations while "destroying all the Cattle & stock they possessed."[21] They killed no one, and they stole no property. Their aims, then, were simply to clear white settlers from the land, though they had travelled south initially to attack Choctaws. The Alabama province of the Upper Towns held primary claim to the lower Alabama River and the Mobile Bay area, yet when Lower Creeks encountered an

MAP 2. Bernard Romans, "A general map of the southern British colonies in America, comprehending North and South Carolina, Georgia, East and West Florida, with the neighboring Indian countries, from the modern surveys of Engineer de Brahm, Capt. Collet, Mouzon, & others, and from the large hydrographical survey of the coasts of East and West Florida" (London: Printed for R. Sayer and J. Bennett, map, chart, and printsellers, 1776). Library of Congress, Geography and Map Division, GM71005467.

unauthorized settlement, they attempted to remove it.[22] This behavior suggests that in 1770 Creeks thought of their territory as the property of the larger confederacy, not merely the hunting grounds of a single talwa or province.

General Thomas Gage, commander in chief of British forces in North America, understood the message conveyed by the Mobile Bay raids. In 1771 he wrote, "I find the encroaching upon the Indians Land an Universal complaint, but did not imagine it would happen so soon in West Florida."[23] The 1770s witnessed increased pressure on Creeks' southern border as the non-Native population of East and West Florida rose. At the end of the Seven Years' War in 1763, Spain and France ceded their Florida claims to Great Britain. Under British rule, the colonial population rose from 3,200 to 4,800. The Euro-American population actually declined from 2,700 to 1,800 while the African American population skyrocketed from 500 to 3,000. British immigrants brought African

American slaves in the hope of establishing plantations, a motive Creeks found worrisome.[24] In the late 1760s and early 1770s, Upper Creeks routinely complained about British encroachment, and they warned settlers to "keep your slaves and cattle" out of Creek country.[25]

British officials worked to stabilize diplomatic relations with Native groups in the eastern woodlands following the Seven Years' War. Under the British Crown's Proclamation of 1763, only Superintendent of Indian Affairs John Stuart had authority to negotiate land cessions with Indians south of the Ohio River. Stuart often opposed demands for indigenous lands to the chagrin of colonial governors.[26] In August 1771, Stuart visited Pensacola for a meeting with several Upper Creek leaders including Emistisiguo. Prior to the meeting, Stuart attempted to dissuade West Florida governor Peter Chester from requesting tracts of land on the Alabama River above Mobile Bay and the Escambia River above Pensacola Bay. Since Stuart had direct contact with Creeks, he had concerns about land issues that Governor Chester did not share. Stuart acknowledged indigenous territorial rights, putting the question to Chester bluntly: "Upon what principles are we to Account to the Indians for having made Settlements so far beyond the Stipulated Boundary upon the Alibama River?"[27]

John Stuart tried several arguments to deter Governor Chester's demand for Creek land. Stuart viewed pressure on Native lands as a widespread problem. He warned Chester that such pressure could push Native people into a pan-Indian alliance that could embroil the colonies in a far-flung Indian war.[28] Sir William Johnson, superintendent of Indian Affairs for the Northern District, agreed with the assessment.[29]

Stuart also cautioned Governor Chester about the incipient dispute between Creeks and Georgians over a ribbon of land bordering the Oconee River valley. Cherokees owned and occupied portions of present-day Tennessee, the Carolinas, and northern Alabama and Georgia. They recently had ceded some of their lands in northern Georgia directly to Augusta traders in payment of debts. Creeks claimed the same tract, located about forty miles northeast of the Oconee River. Stuart feared that "Encroachments" into it could unite Creeks and Cherokees in resistance.[30]

Finally, Stuart informed Chester that the "Creek Nation" treasured the Alabama River lands and were waging war against Choctaws to defend them.[31] Some Creeks saw the lands surrounding the confluence of the Alabama and Tombigbee Rivers as "their most valuable Hunting grounds."[32] Stuart reminded Governor Chester that "the Creek Towns are Situated about 150 miles to the No. of this Bay and they will not be pleased to See our Settlements within fifty miles of them."[33] Both Creeks and Choctaws had solicited British officials to broker an end to the Creek-Choctaw War so they could use the Alabama River lands safely, again indicating that Creeks saw territorial defense as an issue of common concern for the larger polity.[34]

For these reasons, Stuart refused to demand any more Creek land. Governor Chester, displaying a European notion of statehood and property rights, insisted that Great Britain took West Florida from France in the 1763 Treaty of Paris ending the Seven Years' War, not from Creeks.[35] He contended that any British transgression of boundaries had resulted from the mistakes of surveyors and settlers, not from government policy.[36] When Chester learned that Creek raiders were "warning off the Settlers who had encroached," he claimed he would remove the white squatters himself.[37] "I would never allow of any such Encroachments," he insisted.[38] Two months later, however, Chester complained that Creeks had "broke up" several settlements.[39] This suggests that, rather than removing squatters, Chester grudgingly accepted that Creeks had evicted them. The governor attributed this "irregular Behaviour" to drunken young Creeks and British rum traders whose actions "never . . . have been approved by the Leading and Headmen of the Nations."[40] Though biased, Chester's comment illustrates generational tension between young men and miccos. Such tension was a customary element of Creek governance that loomed large as they confronted colonies impinging on their borders.

Creek leaders may have viewed breaking up a few unauthorized settlements in September 1771 as a border patrol success that conveyed the right message without bloodshed. West Floridians, however, were already making the case for additional land cessions. Governor Chester thought that disruptive traders were the real problem, and he argued that land cessions and stricter trade regulations would solve it. Appointing official commissaries to live in Native communities would restrain "unruly traders" accustomed to "cheating the poor Ignorant Indians."[41] Creeks must also cede more land for British planters. Governor Chester's Council convinced the Earl of Hillsborough, secretary of state for the colonies, that Creeks had violated existing treaties. The Council defined Creek raids on Mobile Bay plantations and their evictions of Alabama River squatters as "infractions" rather than a sovereign polity's legitimate right to defend its territory.[42]

As the summer of 1771 faded to autumn, raiders from several Lower Towns struck West Florida. These raids demonstrated that Creeks' coalescent society accommodated local interests and autonomy, yet the people shared a sense of Creek country's territorial integrity. Men from Yuchi and Chiscalaloo struck plantations on Mobile Bay, killing more than a dozen livestock, destroying food stores, and pilfering a copper kettle.[43] Yuchis were a distinct people in Creek country who spoke a unique language and were often marginalized politically. Chiscalaloo, synonymous with Chiscatalofa, likely refers to a subordinate village peopled by Chiscas. Chiscas, Yuchis, and Cheahas derived from Mississippian chiefdoms that had occupied the Appalachian Mountains of northeastern Tennessee and southwestern Virginia in 1600. By 1700, groups of Chiscas, Yuchis, and Cheahas allied with the Apalachicola province and settled towns on the Chattahoochee River.[44]

A group from the Lower Town of Tomatly plundered a plantation on the Pascagoula River in the fall of 1771. They captured a family of indigenous slaves, killed the father and daughter, sold the son to a white trader, and ransomed the mother.[45] Lower Eufaula warriors burned a plantation house on Pensacola Bay and killed an enslaved boy because the house was "on their own land."[46] Tomatly was peopled by Hitchiti-speaking descendants of the precontact Altamaha Chiefdom, a group that had occupied the head of the Altamaha River near present-day Macon, Georgia. As with Yuchis, Chiscas, and Cheahas, early contact with Europeans and the seventeenth-century Indian slave trade destabilized the Altamaha Chiefdom, and refugees migrated widely in the 1600s.[47] Lower Eufaulas, neighbors of Tomatly, were the only Muskogee-speaking town at the southern end of the Lower Creeks. They had been closely associated with the Tallapoosa province town of Atasi since the 1600s.[48] When John Stuart learned of these raids committed by four different talwas speaking four different languages, he understood them as a defense of the larger Creek polity's territorial rights: "Treaties have not been Strictly observed on the part of the government of West Florida."[49]

The 1771 Pensacola Congress and Native Rights

Superintendent of Indian Affairs John Stuart succumbed to pressure and summoned Creeks to Pensacola in the fall of 1771 to discuss land cessions. During the meeting, Emistisiguo of Little Tallassee claimed a role as a national leader. He resisted demands for land by explaining complex Creek property rights to John Stuart. He asserted Creek nationhood yet deferred to autonomous talwas. The 1771 Pensacola Congress stands as a remarkable moment in the long history of Creek coalescence.

Emistisiguo was a new kind of Creek leader, but his mode of executive leadership would become more common. He drew from the deep well of the Mississippian past, yet he also availed himself of new opportunities presented by the British presence on the Gulf Coast. He enjoyed a great deal of influence with Tallapoosa, Abika, and Alabama talwa leaders, as well as with John Stuart. He actively worked to strengthen relations with Lower Towns. To be effective, he drew on the strength of clan kin, the prestige of his military record, and access to European trade.[50] Emistisiguo's mother was a non-Creek slave, ostensibly depriving the man of membership in a matrilineal clan. Emistisiguo, however, appears to have been a member of the prominent Tyger clan, suggesting his mother had been adopted.[51] Success in war had been an important component of Mississippian leadership, and it remained a reliable path to distinction for young men in Creek society. By the 1760s, Emistisiguo could claim the title of "Head Warrior."[52] Mississippian leaders also worked to control access to supernaturally charged, exotic prestige goods such as shell gorgets as symbols of leadership. By the mid-eighteenth century, Creeks and other southeastern Indians used European goods such as medals and silver armbands as leadership symbols. They symbolized access to manufactured goods rather than access to semi-divine ancestors. Emistisiguo became a "great medal chief" in the eyes of British leaders when he accepted a large medal from John Stuart in 1765.[53] Archaeology also suggests that some Mississippian chiefdoms possessed a kind of town council in addition to elite chiefs. Eighteenth-century leaders like Emistisiguo worked through town councils and inter-town alliances to unify Creek country. His leadership is a good example of both continuity and change in Creek governance. His rise also reflects the problems and possibilities of an intruding modern world economic system. Emistisiguo, Little Tallassee, and the Upper Towns more generally owed much of their increasing importance after 1763 to British commerce via to Mobile and Pensacola.[54]

Poised to avail himself of long-term trends and to assert leadership of a more unified polity, Emistisiguo explained Creek concepts of communal land ownership during the meeting in Pensacola in 1771. In the opening session, Alabama, Abika, and Tallapoosa headmen joined him in bestowing ceremonial titles on John Stuart. The titles established a fictive kin bond with Stuart, requiring him to serve as a kind of protector of Creek country. The titles also acknowledged the interests of Lower

Creeks. First, the headmen declared Stuart Alabama Micco. Then they awarded Stuart the titles of Cussita Micco and Apalachicola Micco. The leaders of the Lower Towns of Cussita and Apalachicola may or may not have condoned these gestures, but they were not present in person.[55]

In the talks that followed, Emistisiguo indicated that Creeks viewed their land as an economic resource but also as something far more important. Creek people's relationship with their land was a fundamental component of the society's identity. Land ownership, however, hinged on talwa autonomy and individual independence rather than the authority of a central government.[56] Emistisiguo began by reminding Stuart of the borders established during congresses at Pensacola and Picolata, East Florida, in 1765. Stuart had agreed that those borders "should be a like a Stone Wall not to be removed without Mutual consent."[57] "My Nation is numerous," Emistisiguo explained, "and every Child in it has an equal Property in the Land with the first Warrior, making any alteration in the Boundary without the consent of the Whole will be improper."[58]

Considering Emistisiguo's acknowledgment of Lower Creek interests at the beginning of the Congress, he seems to include all Creeks in "My Nation." However, talks attributed to Emistisiguo often contain the English word "nation" used equivocally. In 1767, Emistisiguo explicitly stated that "we look upon the lower Creeks, to be a different nation from us."[59] At a 1768 council in Savannah, he made it clear that he was authorized to speak on behalf of "the Nation" by "a general Meeting of Head Men of both upper and lower Creeks."[60] In some talks, he includes Alabamas, Abikas, Tallapoosas, and Okfuskees in his nation. In others, he explicitly refers only to Abikas and Tallapoosas as his nation.[61] Emistisiguo did not speak English, so apparent equivocation simply may be the result of inconsistent translation. Muskogee dictionaries consider "nation" and "talwa" synonymous, though "talwa" is also translated as "tribe" or "town."[62] However, it seems more likely that uneven use of the term "nation" reflects the core tension in Creek society between local autonomy and greater unity. Leaders like Emistisiguo presented Creeks as a polity united on the issue of territorial sovereignty.

Communal land ownership was such an important concept that Emistisiguo repeated himself. He explained again fundamental Creek unity as well as generational tension between mature leaders and young hunters. "The lands are not the property of the head Warriors," he insisted, "but of the whole Nation in common every Boy has a right in the disposal of them."[63] Emistisiguo, however, agreed to exercise his influence as a rising national leader to reach a compromise. The Creek leaders present agreed to "lend" some land above Pensacola along the Escambia River.[64] They warned that they had lent the same land to the Spanish who failed "to keep within the Limits . . . the consequence of which was a War."[65] John Stuart complained that the loan was "only four Miles of very Poor land," and he rejected it as "not worth the trouble."[66] Irritated by Stuart's pestering, Emistisiguo replied, "Father, If you had sent us word before we left our Nation that this was to be a Talk about giving more Land, we should not have come down without first having Consulted our people."[67]

Creeks moved to conclude the Pensacola congress, though they agreed to present British land requests to their town councils. Stuart convinced them to stay, ostensibly to discuss other matters, though he continued to bother Creek delegates with requests for land. Emistisiguo countered by stressing the issues of British squatters, trespassing hunters, and disruptive trading stands outside Creek towns. Exasperated, he finally dismissed Stuart: "I find you and I have Talked to no purposes."[68]

The following day, Emistisiguo repeated to Superintendent Stuart that all Creeks would continue to defend their borders. The manner of border defense highlighted generational tension in Creek society. That tension paralleled conflicting desires for local independence and greater unity. Emistisiguo recalled the 1763 Treaty of Augusta when John Stuart had agreed "that all persons found trading in the woods should be considered infringers of the Treaty." Exercising Creek rights, Emistisiguo "caused some such to be plundered to shew them their Error, from which I incurred much reproach from both White and Red people."[69]

Such demonstrative strikes asserting territoriality had a deep history, but Emistisiguo's raid illustrates the political hazards that leaders faced. British hunters, settlers, and rogue traders annoyed Creeks, but harming them could provoke a trade embargo as well as stoking tensions between Creeks themselves. Emistisiguo plundered white trespassers "in company with Sempoyaffe."[70] Like Emistisiguo, Sempoyaffee was a member of the Tyger clan. However, Sempoyaffee was also close kin to Malatchi of Coweta, the most influential national leader of his generation until his death in 1756. Sempoyaffee became a principal headman in his own right, and his brother, Escotchaby of Coweta, was perhaps the most powerful Lower Town leader of his generation. Sempoyaffee and Escotchaby benefited from trade along the path to Augusta, favored opening trade via San Marcos de Apalachee in East Florida, and viewed trade along the path from West Florida to Emistisiguo's Little Tallassee as unwelcome competition.[71] Emistisiguo's men had robbed traders in Lower Creek territory who were employed by George Galphin, a prominent trader married to Sempoyaffee and Escotchaby's sister Metawney. Emistisiguo's action infringed on Lower Creek interests generally and on the trading interests and kin bonds of Coweta's leaders.[72] Moreover, young men preferred to trade raw skins for rum with backcountry traders. Many older town and clan leaders wished to control young men's destructive, intoxicated behavior. When leaders like Emistisiguo attempted to chastise troublesome white traders, they risked reinforcing regional and generational conflict rather than fostering national unity.[73]

In principle, Superintendent Stuart endorsed Creek rights. He reassured Emistisiguo that, "when you meet White Hunters in the Woods, you have a right to the skins of your own Dear and the Guns with which they were Killed." If Creeks encountered unlicensed British traders in the backcountry, they should "discourage that practice by taking their skins."[74] Stuart's position could be no plainer. Creek men should patrol their lands and harass trespassers by confiscating their property.[75] Even General Thomas Gage, commander in chief of British forces in North America, endorsed Creek rights. He suggested they destroy traders' rum casks and any weights and measures inconsistent with those provided by Stuart. Gage observed that "the Nations" must regulate "the Rascally Traders."[76]

The Pensacola Congress concluded on November 2, 1771, with a land grant that illustrated another element of flexible Creek ideas about territorial sovereignty, national identity, talwa autonomy, and regional interests. While Creeks communally owned all lands, each of the major provinces held superior claims to particular areas. Thirteen leaders from Alabama, Tallapoosa, and Abika Upper Towns granted "rights" to some lands on the lower Alabama River, well north of existing Euro-American settlements.[77] The miccos, however, refused to grant lands on the Escambia River. They argued they must first "take the sense of their Nation in a great Council," suggesting they intended to consult leaders from Lower Towns.[78] The Alabama River lands, by contrast, "belong to the Alabama Tribe, all the Chiefs of which being present they could with propriety make this cession."[79] Each province asserted priority control over territories nearest them, yet Creeks simultaneously viewed land as communal property.

To seal the 1771 Treaty of Pensacola, the British adhered to Creek diplomatic protocol by offering substantial gifts that appealed to both women and men. Presents included quantities of cloth such as strouds and duffels, ruffled and plain shirts, scarlet suits, and blue greatcoats. Creeks also received myriad metalware, from butchers' knives and felling axes to needles, scissors, awls, broad hoes, and brass and tin kettles. Perhaps most satisfying to hunters, they received 371 trade guns at a value of ten pounds each plus 1,500 flints, three gross gun worms, 3,000 pounds of gunpowder, and 4,300 pounds of lead ball.[80]

During the final negotiations, Emistisiguo demanded a provision that revealed a key component of Creek territoriality, diplomacy, and gift giving. Though the provision was omitted from the final treaty document, Emistisiguo insisted that West Florida settlers "will use us kindly when we shall happen to go and see them."[81] The language carried more meaning than the British acknowledged. He intended to establish a reciprocal exchange relationship that required settlers to provide gifts. Presents renewed the privilege of using Creek land and resources. From the Native perspective, such hospitality was a routine expectation among friends. A person who withheld hospitality was recategorized as an enemy.[82] The requirement that West Florida settlers "will use us kindly" is similar to demands that Creeks made of Georgians and Cherokees. Such demands were a common feature of Creek negotiating. Indeed, months after the Treaty of Pensacola in February 1772, Emistisiguo required John Stuart's deputy, David Taitt, to provide him with a letter instructing settlers in the Mobile-Tensaw River delta to "use him and his people well" whenever they were "in want of anything." The headman later praised some settlers who had, in fact, "used him very well giving him what provisions he stood in need of."[83]

Emistisiguo also called for caveats regarding cattle and plantations in "our Nation" to be added to the Pensacola treaty. Speaking again for both Upper and Lower Towns on this issue of mutual concern, he reminded John Stuart of a prohibition on driving cattle through Creek country. He offered a sensible compromise that would allow Creeks to maintain territorial integrity yet provide Georgia ranchers with access to Gulf Coast markets. The Indians would be the cowboys. The Creek leaders in Pensacola agreed "they would send people to drive your Cattle."[84]

Emistisiguo asserted the right to break up British slave plantations and ranches in Creek country. He identified several traders by name who were "driving Cattle and settling cowpens on our land without our consent."[85] By provisioning themselves, they disrupted a key segment of the Creek economy. Emistisiguo offered James McQueen as a specific example who "in opposition to our Talks not only brought up Cattle and also Negroes and has made a settlement near the Great Tallassies."[86] This was a problem because older women and "motherless Children" customarily exchanged small quantities of food with traders for goods and cloth "to

cover their nakedness."[87] Emistisiguo's complaints about British plantations and ranches were assertions of territoriality by a national leader as
well as a protectionist economic policy. He spoke on behalf of specific
talwas, and many other talwa leaders would echo his concerns in the
coming years.

At the Pensacola congress, Upper Creek leaders presented themselves
as representatives of a nation with communally owned territory. They
shared the power to govern among the talwas of the Alabama, Tallapoosa,
and Abika provinces, while also acknowledging the interests of Lower
Creeks. Warriors from four different linguistic groups in the Apalachicola province committed the raids around Mobile and Pensacola, but
the Alabama province held primary claim to the area. During the 1771
Pensacola congress Emistisiguo had represented the shared interests of
the coalescent society while respecting local prerogatives. He had reasserted Creek warriors' right to evict squatters and regulate trespassing
traders and hunters by confiscating offenders' property. This policy had
the explicit sanction of John Stuart as superintendent of Indian Affairs
for the Southern District and General Thomas Gage as commander of
the British military in North America. Emistisiguo had acknowledged
that some Creeks and white men alike criticized border defense actions,
but in 1771, the benefits still outweighed the risks.

1773 Treaty of Augusta and the "Ceded Lands"

A few months before Creeks confronted British West Florida's problematic encroachment and trading practices at the 1771 Pensacola congress, similar issues prompted talks between Creeks, John Stuart, and
Georgia governor Sir James Wright. The talks settled nothing. Two years
later, those nagging issues led to a congress in Augusta where Governor
Wright demanded the cession of a long, narrow strip of land between
the Ogeechee and Oconee Rivers, stretching 150 miles from present-
day Athens to Vidalia. Wright's demand inaugurated the first phase in
a dispute over the Oconee River valley that would last three decades.
The dispute defined Creek-Georgia relations and led to political crises
over the nature of authority in both Creek country and the United States.
Creeks refused Wright's request in 1773 and asserted the right to defend
territorial boundaries. Georgians used Creek border actions to justify
continual demands for land. Both positions set long-lasting precedents.

Conflict plagued Creek country's border with Georgia, and the frequency of squatters settling Native lands elicited forceful statements on

territorial rights from Emistisiguo and others. In his talks, Emistisiguo continued to claim a role as executive leader of all the Upper Creek provinces. Such claims were uncommon, though not without precedent. Occasionally, Creek towns appointed the headmen of allied towns to represent them. And in a few cases, leaders temporarily arrogated power as national executives.[88]

In May 1771, Emistisiguo spoke for several Upper Towns in a remarkable talk to Governor Wright explaining Native rights, territorial boundaries, property ownership, and border defense. The meeting occurred at Oakchoy, a Muskogee-speaking Okfuskee province town populated by two hundred to three hundred people. Oakchoy's headmen, the Mortar and the Gun Merchant, were both considerable leaders.[89] While they disagreed on trade issues, Emistisiguo had spoken as "the Mortar's head warrior" in the 1760s and referred to him in translated talks as "my king."[90] The fact that Emistisiguo spoke for all Upper Creeks at Oakchoy indicates his rising level of influence. He acknowledged that there were "a great many mad young people" among Creeks, a phrase often used to describe men who raided British colonists to gain prestige through war honors.[91] Creeks long had used formal rhetoric about their prowess in war to intimidate Georgians yet signal openness to alliance.[92] "The white People were always told by us, that we were a Mad sort of People," Emistisiguo remarked, yet "there were some sensible People amongst us, that would take care to keep the Path white & clean."[93]

Emistisiguo put himself forward as a "sensible" leader who could control "mad young people," provided that Georgians observed Creek borders. He reminded Governor Wright that "the Boundaries were fixed" at the Savannah River by earlier treaties. Creeks eventually had agreed to move the border some thirty miles west to the Ogeechee River, more than doubling the colony's size.[94] Despite such generosity, Georgians had "made a large Step" beyond the Ogeechee that "was not by our consent," yet Creeks would consider allowing it.[95] Emistisiguo was magnanimous in interpreting the boundary and in forgiving the recent murder of a man from his own Tyger clan. He declared that "the great King over the Great Water is of the Tyger Family" and the Tyger clan's headmen "look upon that matter as taking proper satisfaction."[96]

There was a limit, however, to the border transgressions that Upper Creeks would tolerate. Emistisiguo reminded his British audience of the 1763 Treaty of Augusta attended by four royal governors and Superintendent John Stuart. At that Congress, all had agreed that "if we found any white person settling beyond the Boundaries then fixed we should seize all their Effects but not hurt their Persons."[97] Creeks intended to manage their borders, and British officials had acceded to the policy. At the same congress, Emistisiguo noted that British leaders had agreed that colonial ranchers would remove any cattle that strayed over the border, and no cattle would be driven through Creek country without Creeks' permission. "The Govr of Georgia," he insisted, "had given him Liberty to kill any Cattle brought into his nation without his consent."[98] Perhaps most importantly, Emistisiguo declared that "Mr. Stuart then told us, That he should ask no more Land from us."[99]

Emistisiguo then explained some core concepts of Creeks' relationship with their land and resources: retained rights on ceded lands and reciprocal exchange. His words were remarkably consistent with the speeches he gave at the Pensacola congress, suggesting that they reflected commonly held beliefs. Emistisiguo's ideas drew on a deep reservoir that included both recent history and centuries-old Mississippian notions of strong chiefdoms forcing weaker neighbors into tributary relationships.[100] He reminded Governor Wright that, by earlier treaty terms, colonial settlers were required to give supplies to Creek hunters on ceded lands. He insisted, "If any Indian happened to travel in the Land we had granted to the white People they might be supplied with such provisions as they should stand in need of."[101] When Georgia's settlers refused to present Creek hunters with a horse, food, or ammunition, it constituted a breach of the relationship, redefined Georgians as enemies, and justified property taking. This provision did not appear in the final English-language text of the 1763 Treaty of Augusta. Emistisiguo, however, invoked it in his May 1771 talk to Governor Wright, referenced it again during the Pensacola congress in October 1771, and again to deputy Indian agent David Taitt in 1772. These reminders show that Creeks understood the article to be in force.[102]

White squatters concerned Emistisiguo the most, and he assured his audience that Creeks would "assert our native rights" by removing them.[103] Georgians had encroached "two Days March" west of the Ogeechee River boundary, and in accordance with earlier treaties, warriors had "plundered" the trespassers "but did not hurt their persons."[104] Emistisiguo impressed the political nature of these acts on Governor Wright by enumerating the property taken: "two pieces of small Gold about 6 Dollars, some Pewter and one Rifle Gun. We mention these particulars, to convince you that it was not done with a view to Rob but only to assert our native rights."[105]

Governor Wright's solution to trespassing was to demand moving the border dozens of miles west from the Ogeechee River to the Oconee.

This audacious maneuver would have tripled Georgia's size. Governor Wright justified the expansion to his superiors by portraying Creeks as an imminent military threat, and Georgians repeated that depiction for decades. Georgia "lyes greatly exposed to the Invasions of the said Indians," he lamented, and they "often Rob and Plunder His Majesty's Subjects of their Property, and sometimes Murder them."[106] Creeks had broken treaties by stealing "great numbers of Horses and Cattle," he insisted, disregarding Native rights to oust trespassers and confiscate their belongings.[107] Wright stressed Creek violence, specifically noting two settlers "barbarously murdered" near Wrightsborough Township on the Ogeechee River border.[108] Wright accused Creeks of having killed the two men "in Cool Blood, and without any Cause or Reason whatever."[109] In fact, Okfuskee hunters working along the Oconee River had committed the murders following a raid on trespassing settlers. Governor Wright dismissed this justification as "a false report."[110]

In Governor Wright's estimation, land encroachment was not the true problem in Creek-Georgia relations, despite Emistisiguo's talk. The true problem was disruptive trading practices, and, like Governor Chester in West Florida, Wright argued that more land cessions were somehow the solution. Traders were "the worst sort of People," he observed. They "commit every kind of Fraud and Abuse towards the Indians," inciting Creeks to rob and kill "his Majesty's Innocent Subjects."[111] Surprisingly, Wright felt he could turn the situation to advantage. He knew that both Creeks and Cherokees claimed a "very considerable" tract of land lying between Little River (then Georgia's northern border), the Broad River thirty miles farther north, the Savannah River to the east, and the Oconee River to the west. Cherokees had volunteered to cede their claim on the land to clear their debts. Wright believed Creeks could be "prevailed upon" to cede their claim to the parcel in addition to all the lands between the Oconee and the Ogeechee to satisfy their debts.[112]

Governor Wright was convinced that the Oconee lands were critical to Georgia's future as an agricultural colony. He believed the Oconee strip would make Georgia "the most considerable province on the whole continent" because the lands were "of the richest and best Quality and very fit for Tobacco, Indigo, hemp, Flax, Wheat, and every kind of Grain."[113] In 1773, the naturalist and traveler William Bartram described the Oconee valley in similar terms, noting that the river's east bank was "generally very fertile and of good quality for agriculture."[114] Bartram portrayed the west bank more poetically as "a pleasant territory, presenting varying scenes of gentle swelling hills and levels, sublime forests, contrasted by

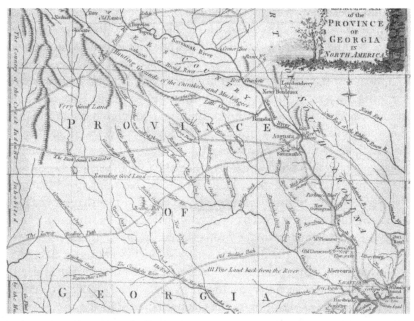

MAP 3. "A New and Accurate Map of the Province of Georgia in North America." *Universal Magazine of Knowledge and Pleasure* 64 (April 1779), facing p. 168. Library of Congress, Geography and Map Division, 2008625108.

expansive illumined green fields, native meadows and Cane breakes."[115] Indeed, a 1779 map of Georgia declared the entire Oconee strip "Exceeding Good Land" and "Very Good Land." Such statements indicate that colonials viewed the Indian trade and Indians themselves as temporary obstacles to the development of a plantation economy in Georgia.

Governor Wright used rare episodes of bloodshed to reinforce his narrative about the Creek threat and cultivate support for taking the Oconee valley. Border conflict, however, showed the limits on both Creek and colonial leaders' control of violence. In the spring of 1772, a Yuchi man from the Lower Town of Cheaha killed a British settler named John Carey on the Ogeechee River border. From London, Colonial Secretary Lord Hillsborough fretted that "the lawless Behaviour of the Back Settlers on the one hand and the Violences and Outrages of the Savages on the other" stymied the Georgia colony's westward expansion.[116] Unruly colonists, Hillsborough insisted, must be "restrained from avenging themselves" in the event of Creek violence and "seek Redress through the Intervention of Government."[117]

A few weeks after the white settler's death, Yuchis themselves captured the man's killer, held him down, and stabbed him to death in Cheaha's square ground.[118] The execution satisfied Lord Hillsborough and Georgia's assembly, yet it threatened the balance between autonomous talwas and the interests of the larger coalescent society.[119] Cheaha was a Koasati-speaking town mostly likely derived from the precontact Cheaha Chiefdom of eastern Tennessee. By 1690, Cheahas had migrated south, joined the Apalachicola province on the Chattahoochee River, and had grown politically close to Muskogee-speaking Ooseechee town and the Hitchiti speakers of Hitchiti town.[120] Cheahas and their neighbors likely resented the Yuchi warrior's disruptive behavior and perhaps pressured his family to give satisfaction for John Carey's death. Just twenty years earlier, Malatchi, the powerful micco of Coweta, ordered the execution of a man named Acorn Whistler under similar circumstances. The action alienated so many Creeks that it nearly ended Malatchi's political career.[121]

Governor Wright's portrayal of the severe Creek threat contrasts with available evidence, yet a few instances of violence and property confiscation confirm Creek devotion to the Oconee lands. Records contain concrete reports of only eleven raids. Nine of them ended in violence, and four included theft. In all, eleven white Georgians and four Creek men were reported killed. To their credit, Superintendent John Stuart and his deputy in Creek country, David Taitt, admitted that border violence stemmed from Creeks' genuine political grievances. Stuart reported the killing of four white men trespassing on the Oconee strip in April 1773, noting they were "Notorious Horse Thieves" whom Creeks had caught "hunting and encroaching on their lands."[122] Such trespassing was common and exposed Creeks to unnecessary risk.[123] British victims of horse theft frequently reported seeing only moccasin tracks leading west, so Creeks could easily be blamed for thefts committed by white bandits. Stuart took the murders as a broader commentary on Creek commitment to the Oconee valley. The killings, he wrote, occurred on "the Land now to be negotiated for . . . which Shows the Jealousy of that Nation."[124]

Other colonists also understood Creeks' devotion to the Oconee lands. A white trader and interpreter named Stephen Forrester reported from Tuckabatchee, a leading Tallapoosa province town in the Upper Creeks, "as for the Land I am sure they never will give up."[125] Even General Thomas Gage at his remove in New York observed that Creeks "appear to be more tenacious of Land than Indians generally are." The experiences of other indigenous people, he supposed, "has shown them, that as the White People advance the natives are annihilated." Gage even commended Creek assertions of sovereignty: "their Policy is good to prevent us from extending ourselves into their Country."[126]

Young hunters throughout Creek country were particularly resistant to ceding the Oconee strip because it was a critical economic resource. "The Creek Indians will never acquiesce in the cession," John Stuart declared to General Gage, because they viewed the land "as their most valuable hunting grounds."[127] Stuart believed that headmen were "the most strenuous opposers of such a cession" in part because they were responding to the will of young hunters. Stephen Forrester warned that Creeks had severely beaten two of his fellow traders and a killed a third along the trading path to Augusta because of traders' persistent demands for land.[128]

Creek leaders grew agitated as Crown officials and Augusta traders badgered them for the land bounded by the Little, Broad, Savannah, and Oconee Rivers.[129] Initially, Upper and Lower Town leaders presented united opposition. Lower Towns held priority claim to the land, but it was critically important to Upper Creeks in the 1770s because the Creek-Choctaw War had rendered hunting around the Upper Towns more dangerous. Emistisiguo acted the part of national leader opposing the cession. In August 1771, he gave a talk in Cussita rejecting Cherokees' cession of the land as "Undervaluing both upper and lower Creeks."[130] He then acknowledged that "our Nation is much in Debt," but Creeks would pay their debts in deerskins, not land. In a remarkable show of unity, Lower Creek leaders from five towns endorsed Emistisiguo's talk, including Escotchaby of Coweta. However, Escotchaby's brother-in-law and leading trader George Galphin began pressuring Lower Creeks to make the cession by threatening a trade embargo.[131]

Emistisiguo reportedly threatened war in August 1772, arguing that white traders should absorb any financial loss incurred from reckless lending to unreliable young Creeks.[132] Second Man of Little Tallassee, also known as Neothlocko, was a close associate of Emistisiguo's by dint of rank.[133] He took a very different and strikingly somber view of the British threat.[134] The two leaders visited the leading Abika province town of Abeecoochee to hear a disquieting Chickasaw talk concerning war with the British. Unaware that white traders were eavesdropping, Emistisiguo and the Second Man remained awake all night discussing the talk's implications. The traders reported the Second Man's bleak assessment. He tried to convince Emistisiguo that Creeks must avoid a war with Georgia. Creeks could not hope to win because they could make neither guns nor ammunition. Worse still, British colonists threatened both Creek country's eastern and southern borders. The Second Man reportedly felt that "it was now too Late. That the White People . . . were all Round them."[135] He dismissed border patrols, saying that even if Creeks destroyed all the livestock and backcountry settlements, they "must be worsted in the end."[136]

In this moment of despair, the Second Man of Little Tallassee accepted that the entire Oconee strip must be ceded, though he expected it would enrage young hunters and trigger an internal power struggle: "The Yong men would Resent the giving of this Land."[137] Older leaders could hope only to channel young men's anger into a manageable war with Choctaws to avoid disastrous conflict with the British. In sorrow and frustration, the Second Man cried out that he "wished that the Great Spirit above would open the Earth & Swallow up all the Lands and themselves too" rather than be dragged into war with Georgia.[138]

The Second Man's grave plea dissuaded Emistisiguo from actively supporting war. The two men, however, understood that leaders from each talwa must consider Governor Wright's demand for the Oconee strip and make their own decisions. As dawn broke, they ended their conversation fearing war was inevitable. Later in the day, Emistisiguo exhibited a flash of the defiance that had made him a great warrior. He taunted the eavesdropping trader, William Gregory, asking the white man if he would like to "fetch him wood & water."[139] Emistisiguo meant the phrase as a threatening euphemism for captivity. Victorious warriors humiliated prisoners by forcing them to do women's work such as hauling firewood and water.[140]

Georgia's pressure on the Oconee lands disconcerted all the provinces of the Upper and Lower Creeks, suggesting that communal land ownership trumped the claims of any single town or province to particular areas. The Lower Towns possessed superior claim to the Oconee strip, yet Upper Town leaders were prepared, if reluctant, to shed blood defending it.[141] Emistisiguo and the Second Man even discussed ceding more land to West Florida if Georgians would drop their demand for the Oconee lands.[142] The Oconee valley was more important to Creek sovereignty because it was the buffer zone between Creeks and the rapidly growing Georgia population.

Nevertheless, Lower Creek leaders soon took the lead in negotiations with Georgia. Escotchaby, also known as Skutchiby or the Young Lieutenant of Coweta, and Niligee, also known as the Head Warrior of Coweta, sent a talk to Superintendent John Stuart in September reluctantly agreeing to cede the land north of Little River "to pay our Traders with."[143] They insisted, however, on setting the tract's border well east of the Oconee River. The Muskogee-speaking towns of Coweta and Cussita dominated the Lower Towns in the 1700s, yet most of the Lower Towns spoke Hitchiti or other languages. Archaeological evidence suggests that, between 1540 and 1600, Muskogee-speaking refugees from disintegrating chiefdoms in the Coosa-Tallapoosa-Alabama River confluence migrated into the Hitchiti-speaking Chattahoochee River valley where they founded Coweta and Cussita. Muskogee speakers and Hitchiti speakers maintained a sense of their distinct identities throughout the eighteenth century.[144] Escotchaby's pretension to speak for the entire diverse Apalachicola province, then, represents another moment of coalescence.[145]

Escotchaby prefaced his proposal to John Stuart with a short history of Lower Creek ownership of the lands between the Chattahoochee and the Savannah Rivers. His talk reinforced Creeks' complex view of communal property rights and reciprocity while emphasizing Coweta primacy. He asserted that "all the Lands on this side Savannah River as far as the foot of the Mountains is ours" as a result of the long-running Creek-Cherokee War. Creek warriors, often led by Cowetas, "drove the Cherokees up to the Mountains & they know the Land to be Ours." Cherokees, however, had "asked leave to Plant Corn near Toogaloo Old Town and promised that our people should have Something to Eat when they meet them a hunting."[146] According to Escotchaby, then, after Creeks took the land by conquest in the Creek-Cherokee War in 1753, they allowed Cherokees to occupy the area. In exchange, Cherokees renewed that right by provisioning Creek hunters who traveled nearby. This is precisely the sort of reciprocity that Emistisiguo had required of white settlers near Mobile in exchange for ceding lands along the Alabama River.[147]

Escotchaby and Niligee's proposed cession to Georgia demonstrated a clear sense of Creek territorial boundaries, the land's value, and the need to garner consent from diverse Lower Towns. Niligee described a significant land parcel that he believed would satisfy Augusta traders without enraging Creek hunters. The parcel would be bounded by the Savannah River on the east, the Little River to the south, and the heads of the Broad River's forks to the west. The northern boundary would run diagonally from the forks of the Broad to Tugaloo Old Town above the forks of the Savannah.[148] The lands to be ceded lay just thirty miles west of the Oconee River.

In addition to satisfying all Creek debts, Escotchaby demanded presents to win the approval of young hunters. He also called for trade regulations that would both benefit hunters and help talwa leaders control them.

He asked for "four Baggs of Powder & Six baggs of Ball," as well as guns, flints, and knives for every Lower Town. Escotchaby then demanded "the Steelyard Trade," that is, traders must adopt uniform steelyard balances for weighing and valuing deerskins. He also declared that Creeks would trade only "drest Leather" rather than raw hides. Trading dressed leather required young men to involve their female kin in processing hides, pulling them into the orbit of civic and social structures. This would discourage young hunters from trading raw skins for rum in the backcountry.[149] "This is what our young men desires," Escotchaby declared to British agents.[150] Conveniently, regulations also would aid miccos who wished to curb young men's alcohol consumption.

After laying out their proposal, Escotchaby and Niligee provided a list of Cherokee and Creek leaders to invite to a congress at Augusta to finalize the cession.[151] Only Creek leaders from the Muskogee-speaking towns of Coweta, Cussita, and their daughter towns appeared on the list, yet Escotchaby and Niligee delivered their talk at Apalachicola town, the founding Hitchiti-speaking town in the province.[152] Leaders from Coweta and Cussita long had dominated Hitchiti-speaking towns, but Hitchiti representatives' total absence from the negotiation is a striking contrast with Emistisiguo's concern for representing each Upper Creek province.

When Deputy Superintendent of Indian Affairs David Taitt consulted Upper Creek leaders about the proposed cession, some of them deferred to Coweta and Cussita. This suggests that, as late as 1772, border issues demanded increasing attention from all Creeks, but regional divisions and talwa autonomy could still take precedence. The Gun Merchant of Oakchoy informed Taitt that "whatever the Lower Creeks & Cherokees should settle at Augusta when they meet, the Upper Creeks would agree to." A headman named Stochlitca, also known as the White Lieutenant of Okfuskee, disrupted this political consensus. In a drunken rage, he railed against any land cessions.[153] The Mortar of Oakchoy and the Handsome Fellow of Okfuskee refused to meet with Taitt at all, suggesting a more serious breach.[154] The dissonance shows that while some talwa leaders were content to defer to their counterparts in other locales, others disagreed, perhaps seeing a need for greater coordination. Indeed, months earlier when Augusta traders began demanding a land cession, the Koasati-speaking Lower Town of Cheaha had summoned Emistisiguo to brief them on the state of border talks with West Florida.[155]

No one was entirely satisfied with Niligee's proposal, yet all parties appeared ready to go through with the cession. Niligee's tract was less than traders and Georgia's government asked for.[156] Creeks were "very much tired with the subject of Land and wanted to have done with it." John Stuart worried the traders who had pushed for the sale were unlikely to "reap much benefit by it" because Governor Wright planned to use revenue from land sales to "maintain Rangers, build Forts, endow schools & churches."[157] General Gage was irritated by the whole affair because it had piqued the Creeks, and he hoped they would "retract the offers."[158]

Over several months of talks, Deputy Superintendent Taitt, Superintendent Stuart, and General Gage had taken Creek assertions of native rights seriously. The leaders of the Georgia colony had not. On December 30, 1772, Creeks attacked a party of speculators that was appraising Oconee valley lands. In the ensuing firefight, two British men and one Creek lost their lives.[159] Georgians were so heedless of Creek resentment that shortly afterward, settlers in the Altamaha River valley at the colony's southern end asked the governor to pressure Creeks for yet another land cession.[160] Deputy Indian agent Charles Stuart reported an alarming rumor from Mobile that Creeks intended to make peace with Choctaws so they could "fall on the White people" because of "Incessant Requisitions for Land."[161]

When the parties finalized the Treaty of Augusta in June 1773, the land cession was virtually identical to Niligee's proposal from eight months earlier. Some three hundred Creeks were present, many of whom were young hunters. Emistisiguo led an Upper Creek delegation, and Niligee spoke for the Lower Towns in concert with the Cussita headman, Captain Aleck and others.[162] William Bartram observed the proceedings and remarked that the young men "betrayed a disposition to dispute the ground by force of arms," especially the area closest to the Oconee.[163] Eventually, however, "the ancient venerable chiefs" prevailed upon them. "Liberal presents of suitable goods" valued at £1,700 sterling—likely the guns, ammunition, and other goods Escotchaby had demanded—appear to have ensured young men's acquiescence.[164]

According to the treaty terms, the New Purchase or Ceded Lands, as Georgians began calling them, stretched from the heads of the Ogeechee River north to a ridge separating the Broad River from the Oconee.[165] The ridge dividing the Broad from the Oconee, however, was so low that it was at points indistinguishable. As surveyed, the Ceded Lands ran all the way to the Oconee River and encompassed a significant portion of the east bank. Indeed, Governor Wright may have altered survey maps unilaterally to add thirty thousand acres to the New Purchase.[166] Ever the keen observer, William Bartram accompanied the surveying party and noted that while marking the boundary, they came within three miles of the Oconee—an area Bartram described as "incredibly fertile."[167] A dozen Creeks in the party likely understood, as Bartram did, that "a very respectable number of gentlemen" followed the surveyors "to speculate in the lands."[168] As the party returned to Augusta, Bartram noticed "a newly settled plantation" on the Broad River in what had been, just a few weeks earlier, many miles deep in Creek country.[169] In fact, there already may have been hundreds of squatters in the New Purchase before Creeks officially ceded it.[170]

In the years from 1770 to 1773, Creeks struggled to manage the geopolitical reality of British colonies pressing on their northeastern and southern borders. Creeks were a society engaged in a long-term process of coalescence. They were devoted to talwa autonomy and divided by language and regional economic interests. Clan kinship, religious practices, material culture, and centuries of shared experiences, cooperation, and competition drew them together. In the 1770s, capable headmen like Emistisiguo and Escotchaby presented Creeks as a unified polity by asserting native rights to communally owned land while deferring to provinces with superior claims to particular territories. To defend Creek land and resources against white squatters, small groups of men plundered, removed, and occasionally killed intruders. British leaders including John Stuart supported Creek efforts to evict squatters, though they did not condone violence. Drawing lessons from these events, Creeks would use similar tactics to assert their native rights in the coming years.

2 / "Neither the Abicas, Tallapuses, nor Alibamas
Desire to Have Any Thing to Say to the Cowetas
but Desire Peace": The White-Sherrill Affair and
the Rise of Border Patrols, 1774–1775

Rumors of Creek dissatisfaction with the land cession defined in the
1773 Treaty of Augusta emerged almost immediately. Governor James
Wright boasted of gaining over 1.5 million acres for the Georgia colony.
He reveled in a spate of land grant applications and was eager for more.[1]
He feared, however, that Creeks could "break up and ruin this province,"
and he called for a troop of rangers to guard settlers in what Georgians
called the New Purchase or the Ceded Lands.[2] Even as Governor Wright
acknowledged the disruptive potential of Creek warriors, he dismissed
their legitimacy. If Creeks committed any violence, it would not be the
lawful action of a sovereign polity defending its borders. Instead, Wright
declared it would be merely "bloody amusement" without which "these
wretches cannot rest."[3]

   In December 1773, the New Purchase erupted in a handful of violent
clashes. Historians have presented these pivotal events in Creek history
as moments when the personal, criminal acts of a few young rogues
ensnared the broader polity in a serious conflict with Georgia. Georgia's response to the attacks forced Creeks to recognize their dependence
on British trade and reduced them to the "politics of insecurity."[4] Until
recently, historians have hesitated to portray the violence as political
protest against the Treaty of Augusta. The initial attacks quickly escalated into a political firestorm that channeled broad-based resentment
against the cession. The violence was meaningful, not random, and combined personal and political motives. It began when young warriors with
ambiguous motives killed settlers William White, William Sherrill, and

their families. Then Lower Creeks from Coweta and a few other towns protested the treaty by forming border patrols, raiding more settlers, and attacking a Georgia militia in the New Purchase. The White-Sherrill affair left an indelible mark in Georgians' minds, crystallizing for them a sense of fear and disgust for Creeks. They expressed those emotions in rhetoric depicting Creek raids as the unprovoked violence of barbarians. Creeks discovered that resisting Georgia's expansion with violence had mixed results. Border patrols also quickly became the vehicle through which Creeks contested tensions between political unity and talwa autonomy, youth and maturity, and competing economic interests. The young warriors who participated in these raids operated within a cultural tradition of violence, but their actions challenged leaders.[5]

The White-Sherrill affair redefined Creek violence, centering it geographically on the Oconee River border with Georgia and politically on border-jumping colonists. Creek violence during most of the eighteenth century had been categorically different. Creeks had fought alongside the British against Spanish Florida and other Native Americans. They had clashed with Georgians in Creek country in trade disputes, but they had not yet contested the border aggressively. The new geographic and political focus alarmed Georgians. The White-Sherrill affair also revealed the leading edge of a disruptive political trend in Creek country. Common young warriors acted independently of both head warriors and older civil leaders. Broad-based support for young raiders led some prominent leaders to embrace them. Others disavowed them and called for their execution. The affair also exposed competing economic interests. Most Upper Towns and Hitchiti-speaking Lower Towns feared a disruption in trade, so they called for the execution of the culprits and sought alternative sources of goods on the Gulf Coast. Conflict between youth and maturity, and between competing economic interests, revealed the limitations of talwa autonomy. Young men long had been admired and rewarded for reckless courage in battle, but older leaders typically had restrained their ferocity. Despite their innovative character, the White-Sherrill killings drew on deep-seated Creek understandings of retributive violence. They were orderly, rule-governed actions saturated with political and spiritual meaning. Warriors intended to restore order by correcting settlers' aggressive behavior and balancing the deaths of Creeks. They did not mean to ignite full-scale war. While attacks were limited and conventional from the Creek perspective, they caused a crisis in Creek leadership and sent shock waves of fear through Georgia. Creeks responded with unprecedented unity to resolve the situation.[6]

Creek Violence, Creek Politics

On December 25, 1773, a group of Creek men attacked the home of William White on the Ogeechee River in the New Purchase. Most of the men haled from Coweta and Cussita, Muskogee-speaking Lower Towns, though most lived in a detached settlement called Pucknawheatley, or the Standing Peach Tree. The settlement lay on the Ocmulgee River between the Lower Towns and the Georgia border. It was associated with Escotchaby of Coweta and home to a trading stand belonging to Escotchaby's friend and brother-in-law, George Galphin.[7] The men killed William White, his wife, and their four children. Shortly afterward, another white man was killed near the Ogeechee. Almost three weeks later, on January 14, 1774, a larger band of Cowetas and others attacked the home of William Sherrill, a neighbor of the late William White. Over the course of several hours, they killed seven people at the Sherrill farm. They lost at least two of their own, and perhaps as many as five. On January 23, a company of Georgia rangers and militiamen escorted survivors back to the Sherrill farm to survey the damage and recover any salvageable property. A still-larger group of Creeks ambushed them, killed four more colonials, and put the militia to flight. Creeks then methodically tortured to death Lieutenant Daniel Grant, a captured officer.[8]

Lieutenant Grant's torture particularly outraged Georgians. The long-standing Creek practice of ritualized torture and execution purified a community spiritually and emotionally, restored cosmic balance, and quieted the crying blood of slain talwa members who were otherwise denied a peaceful afterlife. Southeastern Indian cosmology revolved around a principle of balancing opposing forces that forever threatened to careen into chaos. This balance principle underlay everything from the structure of the universe to romantic relationships. It also extended to untimely deaths, be they accidental manslaughter, malicious murder, or death in combat. When a Creek died at the hands of an outsider, the larger polity demanded a compensatory death in the culprit's community. The victim's talwa and close relations could decide whether to accept some other form of compensation. Killings committed to restore balance, however, were at odds with Euro-American systems of justice and frequently contributed to diplomatic impasse.[9]

A man called Ochtullkee held primary responsibility for the murder of William White and his family.[10] Ochtullkee killed the White family as an act of retributive violence that conformed with Creek cosmology, but the killings also indicated his political ambition. Ochtullkee was most likely a Muskogee speaker from Okfuskee living at Pucknawheatley in 1773. William White and his family were recent settlers in the Ceded Lands near the Ogeechee River. Ochtullkee was reportedly "of Conse-quences in his Village," a member of the powerful Tyger clan, and the nephew or son of the Head Warrior of Cussita.[11] Howmachta of Coweta was headman at Pucknawheatley and supported Ochtullkee's attack on the White family. Deputy Superintendent of Indian Affairs David Taitt reported that Howmachta was a witch, a powerful yet ambivalent role in Creek society that engendered fear.[12] Shortly before their deaths, Wil-liam White and William Sherrill had discovered horses missing from White's farm. They tracked the horse thieves to the Oconee River, where they caught and killed one of them.[13] The survivor, Ochtullkee, escaped to Pucknawheatley, where he recruited Howmachta and five others to return to the White farm.[14]

Howmachta also had personal grievances. In 1767, Georgians burned his village on the Oconee River after accusing him of stealing horses from settlers along the nearby Little River. Governor Wright promised to prosecute the settlers who torched the village, but he demanded that Howmachta's people withdraw from their own land. Wright appre-hended the Georgians who burned Howmachta's village, but a grand jury declined to indict them. Howmachta later founded Pucknawheatley.[15]

Ochtullkee, Howmachta, and their companions killed the White fam-ily to quiet the crying blood of a Creek man slain by White and William Sherrill. Ochtullkee's actions, however, also imply youthful political ambition and highlight conflicting economic interests among Creeks. The seven men who killed William White and his family have been described as "renegades," but they ignited the simmering anger of many young hunters over the 1773 land cession. Ochtullkee's actions accorded with popular sentiment, especially in Coweta. Young men eager to turn back colonial expansion flocked to him. By 1774, young Creeks desper-ately needed lands for commercial hunting so they could purchase the European goods upon which they depended.[16] Moreover, Upper Creeks from the Alabama province (Tuskegee and Coosada) and the Tallapoosa province (Little Tallassee) joined Cowetas in complaining that they had been "cheated in the quantity of ammunition promised them as payment for the land which they ceded."[17]

Ochtullkee, Howmachta, and their followers may have been focused on blood vengeance or personal grievances, but their actions also consti-tuted a broader assertion of leadership that irritated older headmen and jeopardized the flow of trade from Georgia. The victims were symbols of warriors' dissatisfaction with the recent land cession. William White and William Sherrill had moved quickly into the New Purchase, built farms, and killed a Creek man. Georgians had advanced from expropriating Creek resources to killing Creek people. In two attacks following the raids on the White and Sherrill farms, much larger groups of Creeks targeted explicit symbols of Georgia authority and permanent white settlement—a troop of rangers and militiamen and William Sherrill's stockade. These attacks indicate both the political motive of clearing contested lands and the popularity of that cause among Creeks.

On January 14, a group of fourteen to sixty Creeks attacked the home of William Sherrill, William White's neighbor who allegedly participated in the killing of a Creek horse thief. Sherrill built his farm in the Ceded Lands near Williams' Creek, about four miles from White's farm. Coweta warriors found that Sherrill was "enclosing his house with a stockade, one side of which he had completed."[18] They killed Sherrill and four to five other white people, including Sherrill's wife and daughter, as well as two black slaves. Sherrill's plantation was home to "five white men, three Negroe fellows, and 12 women and children of both colours."[19] Several of them escaped. In a firefight lasting six hours, an enslaved black man led two of Sherrill's sons in holding off the Creeks. The black man "shot one of the Head Indians through the eye." Together the settlers killed between two and five Creeks. Before departing, however, the Creeks burned the stockade and one of the houses.[20]

Governor James Wright deployed a company of one hundred rangers and militiamen to Williams' Creek "to protect the settlements."[21] When Creeks encountered a detachment numbering some forty Georgians on January 23, the raiders had increased to "at least 150 in number."[22] The Creeks routed the colonials without firing a shot, and John Stuart believed this led humiliated rangers and militiamen to exaggerate the number of Natives they faced.[23] After colonial scouting parties searched the area for two days ensuring no Indians remained, a detachment of about thirty militiamen escorted the Sherrill family survivors to the farm to retrieve "some provisions and other things which they had left."[24] As they approached the farm, Creeks ambushed. Native warriors killed three militiamen and wounded two more, one of them fatally.[25] The colonials fled to their main camp, where their terror proved contagious. Militiamen "were struck with such a panic that neither fair means nor threats could prevail on them to stay."[26]

Lieutenant Daniel Grant, the detachment's leader, was not so lucky. Creeks captured the wounded and unhorsed officer and ritually tortured him to death. The manner of his death illustrated the personal and political meanings that suffused the White-Sherrill attacks. Creeks captured Grant in large-scale combat with colonial paramilitary on the edge of disputed territory. This demonstrated that the battle was political protest against the 1773 Treaty of Augusta. Grant was "tied to a Tree, A Gun Barrel, supposed to have been red hot, was thrust into, and left sticking in his Body; his Scalp and Ears taken off, a painted Hatchet left Sticking in his Scull, twelve arrows in his Breast, and a painted War-club left upon his Body."[27] Creeks had long inflicted such torture on enemies as ritualistic catharsis to balance the deaths of those killed by outsiders.[28]

Georgia's Narrative of the Creek Threat

Some white observers portrayed the White-Sherrill attacks as the isolated, illegitimate acts of individuals. Led by James Wright, however, the governors of the neighboring colonies anticipated full-scale war with all Creeks. Governor Wright attributed the attacks to Cowetas who opposed the Treaty of Augusta's land cessions. He worried that the attacks would halt "the settling of the late ceded lands . . . [and] has broke up a great many of our old settlements."[29] Both colonials and some Creeks reported shortly after the attacks that "the mischief has been done by a set of renegate Indians who have long frequented the Ceded lands and with a view to prevent their being settled."[30] Lamenting the savvy timing of the attacks, Governor Wright observed that, "had it not happened just now we should soon have had such a number of inhabitants on the ceded lands that they dare not have attempted to disturb us."[31] John Stuart acknowledged Creeks' perspective: "I must observe as I have often observed before that our incessant requisitions for land affords no matter of discontent . . . they cannot see our advances into their most valuable hunting grounds with pleasure."[32] Whereas his colleagues called the perpetrators renegades and villains, Stuart moderated his rhetoric, referring to them simply as "Cowetas" or "Indians." [33]

Governor Wright was mistaken when he identified the culprits as "villains" rather than legitimate political dissenters. The raiders rejected Escotchaby's land cession because it failed to represent their interests.[34] The White-Sherrill affair resulted from bitterness over the Treaty of Augusta. One of the killers went to his grave urging his clan kin to push Georgians out of the New Purchase. The attacks were not merely the acts of "a single Villain or two" or a few "Runegates & Mad Young People."[35]

The White-Sherrill affair instead should be understood as a series of escalating, politically motivated border patrols. Disaffected young hunters from Lower Towns defended lands they depended on economically while Upper Town leaders tried to mitigate conflict and protect the flow of trade. The patrols ignited smoldering popular resentment and challenged older leaders who had consented to the land cession. Even older Creek leaders who cooperated with Georgia and disavowed the White-Sherrill attacks complained of white settlers' failure to abide by existing treaties, boundaries, and trade regulations. The dissidents who struck the White and Sherrill farms used aggressive tactics for a new purpose—to evict squatters—yet the tactics drew on long-standing practices like crying blood vengeance and cathartic ritual torture.[36]

Governor Wright claimed that both "Upper and Lower Creeks disown the murders," but that was not entirely true.[37] While some headmen renounced raiders, the attacks reveal an important trend.[38] A band of seven to fourteen men committed the initial attack on the White farm.[39] A few days later, the raiding party that struck the Sherrill farm had grown to some sixty warriors.[40] This growth shows that more Creeks resented the recent land cession than either Georgians or talwa headmen cared to admit. The popularity of the cause encouraged some reluctant older leaders to support the raiders.

The choice to attack Georgia's militia and rangers in the New Purchase was strictly political. Earlier deaths had satisfied the need to restore cosmic balance. If Creeks' goal had been mere plunder or further blood revenge, poorly defended squatters made easier targets. The Creeks likely knew that the militia detachment was part of a larger force yet chose to attack it anyway. Not only did Creeks rout the combined ranger and militia force, they captured and tortured an officer. Southeastern Indian battle tactics typically called for ambushing small groups with overwhelming force.[41] The Creek patrol was probably smaller than the 150 men that Georgians reported, but they almost certainly outnumbered the 30-man detachment they ambushed. This suggests they were more than simply a few "Mad Young Men" or "Out-casts from the Nation."[42] Their motives went beyond plunder or crying blood revenge. They were attacking symbols of permanent settlement by burning William Sherrill's stockade and killing rangers and militiamen, many of whom likely had settled New Purchase lands themselves.

Shortly after the attacks on White, Sherrill, and the combined ranger and militia force, Georgians determined that only men from Coweta had participated. It is likely, however, that men from other towns joined them.[43] Lower Towns, especially Coweta, long had held primary claim to lands between the Oconee and the Savannah Rivers. Resentment likely would have been greatest in that quarter, despite the roles of Escotchaby and Niligee in negotiating the cession. Coweta and its neighbor, Cussita, were the most prominent towns in the Lower Creeks. Coweta alone may have boasted as many as 130 gunmen, though the town had been declining since the 1750s. During the same period, a multilingual group of Lower Towns had been gaining influence. Known as the Point Towns, the group included Ooseechee (Muskogee speakers), Ocmulgee (Hitchiti speakers), and Cheaha (Koasati speakers). In the following decades, the Point Towns would figure prominently in border raiding.[44]

After the raid on the White farm, established leaders began to participate in border defense, swayed by popular resentment of the 1773 land cession. The initial attack may have sprung from the grievances of young men from the Coweta satellite village of Pucknawheatley, but the number of participants grew with each action. This induced older leaders to embrace the raiders. Escotchaby himself, the Coweta headman who initially proposed the land cession, eventually participated in border patrols.[45] He also continued his attempts to secure trade from Spanish Cuba that would free Lower Creeks from dependence on Georgia.[46] Cussitas likely joined the Coweta warriors. Some evidence even suggests that Creeks recruited Cherokees to help drive colonial settlers out of the New Purchase.[47] By March, Georgians reported that disaffected Creeks possessed an astonishing degree of unity. "Creeks were all ready to take up arms," even if they faced "an army of Red Coats."[48]

Creeks and Georgians alike found that border patrol violence effectively cleared squatters from disputed lands and terrified colonial leaders. "A great Number of People" evacuated the New Purchase, Governor Wright declared, because "the late Murthers have struck such a Panic."[49] Calling for a regular army presence, Wright insisted that, "without some troops People will not think themselves safe."[50] Georgians used fearful language to petition for royal troops to crush the "savages" and prevent any further "wanton and unprovoked barbarities."[51] The Georgia Assembly went further, describing Creeks as "inhuman."[52] The Assembly requested one thousand royal troops because, they argued, Creek warriors "far exceed any force that we can oppose to them."[53] Even if Georgia avoided active combat with Creeks, the Assembly demanded five hundred redcoats "to defend our Frontiers."[54] Governor Wright begged the loan of three hundred soldiers from General Frederick Haldimand, then in New York serving as interim supreme commander of British forces in North America.[55]

Fear quickly spread through East and West Florida. Georgia warned those colonies that they were "in danger of receiving a sudden stroke from the Merciless hands of the Cruel Savages."[56] West Florida's officials took the warning to heart, remembering that Lower Creeks had slain three Englishmen near the Apalachicola River at St. Joseph's Bay in October 1773. They sensed hostility in "the behavior of some Creeks in the Neighborhood" of Pensacola and began to ready fortifications and artillery for "any sudden attack."[57] Georgians did not wait for official action. In late March, they killed and scalped a man they referred to as Big Elk. Purportedly one of leaders of the White-Sherrill border patrols and the man who had scalped Lieutenant Daniel Grant, Big Elk also had threatened to raid South Carolina.[58]

Embargo, Cooperation, Execution

Governor Wright hoped to forestall further violence by embargoing trade until Creeks gave satisfaction for the White-Sherrill attacks. His embargo divided Coweta from the Upper Towns. When Wright invited Creeks to Savannah for talks in April 1774, Muskogee-speakers from six prominent Upper Towns and one Lower Town accepted.[59] Creeks could ill afford trade restrictions.[60] Still, Wright was cognizant that his demand for satisfaction must not be excessive.[61] Emistisiguo and Neothlocko, the Second Man of Little Tallassee, led the tiny delegation. Captain Aleck of the Lower Town of Cussita also attended the meeting. As a headman, Captain Aleck had often complained of English encroachment.[62] James Wright opened talks with a recent history. His version of events, however, ignored Georgians' behavior altogether and focused instead on murders committed by Creeks since 1763. He made no mention of controversial land cessions.[63]

Three Creek delegates responded to Wright in turn. Invoking talwa autonomy, each man declared that his town must not suffer an embargo because of Coweta's actions. Emistisiguo explicitly disavowed the raids on the White and Sherrill farms. He insisted that "the Cowetas have not shut up the path between us . . . and he told Sempiasse, a principal headman in the Cowetas, that the Cowetas . . . should not stop their trade and that they (the Cowetas) must stand for themselves."[64] Emistisiguo emphasized his independence as a town leader, declaring "what he has now said is his own talk and that nobody gave him directions what to say."[65] Captain Aleck of Cussita concurred. When he learned of the White-Sherrill affair, "he went into the town . . . [and] he recommended to most of those who were there to take care of the white people amongst them that no harm happened to them."[66] Wright evidently believed that Cowetas had acted alone, yet he expected Creek leaders to exert central-ized control over men from other towns. He viewed Emistisiguo as a national leader and called on him to put "four of the Offenders to death" since "they have lost four of their People."[67]

Emistisiguo invoked talwa autonomy, yet he also attempted to play the role of national leader, albeit with little success. He passed through the Lower Towns on his way to Savannah in a failed bid to convince Lower Town leaders to join him. Many Lower Creek leaders refused the invita-tion because they feared Governor Wright would imprison them. Emis-tisiguo optimistically believed Lower Creeks would agree to execute four of the White-Sherrill raiders as Wright demanded.[68] When he arrived in Savannah, however, Emistisiguo learned that a white man recently had murdered Mad Turkey, a headman from the influential Upper Town of Okfuskee. The murder shook Emistisiguo, leaving him with "great concern and uneasiness."[69] Escotchaby had requested that Mad Turkey deliver a peace talk to Augusta on behalf of Coweta. Mad Turkey's diplo-matic mission and Emistisiguo's attempt to broker peace demonstrated to Creeks the shortcomings of talwa autonomy. Town independence, however, remained the preferred political principle in Creek country. Contrary to Wright's and Stuart's expectations, the wanton murder of Mad Turkey in an Augusta tavern did not unify Okfuskees and Cowetas, nor did it provoke a coordinated war against Georgia.

Mad Turkey's death certainly angered Okfuskees and Upper Towns in general. Andrew McClean, a white trader, informed Georgia officials that "The Indians in the Upper Towns say a man & not a mean one they will have for the Mad Turkey."[70] Shortly after Mad Turkey's death, Okfus-kees badly beat a trader named Scott with intent to kill. They tracked the unfortunate Scott "Forty Miles to finish him & lay hold of [Thomas] Graham," a partner of Okfuskee trader Robert Rae.[71] After beating Scott and Graham, traders associated with their own town, Okfuskees appear to have been somewhat satisfied. Mad Turkey's close relations, however, threatened to commit further retributive violence.

Upper Towns soon learned that they, too, would suffer the con-sequences of economic sanctions even though they repudiated the White-Sherrill attacks. In early May, a group of men on their way to raid Choctaws stopped in Pensacola to request ammunition and food, but West Florida governor Peter Chester refused them. He announced they would have no presents until Georgia received "satisfaction for the

Murders committed by their Nation."[72] These Upper Creeks evidently reacted angrily, surprised that they would be held responsible for Lower Creeks' actions. As they departed Pensacola, "This Party frightened the Inhabitants so as to make them Subscribe above four Hundred Dollars" to improve the town's defenses.[73]

To resolve the growing problem, Emistisiguo and Neothlocko of Little Tallassee asserted roles as national leaders yet abided by talwa autonomy. They called an unprecedented joint council of twenty-six towns in May and won their consent to execute four ringleaders of the White-Sherrill attacks.[74] Emistisiguo "strongly recommended the measure of stopping the Trade" to all Lower Towns. Without such a measure, he feared they would harbor Ochtullkee, Howmachta, and the remaining leaders.[75] David Taitt reportedly had escorted all traders out of Creek country by April 1774, and by February, West Florida and South Carolina had officially joined the embargo.[76] It remained leaky for months, however, as traders refused to comply.[77] A few substantial shipments slipped through, but Creeks were embroiled in war with Choctaws, and British leaders recognized they were ill-equipped to endure any reduction in the ammunition supply. War with Choctaws concerned Upper Towns the most because of their proximity to Choctaw country, further demonstrating the disparate interests of the two regions. The Mortar of Oakchoy set out for Spanish New Orleans in late 1774 in the hope of increasing trade from that quarter, but Choctaws ambushed his party and killed him.[78] Emistisiguo expected that Georgia could embargo the Lower Towns while Upper Towns traded along the path to Pensacola. Deprived of powder and ball, Cowetas soon would come to heel.[79]

The joint council with representatives from twenty-six towns was extraordinary, suggesting the depth of concern. This protonational body, however, had difficulty imposing its will on the Lower Towns. Some Lower Towns sheltered the White-Sherrill border patrollers.[80] The twenty-six-town council consented to the executions of Ochtullkee, Howmachta, and others, but when deliberations concluded, leaders found that the condemned men had disappeared.[81] The ease of their escape shows that Lower Creeks were unenthusiastic about the death sentences. Indeed, the patrollers were so admired that when they absconded, bodyguards accompanied them.[82]

In addition to Lower Creeks' sympathy for Ochtullkee and Howmachta, other factors reduced the likelihood that Creeks would execute the leaders of the White-Sherrill attacks. Georgians' behavior continued to alienate them. Major General Frederick Haldimand worried that the

"Licentiousness of some of the inhabitants of our Frontiers" would lead them "under pretence of retaliating the Murders committed by a few of the Indians think themselves authorized to assassinate any of them."[83] Trader Andrew McClean agreed and encouraged colonial administrators to restrain the "rascally Crackers."[84] Their concerns were well-founded. In late May, colonial authorities arrested and jailed Thomas Fee, the man who had murdered Mad Turkey in Augusta. A dozen armed Georgians brazenly broke open the prison and rescued Fee.[85] Some Creeks saw the jailbreak as ample reason to pardon Ochtullkee and Howmachta.[86] Also, Governor Wright's trade embargo was increasingly unreliable. Traders regularly set "off for the [Creek] Nation with goods," and Georgia's militia failed to stop them.[87]

Nevertheless, in late May, "a Party from each Town" set out in search of the condemned leaders of the White-Sherrill attacks.[88] Governor Wright's embargo, however leaky, drove Creek leaders to a protonational exercise of power that shocked Creeks. The raiders, they believed, had asserted long-standing prerogatives to restore cosmic balance through retributive violence. They had defended Creek resources as members of autonomous talwas, not citizens of a centralized state.

Within a month, Ochtullkee was dead. Representing the Lower Towns of Hitchiti, Pallachicola, Oconee, and Ocmulgee, the Pumpkin King reported that Creeks executed "one of our Great Warriors named Oktullkee, the Head & Leader of all the Murders in Georgia." They also executed a man responsible for an earlier attack on three Englishmen near St. Joseph's Bay on the Apalachicola River.[89] In the end, Ochtullkee's own father took his life. Ochtullkee lingered for four days nursing a musket wound and went to his grave demanding that "his Relations revenge his Death on the Virginians and not give out until every one of his relations should fall."[90]

The circumstances of Ochtullkee's death highlight the profound tension between young hunters and mature leaders as well as the tension between protonationalist interests and talwa autonomy. Ochtullkee's father, the Head Warrior of Cussita, carried out the execution.[91] His death shows that Creeks remained reluctant to sacrifice their own, but Georgia's pressure was intense enough to drive the Head Warrior of Cussita to an act that is difficult to imagine. He was acting, however, in the best interests of the larger polity.

George Galphin, one of the most influential traders in Creek country since the 1740s, possessed strong commercial and kin relationships in Coweta and the Lower Towns generally.[92] Galphin was eager to end the trade embargo. When the White King of the Muskogee-speaking Lower Town of Lower Eufaula visited his cow pen, Galphin counseled that if the Lower Towns killed Ochtullkee, Georgians would forgo the remaining executions. The White King then called a meeting of Lower Creek leaders at Yuchi town, where he repeated Galphin's advice. Galphin may also have spread his message through the Lower Towns via "his half Breed Factor Cozens" and "an Indian Factor called the Bulley."[93]

Galphin's suggested course of action could restore peace and reopen trade between Creeks and Georgians. The Head Warrior of Cussita responded by taking seventeen men to Oconee town south of Cussita. At Oconee, he burned the house and destroyed the corn "that His Sone and another of the murderers planted." He intended "to kill his son or carry him into his nation which he has effected, and had his Son with him."[94] The Head Warrior's execution of his son, Ochtullkee, was fraught with meaning. The man likely labored under a heavy emotional burden. Under matrilineal kinship rules, one's father was not considered a blood relative, but such relationships still could be close. Since a father was not a member of his son's clan, the execution also risked triggering a retributive murder to restore balance. Ochtullkee belonged to the Tyger clan, whose prestigious members also included Escotchaby, Sempoyaffee, and Emistisiguo.[95] The pressure required to force the Head Warrior of Cussita to transgress so many emotional and social boundaries must have been severe.

The several disparate interest groups involved in the White-Sherrill affair testify to broad cooperation among Creeks. A council of twenty-six Upper and Lower Towns demanded the execution of leading raiders. The Pumpkin King represented four Hitchiti-speaking Lower Towns, and the Muskogee-speaking Head Warrior of Cussita executed his son. Generational tension and economic interests divided Creeks in their responses to the White-Sherrill affair. The Pumpkin King insisted that, even though Ochtullkee was a great warrior, he was merely the leader of "a few Runagadoes" who misled young men into mischief.[96] After Creeks executed Ochtullkee at great emotional, spiritual, and political cost, the Pumpkin King expected that Governor Wright would not "demand any more Blood . . . & let goods come again amongst us with all speed."[97]

Talwa Autonomy, Consensus, and Compromise

Upper Creeks remained united in their desire to end the trade embargo, despite the fact that "a smuggling Trade carried on all along" allowed some goods to reach them.[98] Upper Town leaders appeared eager to renew trade even if it meant forgoing justice for Mad Turkey of Okfuskee in addition to executing the White-Sherrill border patrol leaders. After months of embargo, headmen from several Upper Towns attempted to restore their relationship with Georgia. The Tallapoosa towns of Atasi, Upper Eufaula, and Kialijee joined the Abika town of Hillaubee and Okfuskee in a talk to Georgia urging the renewal of a "straight & white" path to the Upper Towns.[99] They sent formerly aggressive young men to deliver their peace talk.[100] The group's leader, Cujesse Micco of Okfuskee, told Georgians at Augusta that they did not "come with a bad talk for my near relations that fell at this Place."[101] That is, Cujesse Micco had no intention of committing a restitution murder to balance the death of his uncle, Mad Turkey. Indian Affairs agent David Taitt was not entirely convinced of the delegation's peaceful intentions. He noted that Cujesse Micco frequently had threatened to take revenge for his uncle's death. Two other nephews of Mad Turkey accompanied Cujesse Micco. Taitt alleged they had murdered Thomas Jackson and George Beeck, two men from Wrightsborough near the Oconee River, in 1771.[102] A fourth member of the group had assaulted trader Thomas Graham a few months earlier in retribution for Mad Turkey's murder.

Cujesse Micco and his companions delivered a talk at Augusta insisting that the five Muskogee-speaking Upper Towns they represented had neither participated in nor condoned the White-Sherrill attacks. They assured Georgians that "we hope that we may be able to make up peace as we are not concerned with the Cowetas and as we have brought the Path white to this House."[103] Seemingly undisturbed by the loss of the New Purchase and the fate of the Lower Towns, this delegation desired only that "our Trader & Pack Horses" return to the Upper Towns immediately because "we are now very poor for Goods and the Hunting season near at Hand."[104] They claimed to represent all the provinces of the Upper Towns, arguing that neither "Abicas, Tallapuses, nor Alibamas desire to have any Thing to say to the Cowetas but desire Peace" and "hope to have a supply of Goods."[105] By August 1774, the Upper Towns were largely united in their interests yet completely divided from Cowetas. The White-Sherrill attacks tapped into a powerful current of discontent in the Lower Towns and rallied a significant number of young men to action. They also reinforced older patterns of governance based on talwa autonomy. Taitt doubted Cujesse Micco's sincerity and anxiously awaited news from the place he considered the source of strife: the Lower Towns.[106]

Both John Stuart and James Wright were pleased with the news of Ochtullkee's demise. They were also pleased to learn Creeks had executed one of the men responsible for the 1773 murder of three white people on St. Joseph's Bay. Neither Stuart nor Wright, however, was entirely satisfied. Stuart sent a congratulatory talk to Emistisiguo and Neothlocko in Little Tallassee, and he extended his congratulations to the wider cadre of "head Men & Warriors of the Abikas Tallipusses & the Lower Towns."[107] The superintendent was gratified, but he reminded the leaders they had agreed to put four men to death. He was reticent to push too hard, however. He worried that executions could trigger clan-based crying blood killings and understood that Creeks proceeded delicately to avoid such an outcome. "Executions must be performed by the near Relations of the Offender," Stuart explained, "and nothing but the most pressing Exigency can induce such a sacrifice to the public good."[108] Stuart worried that "insisting upon fuller satisfaction" could force Creeks into war "contrary to their Inclinations" and result in an unnecessary expense.[109] Great Britain's secretary of state for colonial affairs, Lord Dartmouth, agreed that peace and limited satisfaction were preferable to full satisfaction at the risk of war. Stuart counseled his superiors to let the matter be, noting that, even in the British Empire, state authority had its limits. Referencing the failure to punish Mad Turkey's killer, Stuart rebuked Georgians: "It seems rather unreasonable to push the Indians who have no police at all in the like circumstances to perform what we find impracticable."[110]

Governor Wright in Georgia, however, continued to demand more executions. He was pleased with Ochtullkee's death and "very hopeful they will for once complete the satisfaction."[111] He warned that, "if they stop here it will not do."[112] Wright renewed his request for royal troops to garrison "2 or 3 Forts on the Frontiers" because even if Creeks completed the required satisfaction, "People will be afraid to Purchase and settle on the late ceded lands."[113]

The embargo's leaks vexed Governor Wright and John Stuart, though only Wright insisted upon further executions before lifting sanctions. In addition to the regular smuggling of goods to the Chattahoochee River reported by David Taitt, Wright complained that 1,400 pounds sterling worth of goods had been delivered to a store on the St. Johns River in East Florida.[114] This, he fumed, "intirely . . . defeated" his work of six months harassing Lower Creek leaders for satisfaction.[115] Stuart joined Wright in excoriating the "Villainy and avarice" of smugglers as well as the abusive practices of traders generally.[116] Stuart believed that the

"Sorded avarice and Licentiousness of Traders and the Brutal Barbarity of our Back Inhabitants . . . were . . . the Chief causes which produced the present disturbances" and prevented "restoring Peace."[117] Essentially, Stuart acknowledged that the White-Sherrill attacks were not random acts of violence committed by renegades, as Georgians claimed. Creek violence was a legitimate response to real political and economic grievances that troubled the Lower Towns more deeply than the Upper Towns.

Governor Wright's complaints about the situation grew more fearful by September 1774 as he clarified his priorities. The White-Sherrill border patrols had driven settlers out of the New Purchase and slowed the pace of land sales. However, by his own admission, there remained 2,600 white men in the New Purchase available for defense—a substantial number considering the lands had been legally available for settlement for just over a year and Creek attacks allegedly caused many to flee.[118] Wright worried that the number of settlers "would not dare be Sufficient to defend and protect their farms and familys and their Blacks would require a number of People to . . . keep them in order."[119] By contrast, Wright estimated that Creeks could field "at least 4,000 gun men."[120]

Governor Wright chided General Thomas Gage for refusing to deploy regular army troops in Georgia. He grumbled that "a total stop has been put to the settlement of our back country . . . and instead of Increasing we have retreated and Suffer many of the calamities of war without the hearty Prospect of obtaining any benefit whatever from it."[121] However, a comparison of the numbers he reported in December 1773 and September 1774 shows that the population nearly doubled from 1,400 to 2,600.[122] Wright argued that, since he had provoked Creeks to war, Great Britain should take the opportunity to seize Creeks' remaining resources. He tried to persuade Gage that frontier Georgians were consumed by fear of Creek attacks: "I . . . suppose in a few months they will begin to murder the King's subjects again, and when our people find they can get no satisfaction, they will take it by killing any Indians they may have an Opportunity of killing."[123]

John Stuart agreed that Georgia and South Carolina together were ill prepared for a war with Creeks, but Stuart's solution to this problem differed greatly from Wright's.[124] In the nine months since the initial attack on the home of William White, British colonists had killed at least a dozen Creeks. Stuart suggested that Georgia formally accept these deaths as full satisfaction, and lift the embargo.

Stuart's idea laid the groundwork for a peace agreement, and on October 20, 1774, a group of Creek headmen visited Georgia's capital to formalize the Treaty of Savannah.[125] Leaders representing each of the provinces signed the treaty. Seven leaders represented at least five Lower Towns, and thirteen leaders represented at least five Upper Towns. The most influential Lower Town leader, Escotchaby of Coweta, was conspicuously absent.[126] A shared problem drove this multitown consensus. The White-Sherrill attacks provoked an embargo that had damaged both Upper and Lower Creek economies. Various talwas had tried and failed to establish alternative trade sources at San Marcos de Apalachee, Pensacola, and New Orleans. The crisis underscored the need for a unified Creek foreign policy.

The treaty held some benefits for Creeks, but it limited their access to the Oconee lands and blamed them for the conflict. The treaty document declared that Creeks must "actually put to death three of the offenders" as they previously agreed to do.[127] Two remaining leaders of the White-Sherrill attacks, Howmachta and Sophice, had escaped to Cherokee country. The treaty signers promised to execute them should they ever return.[128] Moreover, Creeks promised to "deliver up all the fugitive slaves who have taken shelter amongst them, as well all the Cattle which their young people had driven off."[129] The treaty language depicted Georgians as guiltless victims and dismissed Creeks' grievances. The treaty declared that the White-Sherrill attacks had been committed "without any cause or Reason whatever" and that Lieutenant Daniel Grant had been "tortured and put to Death in a most cruel and shocking manner."[130] The treaty language further enshrined Georgia's depiction of the Creek threat by referencing border actions that had received little attention in the preceding months. After the White-Sherrill attacks, "the Indians did plunder and burn Several Houses and did drive & carry away several Horses & Cattle belonging to divers White Persons."[131]

The 1774 Treaty of Savannah reopened trade and promised orderly regulation of abusive white traders. John Stuart was empowered to issue licenses and enforce rules that he had proposed in 1767, but the treaty did not provide for the adoption of uniform steelyard balances for weighing deerskins.[132] It did, however, confirm a preexisting incentive to employ Creeks as slavecatchers. Creeks agreed "not to Harbour any Negroes," and Georgians agreed to pay "for every negroe brought to Savannah Sixty pounds of Leather or the Value there of in Goods" and a reduced rate for black people surrendered to white agents in Creek country.[133] This provision made occasional, uneasy alliances between Creeks and black people less tenable and reminded Creeks that British colonists defined black people as valuable property in their emerging plantation economy.

Perhaps most significant for the future of the Oconee lands, the treaty prohibited any Creek settlement there.[134] More worrisome to young hunters, the treaty signers compromised hunting rights to the Oconee's east bank. The treaty required that Creeks refrain "from Hunting on the North side of the Oconee River or in the Settlements in order . . . to prevent any disputes and Quarrells or any Horses being stolen Either by the Indians . . . or by the White people."[135]

Wright and Stuart both reported to Thomas Gage their satisfaction with the treaty terms.[136] Creek responses were less enthusiastic. Interpreter Samuel Thomas reported "the Coweta Villains are as bad as ever," though Le Cuffee of Coweta had signed the treaty for his town.[137] Escotchaby had grown weary of dealing with British colonists. He sought "the Spaniards to get Ammunition from them," ultimately sailing to Cuba himself aboard a Spanish fishing vessel.[138] Howmachta, the Coweta witch and one of the White-Sherrill border patrol leaders, sent word that he and three others soon would travel east on the Upper Trading Path "to Kill White Men."[139] As the crisis of 1774 seemed to pass for Georgians, Creeks remained hard-pressed. As always, John Stuart worried that squatters and the rapid growth of legitimate settlements "greatly alarmed" Creeks. He reflected that "the Indians can have no such powerfull motive of quarelling with us as our insatiable avidity for land."[140]

The violence of the White-Sherrill border attacks had provoked a ruinous embargo. It also provided Georgians with a political narrative they could use to justify continued pressure for Creek land cessions. Compared with the largely nonviolent evictions on the Creek–West Florida border three years earlier, the White-Sherrill attacks had failed to protect Creek territory. That is perhaps why, after 1774, nonviolent tactics like horse theft became the dominant, character-defining feature of Creek resistance to white encroachment. Upper and Lower Towns apparently collaborated to end the crisis of 1774 with a new treaty, but this short-lived and shallow consensus masked deeper divisions. The post-treaty scramble by competing leaders to develop a new foreign policy suggests that, despite some coordination, Creek towns were still very much politically autonomous. The Revolutionary War created a new political landscape that afforded Creeks new opportunities.

3 /   "Settle the Matter Yourselves": The American Revolution in Creek Country, 1775–1783

The outbreak of the American Revolution initially may have appeared to Creeks as a respite from the difficult decade that preceded it. Any optimism quickly evaporated. There could be no return to the policy of neutrality. Playing the French and British empires against one another had allowed Creeks to protect their borders and present themselves as a unified nation when necessary. Most importantly, diplomatic neutrality allowed Creeks to govern themselves primarily as independent talwas. During the Revolutionary War, two colonial powers once more competed for Creek alliance. Georgians' relentless pressure on Creek lands continued, but the Revolutionary War presented an opportunity to roll back the land losses of the previous decade. The conflict all but destroyed the deerskin trade. British and rebel leaders both used a limited supply of goods to recruit Creek warriors. Backcountry Georgians waged a war of their own against Creeks to secure land. In these shifting geopolitical sands, Creeks with diverse interests pursued multiple strategies to defend their sovereignty, their territory, and to secure trade. Initially, most towns agreed they should remain militarily neutral, yet Creeks almost came to blows over whether to trade exclusively with rebel or British agents. By 1778, many Creeks were conducting raids against Georgia settlers, appearing to favor British interests. In the postwar years, Georgians added that apparent Anglo-Creek alliance to their narrative about Creek ferocity to justify further land taking.[1]

During the Revolutionary War, some bands of Creek warriors attempted to push Georgia settlers out of the New Purchase lands

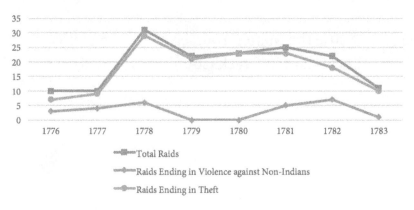

FIGURE 2. Creek Raids in Georgia, 1776–1783

bounded by the Oconee, Little, Broad, and Savannah Rivers. Many Creeks had never accepted the 1773 Treaty of Augusta that ceded the tract. Creeks increased raiding and focused geographically on the New Purchase, incorporated as Wilkes County in 1777. The largely nonviolent pattern of raiding suggests that Creeks altered their tactics to avoid the kind of backlash the White-Sherrill attacks produced. A total of 150 documented raids occurred between 1776 and 1783. Of these raids, 102 occurred in Wilkes County, and the vast majority—93 percent—ended in theft. Only 24 included violence.

During the Revolutionary War, Creeks had an opportunity to reclaim the New Purchase, but they also faced a dual crisis. First, they needed to protect Creek territorial integrity and political sovereignty, and second, they needed to secure reliable trade. Both rebels and British agents recognized the importance of presents and trade to gaining Creek allies. British superintendent of Indian Affairs John Stuart advised his superiors that Native Americans "cannot resist the Temptation of presents." Rebels, he warned, would use that economic vulnerability.[2] Almost immediately, rebel boycotts of British manufactures damaged the Creek economy by obstructing traders' business. Stuart reported that Creeks and Cherokees "complain that they have not a sufficient supply of goods particularly of arms and ammunition; which is the Effects of the non-importation agreement."[3] Stuart's agents in Indian country requested "additional supply of presents" to compensate.[4] Lower Towns continued trading with Cuba, sending another delegation to Havana aboard a Spanish fishing vessel in May 1775.

Neutrality

Rebel and British agents competed fiercely for Creek allies, yet Creeks remained neutral in 1775. John Stuart understood the reasons for Creek reticence, so he did nothing "to interest the Indians in the Dispute."[5] Rumors to the contrary, however, led rebels in Georgia and South Carolina to call for Stuart's arrest. In June, he narrowly escaped Savannah aboard a Royal Navy schooner bound for St. Augustine as boatloads of armed rebels chased him across the harbor.[6]

The Continental Congress and Carolinians quickly recognized that they needed Indian agents of their own and appointed longtime Coweta trader George Galphin.[7] Galphin had profound kinship and commercial ties in Creek country after three decades as a trader. His two sons by Metawney of Coweta, John and George, used their clan affiliation, commercial connections, and language skills to enhance the family's influence. Galphin was close friends with Metawney's relatives Escotchaby and Sempoyaffee, Coweta's most prominent headmen.[8] His impact, however, was not always positive. He led the traders who pushed for the 1773 Treaty of Augusta ceding the New Purchase. Many Creeks resented it. John Stuart and his deputy, David Taitt, focused on working against Galphin's influence.[9]

Rebel and British agents rushed presents to Creek country to curry favor, though both sides encountered difficulty. In the summer of 1775, John Stuart worried that Cherokees and Creeks continued to complain "for want of ammunition and other necessaries." He was "disappointed in the hopes I entertained of being able to supply them with some powder and shot."[10] Creeks were especially "distressed" because of the ongoing Creek-Choctaw War.[11] Shortly before being driven from Georgia, Stuart had arranged a shipment of ammunition for Creeks. Georgia and South Carolina rebels seized Stuart's vessel and confiscated the eight-ton cargo of gunpowder.[12] George Galphin and other rebel leaders then presented Creeks with thirteen horse loads of the confiscated ammunition. Peace talks from Savannah's Council of Safety accompanied the gift. David Taitt reported that Cowetas were "well satisfied" with their share of the present, "but the others condemned it as a mere nothing."[13] Upper Creeks from the Tallapoosa and Okfuskee province towns of Tuckabatchee, Little Tallassee, Okfuskee, and Oakchoy were also disappointed with the paltry gift. Taitt suggested that a modest British gesture would be enough to forestall a Creek-rebel alliance. He also recommended that Stuart pardon Howmachta, the Coweta witch who had helped lead the

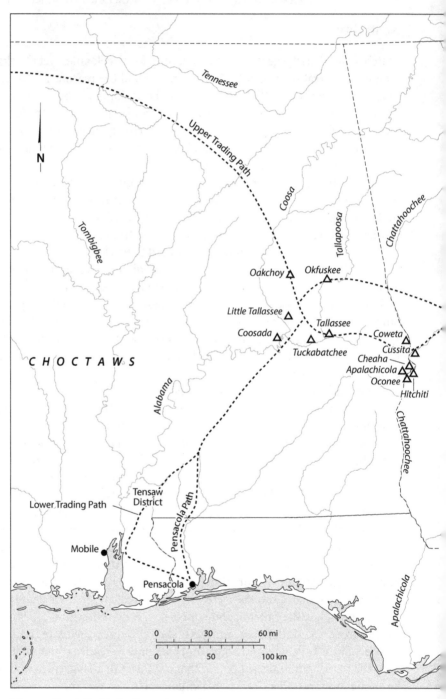

MAP 4. Creek Raids in Georgia, 1776–1783

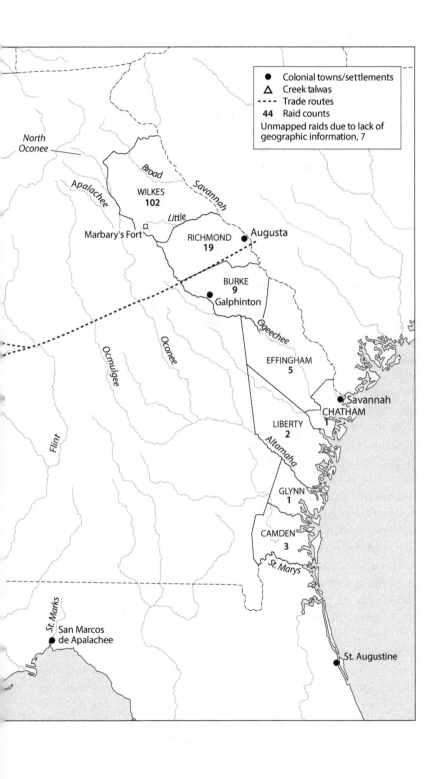

Colonial towns/settlements
△ Creek talwas
--- Trade routes
44 Raid counts
Unmapped raids due to lack of
geographic information, 7

North
Oconee

Broad
Savannah

Apalachee

WILKES
102

Little

Marbary's Fort

RICHMOND
19

Augusta

BURKE
9
Galphinton

Ogeechee

Ocmulgee

Oconee

EFFINGHAM
5

Flint

Savannah
CHATHAM
1

LIBERTY
2

Altamaha

GLYNN
1

CAMDEN
3

St. Marys

St. Marks

San Marcos
de Apalachee

St. Augustine

White-Sherrill attacks.[14] Some Lower Creeks recently had threatened Taitt's life, so perhaps he felt a show of good faith was in order. In the fall of 1775, General Thomas Gage ordered a shipload of ammunition to St. Augustine for Creeks to "bind them more firmly."[15]

Creek towns accepted gifts from both British and rebel agents in 1775 in keeping with their long-standing policy of neutrality. Leaders from several different provinces addressed remarkably consistent talks to British agents. The similarities of those talks suggest some coordination of foreign policy. Each talk declared Creek neutrality, encouraged white people to settle their dispute quickly, and called for regular trade.

In September 1775, Emistisiguo of Little Tallassee spoke at a council of leaders from seventeen Upper Towns, but his message emphasizing neutrality and trade was intended for John Stuart. Emistisiguo advised his colleagues to keep the paths to Savannah and Charleston "clear" and "white," using standard diplomatic language that evoked the Creek Upper World of purity and order.[16] Upper Creek leaders were eager for the British to resolve their differences. Emistisiguo saw no reason for the conflict because "we . . . look upon all the white People as one People." His main concern was trade. "The great King ordered the Ships allways to come over with supplies for us," he said, "and we do not know the Reason why they should now be hindered." He was annoyed that Stuart expected him to pick up presents of ammunition at the distant port of St. Augustine. He had no horses for such a long journey, so he suggested instead that Stuart "come in a Ship" to Pensacola. The Gulf coast port was much closer to Little Tallassee. In closing, Emistisiguo reminded Stuart that "we are not a small people but many in number," so Upper Creeks required a large quantity of ammunition to confirm their friendship.[17]

A leader identified as Jesse Micco gave a talk on behalf of "all the Kings headmen and Warriours of the Lower Creeks" that also emphasized neutrality.[18] Jesse Micco's talk to Georgia's royal governor, Sir James Wright, expressed his hope that "the path between us and you will remain white and Clear," but he proclaimed that Lower Creeks would not "meddle with the Quarrell, we wish all the white people well."[19] Like Emistisiguo, he felt that white people were "all one mothers Children we hope that the great man above will soon make peace between you."[20] Also like Emistisiguo, Jesse Micco worried most about trade. "We hope that you will help us with as much ammunition as you possibley can," he urged, repeating later, "we hope . . . your People will send plenty of goods among us."[21] Jesse Micco closed with a third reminder that "we must again put you in mind that we hope you will send us more amunition."[22]

A few days later, another group of Lower Creek leaders repeated the themes of neutrality, peace between white people, and uninterrupted trade. Sempoyaffee of Coweta; the Blue Salt, King of Cussita; and the King and Long Warrior of Cheaha all agreed that John Stuart's "Talks is good and we Like it vary well."[23] They were not impressed with the rebels' gift of a "hand full of powder and Lead" and were eager to "come Down and Gett some more."[24] The headmen agreed to meet Stuart at Fort Picolata in East Florida to accept presents, despite the onerous trek. As they prepared for the journey, John Stuart's interpreter noticed "much Grumbling" among young men who lacked enough powder to hunt.[25] Their frustration increased tension with older leaders responsible for managing foreign relations.[26] Sempoyaffee and his peers were grateful for the gunpowder but wanted nothing to do with the conflict between rebels and British authorities. They plainly told Stuart the white people must "Settle the matter yourselves."[27]

When young Lower Creek men arrived in St. Augustine to accept John Stuart's gift of gunpowder, the agent blamed rebels for the interruption in trade. He reminded them that his role had always been to "Talk to you of Trade . . . to remove all thorns and Bryars out of the paths to Savannah and Charles Town that you might be supplied with goods."[28] If Creeks wanted manufactured goods, they must remember that "The goods arms and ammunition . . . were made in England . . . for the People of Georgia and Caro[lina] cannot make any."[29] Stuart also observed Creek diplomatic protocol by presenting strings of white beads to symbolize his peaceful intentions and confirm his sincerity. He apologized that he could not smoke "the beloved pipe" with his visitors because rebels had forced him to abandon his calumet when they drove him from Charles Town.[30]

Ultimately, Creek neutrality was impossible because rebel Georgians consistently viewed Creeks as enemies. Backcountry Georgians also distrusted rebel commissioner of Indian Affairs George Galphin because of his close ties to the Lower Towns. Nevertheless, Galphin attempted to recruit Creeks to the rebel cause at a May 1776 congress in Augusta. The congress ended in failure because of Georgians' contempt for Creeks. Many Lower Creeks made the trip, including representatives from the key Muskogee-speaking towns, Coweta and Cussita.[31] A group of white Georgians led by Thomas Fee plotted to waylay and murder the entire delegation. Fee was the same notorious Indian hater who in 1774 murdered the Okfuskee headman, Mad Turkey, in an Augusta tavern. Fee's party ambushed the Creeks and killed a young Coweta man, but, astonishingly, the majority of the delegation continued on to Augusta. Speaking for the group, Niligee, the Chewacla Warrior of Coweta, asserted neutrality and demanded satisfaction for the murder. He also demanded to know why "Virginians" had crossed beyond the 1773 boundary and built forts.[32] Rather than offering satisfaction, Galphin justified Fee's ambush as retaliation for a horse theft. To its credit, Georgia's Council of Safety ordered two troops of light cavalry to "apprehend the man," but the likelihood of capturing Fee was slim.[33] Galphin insisted that, even if captured, Thomas Fee must be taken to Savannah for trial. He blamed the backcountry forts on British treachery: British Indian agent David Taitt had spread rumors that Creeks planned to attack settlers.[34]

White settlers in the New Purchase were concerned more with defense against Creeks than with Whig ideology, and rebel leaders capitalized on their fear.[35] British governor Patrick Tonyn observed from East Florida that "The Americans are a thousand Times more in dread of the Savages, than of any European Troops."[36] Rebel officials comforted settlers, proclaiming they were ready "to defend and protect them from those merciless Savages."[37] Indeed, in May 1776, Georgia settlers in the New Purchase petitioned the Council of Safety for another troop of cavalry "for the defense of the back settlement."[38] Rather than accepting Creek declarations of neutrality, the Council of Safety assumed Creeks' "natural principle of infidelity" would allow British agents to "purchase their friendship by presents" leading to war.[39]

Rebel Georgians also feared potential alliances between enslaved people and Native Americans, and this reinforced their hatred of Creeks. The Council of Safety fretted that there were enough slaves in Georgia "perhaps of themselves sufficient to subdue us." In July, the Council suggested that, "In point of number the blacks exceed the whites," rendering them "much to be dreaded."[40] They proposed deploying six battalions to the backcountry to prevent contact between slaves and Creeks. They also requisitioned funds from the Continental Congress for forts and guard boats to cut off access to Florida. The Council hoped to use some of those funds to bribe Creeks, who, they believed, "expect to be well paid, even for neutrality."[41]

Creeks often viewed black people as property that could be ransomed, sold, or used for labor, though alliances between Creeks and black people also existed.[42] During the Revolutionary War, Creek theft of black people increased. There were no reported slave thefts from 1770 to 1774, but from 1775 to 1783, Georgians reported fourteen Creek raids in which they lost forty-six slaves. At least some of those reported thefts could be better described as rescues. Lachlan McIntosh complained in July 1775 that his two most valuable slaves had become "acquainted with that Villain the Indian Doctor who conveyed them to the Nation."[43] McIntosh valued the two men, Ben and Glascon, as sawyers, carpenters, coopers, and boatmen, and he was eager for their return. Ben and Glascon soon were arrested and confined to the Charleston workhouse, but McIntosh blamed the Indian Doctor entirely for the escape. They were "no runaways" until meeting him, nor could they have escaped on their own, "as neither of them are Woodsmen."[44]

Throughout 1775 and early 1776, both rebel and British agents worked to recruit Creeks. Many talwa leaders agreed on the policy of neutrality. Their primary concern was secure trade, but it was unclear whether either side could provide it. Some Lower Creeks appeared most attached to rebel Georgians because of George Galphin's commercial and kinship ties, but the hostile behavior of backcountry settlers threatened to shift Creeks' focus from neutrality and trade to territorial integrity.[45]

Reclaiming the New Purchase

Creeks remained mostly uninvolved in the Revolutionary War before 1778 despite overtures from both rebel and British leaders. Thereafter, both Upper and Lower Towns grew more active. Georgians reported only nine raids in 1776 and just eleven in 1777. In 1778, however, raiders struck at least thirty times. From 1779 to 1782, each year witnessed twenty-one to twenty-three raids. A few Creeks participated in British-led actions, but it would be inaccurate to describe Creek raids as "pro-British" or dismiss them as merely opportunistic plundering.[46] Settlers in the New Purchase spent much of their time in forts and blockhouses because "the Creek Indians particularly from the Coweta and Cusseta towns were extremely troublesome and daring."[47] Between 1775 and 1783, 71 percent of reported raids occurred in the New Purchase or adjacent Creek lands. This geographical focus indicates that raids are best understood as a Creek attempt to reclaim the New Purchase.[48]

The rise in raiding after 1776 was an expression of Creek towns' political agendas rather than support for the British or patriot causes. Each talwa acted autonomously, often in ways that frustrated one another's designs. Conflicting strategies speak to the endurance of talwa autonomy, linguistic diversity, disparate economic interests, and tension between older leaders and younger hunters. Perhaps counterintuitively, the uptick in raiding also hints at a trend toward greater unity of purpose among Creeks determined to assert a national boundary. For example, Koasati speakers from the Lower Town of Cheaha killed four rebel rangers on the Altamaha River in the fall of 1776. At the same time, Muskogee speakers from the neighboring town of Cussita negotiated with rebel commissioner of Indian affairs George Galphin. The Upper Town of Okfuskee had long-standing ties to Augusta trader and rebel agent Robert Rae. Okfuskees murdered two Englishmen on the path to Pensacola and volunteered to attack Pensacola itself in exchange for goods from Rae and Galphin. Cheahas were not supporting the British cause by killing rebel rangers, nor were Okfuskees supporting rebels by attacking Englishmen. Each town advanced its own interests while defending Creek territory. Okfuskees obstructed the Pensacola path to maintain their home talwa's prominence by confining trade to the path from Okfuskee to Augusta.[49] Galphin conceded that a reliable supply of goods tied most Upper Towns and some Lower Towns like Cheaha to British Pensacola. However, he hoped to deliver enough goods to Okfuskee, Cussita, and other towns to preserve their neutrality.[50]

In their attempts to recruit Creek warriors, British leaders emphasized the rebel threat to Creek life and territory. Secretary of State for the Colonies Lord George Sackville Germain provided John Stuart with presents and valuable information in November 1776. He wrote the superintendent that a "very liberal supply of Goods for Presents to the Indians" was bound for Pensacola. He also informed Stuart that rebel leaders in other colonies were fighting vicious campaigns against Native Americans. Virginians had offered "considerable rewards for the scalps" of adult Cherokees. They had declared that captured Cherokee children could be enslaved.[51] Germain expected this news to "inflame" Cherokees and "excite the resentment of all the other Indians."[52]

Rebels mercilessly attacked Cherokees, and hundreds of Cherokee refugees flooded Creek country. This refugee crisis made a powerful impression on Creeks. During the late summer and fall of 1776, thousands of rebel militiamen from Georgia, South Carolina, North Carolina, and Virginia invaded Cherokee country. They methodically burned dozens of towns, destroyed vast quantities of stored corn and other provisions, and ruined remaining cornfields.[53] Five hundred refugee Cherokees found temporary relief in Creek country and ultimately sought British protection in Pensacola.[54] George Galphin publicized Cherokee suffering to terrify Creeks into continued neutrality rather than fearing their resentment.

The hostile actions of both white Georgians and Creeks from several towns undermined Galphin's efforts to maintain Creek neutrality. In

June 1777, Galphin invited Creeks to another congress to be held at his Ogeechee River plantation. He hoped this location on the Creek-Georgia border would prove beyond the reach of most Indian-hating settlers. The Handsome Fellow of Okfuskee, a close friend of Robert Rae, led the Creek delegation of nearly five hundred men. Headmen from several Upper and Lower Towns attended the congress. The Old Tallassee King represented his Tallapoosa province town, and the Cussita King and Yahola Micco of Coweta represented Muskogee-speakers of the Apalachicola province. Okfuskee, Cussita, and Coweta all had long-standing commercial and kinship ties to Galphin and Rae.

While the headmen at George Galphin's Ogeechee congress in the summer of 1777 confirmed their towns' neutrality, young Creeks from some of those very towns went raiding. Hostile white Georgians also proved disruptive. Galphin had few presents to offer, but he invited the Handsome Fellow and nine others to be feted in Charles Town. Meanwhile, some Cowetas raided alongside loyalist Georgia planter Thomas Brown and his East Florida Rangers. Three Cowetas and several Georgians were killed. Other Creeks from Little Tallassee, Coweta, and Cheaha raided the New Purchase using ammunition supplied by John Stuart. As Handsome Fellow's party returned home in August, Georgians imprisoned them in retaliation for the raids.[55]

The imprisonment of Handsome Fellow's party in Augusta in August 1777 alienated the Creeks most likely to advocate neutrality. During their detainment, rebels demanded that the Creek leaders assassinate British agents in Creek country, some of whom, such as David Taitt, had kin ties to Creeks.[56] Rebel Colonel Samuel Elbert harangued the Handsome Fellow of Okfuskee, the Head Tallassee Warrior, the Oakchoy Warrior, the Cussita Second Man, Yahola Micco of Coweta, the Apalachicola Second Man, and others representing most of the provinces in Creek country. He urged them to ignore British agents, boasting that rebels would "crush you . . . to Atoms."[57] Elbert demanded satisfaction for a Coweta attack on a rebel fort in the New Purchase that had killed a Georgia officer, a woman, and her child.[58] Instead of calling for the execution of the Cowetas, however, Elbert wanted "the Lives of those white-men in the Nation who set them on."[59] Elbert wanted Creeks to assassinate David Taitt, Thomas Brown, John Stuart, and other British agents. He insisted there was "no method for you to save your Country from ruin, than to *Kill* those men, who the King sends amongst you."[60]

George Galphin secured the release of the Handsome Fellow's party, but the situation worsened. Elbert sent a detachment to escort them to the Ogeechee River border and warned his troops to be "always on your Guard as the Savages come as a Thief in the Night."[61] As was so often the case, however, Creeks had more to fear from Georgians than the reverse. Georgians ambushed the Creeks and their guards, killing a white man they mistook for Galphin.[62] The Handsome Fellow died of natural causes during the journey home.

This pressure on Creeks further divided talwas as they struggled to secure trade. Small raids in the summer of 1777 had undermined head-men's negotiations with rebel commissioner George Galphin. Such raids, however, failed to satisfy British leaders who demanded that large numbers of Creek warriors serve under British command. John Stuart claimed by September 1777 to have a force of two hundred white traders along with some Creeks ready to attack rebels in Georgia's backcountry.[63] A rising star from Little Tallassee, Alexander McGillivray, was among them. Stuart appointed him as David Taitt's deputy commissary.[64] Okfuskees and a group of Lower Creeks, on the other hand, attempted to assassinate Taitt in response to rebel Colonel Samuel Elbert's demands. Alexander McGillivray foiled the assassination, narrowly averting a potential explosion of crying blood killings tantamount to a Creek civil war.[65]

John Stuart embargoed the towns of the would-be assassins, and they quickly learned that Americans could not provide adequate trade.[66] Stuart was confident that Emistisiguo could restore Okfuskees to Brit-ish alliance with the help of Alexander McGillivray and a steady supply of presents. The deprivation of the embargo brought some six hundred Lower Creeks, mostly from Cussita and Hitchiti, to British Pensacola seeking gifts and reconciliation. McGillivray reported to Stuart that Okfuskees were contrite and desired a resumption of trade. In a ges-ture of atonement, the leader of Hitchiti town reported that he had con-vinced "the principal disaffected chiefs" to join him in attacking "Rebel Towns."[67] Satisfied that most talwas had been brought to heel by March 1778, Stuart reopened trade.[68]

Creeks came to two realizations that led to more active raiding. George Galphin and other rebel leaders could not provide sufficient trade, yet backcountry settlers remained committed to expropriat-ing Creek land. As Great Britain prepared for a major invasion of the southern colonies in the spring of 1778, some Creeks moved to reclaim the New Purchase.[69] Colonial Secretary Lord Germain and General Sir Henry Clinton planned the invasion. They agreed that prior to the assault, redcoats, Florida Rangers, and "a Party of Indians" would march from St. Augustine and "attack the Southern Frontiers, while Mr. Stuart brings down a large body of Indians towards Augusta."[70] British officials carefully planned how they would use Indians, but Creeks followed their own interests.

Creeks directed their raids against those they considered squatters in the New Purchase. In early August 1778, they launched a devastating attack that inflicted more casualties than any raid in decades, including the White-Sherrill affair. Georgia's rebel Executive Council reported that as many as twenty people might have been killed.[71] Creeks also took some horses and cattle.[72] Militias throughout the state received orders to scout for signs of additional Indian attacks.[73] The rebel militias of Wilkes and Richmond Counties—counties that encompassed the New Purchase and adjacent lands—scouted constantly "towards the frontier."[74] Rebel Colonel Andrew Williamson brought five hundred South Carolina militiamen to Georgia's aid. Williamson had commanded South Carolina's militia during the razing of Cherokee towns in 1776, proving himself a vicious Indian fighter.[75] George Galphin warned Georgians to respond carefully, stressing that Creeks intentionally left unharmed any white settlements that "had not shown hostility."[76]

Creeks continued harassing settlers in the New Purchase with the intent to expel them, though 1779 witnessed a decline from thirty to twenty-one raids. None resulted in confirmed fatalities. Raiders used a variety of tactics from besieging forts to theft, kidnapping, and property destruction. For example, in a 1779 raid, Creeks stole horses and captured two white boys, but after taking them more than a hundred miles toward the Lower Towns, the patrol released the boys to white traders.[77] The same year, Creeks burned the home of John O'Neal near Marbary's Fort in the New Purchase.[78] Witnesses reported that three hundred Creek warriors besieged the fort for eleven hours.[79] From the fort, O'Neal's daughter watched Creeks set fire to her home and outbuildings while her father and another person fled, reaching the fort unharmed.[80] During the night, Creeks slaughtered some cattle and withdrew the following day after confiscating horses. A council of several Upper Towns condoned sending up to five hundred raiders to the New Purchase, indicating substantial support. Alexander McGillivray reported to British agents that he led a huge force himself, thereby enhancing his prestige.[81] The rise of such concerted action in the New Purchase should be seen as an attempt to reclaim the disputed territory. Creek and British interests may have converged for a moment, but reclaiming the New Purchase was not a pro-British policy.

British Lieutenant Colonel Archibald Campbell's campaign to take Georgia in early 1779 demonstrated just how quickly Creek and British interests could diverge. Campbell restored Savannah and Augusta to Crown control in February. However, when he attempted to take Augusta, Georgia and South Carolina rebels forced him to retreat. David Taitt promised to deliver one thousand Creek warriors to help Campbell retake Augusta, but a British ban on plundering the New Purchase discouraged Creeks.[82] Major General Augustin Prevost declared that "No Hostilities" could be committed in Georgia, but Creeks could "act in their own desultory way on the Frontiers of Carolina" because South Carolina had not yet returned to "the King's peace."[83] When Creeks accompanying Taitt learned of Prevost's policy, they balked.[84] Creeks were free to raid South Carolina in support of British war aims, but they initially declined because it would have done nothing to help reclaim the New Purchase. Some weeks later, however, four hundred Creeks agreed to attack South Carolina only after pausing to destroy an abandoned fort in the New Purchase.[85]

At the same time, a contingent of seventy men including Alexander McGillivray raided near Augusta without British support.[86] The raid ended in disaster. On March 29, 1779, a force of four hundred rebels fell on McGillivray's camp. While McGillivray rode to safety, rebels killed two white traders and six Creeks. They also captured three white men and three Creeks.[87] It was, no doubt, a humiliating episode that the young McGillivray would have difficulty explaining to the relatives of those slain and captured.

David Taitt failed to deliver the one thousand Upper Creeks he had promised Lieutenant Colonel Campbell, but in April 1779, some 120 Lower Creek warriors joined a British feint at Charles Town. During that action, Creeks witnessed the ferocity of white loyalists. Taitt reported that while Creeks "behaved extremely well," Georgia volunteers "committed shocking outrages & have set a bad example to the Indians, who cannot now be restrained from taking Negroes."[88] White loyalists did not give Creeks the idea to steal slaves, but observing their behavior may well have encouraged Creek men to expand the practice.[89]

Creek raids in the New Purchase and the British invasion of the southern colonies reinforced Georgians' fear and hatred. A new rebel government briefly seated itself in Augusta in July 1779 while royal governor Sir James Wright and a contingent of redcoats occupied Savannah.[90] Rebels in Augusta feared the British army, but they expected a Creek onslaught first. They learned that "Indian goods are now imported at Savannah," and they expected loyalists to use them in "bringing the Savages upon the frontiers."[91]

Settlers in the New Purchase feared Creeks, yet they worsened the conflict through continued encroachment and violence. George Galphin charged in October 1778 that "the most of the people in the Ceded Land has wanted an Indian Warr Ever Since the Difference between ameraca & England & Did Everey thing in there power to bringe it on there was 4 or 5 Indians killd before there was one white man killd upon the fronteres."[92] Despite Creek border patrols, Galphin reported that white settlers had "run most of the good land between the Line & the Oconee which was cause enough to bring on a war without any thinge else." Not satisfied with this encroachment, Georgians also "raided the Indians in their hunting grounds & beat them."[93] Galphin had been warning at least since 1776 that backcountry Georgians were provoking Creeks intentionally "on acount of getting their Lands."[94] Reports of white violence and land lust contextualize the testimony of white settlers. New Purchase settler Noah Cloud recalled that, in 1780, Creeks continually patrolled the area and confiscated property. He complained that white people "were frequently killed & murdered by said savages insomuch that the Country thereabouts might well be said to be in a state of continual Warfare," forcing settlers into forts and blockhouses.[95] Considering Galphin's accusations, Creeks' insistence on burning an empty fort in 1779 to deprive squatters of refuge seems sensible.

For Creeks, Augusta was the most important trade hub in Georgia. The town changed hands several times during the Revolutionary War. The experience of Creek warriors during the First Battle of Augusta in 1780 shows that Creeks could trust neither rebels nor loyalists. After Charleston fell to British forces in May 1780, General Sir Henry Clinton gave command of British troops in the South to Major General Lord Charles Cornwallis. Cornwallis had orders to secure the backcountry, including Augusta. He offered pardons to all rebels, and this allowed Thomas Brown to take Augusta peacefully in June.[96] Hundreds of rebels, however, retreated into the New Purchase, where they rallied under Colonel Elijah Clarke and Governor Stephen Heard.

After John Stuart's death in 1779, loyalist ranger Thomas Brown replaced him as superintendent of Indian affairs. As superintendent, Brown invited Creeks to loyalist-controlled Augusta for a congress in September 1780. When Elijah Clarke learned that Brown intended to hold an Indian congress at Augusta, he made it his mission to destroy Creeks. In late August, 250 Creeks arrived in Augusta, likely dominated by Upper Creeks led by the Little Prince of Tuckabatchee, a Tallapoosa town. While the Creeks were encamped outside Augusta, Clarke's force of six hundred rebels fell upon them, "killed a number of Indians," captured some artillery, and forced loyalists to take cover.[97] Thomas Brown's loyalist rangers and Creeks withstood a siege for several days until British reinforcements arrived and routed Clarke's men.[98] Native Americans, as one historian described events, "pursued the Georgians, and, out of Brown's sight, they resorted to the savage warfare dreaded by backcountry people."[99] Rebel leader James Jackson declared that Brown handed rebel captives over to Creeks "who tortured them & burnt them alive."[100]

British officers, however, painted a very different portrait of Creek behavior after the First Battle of Augusta. General Cornwallis believed that Creeks and Cherokees were simply unlucky. They accepted Brown's invitation to receive presents and soon found themselves under attack.[101] Brown insisted that no "Indian barbarities" had taken place.[102] Thomas Brown never trusted his Native allies and likely would have reported any atrocities.[103]

After losing the First Battle of Augusta, rebels retreated into the New Purchase and northward to the Appalachian Mountains.[104] Elijah Clarke accused Creeks of unleashing a reign of terror, scalping and torturing women and children, rebel and loyalist. However, other evidence suggests that in 1780 and 1781, a total of only three Creek raids ended violently. Some observers claimed that, in fact, loyalist forces harried rebels through the New Purchase, destroyed more than one hundred plantations, burned houses, drove off cattle, took captives, and "Distressed the Inhabitants Cruelly."[105] Thomas Brown attacked rebel squatters on Creek lands between the Ogeechee and Oconee Rivers, earning their enduring hatred.[106] Some rebel leaders even blamed Elijah Clarke for causing this retribution by committing atrocities of his own during his attack on Augusta.[107]

Creek raiding in the New Purchase lands from 1778 to 1780 constituted an attempt on the part of Creeks to reclaim that territory. The hundreds of Creek warriors involved appear to have represented primarily Upper Towns from the Okfuskee, Tallapoosa, and Alabama provinces and Muskogee-speaking Lower Towns, especially Coweta. Ironically, Okfuskee and Coweta were the towns most closely tied to rebel Indian Affairs agents. George Galphin's inability to provide secure trade coupled with the belligerence of backcountry Georgians and British presents persuaded them the time was right to retake the New Purchase. The participation of hundreds of warriors from multiple towns, provinces, and language groups suggests there was broad support for reclaiming the New Purchase, yet Alexander McGillivray took credit for the raids with British officials. This left some white people, rebel and loyalist alike, with the mistaken impression that Creeks as a whole were pro-British.[108]

The Noose Tightens

When Spanish forces besieged British Pensacola in March 1781, Creeks confronted new possibilities. Their behavior appears ambivalent at first blush, but it was consistent with talwa autonomy and disparate economic interests. Creeks initially seemed eager to protect the port city from which British goods flowed. Spanish forces commanded by Governor Bernardo de Gálvez of Louisiana already had driven the British from Mobile in March 1780, so Creeks recognized a credible threat. An unprecedented force of 1,700 Upper Creeks and 200 Lower Creeks made their way to Pensacola, where they remained for two months. Alexander McGillivray led the men as a headman from Little Tallassee and as British deputy commissary in the Upper Towns. Deputy Superintendent of Indian Affairs Charles Shaw suspected that McGillivray's influence rested solely on his access to British goods, and newly available Spanish goods threatened that influence. "Spanish emissaries" already had induced leaders from two Alabama towns to visit Mobile, where Governor Gálvez "promised to load them with Presents and Rum."[109] Shaw warned that John Galphin, son of Metawney of Coweta and George Galphin, was emerging as a rival to Alexander McGillivray. John Galphin reportedly urged Creeks to visit Mobile and pledge themselves to the Spanish "at the insistence of his father."[110]

The Spanish did not attack Pensacola in the spring of 1780 as expected, so Creeks slowly returned to their homes upriver. When Bernardo de Gálvez's troops finally invaded Pensacola a year later, Alexander McGillivray could not convince Creeks to defend the port town. Many had not yet returned from winter hunts, and others were unsatisfied with the British presents received on their previous visit. They were annoyed by repeated British requests for help over the past year. Alexander McGillivray finally managed to persuade some eighty Upper Creek men to accompany him to Pensacola in April 1781. Leaders from several Upper Towns were already offering their service to Governor Gálvez at Mobile. McGillivray himself soon would follow suit. Creeks seem to have concluded quickly that the Spanish were acceptable neighbors and trade partners.[111]

After the Spanish conquest of Pensacola in May 1781, Creeks continued raiding the Georgia border with Alexander McGillivray's encouragement. Long after the Revolutionary War, Georgians still resented what they remembered as Creek support for the British. Such support, however, was limited, sporadic, and contingent on Creek interests. The Second Battle of Augusta in the spring of 1781 illustrates the same pattern of self-interested decision making that Creeks displayed in the First Battle of Augusta and the Siege of Pensacola. Following victories at King's Mountain and Cowpens, South Carolina, rebel general Nathaniel Greene ordered Colonel Henry "Lighthorse Harry" Lee, Andrew Pickens, and Elijah Clarke to take Augusta. As in the First Battle of Augusta, a small number of Creeks fought alongside loyalists and were accused of wanton barbarity afterward. Early in the campaign, Thomas Brown requested that Upper Creeks send more warriors to help defend Augusta. He may have believed rumors that an enormous force of one thousand Creeks was en route.[112] By May, however, a vast rebel force besieged Augusta.[113] Colonel Lee offered Brown the opportunity to surrender. Brown declined because he believed Elijah Clarke commanded. He considered Clarke a brigand. Lee thought even less of Clarke, depicting him as nothing more than a plunderer and murderer.[114]

Thomas Brown finally surrendered Augusta on June 5, 1781. He requested parole for officers and Native American warriors, some of whom had their families with them. The outcome remains unclear, but Georgians executed some of their white loyalist prisoners, suggesting that Native captives could expect the same. One observer excoriated rebels, writing that Native "cruelties in this part of the continent have been exceeded in number at least four-fold by those of the Rebels. Putting a man to Death in cold blood is very prettily nicknamed giving a Georgia parole."[115]

After the fall of Pensacola to the Spanish and the fall of Augusta to rebels, Creeks found themselves in a new economic and diplomatic position. Rebels and loyalists alike continued using a combination of intimidation and gifts to manipulate Creeks. Rebel Georgia governor Nathan Brownson threatened that "Our brothers of Virginia have heard that your Tomahocks have drank our blood, they Sent us a talk that they had whet their Swords and cleaned their riffles and only waited for us to give the word, and they would- come and make your women widdows and your Towns Smoak."[116] Brownson, however, would forgive Creek violence and attribute it all to "mad young fellows, set on by Brown's lying people."[117] He promised to resume trade if Creeks surrendered Thomas Brown and his loyalists, warning that Spanish Pensacola could not provide sufficient goods. Royal governor James Wright also recognized Creeks' vulnerability. Wright bought presents for Creeks and organized Thomas Brown's rangers to deliver them. According to an early Georgia historian, Creeks then resumed raiding the backcountry at Brown's behest, though the number of reported raids did not change from 1780 to 1782.[118]

As 1781 drew to a close, so too did the Revolutionary War. The Battle of Yorktown in October proved decisive in the broader conflict, but hostilities in Georgia culminated with the rebel siege of British-held Savannah in May and June 1782. Some Creeks continued striking the New Purchase, and rebels under General John Twiggs clashed with them.[119] Over 80 percent of raids in 1781 and 1782 occurred in Wilkes County or adjacent Creek lands. Other Creeks, sensing the war's end, worked to improve relations with Georgia. The Head Warrior of Tallassee, for example, visited the rebel government in Augusta.[120]

Georgians continued to conflate Creek raids in the New Purchase and British war aims. This reinforced the perception that Creeks had no legitimate political agenda of their own. Outraged rebel leaders claimed that Thomas Brown and his loyalists had used "a few trifling presents" to persuade some "mad people" among the Creeks to "murder 7 or 8 of our people in the back settlements," capture women and children, and steal horses, cattle, and slaves.[121] One rebel officer in the New Purchase requested additional ammunition so he could pursue "Indians and Toreys" who had killed a settler named Henry Gold, plundered his home and horses, and captured two white girls from a neighboring home.[122] Georgia's Executive Council expressly ordered a scouting party under Colonel Elijah Clarke to patrol the Oconee River's east bank.[123] Rumors held that Thomas Brown had provided ammunition to one hundred Cherokees and Creeks in Savannah.[124] Georgians continued threatening to invade Creek towns and "lay them in ashes" unless Creeks returned captives and stolen property and surrendered "all those torys & Bad people & Kings men."[125]

Backcountry Georgians continued their separate war against Creeks even after a Continental Army under General Anthony Wayne besieged Savannah in May 1782. Elijah Clarke invaded Creek country west of the Oconee River, killed several Indians, and hung two white loyalists.[126] He reported in May that Creeks again had struck the New Purchase, killing two, wounding three, and capturing four.[127] Rather than supporting the Continental Army's siege of Savannah, Clarke raised "Three Ranging Companies to Act on the Frontiers" against Cherokees, Creeks, and Torys.[128] Micajah Williamson refused to lend his volunteer militia's support to the siege because of two additional Indian raids in the New Purchase.[129]

Leaders from different towns in Creek country continued pursuing local interests rather than a unified Creek foreign policy. Hoboithle Micco of Tallassee, a Tallapoosa town in the Upper Creeks, led a group of two Upper Towns and six Lower Towns in a meeting with rebel governor Jonathan Martin in Augusta in late May 1782.[130] The Head Warrior of Tallassee had approached Georgians in January, and Hoboithle Micco built on that foundation by offering Governor Martin white beads, a white pouch filled with tobacco, and a white wing as spiritually charged symbols of peace and friendship. Hoboithle Micco also offered information. He alerted Governor Martin that William McIntosh, British commissary to the Lower Towns, was moving east "with a strong party of Cowetas." They intended to rendezvous with Cherokees and attack "the Okonnys on our Frontiers."[131] It did not occur to Martin that, under the 1773 Treaty of Augusta, the Oconee valley remained Creek country and not Georgia's "back Settlements."[132]

By early June, a cease-fire was imminent, and General Anthony Wayne was eager to capture Savannah before peace deprived him of that honor. In a rare moment of clear support for the British war effort, Emistisiguo and 150 Creeks attacked Wayne's siege lines. Creeks drove Continentals from their camp, overran American artillery, and destroyed ammunition and supplies. Most of the Creek warriors punched through Wayne's lines and entered Savannah, but eighteen perished, including Emistisiguo himself. The Creek presence made little difference. The British cause was lost, and Savannah formally surrendered to Wayne on July 11, 1782.[133]

Creek survivors of the Siege of Savannah evacuated with loyalists to St. Augustine. In September, as they departed for their homes, Thomas Brown gave them presents. He later reported that some of the Creeks had vowed to continue fighting Georgia squatters.[134] Peace negotiations between Great Britain and the United States dragged on for another year.

With Emistisiguo gone, Alexander McGillivray filled the leadership vacuum in Little Tallassee and, more broadly, in the Upper Towns. Responding to talks from rebel authorities, McGillivray claimed that he commanded Creeks to keep peace in August 1782.[135] Many Creeks sought trade with loyalists in West Florida. Thomas Brown sent word that supplies would be available at St. Augustine, and late in the year, some three thousand Creeks visited the town to trade and receive presents. Delegations from other Native polities throughout the eastern woodlands also visited St. Augustine. Brown's final advice to Creeks at the end of the Revolutionary War already had become self-evident to many: Defend your borders.[136]

Throughout the Revolutionary War, various interest groups within Creek country pursued multiple strategies to maintain trade and territorial integrity. Initially, most Creeks favored neutrality. By avoiding participation in the conflict, they hoped to secure trade and presents from both rebel and British sources. As the factions pressured Creeks to choose a side, Creeks almost came to blows over whom to favor. Rebels proved unable to provide manufactured goods, and belligerent backcountry Georgians alienated Creeks with kinship and commercial ties to rebel agents such as George Galphin. British agents increased pressure on Creeks to participate militarily. In response, some Creeks, especially the Upper Towns of Little Tallassee and Okfuskee and the Lower Town of Coweta, attempted to reclaim the New Purchase by raiding white settlers they considered squatters. Squatters led by Elijah Clarke struck back ferociously, invading Creek country and plunging the Oconee lands into unprecedented violence. In the waning years of the war, the noose tightened when rebels took Augusta and besieged Savannah as Spanish forces ousted the British from Pensacola. At war's end, Creeks found themselves starved of trade and forced to consider a new, coordinated foreign policy to deal with another massive geopolitical shift.

4 / "We Mean to Have the Consent of Every Headman in the Whole Nation": Treaties, Resistance, and Internal Creek Political Conflict, 1783–1785

After the fall of Savannah to rebel forces in July 1782, a new era of Creek-Georgia relations began. Georgians imposed a series of illegitimate treaties, and Creeks responded with border raiding throughout the 1780s. The treaties of the 1780s inaugurated an expansionist United States policy that embodied long-held Anglo-American assumptions that the rights of cultivators trumped the rights of savage hunters.[1] The Creek-Georgia treaties of the 1780s left the exact location of the border between Creek country and Georgia in question, and white people settled where they dared. As white slaveholders imposed a plantation economy on the Oconee River valley, Creeks understood that their territorial integrity, the deerskin trade, and perhaps their very existence as a sovereign polity, depended on managing their border with Georgia.

U.S. expansionism also challenged Spain's ambitions, leading to a formal Creek-Spanish alliance. Spain controlled the Louisiana territory and took East and West Florida from Great Britain in the Revolutionary War. The Spanish Crown was eager to expand its claims as far north as the Tennessee River. In an increasingly acrimonious contest, Spain obstructed U.S. expansion by cultivating alliances with Creeks, other Native Americans, and Euro-American settlers who saw Spain as a protector of their economic interests.[2] From 1784 to 1788, Louisiana governor Estevan Miró closed the Mississippi River to U.S. trade. Even after reopening this essential commercial artery, Spain imposed a stiff duty on U.S. goods passing through the port of New Orleans. Throughout the 1780s, however, Spain actively recruited loyalists and other American immigrants into the Mississippi Valley. American immigrants were required to settle under Spanish supervision and take an oath of allegiance. In return, Spain guaranteed their land claims and opened ports and rivers to immigrants' trade, hoping to win their loyalty and use them as a barrier to U.S. expansion. Thousands of American immigrants settled the plantation district around Natchez, and West Florida offered land grants on the Tensaw River above Mobile Bay on the Creek–West Florida border. In 1783, rising Creek leader Alexander McGillivray and several relatives built cow pens and slave plantations on the Tensaw just north of the border. Though divided by an international border, the Anglo-American and Creek halves of the Tensaw district came to function as an economic unit tied to Spanish Mobile and Pensacola.[3]

Spanish agents also cultivated secessionist movements in the Cumberland, Franklin, and Kentucky settlements of present-day Tennessee and Kentucky by offering free navigation of the Mississippi.[4] In the 1780s, the development of American settlements on the Cumberland and Tennessee Rivers concerned Creeks somewhat, though Georgia remained the key threat. Settlements on the upper Tennessee River known initially as Wautauga and, later, as Franklin, enjoyed a population of around two thousand people before the American Revolution and grew rapidly thereafter.[5] The Cumberland settlement founded at present-day Nashville in 1779 had a population of only about forty people, though it also grew quickly to more than seven thousand by 1790.[6] Cumberland and Franklin settlers depended on access to the Mississippi River for commerce. They also focused on taking land in the Cumberland and Tennessee River valleys that belonged primarily to Cherokees, though many other Native peoples, including Creeks, used it. Some Cumberland and Franklin settlers believed the Confederation government in the 1780s was too weak to secure the right of navigation on the Mississippi and unwilling to defend their settlements against Native American raids. Ultimately, however, Spain could not maintain simultaneous alliances with Native people defending their land and Anglo-Americans bent on taking it. By the 1790s, Cumberland and Franklin settlers were pleading for U.S. government intervention.[7]

The struggle to manage their borders ignited a period of political conflict in Creek country. Creeks protested Georgia's encroachment in different ways, opening a contest for leadership between those who preferred talwa autonomy and those who advocated for a more centralized government. The treaties of the 1780s, as Creeks understood them, confirmed their rights to hunt ceded land, but Georgians routinely violated treaty terms. Some talwa leaders rallied behind Alexander McGillivray of Little Tallassee. They rejected the treaties, arguing that the treaty signers did not represent Creeks as a whole. Treaty signers were led by Hoboithle Micco of Tallassee, another Muskogee-speaking Upper Town in the Tallapoosa province. Hoboithle Micco usually partnered with Neha Micco of Cussita, a Muskogee-speaking Lower Town. Under the principle of talwa autonomy, individual towns had every right to repudiate the agreements, but as McGillivray rejected the treaties, he strove to centralize the power to govern in his own hands.[8] Claiming to represent a unified Creek Nation, he ordered expanded border patrols to clear settlers from the Oconee River's east bank. He sought Spanish trade and political support. Hoboithle Micco and his allies insisted on peace and trade with Georgia, cost what it may. They confirmed their cession of the Oconee's east bank, urged Georgia's leaders to gain each talwa's consent, and insisted that Georgians allow Creek hunters to continue working ceded lands.[9]

The tortuous path to completing the 1783 Treaty of Augusta, the treaty's contentious aftermath, and the 1785 Treaty of Galphinton expose a paradox of Creek life. Creeks continued adhering to the principle of talwa autonomy, yet dealing with Georgia and the United States resulted in border patrols that diminished differences between talwas and fostered coalescence.[10] Disagreements between diverse talwas with differing economic interests were not new, nor was conflict within talwas between mature leaders and ambitious young men.[11] There were precedents for temporary assertions of nationhood as well, but Creeks who worked to centralize government in the 1780s acted in a new and dangerous political and economic climate.

A Shifting Economy, a Contraband Slave Trade

The Revolutionary War profoundly disrupted the deerskin trade. Georgians and some Creeks emerged from the conflict convinced there could be no return to a deerskin economy.[12] During the war, some Creeks and loyalist traders in Creek country, so-called Indian countrymen, profited from the growing importance of slavery in the region by selling stolen slaves in Spanish Pensacola.[13] Others were eager to return all contraband in order to renew trade with Georgia. Even as Emistisiguo's Upper Creeks had attacked U.S. lines during the May 1782 Siege of Savannah, Hoboithle Micco of Tallassee led eight Upper and Lower

Towns to Augusta to restore peace with rebel governor Jonathan Martin. In the metaphorical language of Creek diplomacy, Hoboithle Micco had vowed to keep the path "white and straight" and hoped "the cloud is breaking and that soon it will be all calm and clear."[14] To seal the alliance, he had offered gifts, and, more importantly to Martin, Hoboithle Micco's cohort had agreed to return stolen horses and surrender white and black captives. They also had signaled openness to a modest land cession.[15]

Upper Towns such as Tallassee and Okfuskee opposed the traffic in contraband slaves because they gained nothing from it. By contrast, returning slaves promised twin benefits: immediate ransom for captives and the restoration of regular trade with Georgia. In September 1782, Upper Creeks from the Okfuskee and Tallapoosa provinces joined Muskogee speakers and Hitchiti speakers from Lower Towns to visit Georgia. They intended to negotiate the return of some white and black captives. The delegation included more than two hundred Okfuskees led by White Lieutenant and ninety Tallassees led by Hoboithle Micco.[16] These men expected compensation for any captives returned.[17] Presents of corn, gunpowder, lead ball, and salt would confirm friendship and facilitate captive return, but they would also maintain Hoboithle Micco's leadership position. Deputy Indian Affairs Superintendent Richard Henderson noted that Hoboithle Micco was increasingly vulnerable: "His men who has turned to him begins to upbraid him, they tell him he is all talk and no goods."[18] Giving presents and restoring trade also served Georgia's interests by thwarting the Spanish and loyalists. Henderson pointed out that "if the Others are admited to Carry goods to that land and we send them none we have lost them for ever."[19]

Creeks running the contraband slave trade and those such as Hoboithle Micco who opposed it were on the verge of "an Open Rupture" by December 1782.[20] Georgia Ranger captain Patrick Carr received intelligence from Pensacola that "the Indians and White Peple is Constantly Carying Droves of Negroes . . . & that the Spanish Govener buyes the Chief of them," paying cash. Hoboithle Micco and his allies impeded this traffic by "Seezing opon some Negroes" to return to Georgia.[21] Some Creeks feared the contraband slave trade would provoke Georgians to violence. Before Hoboithle Micco sent men to repatriate white and black captives, he requested that Governor Martin restrain Colonel Elijah Clarke's men. Clarke's militia had slaughtered Creeks and stolen their horses at the First and Second Battles of Augusta in 1780 and 1781, and they had invaded Creek country in the spring of 1782, continuing their war against Indians. Creeks lived in "Constant Alarm" because three hundred militiamen reportedly had marched to the Oconee River.[22]

While Hoboithle Micco and others were working to end the contraband slave trade, return stolen property and captives, and restore trade with Georgia, Creeks such as Boatswain undermined them. Hoboithle Micco told Deputy Superintendent Henderson that "the Nation in general were entirely devoted to deliver up the Prisoners and negroes &c excepting some Roguish disposed Indians Boatswain by name being one who has carried numbers to Pensacola and sold them to the Spaniards."[23] One historian described Boatswain as a "typical Creek war profiteer."[24] By 1774 he had made a fortune trading a variety of goods down the Altamaha River. He used the fortune to capitalize a hundred-acre fenced plantation near the Lower Town of Hitchiti cultivated by fifteen black slaves.[25] Considering the wealth at stake, the conflict over the contraband slave trade was unlikely to end quietly.

The 1783 Treaty of Augusta

The 1783 Treaty of Augusta following the American Revolution was the first of a series of problematic treaties that shaped Creek-Georgia relations and exacerbated Creek internal political conflict. The parties intended the treaty to establish a border, clarify hunting rights, and arrange the return of stolen property. The treaty, however, was illegitimate by both Creek and U.S. standards. This stoked smoldering conflict between the two polities and caused tension within them. Creeks agreed to a stinging land cession to restore the flow of manufactured goods. Goods had been scarce for a decade in Creek country because of the White-Sherrill affair and the Revolutionary War. During treaty negotiations, Georgians accused Creeks of unanimously supporting the British during the war in order to justify punitive land taking.

Despite Hoboithle Micco's diplomatic efforts in the spring of 1782, in the fall, some four hundred South Carolina and Georgia militiamen under General Andrew Pickens and Colonel Elijah Clarke attacked Creek and Cherokee towns and hunting camps. Ostensibly, they were pursuing fugitive Tories. They found no loyalists, but they forced Cherokees to cede their claim to the Oconee's east bank from the source of "the most Southern branch of the Okoney river" to its confluence with the Altamaha.[26] Gaining the Oconee strip nearly tripled Georgia's size. Cherokees insisted on retaining hunting rights in the area, and Georgians consented. Cherokees would "hunt as Usual, on the lands, which they

Ceded to us, Untill we should make Settlements thereon."[27] The retention of hunting rights was a common provision in land cession treaties.

Just months after Cherokees ceded their claim to the Oconee's east bank, Creeks ceded their claim to the same land in the November 1783 Treaty of Augusta. This brought to fruition a goal Georgians had pursued for more than a decade. Creeks initially refused to treat with Georgia because, compared with Cherokees, they had emerged from the Revolutionary War relatively unscathed. As Pickens's and Clarke's attacks demonstrated, however, they were under pressure.[28] Fourteen Creek leaders representing only about 10 percent of Creek towns agreed to the ill-defined land cession. They also agreed to arrange the return of stolen property.[29] Creek negotiators, however, managed to secure two critically important concessions: well-regulated trade and retained hunting rights on the Oconee lands. The concessions and a "considerable amount" of presents made the treaty acceptable to some Creeks.[30]

From the Georgia perspective, it was a complete victory. All "Negroes, horses and other property" would be "restored." Creeks ceded the Oconee strip from the source of "the most southern branch of the Oconee river" to its confluence with the Altamaha, though the precise location of the Oconee's southern branch later became a point of contention.[31] Georgians agreed that Creeks, like Cherokees, could continue hunting the Oconee's east bank. Only a year after signing the treaty, however, Hoboithle Micco found it necessary to remind Georgians that he "expected his people would be allowed to hunt on this side of the river."[32]

Georgians viewed the Oconee River valley and all other Creek lands as theirs by right of conquest. Treaties merely confirmed a fait accompli. Months before the Treaty of Augusta, the state Assembly began reviewing petitions for land grants on the Oconee River.[33] They considered reserving twenty square miles for granting Continental Army veterans the bounties promised by the state and central government.[34] Nearly a year before the treaty, Captain Patrick Carr suggested he could secretly plant a settlement on the Oconee without being discovered by Creeks.[35] The Assembly even granted "2000 acres of land in the Forks of the Oconee and Ocmulgee rivers" to one man "for past services."[36] Creeks did not cede the Oconee-Ocmulgee forks in the 1783 Treaty of Augusta. They would not do so for another two decades.

During the Revolutionary War, Creeks vigorously had attempted to reclaim the New Purchase lands, controversially ceded in 1773. Considering that recent experience, it seems strange that Georgians sensed no potential for conflict following the 1783 Treaty of Augusta. George

Walton served as chief justice of Wilkes County, the county created from the New Purchase that Creeks had raided hardest in the 1770s. Even Chief Justice Walton celebrated the 1783 cession. He declared that "the Creek Indians have consented, without trouble, to circumscribe their hunting grounds," and he looked forward to the "speedy settlement of an extensive country" where Georgians could enjoy "the pursuit of happiness undisturbed."[37] By April 1784, speculators were selling certificates for land in the Oconee strip.[38]

Multilateral Resistance: Talwa and Nation

Some Creek men began to resist the cession of the Oconee's east bank almost immediately. Their varied methods and motives illustrate the emergence of a political conflict between those who favored talwa autonomy and those who believed Creeks must adopt a central government to defend their territory. Older talwa leaders protested via diplomatic channels, urging Georgians to obey the terms of the 1783 Treaty of Augusta. Eager young men repudiated the treaty and launched raids to evict people they considered squatters. Alexander McGillivray's bicultural skills allowed him to ascend to leadership in Little Tallassee after Emistisiguo's death in the Siege of Savannah. McGillivray claimed responsibility for border patrols in a bid to unify Creek country under his leadership. Other Creeks insisted that McGillivray and his supporters did not represent consensus. Creek complaints against the Oconee cession sharpened customary forms of political conflict between talwas and factions within talwas who had differing economic priorities. Popular dissatisfaction with the land cession grew because of Georgians' encroachment and interference with Creek hunting rights. This stoked political conflict as young men resisted the persuasions of headmen.[39]

Still, Creeks displayed an uncommon degree of restraint in the two years following the 1783 Treaty of Augusta despite continual provocation. They used diplomacy and nonviolent border patrols to prevent white settlers from overrunning the Oconee lands. At least thirty-three raids occurred during the two-year period, and twenty-five of them struck the Oconee valley. Only four ended in bloodshed. Creek resistance convinced Georgia governor John Houstoun to issue a proclamation in 1784 forbidding settlement west of the Oconee River.[40] In November 1785, new talks yielded the Treaty of Galphinton, but the new treaty also failed to resolve the Oconee boundary dispute.[41]

The most important development in Creek politics in the 1780s was Alexander McGillivray's drive to centralize Creek government. He offered an alternative to talwa autonomy that undermined local leaders including Hoboithle Micco. As the son of a Scottish trader and a prominent Creek woman who spent much of his youth in colonial port cities, McGillivray had tenuous relations with common Creeks. Like other aspiring Creek leaders, he depended on alliances with talwa miccos, clan kin, and reciprocal gift giving to sustain his leadership claims. Unlike other Creek leaders, he lacked war honors, spoke the Muskogee language poorly, and, most importantly, he used literacy and experience in trade to monopolize relations with non-Indians.[42] In January 1784, McGillivray wrote to Spanish East Florida governor Vizente Manuel de Zéspedes to solicit a Spanish alliance in defense of Creek sovereignty and territory. He promised that "Indians will attach themselvs to and serve them best who supply there necessitys" though trade.[43] He then tried to control that trade by importing goods from Pensacola up the Alabama River to his plantation at Little Tallassee, and he offered his services as an Indian Affairs agent to "his Most Catholick Majesty."[44] Viewed from one perspective, McGillivray behaved as any micco must by securing a supply of goods to redistribute to his people.[45] Viewed from another perspective, he behaved in his own interest by securing trade from Florida while using Creek border patrols to stem the flow of goods from Georgia. McGillivray and a pair of white Indian countrymen, Richard Bailey and Joseph Cornel, reportedly encouraged Creek warriors to raid the Georgia frontier during the summer of 1784.[46] Patrick Carr was so incensed that he advised Governor Houstoun to charge McGillivray and his allies with an unrelated murder so that "they may be Easly Removed or Kiled on account of that womans Death."[47]

Despite Alexander McGillivray's apparent attempt "to Sett the Indians on," Creeks primarily resisted the 1783 Treaty of Augusta through diplomatic channels in 1784.[48] Treaty signers led by Hoboithle Micco protested Georgians' interpretation of the terms, emphasizing talwa-based understandings of leadership, territorial boundaries, and retained hunting rights on ceded lands. Alexander McGillivray sought an alliance with Spain that would recognize the legitimacy of a unified Creek Nation, secure its protection by a European nation-state, and ensure a steady flow of weapons and other goods. Hoboithle Micco and Alexander McGillivray both claimed to speak for all Creeks during 1784, yet they pursued very different diplomatic strategies.

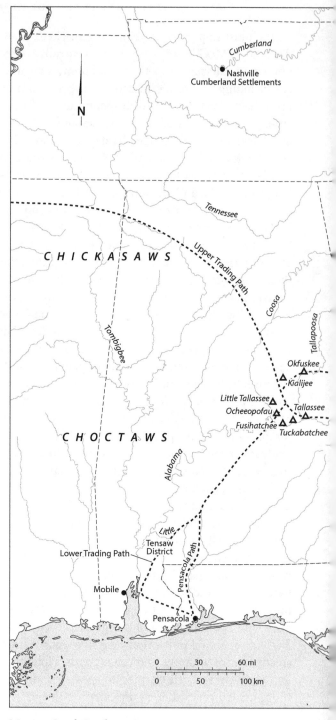

MAP 5. Creek Raids in Georgia, 1783–1785

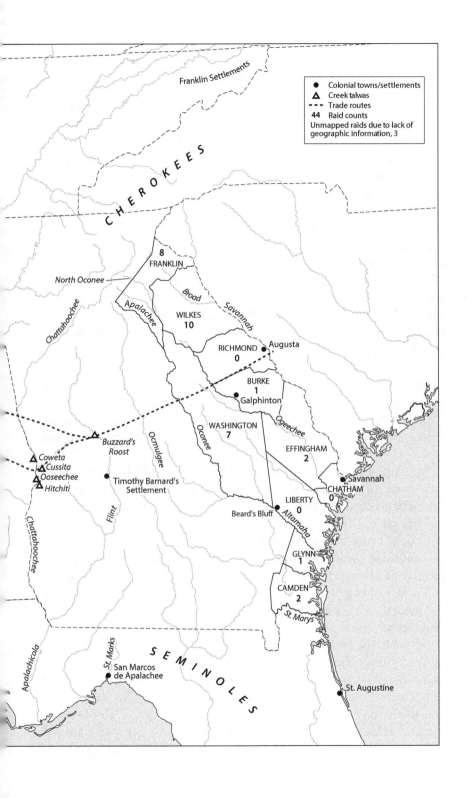

Colonial towns/settlements
Creek talwas
Trade routes
44   Raid counts
Unmapped raids due to lack of
geographic information, 3

Franklin Settlements

C H E R O K E E S

8
FRANKLIN

North Oconee

Broad

Apalachee

Savannah

WILKES
10

RICHMOND
0

Augusta

Chattahoochee

BURKE
1
Galphinton

WASHINGTON
7

Ogeechee

Oconee

Buzzard's
Roost

EFFINGHAM
2

Coweta
Cussita
Ooseechee
Hitchiti

Ocmulgee

Timothy Barnard's
Settlement

Savannah
CHATHAM
0

LIBERTY
0

Flint

Beard's Bluff
Altamaha

Chattahoochee

GLYNN
1

CAMDEN
2

St. Marys

Apalachicola

S E M I N O L E S

St. Marks

San Marcos
de Apalachee

St. Augustine

Hoboithle Micco's Talwa-Based Resistance

Hoboithle Micco and his allies met Georgians in March 1784 to urge them to abide by the terms of the 1783 Treaty of Augusta. They framed their diplomacy in terms of talwa autonomy. Hoboithle Micco argued that he had intended to cede only the land "as far as the main stream of the Oconee River," rather than lands all the way to its southernmost branch, the Apalachee.[49] He complained that Georgians had been surveying land as far as the Ocmulgee River, some forty miles west of the Oconee in undisputed Creek territory. Moreover, Hoboithle Micco explained that, under the principle of talwa autonomy, town leaders like himself "could only give up their own right and the rights of the people of the towns they represented." Recalling Emistisiguo's explanation of communal land ownership, Hoboithle Micco explained that "the land was not his." Creeks retained hunting rights on the Oconee's east bank because he lacked authority "to say to a man of any town who had not ceded his right to that ground . . . you shall not a kill a deer on that ground."[50] Neha Micco of Cussita concurred that hunters retained free access to the Oconee's east bank, and that whenever "the white and red People might meet on the Land . . . they should shake hands together."[51] Creeks "will be suffered" to hunt the Oconee's east bank, insisted the Second Man of the Cussetaws. If they met Americans, "they may eat out of the same Pan together."[52]

In addition to talwa autonomy, Hoboithle Micco also appealed to long-standing Mississippian concepts of diplomacy based on reciprocal exchange, mature civil leadership, and the accumulation of exotic prestige goods.[53] He proposed that "a few presents should be provided and all the towns invited to a talk and that the gift of that ground should be confirmed by all the Towns in the nation."[54] He requested specific prestige goods to reinforce his own authority, including a silver gorget and a pair of engraved silver armbands to illustrate his "indeavors for the success of the American arms."[55] Archaeology from the Tallapoosa province towns of Fusihatchee and Ocheeopofau, or Hickory Ground, show that in the late eighteenth century, the possession of prestige goods, especially silver, remained a critical marker of status.[56] Hoboithle Micco also insisted on the delivery of a drum, American flag, and greatcoat he had been promised during the Revolutionary War.[57] He needed symbols to reinforce his leadership because of the growing rivalry between older talwa leaders and men such as Alexander McGillivray who favored more centralized government. Patrick Carr reported that Hoboithle

Micco's allies were "very angry with McGilvery for attempting to send down talks without there knoledg."[58] Hoboithle Micco also recognized divergent economic interests between himself and men like McGillivray. Referring to Creek-owned slave plantations in the Tensaw district, he warned that McGillivray and longtime trader and planter Joseph Cornel "strives to spoil" Creek-Georgia relations *Because they have a great number of stolen Negroes which they have sent and settled near Mobille.*[59]

In September 1784, Hoboithle Micco claimed to speak for all Creeks when he renewed his demand for trade and border management on Creek terms. He explained that Creeks preferred trade with Georgians over "the French & Spaniards . . . at Pensacola and Mobile" because "they deal for money, that the Indians can't deal with them." Hoboithle Micco assured Georgia's leaders that, concerning trade, his words were "the voice of the whole nation," including "all the beloved men" and "the lower sort."[60]

However, Hoboithle Micco also reminded Georgians that many Creeks had not ceded their rights to the Oconee's east bank. He explained that all towns must confirm the cession before Georgians settled. Appealing to talwa autonomy, he noted that for him and his allies alone to give up the Oconee strip "would not be proper, but if a person was sent to the headmen of the nation with some goods the land might be obtained."[61] Hoboithle Micco suggested in particular sending a high-ranking official to Okfuskee to request that prominent Upper Town's consent to the Oconee cession. If Georgia did so, he believed, "the land would be given up peaceably."[62] Hoboithle Micco conspicuously failed to mention Alexander McGillivray and Little Tallassee.

Hoboithle Micco rebuked Georgians for willfully misinterpreting the Oconee boundary and interfering with Creek hunting rights. "When friends gather together," he told them, "it is customary not to throw each others' talks away."[63] The leader insisted that "he never mentioned giving up the land in the forks of the Oconee & that the white people have been there marking the trees & running their lines."[64] Trespassing was a sensitive issue that undermined his leadership. He warned Georgians that some Creeks were "dissatisfied" and blamed him for "giving away their rights." Hoboithle Micco repeated that he "intended the first water of the Oconee for the line," that is, the North Oconee River, rather than the Apalachee River, some thirty miles west.[65] Creeks valued the forks of the Oconee as an economic resource and, perhaps, imbued the area with special spiritual significance. All the presents Georgians offered in payment "would soon be gone, but the land still continue," Hoboithle Micco argued. "The Trees that grows in the woods are beloved & the grass."[66] He again asserted that once all talwas agreed on the border, Creeks would still retain hunting rights to any ceded land.[67]

A group of Lower Town leaders added their voices to Hoboithle Micco's refrain regarding the Oconee boundary, hunting rights, and talwa autonomy. Likely led by Neha Micco, they informed Governor Houstoun that they planned to hunt across the Oconee during winter. They asked Houstoun to notify white settlers so they could hunt "over the hocones [Oconee] without any dread."[68] Months later, Lower Town headmen agreed that representatives from all the talwas should meet with Georgians to define the border clearly. "As it is a matter that concerns the whole nation of us," they declared, "we mean to have the consent of every headman in the whole nation that there may be no more after Claps or Disputes for the future."[69]

Alexander McGillivray's Nation-Based Resistance

Alexander McGillivray pursued a different diplomatic path. He advocated that Creeks adopt a centralized government for their coalescent society and ally with Spain to defend Creek land and sovereignty. Spain and the United States were engaged in their own tense debates over territorial boundaries between the Appalachian Mountains and the Mississippi River. As those tensions increased, some Georgians and some Creeks expected a war that could bring much of present-day Georgia, Alabama, Mississippi, Tennessee, and Kentucky under Spanish authority. Georgia prepared by expanding toward East Florida, reportedly prompting the deployment of more than a thousand Spanish troops along the border.[70] McGillivray reasoned that an alliance with Spain in the expected conflict would afford Creeks the opportunity to push back the tide of white settlers and assert sovereignty under Spanish protection.[71]

McGillivray established a formal alliance with Spain in June 1784 with the Treaty of Pensacola. He claimed to represent an astonishing thirty-six towns from every province and linguistic group including Seminoles and Chickasaws, though many of the town leaders were "not present" in Pensacola, having elected to "remain in the nation."[72] A representative from Tallassee endorsed the Treaty of Pensacola, but it was not Hoboithle Micco. A few weeks later, Spain closed the Mississippi to American navigation.

Emboldened by Spanish support, McGillivray explicitly rejected all the terms of the 1783 Treaty of Augusta and claimed to speak for all Creeks. He argued that Creeks were "tenacious of their hunting grounds," especially the Oconee strip where they took "three thousand Deer Skins yearly."[73] He demanded that Georgia authorities "strectly forbid encroachments" along the Oconee and warned that only Georgia's legislature could "remove the horrid effect of a savage war."[74] Georgians accused Alexander McGillivray of encouraging young warriors to raid the Oconee lands. McGillivray, however, claimed that he "restrained my warriors," and Georgians acknowledged that some young men stole horses against the wishes of talwa leaders.[75]

McGillivray attempted to centralize power over Creek foreign affairs by monopolizing communications. In 1785, interpreter and trader James Durouzeaux delivered a talk from Georgia governor Samuel Elbert to McGillivray in which the governor called for a new round of negotiations. The ambitious Creek headman took advantage of the situation by withholding Elbert's talk from the public. Instead of gaining the support of talwa leaders from every division as he had done with the Treaty of Pensacola, McGillivray "had the Advise of a few that was [at] hand and has taken upon himself to Writte in the bahalfe of the upper Towns."[76] Durouzeaux, however, also presented the governor's talk in the Lower Towns. This presumption offended McGillivray. He argued the talk was a response to his own letter to the previous governor and so was meant for his eyes only.[77]

Hoboithle Micco and his allies in the Lower Towns grew impatient with McGillivray. Favoring localism, they called for a resolution of the Oconee boundary dispute based on the consent of all talwas. A group of Lower Town leaders gathered at Cussita and insisted that all Creeks must agree on a boundary. They believed that Upper Towns had chosen McGillivray "to act for them in this Matter," but Lower Towns felt a sense of urgency to resolve the dispute.[78] "Thair is Several places on this side of the Oconey River been marcked out with Blased Trees," the leaders noted anxiously. They protested that it "has given our people a graett concern" that unauthorized leaders "should give all the Hunting Ground away."[79] Expressing clear economic concerns, these Lower Town headmen feared that Georgians' encroachment would leave them with too few "Skins to by the Goods with."[80] Hoboithle Micco and several Lower Town headmen dismissed McGillivray. They informed Georgians they would meet with William Clark, a trader at Beard's Bluff on the Altamaha River, to "Setle Every point of the Line and Boundary." They declared that "the Nation has Laeft the wholle to them to act."[81] Excited by the prospect, William Clark's only concern was finding enough presents to satisfy his guests.[82]

Violence against white frontiersmen was far from the minds of most Creeks in 1784 and 1785.[83] James Durouzeaux reported, "The Nation at this present is as Quiett as posable," though famine had struck several towns.[84] A few horse theft raids had occurred, but Durouzeaux dismissed them as "villins" acting "Mutch against the consent of the Haed men."[85] Acknowledging that headmen lacked the authority to command young hunters, Durouzeaux wrote that "some rascals" insisted on stealing horses "even amongst themselves," in spite of leaders' "strong talks against it."[86]

Nearly 80 percent of the thirty-three recorded raids between 1783 and 1785 struck the Oconee valley. This geographical focus on disputed lands suggests raids were politically motivated rather than the opportunistic acts of rascals and villains. For example, in January 1785, Cowetas robbed John King in the forks of the Oconee, designated by Georgians as Franklin County. They relieved King of a rifle, six steel traps, and a beaver skin. The property suggests that King was a white hunter putting pressure on Creek resources.[87] Surveyor Robert Flournoy was robbed in July 1785 while marking out the lines of Washington County near the Oconee's east bank. As a surveyor, Flournoy was the perfect human symbol of the Oconee boundary dispute, yet Creeks did not harm him. Instead, Flournoy camped with a group of Creek hunters until they suddenly disappeared with his horse.[88]

U.S. Intervention: The Results of Multilateral Resistance

In the summer of 1785, the Confederation Congress intervened in the Oconee boundary dispute because it feared escalating conflict with Spain. Creeks were initially pleased with the intervention, viewing it as the result of their diplomacy and modest border raiding. Congress appointed commissioners to negotiate a firm border, and Alexander McGillivray announced that he had ordered Creek warriors to cease "predatory excursions" against Georgia settlers.[89] In reality, few raids had taken place since November 1783. McGillivray largely lacked both the coercive power and the persuasive influence to cause or end raiding. In the negotiations for what became the 1785 Treaty of Galphinton and its aftermath, Creek leaders became more divided as McGillivray grasped for authority to command border patrols.

While awaiting the arrival of U.S. treaty commissioners during the summer of 1785, Alexander McGillivray continued to work for better trading terms as a partner with Panton, Leslie & Company, a Scottish firm operating out of Spanish Pensacola with a near-monopoly in Creek country.[90] McGillivray asked for discounts on Spanish export duties for deerskins. He warned that Americans continued to "seduce" Creeks with "liberal trade," though he insisted Creeks "will continue to Refuse" such offers.[91] James Durouzeaux counseled Governor Samuel Elbert that Upper Creeks might follow McGillivray's lead and trade exclusively through Pensacola, but he had no influence with the Lower Creeks.[92]

Despite border conflict, proximity to Augusta along the Creek Path still made trading with Georgia attractive to Lower Creeks. James Durouzeaux remarked that Lower Towns were "Very Letle Concerned" with the Spanish.[93] Escotchaby of Coweta and others had worked to establish a thriving trade in East Florida during the 1770s, but Spanish alliance evidently held little allure. Cuban vessels still made regular visits to the Gulf Coast, but Creek access to Spanish goods remained problematic. Authorities were unable to provide adequate presents to renew the relationship. West Florida governor Arturo O'Neill reportedly discouraged Creeks from visiting Pensacola because "he haed Nothing to Give them," not even a small supply of food for their journey home.[94] Trading at San Marcos de Apalache in East Florida was hampered by the interference of Georgia traders, navigational difficulties, and foul weather.[95]

During the late summer of 1785, different leaders claiming to represent Coweta sent opposing talks. The situation illustrated Creeks' diffuse, multilateral leadership structure, talwa autonomy, and communal land ownership. A group referring to themselves simply as "We the Coweitter people" sent a talk to Governor Elbert disavowing horse theft committed by young Creeks and urging him to control backcountry Georgians. They warned that if encroachment "on our hunting ground" west of the Oconee River continued, "our peace, can Not Be Long." If Georgians impeded Creek hunters, they argued, "Whaer . . . Shall we Get Skins to buy what Good' our traeder Shall bring?"[96] The talk conveyed the importance of the faltering deerskin trade and, by extension, commitment to communal land ownership and retained hunting rights on the Oconee lands. "The Coweitter people" even reminded Governor Elbert that, "although it is . . . our hunting ground We are not all the people that hunts thaer."[97]

"The Coweitter people" promised that, if Georgia controlled its own aggressive hunters and settlers, Cowetas also would restrain their "young people . . . for the better keeping our path White and Strait."[98] To demonstrate their commitment, they returned to Georgians some horses recently stolen by "Maed young people."[99] This affirmed the Creek political pattern of dynamic tension between the white path of peace and persuasion pursued by older headmen and the red path of aggression traveled by young men. Cowetas understood that young hunters had legitimate grievances against white border jumpers, but horse rustling provoked Georgians. Returning the property could preempt violent retaliation.

"The Coweitter people" reassured Georgians they were eager to establish a firm border. Once lines were run, however, Cowetas expected that any white people settled over the line "would obey ther Governor and move from all Sutch places."[100] On the whole, then, these Cowetas appeared optimistic that a clearly surveyed boundary would prevent Georgians' encroachment west of the Oconee, clarify Creek hunting rights, and remove the aggravation that led some young men to confiscate white people's horses.

Alexander McGillivray also claimed to speak for Coweta and several other towns, taking a markedly more aggressive tone. He claimed to declare war between the Creek Nation and Georgia, but evidence suggests only modest border patrols resulted.[101] He again renounced the Oconee cession, and, in September 1785, he commanded Creek warriors to sweep white settlers from the Oconee strip by force. He directed his orders to men from the Lower Town of Coweta, the Upper Town of Tuckabatchee, and others. Border patrols were to carry his written orders with them as they "move[d] off the Okonee settlers," and McGillivray required that "The houses of such as are moved must be destroyed to prevent others coming on."[102]

"The Coweitter people" already had promulgated their own, milder approach to the boundary dispute, and the manner in which McGillivray delivered his orders suggests that his command fell on deaf ears. McGillivray depended on the prestige of other headmen to motivate young warriors. Rather than delivering his talk orally on the town square ground at Coweta, McGillivray wrote to white interpreter James Durouzeaux, instructing him to pass the orders on to Yahola Micco of Coweta. Yahola Micco, then, carried the burden of persuading young warriors to follow him.[103] From the comfort of his slave plantation more than a hundred miles west, McGillivray, who had never led a successful raid himself, instructed Durouzeaux to order Yahola Micco to "call your Woriors together and tell them this Talk." He reiterated that warriors should "drive off from the Okonee all encroachers," but they must "Not to Molest any white person or thaer property."[104]

It is unlikely that McGillivray's words carried much weight with warriors. There is no correlation between reported raids and his commands. McGillivray sent his talks in September 1785, but in the following eight months, only six to twelve raids occurred. Creeks stole some two dozen horses, but they destroyed no houses. This suggests the raids were unrelated to McGillivray's orders. By comparison, in the eight months preceding September 1785, Georgians reported six to twelve raids on white settlers in the Oconee valley. These, too, consisted mostly of horse thefts. There was no change in the frequency, location, or nature of raids before and after McGillivray's orders.

McGillivray's letters from September 1785 reveal some discomfort with his claims to national leadership. Initially, he attributed command of border patrols to a Creek national council, but later he suggested he alone commanded them. For most of the eighteenth century, there was no national council with authority over talwas and their residents, though the provinces and the broader confederacy held multitown councils with increasing frequency.[105] McGillivray wrote to U.S. treaty commissioner Andrew Pickens explaining that "a meeting of the nation" had decided "to send out parties" to evict squatters from the Oconee strip.[106] Once commissioners appointed by the Confederation Congress arrived to restrain wayward Georgians, however, McGillivray volunteered as a show of good faith to "prevent any future predatory excursions of my people."[107]

McGillivray initially succeeded in shaping the talks that led to the Treaty of Galphinton. Always an enigmatic figure, it remains unclear whether he was a Creek patriot, a shrewd opportunist, or some combination of the two. It is apparent, however, that he believed U.S. commissioners would be more conciliatory than Georgians. He instructed James Durouzeaux to tell Lower Creek headmen that he would "accompany the chiefs" to the upcoming talks.[108] As late as November 4, McGillivray still planned to attend the meeting personally and noted that "the talks are very good in the nation."[109]

Over the following week, McGillivray decided to absent himself from the Galphinton talks. Hoboithle Micco of Tallassee, Neha Micco of Cussita, and about eighty warriors assembled at the former trading post and settlement on the Ogeechee River near present-day Louisville, Georgia.[110] Commissioners appointed by the Confederation Congress left the Galphinton talks because the small Creek delegation could not legitimately speak for all towns.

Georgia's representatives moved forward, despite the absence of both McGillivray and the U.S. commissioners. Georgians signed the Treaty of Galphinton with Creeks on November 12, 1785. Alexander McGillivray quickly rejected the new agreement and redoubled his resistance. He ordered more raids to oust settlers from the Oconee's east bank, again admonishing warriors to refrain from violence unless in self-defense.[111] Just as in previous months, however, McGillivray's claim to command likely outstripped his real influence.[112]

1785 Treaty of Galphinton: Complications of Conflict

Secretary of War Henry Knox reflected in 1789 that, despite Creek dissatisfaction with the 1783 Treaty of Augusta, "it was not until a few months after the treaty of Galphinton, that uneasiness began to be fomented in the nation, and some murders were committed."[113] The Treaty of Galphinton confirmed the Oconee River boundary to its "most southern branch," which Georgians defined as the Apalachee River.[114] It also secured a large, new cession of land in south Georgia between the Altamaha River and the St. Marys, the border with Spanish East Florida.[115] White travelers and traders were to be granted free passage through Creek country, a privilege of great importance to the thousands of Americans then settling the plantation district around Spanish Natchez.[116] Creek authorities retained the decisive right to evict any white people who "shall attempt to settle or run any of the lands reserved to the Indians."[117] Moreover, the treaty affirmed Creek rights to arrest Americans who committed crimes in Creek country, though any alleged white criminals must be tried under Georgia law.[118] These two stipulations conveyed Georgia's tacit approval of limited border patrols, though they did not condone property confiscation as John Stuart had in the 1770s.

The list of seventeen Creek leaders who signed the Treaty of Galphinton illuminates the depth of Creek commitment to talwa autonomy and the limits of Alexander McGillivray's influence. Signers included headmen from the Abika, Okfuskee, and Tallapoosa provinces of the Upper Creeks and both Muskogee and Hitchiti speakers from the Apalachicola province of the Lower Creeks.[119] McGillivray claimed to represent all Creeks and especially to command the Upper Towns, yet he boycotted the Galphinton talks. Even some Lower Town headmen agreed that McGillivray acted for all Upper Towns, yet five Upper Towns consented to the new treaty, including the prominent town of Okfuskee that long had enjoyed close trade ties with Georgia. At the height of Alexander

McGillivray's claims to lead Creeks, and at the peak of Georgians' and Spaniards' ascription of national leadership to him, this evidence shows that many Creeks chose the principle of talwa autonomy over centralized power. Perhaps more revealing is that Coweta and Cussita, the two most powerful Lower Towns, consented to cede the Oconee strip in both the 1783 Treaty of Augusta and the 1785 Treaty of Galphinton. Even Yahola Micco of Coweta signed at Galphinton, the very man Alexander McGillivray had ordered to raid the Oconee lands just three months earlier. Lower Towns long had asserted primary authority over the lands in present-day Georgia, and Upper Towns often had deferred to their wishes.

Georgia prepared to occupy the Oconee strip systematically with a new "seat of government," yet McGillivray claimed victory over both Americans and his Creek rivals.[120] He informed Spanish West Florida governor Arturo O'Neill that "there was not twenty Indians in the whole" who attended the congress at Galphinton, and those who went "were not of any consequence."[121] McGillivray directly insulted Hoboithle Micco, calling him a "roving beggar, going wherever he thinks he can get presents."[122] He claimed that U.S. treaty commissioners had quarreled openly with Georgia commissioners, and "thereby rendered themselves Completely ridiculous" to Creek leaders who mattered.[123] McGillivray even took perverse pleasure in the notion that Americans intended to murder him. He gloated that Americans all agreed "it is my fault that they cant bring their Schemes to bear," so they fixated on "Contriving . . . my assassination."[124]

One might expect that violence increased between the 1783 Treaty of Augusta and the 1785 Treaty of Galphinton, but it did not. Heated rhetoric, tense diplomacy, and a few raids targeting property took place throughout 1784 and much of 1785. The Treaty of Galphinton simply confirmed the Creek border as the southernmost branch of the Oconee River with no mention of retained Creek hunting rights to the east bank. The new treaty secured an additional land cession farther south yet acknowledged Creek rights to arrest Georgians trespassing in Creek country.[125] In the years between the treaties, Georgians accused Creeks of just four violent incidents, a marked decline from the Revolutionary War years. During the same period, white men murdered at least two white Georgians and one Creek hunter in frontier counties, and grand juries constantly complained about the theft and violence of non-Indian criminal gangs. White settlers had as much to fear from one another as from Creeks.[126]

The contested treaties of 1783 and 1785 produced little bloodshed, but they sharpened the outlines of internal Creek political conflict. Alexander McGillivray and his allies led a drive to centralize Creek government, but many Creeks remained committed to independent talwa governments. While McGillivray summoned a national council and commanded Creeks to raid the Oconee strip, several translated talks from talwa leaders show that they were willing to allow Georgia settlers to remain in the Oconee valley. Talwa leaders criticized Georgians, however, for willfully misinterpreting treaty terms by claiming land west to the Apalachee River, trespassing west of the Oconee, and harassing Creek hunters on the Oconee's east bank. Despite opposing political ideals and economic interests, talwa leaders found themselves constantly addressing the same issues, and that shared experience ultimately led to greater coalescence.

5 /   "Always in Defense of Our Rights":
The Creek Threat, Real and Imagined, 1786

The year 1786 was a turning point for Creeks committed to talwa autonomy. The 1785 Treaty of Galphinton did little to restrain Georgians' encroachment, and 1786 witnessed a small but significant increase in border patrols. A few of them ended in violence, representing a real but limited Creek threat to Georgia's expansion. Alexander McGillivray claimed responsibility for these raids while a diverse group of talwa leaders rejected his claim to leadership and disavowed the patrols. Young men from many different geographic and linguistic divisions in Creek country raided Georgia settlers for a variety of reasons, often without support from McGillivray or older talwa leaders. Georgians, however, found it politically expedient to view McGillivray as the dominant force in Creek country bent on invading the state and destroying Oconee valley counties. They crafted a political narrative around this imagined Creek threat, misrepresenting border patrols and ignoring white settlers' provocations. Georgia leaders used that political narrative, official intimidation, and the menace of ungovernable settlers to extract concessions from Creeks in the 1786 Treaty of Shoulderbone Creek. The unsatisfying agreement at Shoulderbone forced talwa leaders to recognize that negotiating with Georgia as independent towns had failed, yet they continued to resent Alexander McGillivray's attempt to centralize Creek government. The turmoil of 1786—a few violent raids, young men's rejection of older headmen's authority, Alexander McGillivray's arrogation of power, and Georgia's misrepresentation of the Creek threat—left Creeks grasping for a solution that suited the diverse needs of their coalescing society.

The Creek-Spanish alliance formally secured in the 1784 Treaty of Pensacola remained central to obstructing U.S. expansion, but Spain's goals ultimately conflicted with those of Creek leaders. In 1786, the alliance still benefited both Creeks and Spaniards. Creeks needed trade goods imported through the Spanish Gulf Coast, and Spain hoped to use its Creek, Cherokee, and Chickasaw allies to limit U.S. growth. Spain, however, also continued recruiting American immigrants to Natchez and Tensaw as well as cultivating secessionist elements in Cumberland and Franklin. In 1786, Cumberland settlers named their Superior Court district Mero in honor of Spanish Louisiana's governor.[1] Franklin's leader, John Sevier, negotiated directly with Governor Estevan Miró and Diego de Gardoqui, Spanish minister to the United States. While Creeks continued to focus on the Georgia border, a few raiders struck the growing Cumberland settlements, and Franklinites corresponded with Georgians about the Creek threat. Spanish support was critical to Creek resistance in 1786, but Creek sovereignty was not Spain's priority.[2]

Creeks committed little bloodshed in 1786, though border raiding increased somewhat over the previous two years. Between the 1783 Treaty of Augusta and the 1785 Treaty of Galphinton, Georgians reported thirty-three Creek raids, whereas twenty-five raids occurred in 1786 alone. With Spanish alliance and the growth of McGillivray's kin network at Tensaw, the West Florida border seemed more peaceful and more secure than ever. The growing Cumberland settlement to the north caused some concern, but Cherokees held primary claim to that area. As in previous years, raids focused geographically on the Oconee River valley and usually resulted in horse theft. In eight violent raids, Creeks killed six to ten white Georgians.[3] Two of those were in retaliation for unprovoked murders of Creeks. Common Creeks widely endorsed the religious duty to satisfy the crying blood of the slain by committing retributive violence, so such cases could diminish differences between talwas. However, Georgians used retaliation killings to justify their own retributive violence and pressure Creek leaders for concessions, worsening tensions between young warriors and older headmen. Settlers lashed out, killing at least six and perhaps as many as fifteen Creek men in 1786.[4] Such numbers show that Creeks had as much to fear from white Georgians as the reverse.

The constant threat of violence compelled some talwa leaders to assert leadership of entire provinces, furthering regional coalescence yet increasing factionalism in the larger polity. After months of heightened tension on the border, some Creek leaders called for peace and signed the controversial Treaty of Shoulderbone Creek in November. The Treaty of Shoulderbone Creek became a major turning point. In the months leading up to Shoulderbone, Alexander McGillivray and his allies continued their efforts to present Creeks as a unified nation under his leadership. He convinced Georgians that he had the power to launch a full-scale war. Other miccos argued that McGillivray had little influence beyond a few Tallapoosa and Abika Upper Towns, so he must be ignored. Over the course of 1786 even some headmen who resented McGillivray's claims to national leadership concluded that the system of talwa autonomy was not effective in dealing with Georgia. In response, a cadre of talwa leaders claimed to represent multiple towns during the Shoulderbone talks. In this limited move toward political consolidation, Lower Town leaders asserted primary control over the Georgia border. Emistisiguo had used a similar strategy in the 1770s: encouraging greater coalescence while deferring to divergent local interests. The onerous terms of the Shoulderbone treaty, however, alienated most Creeks. More than any event in the previous two decades, Shoulderbone united people across the talwas.

The Creek Threat in Reality: McGillivray's Gambit, Divided Talwas, and Mad Young Men

In February 1786, Alexander McGillivray declared that, after repeated warnings, Georgia's encroachment had left him no choice but to call "all the Chiefs of the Nation to assemble" and organize border patrols for national defense.[5] McGillivray's national council took place in March at Tuckabatchee and included delegates from twenty-three talwas representing the Upper Creek provinces of Abika, Tallapoosa, Alabama, and Okfuskee, as well as Muskogee, Hitchiti, and Koasati speakers from Apalachicola province Lower Towns. McGillivray reported that representatives "unanimously" agreed to his proposal for new border patrols.[6] This national council determined as a group "to take arms in our defence & repel those invaders of our Lands, to drive them from their encroachments & fix them within their proper limits."[7] This meeting of leaders from twenty-three talwas represents McGillivray's most successful attempt to establish a national council under his leadership. By comparison, representatives from twenty-six talwas met in 1774 to address the White-Sherrill affair.[8]

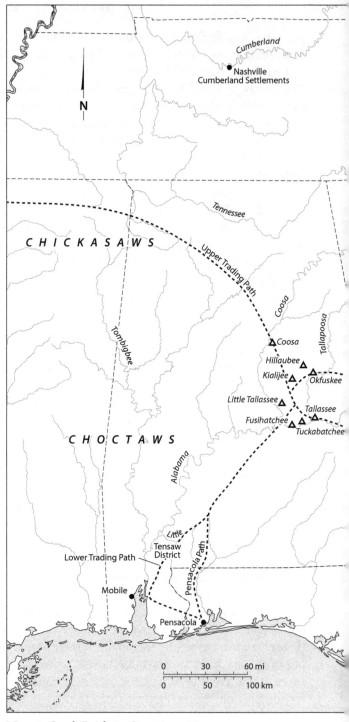

MAP 6. Creek Raids in Georgia, 1786

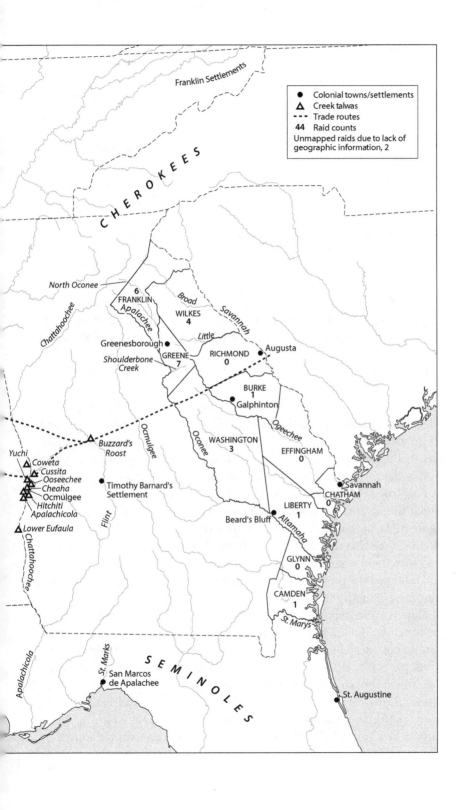

Colonial towns/settlements •
Creek talwas △
Trade routes - - -
44 Raid counts
Unmapped raids due to lack of
geographic information, 2

Franklin Settlements

C H E R O K E E S

North Oconee

6
FRANKLIN

Chattahoochee

Apalachee

Broad

Savannah

WILKES
4

Little

Greenesborough •

Shoulderbone
Creek

GREENE
7

RICHMOND
0

Augusta •

BURKE
1

Galphinton •

Ocmulgee

Oconee

Ogeechee

WASHINGTON
3

EFFINGHAM
0

Buzzard's
Roost △

Yuchi
△ Coweta
△ Cussita
△ Ooseechee
△ Cheaha
△ Ocmulgee
Hitchiti
Apalachicola

Timothy Barnard's
Settlement •

Flint

LIBERTY
1

Beard's Bluff •

Altamaha

Savannah •
CHATHAM
0

△ Lower Eufaula

Chattahoochee

GLYNN
0

CAMDEN
1

St. Marys

Apalachicola

St. Marks

S E M I N O L E S

San Marcos
de Apalachee •

St. Augustine •

In April and May 1786, modest border patrols resulted from McGillivray's national council, hinting at his limited influence. Writing from the Tallapoosa province Upper Town of Tuckabatchee, McGillivray ordered four men by name to undertake patrols in Georgia while others struck the Cumberland settlements.[9] The first of these, Hopoy Micco, hailed from McGillivray's own Little Tallassee town. As a slave owner and cattle rancher, Hopoy Micco stood to gain personally from border raids.[10] The Second Man of Ooseechee and Yahola Micco of Coweta both led Muskogee-speaking Lower Towns, and Yahola Micco himself would later sign the Treaty of Shoulderbone Creek. Efau Hadjo, the Mad Dog, represented Tuckabatchee. Like Yahola Micco, Efau Hadjo was an ambivalent ally to McGillivray.[11] McGillivray reported that "it is the Mad Dog's desire" that participating warriors assemble at Kialijee on the Upper Trading Path "that the matter may be properly conducted."[12] This suggests that Efau Hadjo led the two raids that followed. In those raids, Creeks stole fourteen horses and destroyed a few buildings in Franklin County between the Apalachee and Oconee Rivers.[13] Put another way, only two raids directly resulted from McGillivray's national council and his command to all Creeks.[14]

Headmen of Cussita and its daughter town, Buzzard's Roost, quickly rejected Alexander McGillivray's claim to leadership and disavowed all involvement in border patrols. Their talk to Georgians in early May reveals ongoing political conflict between towns and growing conflict within them. They acknowledged that "Some of the mad people" from Upper Towns conducted raids "by Mr. McGillivereyes orders" during which they plundered and burned houses on the Oconee's "big shoals." Those raids, however, were "unknown to us your friends."[15] Cussitas were so concerned that they actually confronted one patrol, "took all we could find with them wich consist of two rifle guns and a great many Cloaths," and returned the property via longtime Indian countryman, trader, and translator Timothy Barnard.[16]

Cussitas also reported that they had received a talk from Cowetas renouncing McGillivray's border patrol and assuring Cussitas they "would not interfear and that they mean to remain in friendship with the white people."[17] This suggests that, McGillivray's orders notwithstanding, Yahola Micco and common Cowetas may have ignored the call to action. Moreover, Cussitas pledged that any stolen horses brought into town "shall all be taken and Delivered to there owners at Augusta."[18] The Cussita headmen pledged to restrain any young men tempted to raid to prevent any "spilling of Blood."[19]

Cussitas perhaps expected that curbing border patrols before bloodshed occurred would be a relatively easy task. Few raids occurred in April and early May, and even Alexander McGillivray's orders prohibited violence. McGillivray insisted that raiders must "kill no one," but "burn houses bring of[f] Every thing they find on their lands and drive the people of[f]."[20] This tactic conformed to long-standing practice. Escotchaby of Coweta had been warning illegal settlers since 1767 that Creeks would evict them and burn their homes. He had conducted nonviolent patrols of his own after the bloodshed of the White-Sherrill affair.[21] When John Trice and other members of his Greene County household reported the border patrol raid that struck them in May, all acknowledged that Creeks committed no violence. Trice provided a detailed account of damaged and stolen property, including the two rifles that Cussitas later confiscated from raiders and returned.[22] Two women were present in the Trice home when raiders struck, and they reported that the party "seemed to be entirely in quest to plunder, having made little or no attempt to kill or otherwise injure any of the family."[23] Instead, Creeks allowed the women to flee before they burned the house. The raid on the Trice home shows that even those few Creeks involved in McGillivray's border patrols in the spring of 1786 intended to evict settlers by confiscating or destroying their property rather than harming them.

McGillivray pushed for a national policy to harass settlers in the Oconee valley, but he apparently failed to gain the support of Coweta and Cussita, the two most prominent Lower Towns with the strongest claim to the Oconee lands. He influenced several Upper Towns but convinced only a handful of warriors to patrol the border. Cussita headmen reported that three of the five men who "Burnt the house on the Ocones" were from McGillivray's own household.[24] Emphasizing talwa autonomy, Cussitas advised that if McGillivray claimed "all the town has takin his talk in this affair . . . that it is not the case." They assured Georgians that "it is only a few towns aboute himself."[25]

Cussita headmen affirmed their friendship with Georgians in a characteristically Creek manner that further demonstrates their political commitment to talwa autonomy and their cultural distance from McGillivray's claim to national leadership. They renewed friendship using a custom that had been documented by Europeans since the 1500s and that Hoboithle Micco had used with Georgians in 1782.[26] In keeping with Creek color symbolism in which white denoted peaceful alliance and feathers conveyed spiritual power drawn from the upper world of order and perfection, Cussitas presented "as full tokin of our friendship . . . a white wing," and, they hoped, "wen you see this with our talk that you will be fully convinced that we are not madmen."[27]

McGillivray lived in a world where negotiations took place via written correspondence. Treaties were concluded by drawing maps and signing documents. Many Creeks practiced politics by other means. They believed that negotiations were best conducted through ritualistic oratory. Treaties should be struck through the reciprocal exchange of objects charged with spiritual energy. When McGillivray attempted to discredit Hoboithle Micco by calling him a beggar who sought presents, there was a kernel of truth in that criticism. Hoboithle Micco combined older forms of ritual gift exchange with newer forms of commercial trade. By the 1780s, southeastern Indians had been combining indigenous and European forms of exchange to create alliances for two centuries, but they had been doing it as representatives of autonomous towns.[28] Creek leaders' behavior from 1783 to 1786 suggests they still preferred this older form of governance, despite Alexander McGillivray's assertions that he led a centralized nation.

A few more violent incidents occurred in May and June as Creek dissatisfaction with the Oconee cession continued. Violent raids elicited dramatically exaggerated responses from Georgians, and for that reason, more talwa leaders disavowed them. The raids, however, involved men from several different provinces and linguistic divisions within the Upper and Lower Towns. This suggests widespread disagreement between young hunters and talwa leaders. Georgians' responses began with rhetoric but escalated quickly.

Just days after Cussitas sent a white wing to Georgia governor Edward Telfair, a border patrol killed and scalped one white Georgian near the Oconee River in Washington County, a large swath of land encompassing the lower half of the river's east bank. Militia Colonel Jonathan Clements of Burke County, just west of Washington, wrote to Governor Telfair requesting ammunition so he could march to the neighboring county's aid.[29] Overstating the Creek threat, Clements declared that "unless the people of Washington County get a reinforcement it will be Impossible for them to withstand the enemy."[30] A few days later, Clements again warned of "the Hostile Intention of the Creeks and I expect every day to hear more people being killed by them."[31]

John Galphin explained to Colonel Clements that a small but diverse group of thirteen to fourteen young warriors were responsible for the May raid on Washington County. Galphin was the son of the late trader and patriot superintendent of Indian Affairs George Galphin and Metawney, a Coweta woman of the Wind clan. His testimony revealed that resistance to the Oconee cession was growing even among men whose talwa leaders had signed the Treaties of Augusta and Galphinton. The diverse group of border patrollers who struck Washington County included Upper Town men from Tuckabatchee in the Tallapoosa province as well as Lower Town men from Koasati-speaking Cheaha, Muskogee-speaking Lower Eufaula, and Yuchi speakers.[32] Efau Hadjo of Tuckabatchee already had answered Alexander McGillivray's call for border patrols, so continued raiding from that town is unsurprising.[33] A representative from Lower Eufaula, however, had signed the Treaty of Galphinton. The participation of Lower Eufaula warriors shows that some regretted the choice.[34] The patrollers told John Galphin that they would "drive all the cattle and horses they could find and kill all the people they could find in Washington county," contrary to Alexander McGillivray's orders to evict settlers and burn their homes without bloodshed.[35] Galphin's testimony illustrates that the warriors were acting independently of their own talwa leaders and McGillivray. Ironically, John Galphin continued collaborating with Georgia as an interpreter and informer in 1786, but a few short years later, he became a notorious border raider himself.

Rather than responding to Alexander McGillivray's call for border raids, the Lower Creeks whom Galphin encountered likely were influenced by Neha Micco of Cussita. Neha Micco was one of the most influential men in the Lower Towns. He had been a part of every negotiation with Georgians in the 1780s, and he had signed both the Treaty of Augusta and the Treaty of Galphinton. But on May 14, one Georgian reported witnessing Neha Micco urging young men to raid the Oconee valley, "Drive the inhabitants, and take their property."[36] The informant also reported that Creeks recently had fired at Georgians while patrolling Oconee River tributaries in Greene and Washington Counties near present-day Athens.[37] Neha Micco's promotion of border patrols confirms that, by late spring of 1786, some Creeks who had signed the treaties of the 1780s were frustrated with Georgia's failure to abide by the boundary and respect Creeks' retained hunting rights on the east bank.

When white settlers killed Creeks, Georgia's justice system usually failed to provide satisfaction, giving young warriors additional reason to raid. The Creek concept of domestic and international justice referred to as crying blood or the law of blood imposed a religious duty on Creek men to restore cosmic balance. If an outsider killed a Creek person, all Creeks were bound to cause an equivalent death in the offender's community. The victim's close clan kin in his or her home talwa likely led calls for satisfaction, and Creeks could decide at the talwa level to abstain from the process. Many Creeks supported crying blood killings, yet the practice widened divisions between young men and talwa leaders. It frustrated those who wanted a national government capable of restraining young men.[38] In May, for example, white men at Beard's Bluff on the Altamaha River in southern Washington County murdered two Cheaha "men of note."[39] This all but guaranteed their clan kin in Cheaha would kill Georgians to balance the deaths. Headmen from Cussita and its daughter town, Buzzard's Roost, soon reported that "some of the mad people has Spilt Blood on the land by killing two white people."[40] Cussita headmen feared indiscriminate retaliation from Georgia, so they hurriedly informed Governor Telfair that only "a few men oute of five towns" had committed the bloodshed. They insisted that "the other towns have scolded them so much . . . that they doe not intend to goe oute any more."[41]

Cussita headmen disavowed the violence, but they also tried to protect those responsible. In doing so, they asserted talwa autonomy and admitted that retribution killings enjoyed popular support. They acknowledged that the Treaty of Galphinton called for "Satisfaction" in the event of murders committed by "mad people," but they argued that murders had occurred on both sides.[42] This met the Creek standard of justice, but it left Georgians seething. Cussitas initially volunteered to provide satisfaction by killing one of the leaders "of all this mischief," but they reminded Georgians that "two of our people is likewise fell."[43] Georgia Superintendent of Indian Affairs Daniel McMurphy acknowledged it would be impossible to apprehend the Creek killers until Georgians captured the white men who had murdered Cheahas.[44]

Daniel McMurphy, a vociferous critic of McGillivray, the Spanish, and Creek border patrols, reported a more serious raid in late May that strains credibility. According to McMurphy, a large force of one hundred men from the Okfuskee province Upper Town of Hillaubee and the Tallapoosa province Upper Town of Kialijee struck the "upper Settlement," killing five Georgians.[45] Citing the killing of "four or five of our people," in Washington and Greene Counties, Governor Telfair encouraged local militiamen to take up their guns and respond in kind.[46]

Ironically, in the early months of 1786, even experienced Indian fighter Elijah Clarke admitted that there was little reason to fear Creek raids. In May, he noted that twenty Creeks had evicted a settler from Greene County and burned his house, but otherwise there was "little news."[47] By contrast, the Georgia Gazette reported about the same time that "an

Indian war seems to be inevitable. Several people in the upper counties have been lately murdered."[48] Taking no chances, Clarke requested additional arms, ammunition, and men because "I am of the opinion more mischief is Intended."[49]

Creeks risked their lives when they attempted to clear settlers from disputed land. As militia officers fretted about the threat of Creek invasion, the *Gazette* celebrated Elijah Clarke's attack on a retreating border patrol that resulted in the deaths of two Creeks. The *Gazette* boasted that Clarke had "put a stop to their murders, and prevented their again entering the frontier settlements."[50] Indeed, Clarke's "Gall and brave conduct" in assaulting Creeks would be praised later as the only thing that had saved Georgia's frontier.[51]

In light of the spring patrols, Georgians struggled to gauge Alexander McGillivray's threats to resist land cessions through raiding. Indian countryman Timothy Barnard suggested that McGillivray had far less influence in Creek country than Georgians commonly believed. He reported to Governor Telfair that "the whole nation I hear seems to be offended with Mr. McGillivray," and most Creeks desired peace.[52] By contrast, trader and interpreter James Durouzeaux pointed to growing regional factionalism when he claimed that McGillivray had called for a new national council meeting in June where he hoped to convince all Lower Creeks to join Upper Creeks in efforts to reclaim the Oconee strip.[53] Durouzeaux believed that most Lower Creeks had accepted the cessions despite recent events. In the 1780s, Creeks also periodically raided white settlements that encroached on their northern hunting grounds in the Tennessee and Cumberland River valleys. McGillivray claimed responsibility for those raids, too. Spanish and American agents generally accepted his claim.[54]

Creek behavior makes clear that young men raided the Oconee lands of their own volition, often in opposition to the wishes of headmen, and with potentially disastrous consequences. McGillivray declared a cessation of border patrols in June, but some Creeks continued striking settlers. McGillivray cautioned warriors "to be Stil & mind Nothing but thaer planting & hunting," yet James Durouzeaux warned that men from the Lower Town of Yuchi had travelled to "the frontaers to Comitt Murder."[55] It is unclear whether Yuchis actually committed any violence in June 1786, but Georgians responded to the rumor with overwhelming violence. Lower Creek hunters soon discovered the bodies of nine of their people murdered by Georgians. Town sizes varied in the late eighteenth century, but the average talwa population included around one hundred adult men. The deaths of nine men could be a proportionally staggering loss.[56] Georgia's violence shocked the Lower Towns, putting "the whole of the Lower in fright."[57] Indeed, the loss of Creek life may have been greater than initially reported because several hunters remained missing after the discovery of the first nine victims.[58]

In late June, Georgians accused Creeks of murdering and scalping a white girl. In a message disavowing responsibility, a group of Lower Creek headmen reasserted talwa autonomy and priority claims to particular territories. They distinguished themselves from mad young men in other towns as well as Alexander McGillivray's leadership claims. Headmen from Koasati-speaking Cheaha, the Hitchiti-speaking towns of Ocmulgee and Hitchiti, and Muskogee-speaking Ooseechee insisted that they must not be held accountable for the violence of others. "Our Young Warriors are inclineable to go to their hunting Grounds in peace, and expect to be dealt with as friends."[59] Far from protesting land cessions, these headmen invited Georgia settlers who had fled to return to their farms on the Altamaha River at the south end of Washington County. "Upon the Alatamaha," they assured settlers, "is the Cheehaws hunting Ground and they will not molest the White Inhabitants."[60] Further distancing themselves from the killing, the headmen suggested that Seminoles urged on by white trader James Burgess were responsible for the white girl's death.[61]

In addition to promoting Creek border patrols, Alexander McGillivray energetically cultivated non-Creek allies to help defend his country's borders and centralize its government. Georgians perceived his assertions of leadership, his quest for allies, and his encouragement of border patrols as the opening gambit in a full-scale war. White Indian countrymen like James Burgess often supported McGillivray and his efforts to resist the Oconee cession. Their economic influence as traders deepened Creek political conflict because talwa miccos resented the challenge to their authority and local autonomy. Indian countryman Richard Bailey, for example, had allied with McGillivray to encourage border patrols into the Oconee valley since 1784, and he continued to do so in 1786.[62] Creek headmen sometimes blamed Indian countrymen for causing violent raids, and they later called for the deaths of McGillivray, Bailey, and trader John Francis.[63] Georgia tried to control such men by requiring trading licenses, but Daniel McMurphy reported in July that when he demanded Lower Town traders present their credentials, they "produced their Licence from McGilvery." Perhaps because traders' livelihoods were tied as closely to deerskin as Creek hunters, they too warned that "if the people did not move off the Oconey River there would be a war."⁶⁴

Other white people in Creek country, however, worked to undermine McGillivray and his allies. Daniel McMurphy visited Tallassee in July and insisted that Hoboithle Micco call "all the Indians of the different Towns to meet" so he could remind them that they had ceded the Oconee lands with "the consent of the whole Nation."⁶⁵ He also threatened that, if border patrols continued, Georgia was prepared for war. Trader James McQueen reassured McMurphy that Alexander McGillivray and his allies lacked the power to invade the Oconee valley. McQueen believed most Creeks would ignore McGillivray because Georgians had shown their ferocity when they killed nine Lower Creeks a month earlier. McGillivray claimed that he would drive squatters from the Oconee valley even if it meant the "Ruin of the Whole Nation," but McQueen dismissed such bravado.⁶⁶ "McGilvery was much mistaken," the trader opined, "for he could never get the whole nation to take his talk."⁶⁷ McQueen's words may have comforted McMurphy, but a warrior identified as "Colo." cautioned the agent that "if the Georgians were for war," McGillivray "was Ready for them" with rum and gunpowder to encourage young warriors.⁶⁸

Seeking strategic alliances to bolster his power, McGillivray attempted to exploit the political conflict between Georgia and the Confederation Congress. "The Commissioners of Congress," McMurphy fretted, "had wrote him [McGillivray] that Congress will not allow the Georgians to hold any Lands of the Indians without the consent of the whole nation."⁶⁹ Since McGillivray rejected the Treaties of Augusta and Galphinton because only a few headmen had signed them, this put Georgia's ambitions at odds with United States policy. McGillivray used that breach to insist that Georgians "move off all settlers" from the Oconee strip.⁷⁰ Paradoxically, McGillivray's bid for leadership and hard-line resistance ultimately served Georgia's interests because he presented himself as an adversary on whom white Americans could focus.

McGillivray also renewed his appeal to Spain. In mid-August, Timothy Barnard alerted Georgia's governor that McGillivray was again promoting border patrols backed by Spanish powder and ball. McGillivray reportedly intended to issue a final ultimatum to Georgia settlers: "The people are to be all Ordered off the Oconee land and if that is done the Indians are all to lay quiet, if not when the limited time is expired which is til the last of September then they are to fall on the White People."⁷¹ Barnard viewed this as a credible threat because he believed

Spain could supply limitless gunpowder, not because McGillivray possessed the authority to command Creek warriors. By September Spanish West Florida governor Arturo O'Neill reported that he had distributed to Creek visitors in Pensacola "3750 Pounds of powder 7400 of balls 3370 flint-locks," and Louisiana governor Estevan Miró in New Orleans had provided another five thousand pounds of gunpowder, with lead balls "and flint-locks in proportion."[72] McGillivray hoped to use his close relationship with O'Neill and Miró to convince all other southeastern Indians to join a great Southern Confederacy led by him and allied to Spain. The idea never came to fruition, but McGillivray occasionally presented himself as the leader of a Southern Confederacy for political effect.[73]

As Alexander McGillivray thanked Spanish leaders for the ammunition they gave to talwa leaders from Coweta, Ooseechee, Okfuskee, and other towns, he again attempted to gather "all the Chiefs of the Nation" in a national council at Tuckabatchee in July to meet with Daniel McMurphy.[74] That council decided only that Georgia must "send us an answer" regarding "the usurpations" of the Oconee lands.[75]

Timothy Barnard believed that McGillivray's claims to leadership could be undermined by taking advantage of the long-standing principles of talwa autonomy, regional divisions, and leadership by persuasion. Essentially, Georgia should support other Creeks with claims to leadership positions. Barnard recommended the mestizo John Galphin of Coweta. He believed that Galphin, "if he was properly encouraged," and if he had "any sharp person to back him, could do a great deal towards settling matters in the Nation."[76] Galphin was ideal because "he is an Indian as well as Mr. Gillvrey and can attack him with his own weapons."[77] John Galphin possessed many of the same bicultural skills on which McGillivray relied. Both Galphin and McGillivray belonged to the Wind clan. McGillivray's assertions of leadership depended in part on the support of clan kin, but John Galphin also could claim that support, undermining a key source of McGillivray's influence. Galphin grew up working in his father's successful deerskin trading business just as McGillivray had. In addition, John Galphin had skills that McGillivray lacked. He could hunt and fight like a Creek man and was fluent in the Muskogee language. If Galphin failed to undermine McGillivray, Barnard brooded, "there is no other way to manage him, except by having a War."[78] The Spanish were prepared to build a fort near McGillivray's plantation on the Alabama River near present-day Montgomery. From there, they could provide him with cannon and ammunition by water transport from Mobile.[79] Heavy armaments, Barnard implied, might render Creeks capable of permanently reclaiming the Oconee strip.

Georgians began simultaneously preparing to negotiate peace and wage war with Alexander McGillivray. They fixated on the few instances of Creek violence that had occurred in the spring while discounting their own provocations. From Georgia's perspective, Creek raiders "did fall upon several peaceable Inhabitants and cruelly and barbarously murder to the number of six, besides burning and destroying divers houses and buildings, and stealing and carrying off a number of Horses."[80] Georgians responded out of proportion to the scale and conduct of border patrol raids. They ignored the fact that most Creek towns neither participated in nor condoned the raids. Georgians interpreted the actions of the minority as the leading edge of a unified Creek invasion. Violent raids, Georgians concluded, "were done by the authority of the major part of that people," and Creeks "were resolved upon a general attack . . . from whose savage warfare even innocent women & helpless Children are the least secure."[81] Georgia rejected legitimate Creek concerns and their right to territorial self-defense in order to justify military mobilization in expectation of "an Indian War."[82]

The Creek Threat Imagined: Georgia's Narrative

In August, the Georgia Assembly authorized 1,500 militiamen to accompany nine treaty commissioners to Shoulderbone Creek on the Oconee River just below Greenesborough.[83] The few violent incidents in the spring of 1786 shaped each side's negotiating position at the Shoulderbone talks. Georgians assumed that Creeks had no right to use the Oconee's east bank. They depicted border patrols as an unprovoked invasion that threatened to destroy every county in the Oconee valley. This discourse constituted a political narrative depicting Creeks as a stateless people whose random theft and violence proved they possessed neither a credible government nor a polity's right to territorial integrity. White settlers in the Cumberland and Tennessee River valleys crafted similar narratives about Creek and Cherokee threats to justify their own violence and land taking.[84] By contrast, Arturo O'Neill offered a more moderate assessment, arguing that "various bands of the Upper Creeks and Cherokees patrolled their frontiers, expelled the Americans settled on the banks of the Oconee River and the Altamaha, and forced these emigrants to return precipitately to Georgia."[85]

During the Shoulderbone talks in October, Georgians concentrated on six reported deaths. Alexander McGillivray acknowledged them, but he insisted that only mild violence had followed the Treaty of Galphinton. He blamed truculent white squatters for the few incidents that occurred. He wrote that Creeks had met "in general convention" in the spring of 1786 to devise a plan to resist Georgia surveying parties who "uniformly attacked any of our people who chanced to fall in their way, although peaceably hunting game on our own grounds." Far from committing unprovoked acts of savagery, Creeks reacted with "humanity." McGillivray sent warriors "to drive from off our Oconee lands all intruders," and he ordered border patrols to avoid violence except in self-defense. As a result, "only six persons lost their lives on the part of the Georgians, and these fell victims to their own temerity." McGillivray bluntly accused Georgians of using inflammatory rhetoric to exaggerate the bloodshed. "This affair, which their iniquitous proceedings had drawn upon them," he wrote, "has been held forth by the Georgians as the most violent unprovoked outrage that was ever committed, and for which nothing can atone but my life, and the lives of a number of our Chiefs."[86] McGillivray was not alone in his condemnation of white frontiersmen's behavior. His brother-in-law, the French adventurer Louis le Clerc Milfort, described Georgia settlers as "vagrant and dishonest people," "vagabonds," and "Crackers" who would not "submit to any government." They were "addicted to idleness and drunkenness."[87] Indeed, U.S. leaders often shared such low opinions of frontier settlers.[88]

Georgians characterized the deaths of the six white settlers as proof of the Creek threat. Treaty commissioners fixated on them at Shoulderbone, referenced them repeatedly, and demanded satisfaction. Commissioners insisted on a land cession, indemnity for property confiscated by border patrols, and the execution of the killers. Georgia's Committee on Indian Affairs admitted this move to make a new treaty could be construed as baseless land taking, but they persuaded the Confederation Congress that "we have undertaken these measures not from a desire of making any addition to our settled Territory, but altogether on principles of self defence." From the Georgia perspective, the Oconee strip was "indisputably our own and voluntarily relinquished by the Indians whatever may now be pretended to the contrary."[89]

During the May raids, leaders from Oconee valley counties had repeatedly requested state assistance to meet an expected Creek invasion. This, too, shaped Georgia's aggressive posture at Shoulderbone. Robert Middleton, who would soon represent Greene County in Georgia's Assembly, wrote that "the people are all alarmed with the Indians burning several houses and plundering the people." Many settlers fled, and Middleton was sure the county would "intierly brake with out Sum incoragement."[90] Middleton's letter conveys a sense of shock and desperation, yet he described precisely the sort of nonviolent tactics that border patrols had used for years and that Alexander McGillivray openly advocated. Leaders such as Hoboithle Micco had encouraged white settlers to remain on the Oconee's east bank but insisted that Creeks retained the right to hunt there. Middleton disingenuously implied that Creek raids were random, unprovoked, and surprising. He was not alone in communicating that duplicitous message.

Militia officers from Franklin County in the forks of the Apalachee and North Oconee Rivers had despaired that "Our people is much alarmed at the late hostilities acted by the Creeks on the Oconee and expect every Moment when it Will be our unhappy fate."[91] They were convinced that they soon would face an overwhelming Creek invasion. "The Consequence Will certainly be Desperate," they wrote, because, "Our Settlement at this time is Verry Weak not consisting of more than 45 men."[92] Excluding a handful of questionable reports of patrols numbering in the hundreds, forty-five was a number greater than double the size of any recorded Creek border patrol since the White-Sherrill affair.[93] Militia leaders reported that settlers fled Franklin County just as Creeks intended, and militiamen were "Doubtfull we Shall be Able to Stand through Weakness and Scarcity of Provisions."[94] Captain Joshua Inman struggled to articulate the combination of fear, aggression, and disgust for Creeks that many frontier Georgians felt: "We have grate alarms hear and the people drove off from their small farms the Indians said to be very sassy. I have not taken my gun in my hand yet. . . . I am partly shore that there will be a war. . . . [T]hey have been with[in] ten miles of me. . . . I shall be glad to heare from your Honnour befor I take up my gun but cannot suffer them [to] come much near this farm."[95] Militia officers in eastern counties began raising units to aid Oconee settlers "in case of any approaching invasion."[96] Viewing largely nonviolent border patrols as an army of conquest served Georgia's political interests. General John Twiggs organized deployment, and Colonel Elijah Clarke based in Wilkes County was available to respond to emergencies. From Washington County, stretching along some eighty miles of the Oconee's east bank, an anxious Captain William Thompson requested arms and ammunition, reporting that "there was an alarm given on Sunday last which broke all inhabitance south of Ogechee."[97]

So terrifying was the volume and repetition of invasion rumors that Governor Telfair had written to Virginia's governor in June informing him that Georgia had declared war on Creek Indians. He requested that Virginia send five hundred muskets and swords to arm Georgia's cavalry.[98] Georgians plotted with leaders from the Cumberland and Franklin settlements to invade Creek country, though such a coordinated attack never materialized.[99] Indeed, a representative from Cumberland traveled to Creek country in October to propose a trading alliance with Creeks. Alexander McGillivray accepted the offer.[100]

Georgians' specious and occasionally contradictory discourse heralding total war with Creeks was, in part, simple dismissal of Creek sovereignty and territorial rights. For months, Georgians had insisted that total war loomed despite Creek rhetoric and action focused on the more modest goals of removing squatters. Even Alexander McGillivray, the most aggressive advocate of border raiding, did not view such raids as an invasion, nor did he desire war with Georgia.[101] From Georgia's perspective, however, the Treaties of Augusta and Galphinton constituted binding conveyance of all use and ownership rights to the Oconee's east bank. Any attempt on the part of Creeks to use those lands, and any assertion of Creek sovereignty within them, was tantamount to an act of war. In September 1786, the *Georgia Gazette* communicated this perspective by equating Creeks' assertion of rights with warfare. "The Creek Indians have lately received large supplies of ammunitions from Pensacola," the story read, "which, with their having warned the settlers to remove from the Oconee lands by the first of October, next, leaves little or no room for doubt of a war taking place immediately."[102]

Citizens of Georgia's eastern counties sometimes rejected the narrative about the Creek threat, suggesting they understood the duplicity of frontier leaders' exaggerations of Creek violence and dismissal of Creek rights. Some residents of Chatham County on the Atlantic coast, for example, opposed a law raising a militia to defend Savannah against Creek invasion. One outraged Savannah resident excoriated his fellow citizens, assuring them that failure to raise a militia would "risk the existence, not only of ourselves, but our wives and our little ones, with the loss of all our properties."[103] He insisted that Alexander McGillivray soon would attack "the heart of Savannah."[104] "God forbid my eyes should behold the scene," he inveighed, "but I fear the time when our houses will be set on fire, our wives and daughters violated, and our children dashed in pieces before us, as preparative for the dreadful fate that will await ourselves."[105] Rape was a rare tactic in Native American warfare, and Creeks posed no threat to the city of Savannah. The author's dema-goguery was meant to evoke fear and aggression and thereby garner support for the new militia law. Descriptions of Creeks' "rage of barbarity" and their "savage . . . appetite for blood" masked Georgians' violations of Creek sovereignty and territorial integrity.[106] Georgians in eastern counties, however, did not always buy the pitch. Many ignored the call for militia muster because their economic interests were tied to coastal plantations and commerce rather than frontier expansion.[107]

Frontier rumors contributed to Georgians' irrational fear of Creek invasion.[108] Joseph Martin demonstrated the power that rumors could wield, especially when mixed with elements of truth. Martin reported to Governor Telfair secondhand news of Alexander McGillivray's September 1786 trip to Pensacola. McGillivray hired Joseph Syers, an experienced packhorseman, to assist with a packhorse train bringing a shipment of Spanish arms and ammunition into Creek country.[109] While in Pensacola, Syers witnessed several Creeks receiving "Arms & Ammunition to go to war against the Georgians."[110] He claimed that "the Creek Indians have Unanimously agreed to strike on our Frontiers this fall," with the exceptions of Hoboithle Micco's Tallassee, Neha Micco's Cussita, and Timothy Barnard's town.[111] Multiple reports confirm that McGillivray was importing Spanish weapons and thousands of pounds of ammunition, but it is unlikely that Creeks were unanimous about anything. If true, Syers's report would indicate that McGillivray had tremendous influence over thousands of Creek warriors in some fifty towns, but the pattern of raiding over preceding years gave no such indication. Syers also contradicted months of talks from Lower Creek leaders and several white traders and agents living in Creek country. Accepting Spanish arms could indicate simply that men were gearing up for extended winter hunts. McGillivray himself complained that many Tallapoosa province men "squandered" their ammunition instead of saving it "for meeting the Hostile attacks" of white invaders.[112] Receiving ammunition did not necessarily mean all Creeks intended to wage war, but believing otherwise served Georgia's expansionist agenda.

Other frontier rumors also reinforced Georgia's expectation of Creek war. An anonymous correspondent from the Franklin settlements warned a friend in Savannah that Georgia was in perpetual danger of Creek attack. He wrote that during the spring of 1786, "Creeks were unanimously determined to destroy the upper part of Georgia."[113] A year later, in the spring of 1787, Franklin leader John Sevier relayed a rumor from "the Grand Chief of the Chactaws" that Creeks again planned to invade Georgia.[114] Sevier's endorsement elevated the rumor to the status of fact. Such intelligence, though dubious, reinforced Georgians' narrative about the Creek threat.

Georgians embraced their narrative about the Creek threat even when they received credible reports of Creeks' desire for peace. White agents in Creek country determined that many Creeks accepted earlier treaties, and, while they resented settlers' violation of those treaties, they preferred a diplomatic solution to raiding. James Durouzeaux informed John Habersham, Georgia's chairman of the Board of Commissioners of Indian Affairs, that Lower Creeks eagerly accepted an invitation to the Shoulderbone talks.[115] Muskogee speakers from Coweta and Cussita accepted gunpowder and lead in Pensacola, but, along with Hitchiti-speaking Palachicolas, they disdained McGillivray's call for border raids.[116] Even some Upper Creeks planned to attend the talks, though McGillivray intended to prevent them.[117]

Throughout 1786, Alexander McGillivray was less influential than he claimed. The volume of his correspondence with Spanish and American leaders made his role appear more substantial than it was, despite contrary reports from white agents and opposing talks from other talwa leaders. Georgians seemed eager to accept McGillivray's claims to leadership when it was convenient to do so. Positioning McGillivray as an all-powerful and hostile leader allowed Georgians to justify retaliatory violence and push for larger concessions at Shoulderbone. For years McGillivray had claimed to speak for a majority of Creeks. He claimed to command border patrols to drive settlers from the Oconee, "always in defense of our rights."[118] He repeated this assertion in October, demanding again that Georgia remove settlers from the Oconee valley. "It is the wish of the nation," he proclaimed, "to see the settlements on the Oconee lands abandoned." Once that occurred, Georgians would find Creeks to be "sincere friends."[119]

As the date for the Shoulderbone talks approached, new rumors held that McGillivray planned to thwart the proceedings by ambushing Georgia's treaty commissioners and their militia escort of 1,500 men. Spies reported the unlikely rumor that "the Creeks were waiting for the army, which they seemed determined to attack."[120] Several sources confirmed that Creeks had a large supply of Spanish powder and ball for "the war against Georgia," perhaps lending credence to the rumor in Georgians' minds.[121]

The Treaty of Shoulderbone Creek

The October 1786 talks that yielded the Treaty of Shoulderbone Creek illustrated Georgians' dismissal of Creek sovereignty and territorial rights and left Creeks questioning the efficacy of negotiating as independent towns. Concentrating on a few acts of violence, Georgians demanded punitive terms that exacerbated internal Creek political conflict. In the months leading up to the Shoulderbone talks, Alexander McGillivray consistently declared that he spoke for all Creeks. He repudiated the Treaties of Augusta and Galphinton, and he threatened to clear settlers from the Oconee valley by force, if necessary. Learning that Georgians had no intention of restoring the Oconee strip, McGillivray ultimately declined to attend the talks.[122] A cadre of leaders from Muskogee- and Hitchiti-speaking towns in the Tallapoosa, Abika, and Apalachicola provinces of the Upper and Lower Creeks also claimed to speak for the majority at Shoulderbone. A surprising number of them chose to sign the Treaty of Shoulderbone Creek, motivated by a combination of hope, fear, and, perhaps, a lack of alternatives. They repudiated McGillivray, even calling for his death, yet some of them claimed to represent multiple towns in their own limited move toward more centralized government. Leadership by persuasion and talwa autonomy remained key principles in Creek governance, yet Georgia's rigid posture seemed to persuade some headmen that dealing with the state required greater coalescence.

Despite evidence that Creek people had more to fear from settlers than the reverse, Georgians exaggerated Creek violence to justify their demands. It suited their expansionist interests to characterize Alexander McGillivray's promotion of border patrols and his alliance with Spain as full-scale war. By October, Georgians had latched on to a few instances of violence, some theft, and rumors of invasion to craft a narrative of victimization at the hands of a villainous Alexander McGillivray.[123]

Georgia's negotiators coerced Creeks into signing a punitive treaty at Shoulderbone in November using their narrative of Creek violence, the threat of 1,500 militiamen, and hollow promises to govern white border jumpers. Governor Telfair urged Alexander McGillivray to attend the talks, hoping to intimidate him in particular with the massive militia force.[124] Telfair wanted only "a few of the principle men" to attend treaty talks, but he insisted that McGillivray be among them. The Creek leader even accused Telfair of planning to have him arrested or assassinated.[125] Governor Telfair assured Creeks that "no further encroachments will be suffered," though similar proclamations and acts of the assembly had proven ineffective in the preceding years.[126] The Shoulderbone treaty itself empowered Creeks to detain anyone found surveying Creek lands, but such border jumpers must be turned over to Georgia authorities for prosecution. The treaty also acknowledged Creek rights to detain any white people who harmed Creeks or stole their property. Those offenders, too, must be turned over to Georgia, virtually guaranteeing they would face no consequences. The treaty restored trade, but it left Creeks little recourse to challenge unethical trading practices.[127] The Treaty of Shoulderbone Creek's failure to address Creek concerns in a meaningful way alienated those who ceded the Oconee strip and further outraged those who rejected the cession.

The Shoulderbone treaty offered Creeks little, and Georgians demanded several concessions as recompense for Creek violence. Georgia's commissioners ignored the bloodshed committed by white settlers. They declared only that "acts of hostility have been committed by parties of the Indians on the Inhabitants of the said state, in violation of the said treaty [Galphinton]."[128] Like its predecessors, Shoulderbone required that all white captives and stolen property be returned.[129] Perhaps most egregiously for those who had supported earlier treaties, Shoulderbone explicitly prohibited Creeks from hunting the Oconee River's east bank for the first time. In fact, both Creeks and Georgians would now be prohibited from crossing the border without a "special license" issued to Creeks by Georgia's Indian Affairs agents and to white people by the governor.[130] The provision intended to give Georgians authority to keep Creek hunters out of the Oconee strip. Commissioners pressured Creeks to acknowledge that the deaths of six Georgians in 1786 violated the Treaty of Galphinton, though they made no mention of the six to fifteen Creeks killed that year.[131] In a harsh exercise of power, the treaty specifically required the executions of six of the Creek border patrollers responsible for Georgians' deaths. Superintendent of Indian Affairs Daniel McMurphy was to bear witness to the executions, or at least "obtain the clearest and most indisputable evidence" of their deaths.[132] The treaty made no attempt to satisfy Creeks for indiscriminate murders committed by Georgians. The treaty also required the banishment of the white Indian countrymen whom Creek headmen blamed for provoking the violence of 1786.[133] Finally, Georgians took five Creek hostages to guarantee adherence to the terms.[134]

The lopsided treaty held little promise of ending border conflict because Georgians extracted concessions based on the fiction that Creeks had committed unprovoked violence. Georgians wanted contrition, not resolution. Governor Telfair dismissed McGillivray's alliance with Spain as "absurd."[135] This contempt suggests the governor understood that concerns about a Creek invasion were exaggerated. He saw neither Creeks nor Spain as genuine threats to the state's eventual expansion, let alone its survival, but the narrative about the Creek threat was politically useful.

Despite onerous terms, fifty-eight Creek leaders from approximately fifteen talwas signed the Treaty of Shoulderbone Creek. Alexander McGillivray was not among them. He chose not to attend, and after the treaty's completion, he characteristically declared it invalid. He claimed that Georgians had merely intimidated a minority of Creek representatives into agreement.[136] Georgians were well aware of vocal dissent against the Oconee boundary during the Shoulderbone talks.[137] Still, the fifty-eight signers from fifteen Upper and Lower Towns appeared to represent a growing consensus. By comparison, leaders from only six towns signed the Treaty of Augusta, and just eight towns approved the Treaty of Galphinton. The fifteen towns represented at Shoulderbone indicate a growing fear that the Oconee strip could not be saved, yet they constituted a fraction of the fifty to sixty talwas in Creek country. A talk delivered primarily by Lower Creeks bluntly repudiated McGillivray: "The Talks and letters that have been sent you by McGillivray as the voice of the Nation are not so. They are of his own making, and to suit his private purposes."[138] Indeed, they observed that McGillivray must be banished, flee to Spanish Florida, "or else he must also be killed."[139]

Some Creeks at Shoulderbone appeared frustrated with their inability to resolve the Oconee boundary dispute acting as representatives of independent towns. They asserted authority beyond their talwas in a limited push for more centralized government while respecting differing regional interests. Lower Creek representatives dominated the Shoulderbone talks, asserting their superior authority over the Oconee strip. They explained that the political situation was "well known to those present who are from the Upper Creeks," implying that, with the exception of Alexander McGillivray's Little Tallassee, Upper Creeks deferred to them regarding the Georgia border.[140] The list of fifty-eight signers includes men from at least four Upper Towns representing the Tallapoosa and Abika provinces and five Lower Towns representing Muskogee and Hitchiti speakers.[141] Several of the Lower Creeks present claimed "to speak for other Towns, than those they immediately represented, and that such Towns would consequently be bound by what ever was concluded upon."[142]

Despite indications that many Creeks assented to the terms, after the November 1786 Treaty of Shoulderbone Creek, border patrols skyrocketed to a thirty-year peak. The dramatic increase in patrols suggests that the unsatisfying treaty and Georgia's expansionism produced widespread backlash. White Georgians' melodramatic narrative of Creek violence became a self-fulfilling prophecy as Creeks, pushed to the brink, began to push back. In the four years between 1783 and 1786, there were fifty-eight Creek raids. Over the subsequent four years, the number increased by a factor of six. The *Georgia Gazette*'s reporting on frontier violence increased in 1787, but stories often celebrated Georgians' violence against Indians rather than denouncing Creek ferocity. For example, the *Gazette* described a September 1787 incident in which Georgians trespassing in Creek territory met a band of Creeks, and "nine of the savages were killed."[143] A month later, in response to the murder of four white settlers, General Elijah Clarke invaded Creek country and reportedly killed twenty-five to fifty Indians.[144]

At first blush, it is unclear why the Treaty of Shoulderbone Creek represented a turning point in Creek-Georgia relations, yet it clearly did. It shared many of the characteristics of its predecessors. Shoulderbone fixed the Oconee River border between Creek country and Georgia. It was ratified without consulting some Creek leaders and over the objections others. It lacked the approval of the Confederation Congress. The punitive treaties of the 1780s constantly aggravated internal Creek political conflict. Alexander McGillivray led an opposition group that wholly rejected all of the treaties. He represented a rising elite invested in the expansion of Euro-American trade, the accumulation of private property, and the establishment of centralized government. Many older talwa leaders such as Hoboithle Micco, Cusa Micco, Yahola Micco, Neha Micco, and Hitcheta Micco signed the treaties. Their assent indicates that many members of the diverse, polyglot Creek polity still preferred the long-standing system of governance based on talwa autonomy, reciprocal exchange diplomacy, and a deerskin economy.[145] Some aggressive young men disrupted Creek-Georgia relations by seeking war honors and wealth without the consent of talwa leaders, though this, too, was in keeping with long-standing Creek practice. Treaty signers came to recognize the limitations of talwa autonomy in the face of an unprecedented threat, and this led them to assert authority over multiple towns. Signers like Hoboithle Micco and Neha Micco exerted diplomatic pressure when Georgians obstructed Creek hunting rights and trespassed beyond agreed-upon boundaries.[146]

Following the Treaty of Shoulderbone Creek, even men like Hoboithle Micco who had made every effort to settle matters reasonably were forced to confront the border dispute's intractability. Georgia's leaders were unable or unwilling to control white settlers who harassed Creek hunters and encroached west of the Oconee River. In light of the contested treaties of the 1780s, the pattern of increased border patrols after Shoulderbone should be viewed from the Creek perspective as a nation-building exercise that harnessed a powerful spirit of unity to defend communal land rights and political sovereignty. As diplomatic efforts consistently failed, border patrol as a form of resistance gained popularity with profound implications for the struggle over leadership in Creek country.

6 / "An Uncommon Degree of Ferocity":
Border Patrols and the Oconee War, 1787–1790

Hundreds of reports filed by Georgians confirm a kernel of truth in Commissioner James P. Preston's 1822 statement that Creeks raided the Oconee valley with an "uncommon degree of ferocity" in the late 1780s.[1] The Treaty of Shoulderbone Creek's onerous terms and Georgia's continued expansion provoked a surge in Creek raiding. From a total of 58 raids in the four years prior to Shoulderbone, the number leapt to 379 between 1787 and 1790, an increase of more than 600 percent. Of those 379 raids, 70 ended in death or injury. Greene County in the upper Oconee River valley was the most active zone of conflict in those years. Of the 131 raids that struck the county, 13 of them resulted in bloodshed, making Greene the most violent place in Georgia. This peak in violence, however, must be put into a larger context. Greene County was home to 5,405 non-Indians.[2] During the four most violent years of the 1780s in Georgia's most violent frontier county with a population well over five thousand, Creek raiders killed 19 people— that is, less than one half of 1 percent. Statewide, Creeks killed 113 people, or slightly more than one-tenth of 1 percent of the total population.[3] Georgians felt this as a significant loss, but, as a proportion of their population, Creeks suffered far greater losses. Georgians killed 83 Creeks during the same period and likely many more that went unrecorded. While Georgians lost less than one-half of 1 percent of the people in a single county, Creeks lost one-half of 1 percent of their entire population.

The spike in border patrols represented growing unity among Creeks. Men from all the provinces and linguistic groups in Creek country undertook raids. Because of that unity of purpose, border patrols represent a key protonational institution fostering Creek coalescence. They united both young men and talwa leaders from all divisions in the struggle to defend the border, and they created a legacy of shared experiences.[4] Men, however, operated as warriors from independent talwas with a mix of political and economic motives. Brutal responses from Georgians only increased consensus and gave nationalists like Alexander McGillivray an issue they used to rally Creeks. Most Creeks wanted talwa autonomy, but to meet the threat from Georgia, they needed greater coalescence.

Mounting death tolls in the Oconee lands allowed Georgia authorities to claim that the state's very survival was threatened, though they almost certainly knew that was not the case. Georgia's Executive Department calculated that between 1787 and 1789, Creeks killed 72 white people and 10 black people.[5] Evidence collated from multiple sources suggests a higher number—97 white people and 16 black people killed. Georgia's Executive Council informed the Confederation Congress in 1788 that "the settlements of four of the exterior counties are almost entirely broken up," including Greene County.[6] Population numbers show a very different reality. Georgia's population exploded from approximately 23,000 non-Indians in 1775 to nearly 83,000 by 1790. Of those, 11,000 people occupied the Oconee River valley counties of Franklin, Greene, and Washington. Such rapid growth must have deeply threatened the Creek population that totaled only 17,000 people. The majority of Creeks—nearly 9,000—lived in the Upper Creek provinces of Tallapoosa, Abika, Okfuskee, and Alabama along the Coosa and Tallapoosa Rivers, hundreds of miles from the Oconee border. Around 6,000 people lived in Muskogee-, Hitchiti-, Koasati-, and Yuchi-speaking Lower Towns, far closer to the Oconee. They likely felt Georgia's threat more acutely.[7] Because of that proximity and the peak violence of the late 1780s, some Lower Creek leaders began to work with Alexander McGillivray and other Upper Town headmen to resolve the Oconee boundary dispute and assert Creek national sovereignty.

Creeks focused on patrolling the border with Georgia in the late 1780s, but they also opposed encroaching American settlers in the Cumberland and Tennessee River valleys and Spanish West Florida. The Franklin settlements of the upper Tennessee River valley continued to grow, reaching 28,649 people by 1790. The Cumberland River valley settlements,

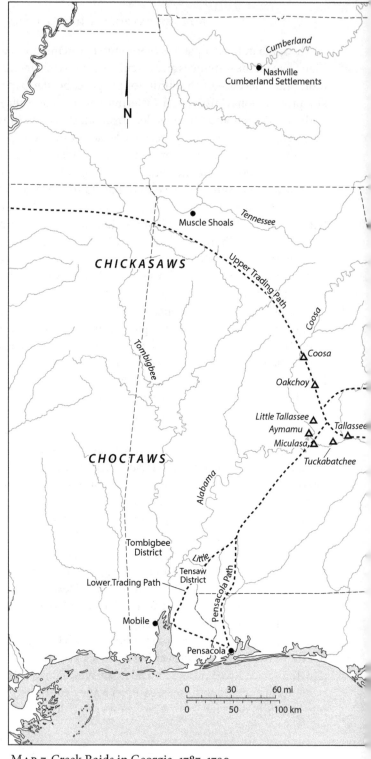

MAP 7. Creek Raids in Georgia, 1787–1790

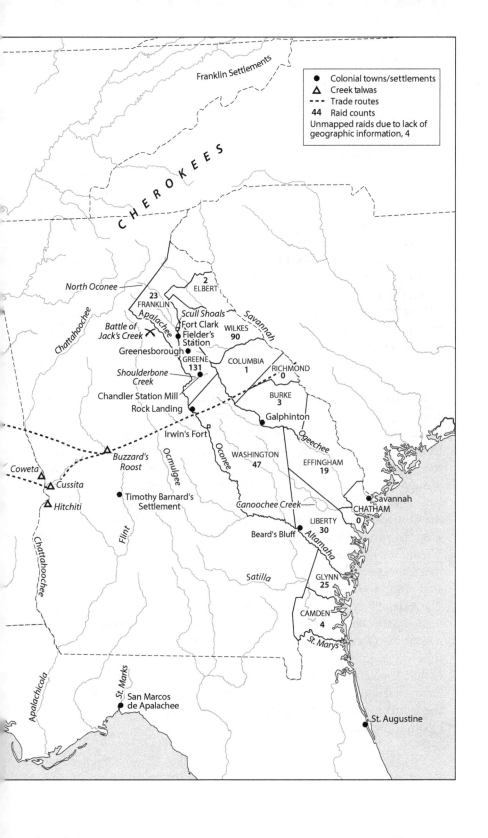

Franklin Settlements

● Colonial towns/settlements
△ Creek talwas
- - - Trade routes
44 Raid counts
Unmapped raids due to lack of
geographic information, 4

C H E R O K E E S

North Oconee

2
ELBERT

23
FRANKLIN

Apalachee

Scull Shoals

Battle of
Jack's Creek

Fort Clark
Fielder's
Station

Savannah

WILKES
90

Greenesborough

GREENE
131

COLUMBIA
1

RICHMOND
0

Shoulderbone
Creek

BURKE
3

Chandler Station Mill

Rock Landing

Galphinton

Ogeechee

Irwin's Fort

Oconee

WASHINGTON
47

EFFINGHAM
19

Buzzard's
Roost

Coweta

Cussita

Timothy Barnard's
Settlement

Canoochee Creek

Savannah

CHATHAM
0

Hitchiti

Flint

LIBERTY
30

Beard's Bluff

Altamaha

Chattahoochee

Satilla

GLYNN
25

CAMDEN
4

St. Marys

St. Marks

San Marcos
de Apalachee

St. Augustine

Apalachicola

Chattahoochee

Ocmulgee

while smaller, grew to 7,049 people. These communities posed a more critical threat to Cherokees, but Creeks collaborated with Cherokees to raid them in the late 1780s, reportedly killing as many as 48 people. Cumberland and Franklin settlers remained disappointed in the U.S. government's refusal to support their provocative land speculation and violence against Indians. They pursued secessionist schemes and alliance with Spain and, ultimately, proposed an alliance with Creeks.[8] Many Cumberland settlers abandoned the region and settled in West Florida north of Mobile along the Tombigbee River. American immigrants rapidly settled the Tombigbee district, just twenty miles west of the Tensaw district and the Creek–West Florida border. American immigrants only nominally accepted Spanish authority, and they rapidly encroached on Creek country. By 1788, they were surveying lands within ten miles of Alexander McGillivray's Little Tallassee. Alabama towns, the southernmost province of the Upper Creeks, led raids against the Tombigbee District in collaboration with Choctaws.[9] The steadily increasing American threat emanating from Cumberland and West Florida contributed to unprecedented unity among talwas.

Like their neighbors in Cumberland, Georgians demanded U.S. government support for an expansionist war against Indians, arguing that Creek ferocity threatened the state's existence. In doing so, they challenged the central government's authority in Indian Affairs and contributed to a growing rift between state and federal authority. Instead of supporting a war against Creeks, however, James White, a Cumberland land speculator appointed as superintendent of Indian Affairs by the Confederation Congress, returned from "the Creek Nation" in May 1787 claiming he had "appeased the minds of the Indians" and secured a temporary truce.[10] In early fall, the Georgia Assembly announced that Creeks again had committed several murders. Settlers had retaliated, and "a war, by the savages, is now raging with all its horrors."[11] The Assembly suggested that, far from securing peace, James White had incited Creek border patrols by implying that the U.S. government might restore the Oconee lands to Creek possession. In reality, Creek raiders simply were responding to continued encroachment and the harsh terms of the Shoulderbone Treaty, including the taking of hostages from Lower Towns. Georgians resented the U.S. government agent's intervention in the conflict, yet they demanded federal funding "for suppressing the bloody violences of the Indians."[12]

McGillivray's Letters, Hoboithle Micco's White Wing: National Consensus and Talwa Autonomy

The frequency of Creek border patrols protesting Shoulderbone quickly increased in the spring of 1787, spiked in 1788, then steadily declined over the course of 1789 and 1790. Raiders continued to display an overwhelming preference for horse theft over bloodshed. When violence occurred, it was often opportunistic rather than the primary intent. For Creeks, confiscating settlers' horses contested white encroachment without provoking violent retaliation in most cases. Horse rustling allowed young men to gain prestige as warriors and potentially improve their economic standing.[13] Occasionally, Creeks simply destroyed settlers' property. As a system of border patrol, few actions could have sent a clearer message than burning squatters' homes. Burning buildings held no economic value for warriors, yet driving settlers out of the Oconee valley was a statement of territorial sovereignty from which one could gain war honors.[14] Such raids show that Creek border patrols targeted Oconee valley settlements because of their location rather than simply the potential spoils.

Dissatisfaction with the Treaty of Shoulderbone Creek resulted in broad-based opposition to white settlement in the Oconee River valley, yet many miccos remained committed to the principle of talwa autonomy. They acted independently even as Alexander McGillivray asserted total command and control of all Creeks. Headmen such as Hoboithle Micco and Neha Micco, for example, resented the treaties they had signed and continued to speak against them.

A talk from the headmen of Cussita and its daughter town, Buzzard's Roost, illuminates the reasons for growing frustration with white settlers in the spring of 1787.[15] The headmen affirmed their consent to the terms of Shoulderbone and swore to assist with the return of any stolen property and the surveying of boundary lines, as stipulated. They complained, however, that the hostages Georgia had taken at Shoulderbone were "your friends" rather than men who objected to the Oconee boundary.[16] "Detaining them," the headmen cautioned, "is only distressing your friends" but would do nothing to prevent raids by "the Bad inclined people of the upper Towns."[17] On the contrary, any accidental harm that befell the hostages would be "attended with very Bad consequences."[18] The headmen demanded that the hostages be released to John Galphin, the mestizo son of the late trader George Galphin and Metawney of Coweta. Once released, John Galphin would escort the former hostages home.

Georgia's rigidity and failure to recognize legitimate Creek grievances slowly pushed Creeks toward consensus on abrogating Shoulderbone.

As Superintendent James White toured Creek country in the spring of 1787, he struggled to understand growing consensus on the Oconee boundary dispute.[19] Alexander McGillivray and a minority of Upper Towns long had spearheaded resistance to the treaties of the 1780s while a few Upper and Lower Towns had consented to them. White concluded, however, that most Lower Creeks had grown resentful of Georgia's encroachment. They vowed to repel settlers "by force." Frustrated, he grumbled that "the very Indians" who consented to land cessions accused Georgia of "having extorted land from them."[20] Hoboithle Micco offered Governor George Mathews a white wing to confirm peace and alliance, yet James White believed the gesture insincere. White observed that, the previous day, Hoboithle Micco had addressed a Creek council and accused Georgia "of many ungenerous practices" by which it "had wrested from him pretended grants of land, & hostages."[21] White was outraged at what he perceived as "shameless duplicity," yet Hoboithle Micco's duty as a talwa leader required him to criticize Georgians' failure to abide by treaty terms while signaling his desire to resolve issues diplomatically.

By the end of his tour, James White feared Georgia was under threat of "immediate invasion," though he credited Alexander McGillivray with preventing such an onslaught for the moment.[22] As with Hoboithle Micco's gift of a white wing to the governor, White misinterpreted what he saw. The agent believed that McGillivray was responsible for restraining young men, and he accepted McGillivray's warning that he would end the cease-fire in August unless Georgia renegotiated the terms of the Shoulderbone treaty.

McGillivray appeared confident that he had consolidated his leadership of all Creeks, and he intended to order new border patrol raids to hurl Georgians back from the Oconee.[23] He boasted to West Florida governor Arturo O'Neill in Pensacola that, at a recent meeting in the Lower Towns, "I had the Satisfaction to find the whole Nation Now Unanimous," including Cussita and Tallassee.[24] These towns were home to Neha Micco and Hoboithle Micco, men who continued to communicate with Georgians and U.S. agents as independent talwa leaders. The dramatic surge in border patrol raids over the course of 1787 and 1788 might at first appear to confirm McGillivray's claim to national leadership, yet it is likely he exaggerated his authority in hopes of persuading O'Neill to continue providing ammunition.[25] While Creeks reached consensus on opposing white encroachment, only Alexander McGillivray did so claiming to represent a centralized Creek nation.

Raiding Patterns: Motives and Methods

Georgians certainly exaggerated Creek ferocity in the 1780s, but it is equally true that border patrol violence spiked between 1787 and 1790. An analysis of raids in these years suggests they were conducted primarily by Lower Town warriors with a mix of political, economic, and religious motives, yet warriors from all divisions participated, diminishing differences between talwas. Clandestine theft of horses and slaves and more aggressive destruction of property skyrocketed. Creek theft was rampant in both northern and southern frontier counties. Horse thieves focused on Greene, Franklin, Wilkes, and Washington Counties in the upper Oconee valley. Some raiders preferred to steal and aid in the escape of enslaved black people from the southern counties of Liberty, Glynn, and Camden between the Altamaha and the St. Marys Rivers.[26]

Theft easily could escalate to bloodshed, though Creeks seldom set out with violence as a primary goal. Occasional violence was part of the pattern of Creek resistance to Georgia's settlement of the Oconee lands. They used similar tactics, though less frequently, farther south along the Altamaha, Satilla, and St. Marys Rivers. Creek warriors also sometimes killed to achieve war honors or to restore cosmic balance after Georgians murdered Creeks.[27] On the relatively rare occasions when border patrols killed people, it most often resulted from botched raids in which Georgians pursued Creeks to reclaim property. The resulting combat did not necessarily violate Creek rules of war, but it could be vicious. Such violence terrified and enraged Georgians, yet they excused their own brutality. Georgians' fear contributed to exaggerations of Creek ferocity and overwhelming retaliation. Georgians sent more troops to the Oconee valley and increased sorties into Creek territory. Georgians' behavior increased Creeks' willingness to compromise talwa autonomy if a national government led by Alexander McGillivray could protect them.

On the rare occasions when Georgians identified Creek raiders, they blamed men from Lower Towns. This suggests that resistance to settlers' encroachment was increasingly the concern of men unassociated with Alexander McGillivray and his Upper Town allies. Lower Towns had primary claim to the Oconee lands, and they were closest to the boundary, so they had the most to fear from Georgia's relentless westward advance. Border patrols in the late 1780s often originated from talwas that had supported earlier treaties. When diplomacy failed, men from those talwas adopted a different mode of resistance.

Between 1787 and 1790, the Greene County stretch of the upper Oconee River valley was the most violent zone of conflict between Creeks and Georgians, yet a handful of incidents account for most of the bloodshed. Of the 131 depredations reported in Greene County between 1787 and 1790, only 13 included lethal violence—that is, less than 10 percent of raids ended in killings. In those 13 violent raids, Creeks killed eighteen white people and one black slave. A single incident across the border in Creek country, however, accounts for a significant portion of both white and Creek casualties during the period.[28] This event, remembered by Georgians as the Battle of Jack's Creek, resulted in the deaths of nine white Georgians and twenty-five Creeks, more than double the number that occurred in any Greene County incident. This suggests that a few bloody encounters helped Georgians support their narrative of Creek ferocity.

Creeks raided for a variety of reasons, but only rarely did men set out merely for the purpose of killing. Instead, raids that began as slave or horse theft sometimes ended in violence. For instance, the theft of John Long's female slave from his Greene County residence in May 1787 led to murder. Long's neighbor Ezekiel McMichael reported the theft to his own family and then set out to track the raiders. A short while later, McMichael's family heard the report of three rifles followed quickly by the return of Ezekiel's horse without its rider.[29] Worried for Ezekiel's safety, John McMichael gathered some men to search for the source of the gunshots. What they found confirmed their worst suspicions, both of Ezekiel's fate and of the Creeks whom they despised. About four miles east of the Oconee River in land ceded to Georgia, they found Ezekiel "wantonly and Barbrously Murthered and Scalped By the Indians."[30] They tracked the raiders to the Oconee River's edge where they found "3 guns 5 shotbags & 4 pairs of Mocasons."[31] "In one of the shot bags," they reported, "was found 2 scalps which was proved to be taken off the head of the Decest."[32]

The Creek warriors appear to have attacked McMichael opportunistically after having made off with the enslaved woman. Georgians considered these acts a general declaration of war and launched an unauthorized militia invasion of Creek country. The intensity of this type of violence rather than its frequency inflamed Georgians and led to disproportionate reprisals. A small group of warriors ambushed an individual and scalped him, a mutilation that Georgians avowedly found wanton and barbarous. Yet from the Creek perspective, the border patrol's behavior indicates eagerness to avoid further bloodshed.[33] When they were discovered at the river's edge, the Indians retreated so quickly that they abandoned rifles, ammunition, footwear, and the scalps that would have brought them war honors in their talwas.

After Ezekiel McMichael's murder, the *Georgia Gazette* interpreted the slaying as an announcement of "renewed hostilities."[34] Local militia captain Samuel Alexander responded without orders by invading Creek country and killing eight Creeks near the Ocmulgee River, some thirty miles west of the Oconee.[35] Years later, a U.S. Indian agent blamed Alexander for thus starting "a long, bloody, and expensive war with the Creek Indians."[36] In the weeks that followed, Creek leaders berated Georgians, explaining that Alexander's victims had not been involved in McMichael's death.[37] The *Gazette* likely panicked Georgians further when it published an unconfirmed rumor that fifty Creek warriors had set out to avenge Captain Alexander's brutality.[38] Two weeks later, the *Gazette* reported that white settlers had killed thirty-five more Indians, and three hundred Georgians had crossed the border. The column concluded that a "general war is thought to be unavoidable."[39]

Creek raiders struck Greene County repeatedly throughout the spring of 1787. On May 31, the same day that Ezekiel McMichael died, Creeks murdered, scalped, and mutilated William Anderson Jones in another apparently unplanned attack. Jones drifted from his farm in search of a stray horse, and, shortly thereafter, his neighbors heard gunshots. They searched fruitlessly for the source but found only the horse Jones had ridden toward the Oconee in search of the stray.[40] The neighbors searched for Jones for three days. When they found his body, he had been "Barbarously Killed and scalped and stripped naked and a Large Bayonet stuck through his Body which pin'd him to the ground."[41] The torture Jones endured was consistent with long-standing modes of southeastern Indian violence. Cloth was the most popular trade item in Creek country, so raiders frequently stole clothing.

The intensity of the murder, scalping, and pinning of William Anderson Jones can be understood as a vehement assertion of Creek rights to hunt the Oconee River's east bank. Creeks customarily mutilated the bodies of slain enemies as a way of capturing "a portion of the dead individual's spirit or soul."[42] Warriors at once accrued spiritual power and disrespected enemies through this generative spiritual practice with deep roots in the Mississippian Period.[43] Any person obstructing Creek travelers or hunters in Creek country might well suffer a similar fate. Collecting scalps to present to their towns remained a path to prestige and leadership positions for Creek men.[44] Miccos protested to Georgians that such torture and murder were the acts of a few mad young men, but Creek communities admired reckless courage. Opportunistic violence in defense of Native rights was in keeping with customary tension between the brashness of youth and the moderation of age in Creek culture. Indeed, theft raids alone could earn prestige.[45]

Raids in which Creeks killed black people also suggest that violence could be an unintentional result of bungled theft. A Greene County raid in 1787 with the apparent motive of theft ended in the death of an enslaved teenager named Tom. The claimant reported that raiders killed Tom, "a negro boy . . . about Sixteen years old" valued at $450, during the theft of a horse valued at fifty dollars.[46] Tom may well have been attempting to resist capture or protect the horse. If property confiscation motivated the warriors, they likely would have attempted to take Tom, whom Georgians considered the most valuable property available during the raid. Georgians reported that Creeks stole 111 slaves between 1787 and 1790, and, while some resisted, many others absconded voluntarily.

Black slaves also fell victim to politically motivated attacks. In August 1787 in Franklin County, the area between the Apalachee and North Oconee Rivers, Creeks attacked the plantation of Samuel Knox. They killed two black slaves, a man and a woman in their twenties, and they captured a two-year-old girl, presumably the couple's daughter. The raiders then burned Knox's remaining property including three buildings, a wagon, and grain stores. The combination of killing, captive taking, and property destruction suggests a range of motives, but what followed indicates that the highest priority was ejecting the settler from disputed land. Creeks may have killed the enslaved man and woman unintentionally while trying to capture them, and they were careless with the child they abducted. Astonishingly, the toddler somehow escaped or was released and found her way to the fort where Knox had fled. Upon investigating, Knox chillingly reported that he found "the House & other property smoking," including "the bodys of the negroes burning."[47] The attack on Knox's plantation, then, appears designed to destroy the settler's ability to remain on disputed land. By no choice of their own, the enslaved people were part of Knox's economic capacity.

Raids often were simpler affairs in which Creeks, bent on taking horses, briefly exchanged fire with white men reluctant to give up their property.[48] For example, in a November 1787 episode in Greene County, a party of Creeks fired on James Woods and his father while they were camped near the Oconee. The white men returned fire, but they fled after James was wounded.[49] Once they were gone, Creeks stole their horses. In a similar attack in 1789, John Chandler was camping on Richland Creek, an Oconee tributary near Shoulderbone, when he was "fired on and wounded and forced to fly for his life."[50] Chandler lost his horse, saddle and tack, his blanket, and three coats. Chandler's companion, Joel Mabry, lost a rifle worth ten pounds sterling, two pair of saddle bags, one blanket, and three coats.[51] All the men escaped with their lives and a fresh awareness of Creeks' ongoing claims to the Oconee strip. Such incidents help explain why Georgians tended to conflate theft and warfare.

Viewed individually, violent raids appear as isolated, almost random incidents. In the aggregate, however, they reveal a pattern of behavior that furthered coalescence by including young men from every division. Creeks occasionally committed targeted killings to restore cosmic balance, but many occurred during botched thefts. Perhaps the most salient feature of border patrol violence is that it was rarely the primary intent of a raid. Georgians, however, interpreted events differently. They believed themselves to be in a state of war with unpredictable savages. While the hundreds of Creek raids taken together constitute a pattern of both political resistance and economic opportunism, the low level of violence indicates that Creeks did not consider themselves to be at war but instead to be involved in a border dispute with an implacable neighbor.

The Oconee War

The surge in Creek border patrols in early 1787, though predominantly nonviolent, elicited from Georgians a curious mixture of fear, devastating retaliation, and elision of theft's prevalence. Georgians exaggerated raids as the harbinger of what they later called the Oconee War, and they used this perceived invasion to justify their own acts of violence.[52] Georgians had fantasized about the agricultural potential of the Oconee River valley since the 1770s. They forcibly dispossessed Creeks and validated their violence by denying Creeks' right to defend their territory.[53]

Georgians' actions seem almost calculated to escalate the Oconee boundary conflict, rendering their fear of Creek violence a self-fulfilling prophecy. Georgians sometimes pursued horse rustlers deep into Creek country with disastrous results. One such incursion took place in the spring of 1787, touching off bitter correspondence and threats that lasted for years. After Creeks stole a number of horses and committed "some murders" in Greene County, a local militia leader named William Melton raised a party and chased them across the Oconee River.[54] Melton pursued them some thirty miles southwest to the Ocmulgee River, where he "overtook a party of Creek Indians" and killed a dozen of them. Melton, however, "did not recover any of the stolen property."[55] This foray demonstrates that Georgians ignored the Oconee boundary as it suited them. The militia's attack was ostensibly retaliation, but killing a dozen Creeks was a disproportionate response, and their failure to recover any stolen property showed that the victims were innocents. Neha Micco of Cussita soon pointed out that fact.

The raids into Greene County that led to William Melton's incursion may appear random, but they were not. They were targeted, meaningful reactions to settler violence. Many Creeks continued to endorse retributive violence to restore cosmic balance and quiet the crying blood of Creeks killed by outsiders. Neha Micco explained that, the previous summer, Greene Countians had murdered two men from Oakchoy, an Upper Town in the Okfuskee province.[56] In response, Oakchoys killed and scalped two Greene County men, captured one black slave, and stole fourteen horses.[57] Melton then invaded Creek country and murdered twelve people to avenge those deaths, but his victims were not Oakchoys. Neha Micco swore they were Cussitas, "your real friends."[58] Turning Georgians' most frequent reproach of Creeks against them, the headman chided, "'Tis not we that have forgot the talk at Shoulder Bone, but you."[59] Indiscriminate attacks like Melton's pushed independent talwas closer to unity.

Lower Towns represented by Neha Micco and Yahola Micco of Coweta were outraged yet inclined to forego balancing Melton's murders. Asking common Creeks to ignore a deeply held religious duty likely would have undermined the miccos' political influence. A few weeks after Melton's attack, the miccos sent a talk to Georgia declaring that peace existed between Lower Towns and settlers. They reprimanded Melton's men for their failure to recognize their "friends," and they insisted that Georgians had killed Cussitas intentionally for "what other bad people did." Melton's men, they continued, "could not think that it was any of the lower towns did you any mischief, when we were at your houses and living with you in a manner that you might be sure it was not us."[60]

Contrary to the Creek practice of balancing the deaths through retribution killings, Yahola Micco and Neha Micco consented to wait for Georgia's justice before taking any action. They noted grudgingly that "It is not the rule of the Indians to acquaint you of this, but to take satisfaction."[61] Instead, they chose to abide by Article 4 of the Treaty of Shoulderbone: "The Punishing of innocent persons under the idea of retaliation shall not be practiced on either side."[62] The Lower Town miccos shamed Georgia's leaders for their failures, reminding them that "You always promised that the innocent should not suffer for the guilty."[63]

Instead of punishing William Melton, however, Georgia's leaders justified the attack by portraying settlers as guiltless victims defending themselves in the midst of open war.[64] They dismissed the context. Oakchoys had conducted their attack in response to the slaying of two Oakchoys a year earlier, yet Melton's men killed a dozen innocent Cussitas. Georgians ignored differences between talwas as well as legitimate Oakchoy grievances and placed equal blame on all Creeks. They accused all Creeks generally of entering "the most solemn engagements" with white settlers and then violating them. "What had our people to expect," Georgians demanded, "when they saw their peaceable countrymen murdered?"[65] After justifying Melton's attack, Georgia consoled the victims, assuring them that they now could "rest satisfied that we consider you, the Lower Towns, as our best friends and brothers."[66] For good measure, Governor George Mathews threatened the friends and families of Melton's victims. If they contemplated retaliation, he warned, "we will not hesitate to do ourselves ample justice, of carrying war into your country, burning your towns, and staining your land with blood."[67]

As independent talwa leaders, Yahola Micco and Neha Micco may have been inclined to let Melton's attack pass, but, as an aspiring national leader, Alexander McGillivray called a meeting at Cussita and convinced other Lower Creeks to demand satisfaction. Following this affair, one historian claimed that "a more general war began in which the Creeks ravaged with impunity the Georgia frontiers" throughout the remainder of 1787.[68] U.S. Superintendent of Indian Affairs James White hoped to defuse the situation. He wrote to Alexander McGillivray that "among the herd of white people" there were many who wished to provoke war with Creeks, but "To restrain this temper, is the duty of more sober reflection."[69]

The constant violence of late 1787 and early 1788 merits the appellation "the Oconee War," though Creeks also occasionally struck Cumberland settlers.[70] Georgians' perception of themselves as the innocent victims of ungoverned savages was critical to justifying their indiscriminate responses. Creeks continued their patrols, but it was clearly they who needed to worry about an uncommon degree of ferocity. The frequency of violent events and the death toll rose to an unprecedented level. The year 1786 had witnessed 25 raids, with 8 ending in violence. The number quadrupled to 101 raids in 1787, with 20 resulting in bloodshed. The number of raids almost doubled again to 180 the following year, with 34 ending violently. In the spring of 1787, Creeks also killed six Cumberland settlers and one Georgian attempting to build a trading factory on the Tennessee River at Muscle Shoals in present-day north Alabama.[71] The *Georgia Gazette* confirmed that the border zones were becoming more dangerous. In September 1787, the *Gazette* reported an event in which Creeks found a group of white ranchers ranging the Oconee River's west bank, indisputably in Creek country. When they attempted to remove the white trespassers, a melee ensued in which the frontiersmen killed "nine of the savages."[72]

The event Georgians would later refer to as the Battle of Jack's Creek was the largest single episode of violence during the Oconee War. It exemplifies the importance of both Creek border patrols and Georgians' distortions of them. In September 1787, General Elijah Clarke raised 160 volunteers to pursue, he claimed, a party of "50 or 60 Indians."[73] Several days earlier, Creek border patrollers had killed three Georgia militiamen who were part of "a small reconnoitering party of eight" that had crossed the Oconee River into Creek country.[74] The survivors reported that "about 40" Creeks had ambushed them near Big Shoals on the Apalachee River. When Clarke's army found the three militiamen "mangled in a shocking manner," his volunteers pursued the Creeks some fifty miles or more into Creek country all the way to the south fork of the Ocmulgee River.[75]

After reaching the Ocmulgee, however, Clarke gave up the chase for the culprits and returned to the Apalachee, where he discovered the trail of a different, uninvolved group of Creeks. On September 21, he caught them "encamped and cooking" at Jack's Creek, a western tributary of the Apalachee well inside Creek country.[76] Clarke ambushed the innocent campers and later boasted to have "totally defeated" them after a three-hour firefight in which the Creeks largely hid in a canebrake.[77] Clarke withdrew after losing six men killed and eleven wounded, and he claimed to have killed "not less than 25 Indians."[78] He insisted that, had he remained, his troops would have found "40 or 50 dead of their wounds."[79] Clarke's men plundered the Creek campground and reported finding one hundred halters and bridles, which they presented as proof their victims were a horse-rustling expedition.

Elijah Clarke failed to identify his victims as members of any particular talwa, but his attacks show that he considered all Creeks enemies. In

October and November, eight more raids struck Greene County, again resulting in overwhelming retaliation. Two of them ended in bloodshed, but in keeping with the larger pattern, most resulted in livestock theft and property destruction.[80] Less than a week after Clarke's attack, Creeks raided the home of David and Charles Furlow, stealing six horses and burning the family's house, outbuildings, furniture, and flax crop, as well as several nearby houses.[81] The *Georgia Gazette* reported that Creeks had stolen some thirty horses, burned several forts, fences, and houses, in addition to cutting down "a very considerable quantity of corn" and destroying a number of hogs.[82] Creeks and Georgians exchanged gunfire at an Oconee River fort called Scull Shoals Station near present-day Athens. After wounding three Georgians, the Creeks fled.[83] Creeks also killed "two or three men" on Shoulderbone Creek shortly after the Battle of Jack's Creek.[84] Elijah Clarke responded by collaborating with another militia commander to invade Creek country with some five hundred men.[85]

Rumors contributed to Georgians' outsized retaliation. False reports of murders were occasionally corrected. In October 1787, for example, the *Georgia Gazette* conceded that a report of three men having been killed by Creeks near Savannah was "entirely groundless."[86] A correspondent in Greene County reported that there were no Creek raiders on the Georgia side of the river, but that he was "induced to believe, from the frequent firing of guns . . . that they are in large bodies on the south bank of the Oconee."[87] Even the report of Creek people hunting within undisputed Creek territory was enough to convince Georgians of impending invasion.

By late October 1787, Georgians had whipped themselves into a frenzy over the Oconee War. The City of Savannah passed an ordinance requiring all inhabitants to provide slaves for the construction of defensive works around the city due to the "approaching mischief of an Indian war."[88] While the theft and violence of the Oconee War represented a genuine threat in the Oconee valley, only two raids touched the county around Savannah between 1787 and 1790, and neither included violence.

Creeks were capable of the large-scale raids that Georgians feared, but, as ever, they focused on the disputed Oconee lands. In November, Creeks retaliated against the recent militia incursions by attacking the Greene County seat at Greenesborough and burning the courthouse and several other buildings. Although it seems likely that the razing of Greenesborough involved bloodshed, there is no definitive evidence of fatalities.[89] It is unclear which

Creeks conducted this ambitious attack, though one Georgian later claimed that after "Greenesborough was sacked and burnt," there were several signs including "some writing in French left by one Cornells" and "marks left on Trees" claiming responsibility.[90] The attribution to Cornells likely referred to Indian countryman Joseph Cornel, Alexander McGillivray's interpreter. It also may have referred to Joseph's brother George Cornel, his son James Cornel, or his nephew, Alexander Cornel, all of whom lived in the Tallapoosa province Upper Towns of Tuckabatchee and Little Tallassee. Cussitas and Cowetas also may have been involved.[91]

As the situation worsened in the fall of 1787, the Georgia legislature passed "An Act for suppressing the violence of the Indians." It called for three thousand militiamen to fight the Oconee War and appealed to the Confederation Congress for funding, since the state could not support the proposed force.[92] Congress took a two-pronged approach by simultaneously preparing to negotiate peace and wage war. After the Battle of Jack's Creek and subsequent raids, Georgia's delegates convinced the Confederation Congress that "their country is in danger of an invasion."[93] Congress then ordered Secretary at War Henry Knox to deliver 300 pistols, 150 swords, and a handful of small artillery pieces with gunpowder and grapeshot.[94] Congress also organized a new treaty commission under U.S. authority while Superintendent James White labored to convince Alexander McGillivray and others to accept the Oconee cession once and for all.[95]

Confederation government officials bristled at Georgians' exercise of authority in Indian Affairs yet supported the state because they found Georgia's narrative about Creek ferocity compelling.[96] Under the Articles of Confederation, the central government claimed the "sole and exclusive right and power of regulating the trade and managing all affairs with the Indians not members of any of the states."[97] Georgia, however, could define Creeks as members of the state by claiming lands from the Atlantic Ocean to the Mississippi River under its colonial charter.

James White echoed Georgians' characterization of Creeks as a stateless but unified people who posed a potent military threat. He claimed that Creeks could field "6,000 gun-men, mostly well armed with rifles."[98] White's self-interest in frontier expansion likely colored his analysis. He was deeply invested in Cumberland valley lands, and, like other speculators, focused on protecting those investments. As a U.S. agent, he encouraged Congress to defend Georgians' land claims. As a speculator, he advocated Cumberland's secession from the United States and negotiated directly with Spanish officials for an alliance that would guarantee Cumberland land titles and free navigation of the Mississippi River.[99]

Based in part on White's report, Henry Knox later concluded that "hostilities still rage" between Georgians and Creeks, and "the cause of the war is an utter denial, on the part of the Creeks, of the validity of the three treaties, stated to have been made by them with the State of Georgia."[100] His assessment was only partially correct. Some leaders such as Alexander McGillivray had rejected the treaties from the beginning. Other men representing both Lower and Upper Towns had signed the treaties in good faith, including Yahola Micco of Coweta, Neha Micco of Cussita, Hitcheta Micco of Hitchiti, Cusa Micco of Coosa, and Hoboithle Micco of Tallassee. They meant to establish firm borders and protect Creek hunting rights on the Oconee's east bank, and they encouraged Georgians to seek the assent of all Creek towns. They only gradually came to reject the treaties because Georgians failed to abide by them.

Other U.S. agents reinforced the narrative about the Creek menace and overestimated Alexander McGillivray's influence. Amid repeated proclamations of outrageous Indian violence, occasional reports suggested that both Georgians and U.S. officials knew that property theft was the more prevalent concern. In 1788, Governor George Mathews submitted a list to U.S. commissioners that enumerated recent losses to Creek border patrols. The list noted some thirty slaves and eighty-three horses stolen but only one person killed and one wounded. Such occasional admissions suggest that Georgians knowingly exaggerated the threat of Creek violence while deemphasizing the real problem of theft.[101]

Late in 1787, Governor Mathews declared that "the State never can have a secure and lasting peace with that perfidious nation, until they have severely felt the effects of war."[102] The state deployed more troops and built more forts. Each action provoked Creeks, escalating the Oconee War. In 1788, theft and violence on the frontier peaked with 180 raids reported, 34 of which ended in bloodshed. Botched raids more frequently ended in horrific violence, and armed clashes increased with Georgia militiamen who assumed all Creeks were enemies of the state. Over the course of 1789 and the spring of 1790, however, the United States operating under its newly ratified Constitution urged Creeks back to the negotiating table. After the Treaty of New York in August 1790, raiding declined precipitously. By the end of the year, rates were almost as low as they had been prior to the Treaty of Shoulderbone Creek, with only two violent raids occurring in 1790.

The more militia commanders patrolled and built forts and block-houses, the more they incited Creeks. In February 1788, Creeks again clashed with Georgians near Scull Shoals on the Oconee and killed a militia captain. Elijah Clarke sent an agitated letter to Georgia's new governor, George Handley, demanding arms and ammunition and warning that "the Indians will be troublesome."[103] At the same time, fifty miles east of the Oconee within a day's travel of Savannah, Creeks allegedly stabbed and scalped a white boy on Canoochee Creek. A nearby settler cried out for state military aid and angrily wondered whether the "government has or intendes doing anything for the defence of the fruntiers or whether they mean making a sacrafise of all exposed."[104]

Throughout the winter and spring of 1788, Georgians continued ramping up military activity with predictable results. Elijah Clarke insisted that Creeks were "in force" just west of the Oconee River, necessitating a standing army, ammunition, and more firearms.[105] Governor Handley ordered state troops to the southern coastal counties of Glynn, Camden, Liberty, and Chatham, and Georgians patrolled both sides of the Oconee regularly.[106] The upper Oconee saw repeated action. In March in Washington County, a Captain Wood was out with a handful of state troops and militiamen when he discovered evidence of a Creek party of about thirty-five. He and his men made for a nearby fort, but Creeks ambushed them, killing one man. Captain Wood went missing during the fray, but his horse turned up later, "very much bloody." His men concluded Wood had been killed or captured.[107] The *Georgia Gazette* reported that "the savages" burned three houses and slaughtered cattle and hogs at Irwin's Fort, also in Washington County.[108] Captain John Fielder and others were out from the Scull Shoals fort gathering fodder when "they were attacked by a parcel of Creek Indians" who stole Fielder's horse, saddle and tack, firearm, and clothes.[109] Creeks wounded two other militiamen. This was only the beginning for Captain Fielder. He spent five years at Scull Shoals, marched with Elijah Clarke on most of his sorties, and spent much of his time as a spy trespassing the border into Creek country.[110]

March 1788 witnessed the single most violent episode of the year when Creeks raided a settler's farm on Williamson's Swamp, a tributary of the Ogeechee River in Washington County some twenty miles east of the Oconee River. The raid on the home of David Jackson seems to have been a botched theft that ended with the deaths of at least six non-Indians, including several of Jackson's children. Creek raiders attempted to capture two slaves, a forty-year-old woman, and a twelve-year-old

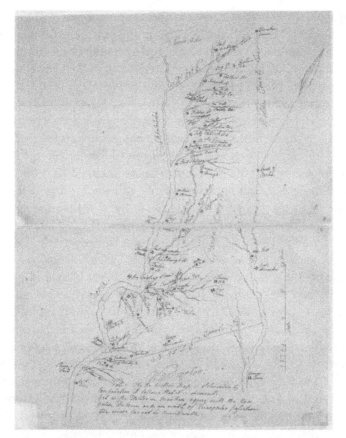

MAP 8. The map depicts dozens of forts and blockhouses built in the upper Oconee River valley in the 1780s and 1790s. Georgia Archives.

girl, perhaps mother and daughter. Instead, they killed the woman and made away with the girl, a rifle, clothing, and furniture. Two of Jackson's neighbors arrived at the house shortly afterward and found the slain and scalped bodies of Jackson's wife, "five or six of his children," and the enslaved woman.[111]

Violent Creek raids on the Cumberland settlements also peaked in late 1787 and 1788. Creeks reportedly killed forty-one Cumberland settlers in 1787 in response to a raid on a large Creek hunting camp at Muscle Shoals on the Tennessee River.[112] Cumberland settlers remained determined to establish a factory at Muscle Shoals to supply Chickasaws. Such a post could serve the dual purposes of securing a Native ally against Creeks and Cherokees and opening a new region for land speculation.[113] Creeks killed at least seven more Cumberland settlers in 1788, and a frontier rumor held that Creeks assaulted a fort in the Franklin settlements, killing 108 people.[114] Creek raids in the Cumberland and Tennessee River valleys left settlers petitioning Alexander McGillivray for peace and alliance.[115]

As the violence peaked in early 1788, Congress authorized a treaty commission under James White with members appointed by Georgia, North Carolina, and South Carolina. Former governor George Mathews served for Georgia.[116] These commissioners assumed that Creeks possessed unity but lacked both sovereignty and the right to defend their territory. The commission initiated talks in April by threatening that "in future it will be considered a war of the Union" if Creeks rejected their "pacifick proposal" by continuing to harass Oconee settlers.[117] In preparation for such an outcome, Secretary at War Henry Knox proposed an invasion plan that would deploy 2,800 U.S. soldiers.[118] By mid-June, "the Chiefs of the Creek Indians" had agreed to a new round of talks to be held in September under Richard Winn, James White's replacement as U.S. superintendent of Indian Affairs for the Southern Department.[119]

Alexander McGillivray declared the proposed talks moot because commissioners already had refused to discuss restoring the Oconee strip and evicting white settlers.[120] Still, Governor Handley declared a truce in August until the conclusion of the proposed talks.[121] Despite the governor's optimism, some Georgians believed that peace was impossible. Creeks could not be "kept in harmony" because of "their great success in the present war" and their "growing lust after property," so easily stolen along the border.[122] One Georgian writing under the pen name Gracchus urged his fellow citizens to view the Oconee War as an opportunity rather than a threat. Georgians must fight "not to conquer but to destroy." "The period has now arrived," Gracchus menaced, "when forbearance becomes criminal."[123]

Attacks like those led by Elijah Clarke and William Melton suggest that there had been little forbearance. By 1788, Georgians had reported killing seventy-seven Creeks. Alexander McGillivray observed that Georgians "warred with an exterminating spirit" in border conflicts, often targeting Creek civilians. Native women were "flayed when partly alive," and "pregnant women were ripped open the men's privates cut off and put in the women's mouths with other monstrosities of the like nature." White men murdered women and children, leaving their bodies "so mangled that they couldn't be known by Relations." McGillivray argued that, beyond simple border jumping, "It is such abominable actions as these that has stimulated the Indians to many cruel but just Retaliations."[124]

Negotiating as Nations

After violence peaked in the first half of 1788, raids declined over the course of 1789 and 1790 as both sides worked toward new negotiations. The treaty talks initially planned for the fall of 1788 were postponed until the spring of 1789 in part to allow the first U.S. Congress operating under the newly ratified Constitution to assume its duties.[125] Newspaper reports, however, led Henry Knox to conclude in July 1789 that Creeks were still "making inroads into Georgia, and that the outrages committed by them have excited an alarm, which has extended itself to Savannah."[126]

Postponing talks may have benefited Georgians. Public opinion outside the state occasionally considered Georgia as the aggressor and favored restoring Oconee lands to Creeks. Continual emphasis on Creek violence, however, was persuasive.[127] The Georgia editorialist writing as Gracchus acknowledged that "it is the fashion of the day . . . to believe Georgia to be in the wrong, and to have provoked by unwarrantable proceedings in respect to land, the present quarrel."[128] Another unnamed correspondent writing in the *Georgia Gazette* observed that Georgia "is reprobated for her conduct with the Creek Nation," but "the first blood drawn, from every reasonable presumption, was by the Indians."[129] Gracchus agreed that not only had Creeks "certainly spilt the first blood," but they had "pushed their ravages" with the goal of "absolute destruction, and not a vindication of their pretended rights."[130] Contributors to the *Gazette* insisted that if other Americans knew about "the cruel ravages of the Indians," they would support Georgia.[131] During the cease-fire, planters complained that slave thefts in particular continued.[132] For his part, Alexander McGillivray accused settlers of ignoring the truce by attacking and plundering Creek hunting camps.[133] Creeks, he warned, would respond in kind.

In October 1788, a few of the most influential leaders from the biggest talwas began collaborating in a move toward greater coalescence. Tallapoosa province Upper Town leaders Alexander McGillivray of Little Tallassee and Efau Hadjo of Tuckabatchee joined Muskogee-speaking Lower Town leaders Yahola Micco of Coweta and several Cussitas. Together, they urged their fellow talwa leaders to meet with

U.S. commissioners as "one people" speaking with a single voice.[134] These talwa leaders believed that the consensus underpinning peak raiding mandated reassertion of Creek rights to the Oconee lands. The border conflict gave miccos a compelling reason to act as a unified polity, but the fact that nationalist leaders still had to persuade their peers speaks volumes about continuing devotion to talwa autonomy. When U.S. Indian agent George Whitefield met with Lower Creeks at Cussita, the town's headmen demanded satisfaction for William Melton's 1787 murder of twelve Cussitas.[135] Whitefield attended a second meeting seventy miles northwest at Tuckabatchee, but the conference was rocky because the interpreter was drunk and McGillivray did not speak Muskogee well enough to make a public presentation.[136] Whitefield, however, noted McGillivray's pleasure that "The Massacre of the Cussitaw people accomplished an end Mr. McGillivary had much at heart, uniting the whole nation."[137] Creeks "only contend for their rights," insisted Yahola Micco, repeating his call to "have the Georgians removed from the land."[138] Efau Hadjo agreed, declaring that Creeks "were all one people" on the question. This unity, however, was fragile in a populace still dedicated to talwa autonomy.

During 1789 and 1790, negotiators on both sides increased their correspondence, yet the Oconee boundary dispute remained intractable. Congress warned McGillivray that if Creeks refused to treat, they would face an American army.[139] McGillivray continued to reject the land cessions of the 1780s, but, recognizing his dependence on Spanish weapons, he began to waver.[140] A precarious truce prevailed in 1789 and 1790, though violations on both sides continued.

Alexander McGillivray approached upcoming treaty talks with an audacious goal: formal U.S. recognition of a sovereign Creek Nation. The parties scheduled talks for the spring of 1789 at Rock Landing on the Oconee River a few miles downriver from present-day Milledgeville. As the forests stirred to life that spring, however, divisions between nationalists and Creeks devoted to local autonomy shone beneath the veneer of unity. Some Creeks demonstrated independence by stealing from Georgia's frontiers.[141] Four violent attacks also occurred, though one later was attributed to white criminals.[142] Elijah Clarke accused McGillivray of ordering the attacks "to break up the new counties at all events, by burning houses."[143] McGillivray denied this, arguing that miccos could not always prevent "disorderly actions."[144] More importantly, Clarke failed to grasp McGillivray's ultimate goal. He and some two to three thousand Creeks intended to appear at Rock Landing, where they would negotiate firm borders, and, more importantly, demand American acknowledgment of "the independency of my Nation."[145]

The planned talks for Rock Landing, however, were again postponed because Creeks feared that, after recent violent raids, they could not travel safely so close to the border.[146] A new date was set for September, and "Mr. McGillivray, and all the Chiefs and headmen of the Nation" again guaranteed an unreliable truce.[147] McGillivray knew that boundaries and trade with Georgia would be key issues. He anticipated that securing Creek trade would be Georgia's priority, and he hoped that, with Spanish backing, he could leverage the issue to regain the Oconee strip.[148] As the Rock Landing talks approached, Georgians' hopes swelled, yet some leaders hedged their bets. In Congress, Georgia representative James Jackson proposed raising an army to invade Creek country should Creeks refuse U.S. terms. The motion failed.[149]

McGillivray worked hard to maintain Creek unity during the September 1789 negotiations at Rock Landing, and he saw the talks as an effective presentation of national sovereignty.[150] U.S. treaty commissioners arrived in September but departed after only a few weeks without a treaty, in part because McGillivray maintained Creek consensus on reclaiming the Oconee strip.[151] He found U.S. commissioners "too agreeable" to Georgia's desire for land.[152] True to his goal of gaining U.S. acknowledgment of Creek national sovereignty, he also balked at a provision that would have prohibited Creeks from making treaties with other nations.[153] Other reports suggested, however, that many talwa leaders disagreed with McGillivray's position and only grudgingly followed his lead.[154] Horse theft and property destruction in the Oconee valley resumed almost immediately after the failed talks. Georgia governor George Walton seemed surprised by this.[155] He had understood from U.S. commissioners that, while they had reached no agreement, Creeks had consented to a cease-fire pending yet another round of talks.[156] Georgia's leaders had agreed to the truce, "taking measures to prevent aggressions or provocations" on the part of backcountry Georgians.[157]

Governing Georgia's white settlers, however, proved more challenging than limiting Creek border patrols. In June 1790, two white men fired on a Cussita headman near the Oconee River. In July, white raiders attacked a Creek hunting camp on the Oconee, killing one man, shattering another man's arm, and stealing the Creeks' guns, horses, and forty deerskins. The hunters reportedly were nephews of the same Cussita leader whom Georgians had attacked two weeks earlier. Some suspected the same two white men were responsible. Governor Edward Telfair reacted by proclaiming it "a measure of the highest concern to suppress . . . acts of violence or outrage." He charged all officers with arresting the white offenders and offered a reward of 150 pounds sterling.[158] In keeping with its efforts to control Indian affairs, the United States deployed federal troops to frontier outposts on the Oconee River at Rock Landing, on the Altamaha River at Beard's Bluff 140 miles downstream, and on the St. Marys River, Georgia's border with East Florida.[159] Telfair claimed this measure actually increased Georgians' fears because federal forces were so inadequate to the task of guarding the border.[160]

By contrast with white Georgia's lawlessness, Governor Telfair observed that Creeks had "preserved the most amicable disposition towards the citizens of this state ever since I have had the honour to preside."[161] The diplomatic conversation increasingly controlled by Alexander McGillivray and U.S. representatives took precedence over local concerns. As spring turned to summer, the United States dispatched Colonel Marinus Willet to Georgia to resume talks, beginning a process that broke the stalemate in the Oconee boundary dispute. Willet bore a letter to McGillivray from Colonel Benjamin Hawkins threatening to destroy Creeks and summoning McGillivray to talks in New York.[162] Despite McGillivray's claim to lead a unified, sovereign polity, Hawkins recognized that talwa autonomy undercut McGillivray's authority. The leader from Little Tallassee possessed only "feeble restraints," so he could not "prevent partial hostilities."[163] Still, Hawkins threatened that the United States would treat Creeks as a unified body if border patrols resumed, warning that Americans "*must punish* . . . the result must be ruin to the Creeks."[164]

Alexander McGillivray traveled to the new U.S. capital in August to conduct talks that resulted in the 1790 Treaty of New York. After the treaty, one historian has argued, the United States considered Creeks to be under "U.S. domination." Georgia could regard Creeks as "spoiled children" and feel "justified in taking the Muskogees' 'vacant' lands."[165] The 1790 Treaty of New York, portrayed as having ended the Oconee War, in fact only exacerbated the conflict leading to another spike in border patrol activity in 1793.

7 /   "The Indians Still Desputed Giving up Their
        Rights to That Land": Renewed Border Patrols,
        1790–1793

The years following the 1790 Treaty of New York witnessed an uneven
decline of Creek border patrols, the rapid growth of America's military
presence in Creek country, and, in 1793, an astonishing new spike in
Creek raids. Both Creeks and Georgians disliked the terms of the Treaty
of New York. The treaty confirmed Georgia's claim to the Oconee's east
bank, and Georgians responded with a massive fort-building project
throughout the valley. The forts were quickly garrisoned, and militia
horsemen frequently patrolled west of the Oconee River dozens of
miles into Creek country. Such intrusions provoked Creeks. Young
men renewed border raids, some of which turned deadly. Creeks cited
their discontent with the Oconee border as the reason for such aggression, and they sought support for bolder action from the Spanish, the
British, and other indigenous groups. Alexander McGillivray passed
away in 1793, and his absence created a new kind of political turmoil.
Older miccos and young warriors often had disagreed with Alexander
McGillivray, but they also acknowledged the value of a highly skilled
executive who could represent Creeks as a unified nation. Still, miccos largely remained committed to town independence. People from
all over Creek country asserted their rights to hunt, trade, patrol their
borders and to commit crying blood killings that balanced the deaths
of those slain by settlers. Georgians used Creek raiding to justify further military buildup and indiscriminate, unauthorized violence. As
bloodshed threatened to spiral out of control, Creek leaders displayed

an extraordinary degree of coalescence when they called a multitown council of unprecedented size and scope to defend their territory and their sovereignty.

The Treaty of New York and Alexander McGillivray's Leadership

In the months before and after the August 1790 Treaty of New York, neither Alexander McGillivray nor the United States could control the aggressive impulses of their people, and McGillivray continued to play an uncertain role in Creek politics. Men from many talwas attacked encroaching Georgians.[1] Georgians regularly attacked Creek hunters, and when Creeks demanded satisfaction, they received none.[2] This failure of his executive power rankled McGillivray, yet he accepted that Creeks' anger at encroaching Americans coupled with the "wide extent" and "distant situation" of towns facilitated raiding and "put it out of the power of the Chiefs to prevent disorderly actions."[3]

In the early 1790s, warriors continued patrolling Creek country's borders with East and West Florida, Georgia, Cumberland, and, briefly, Chickasaw country. Cherokees insisted that the Cumberland settlements must be removed for "outside of this there is nothing that will satisfy the Cherokees and Creeks."[4] Creeks joined Cherokee raids on Cumberland settlements, sparking conflict with Cumberland's Chickasaw allies.[5] White Americans, including many migrating from Cumberland, continued accepting Spain's invitation to settle the lower Alabama and Tombigbee River valleys north of Mobile.[6] The Alabama province towns nearest these settlements long had participated in the Creek confederacy, yet, at least since the 1770s, they had asserted primary claim to lands around the Tombigbee-Alabama confluence. In April 1789, Alabama towns formed border patrols to steal horses and drive away the American settlers.[7] McGillivray cautioned Vizente Folch, Spanish commandant at Mobile, that American encroachment caused "the Indians great fear," and that the Alabama towns refused to be governed by the larger confederacy.[8] Muskogee speakers long had derided Alabama speakers as "stinkards."[9] Acknowledging again the limits of his power and Creek nationhood, McGillivray complained that Alabama province representatives rarely appeared at multitown "assemblies."[10] Alabamas and Choctaws continued raiding white settlements in the Alabama and Tombigbee River valleys for years.[11] They were not alone in asserting control of specific territories within the larger expanse of Creek country. Lower Creeks reminded Spaniards that lands comprising East Florida belonged to them, "only lent to you by us."[12] They implied that the Spanish must behave as good allies, or Creeks would repossess their property.

As Alexander McGillivray prepared for treaty talks in the new U.S. capital at New York in the spring of 1790, he remained committed to goals that had eluded him at the Rock Landing talks a few months earlier. There, he had attempted to forge national consensus around two goals. He wanted the U.S. government to restore the Oconee's east bank to Creek possession and recognize the sovereignty of a Creek Nation. McGillivray had rejected the U.S. proposal at Rock Landing in large part because the terms undercut Creek sovereignty and territorial integrity.[13] At treaty talks in New York, he arrogated the power to compromise Creek territory without seeking consensus among other talwa leaders.[14] This lack of concern for local interests enfeebled the resulting treaty.

Alexander McGillivray and thirty-one other Creek delegates hoped the New York talks would lead to U.S. management of the border. Indeed, three companies of U.S. Army troops had arrived in Georgia in May 1790, but their role was unclear to both Creeks and Georgians.[15] The treaty signers haled from only seven Upper Towns and just three Lower Towns. Hitchiti-, Yuchi-, and Koasati-speaking Lower Creeks lacked representation.[16] McGillivray negotiated the most important treaty provisions in secret. Both he and several other signers received pensions that amounted to bribery.[17] Despite their minimal presence, McGillivray claimed that Lower Towns desired the treaty the most because they had grown "weary" of border violence and believed this new treaty would end strife.[18]

The Treaty of New York centered on three issues: sovereignty, trade, and borders.[19] Despite McGillivray's protests, the treaty declared that the Creek Nation and all its component parts were "under the protection of the United States of America, and of no other sovereign."[20] He later insisted that his acceptance of American protection was limited to lands that fell within U.S. claims. He maintained Creek independence in foreign affairs by reserving the right to ally with Spain because millions of acres of Creek country fell within Spanish claims.[21]

The treaty ceded the Oconee's east bank to the United States rather than to Georgia, but it restored to Creeks those lands between the St. Marys and the Altamaha that Creeks had ceded to Georgia in the 1785 Treaty of Galphinton.[22] The document unambiguously declared that the border ran along the "south branch of the Oconee river, called the Appalachee," to be marked with an alley of felled trees twenty feet wide.[23] Much more importantly, McGillivray only gained the Creek delegation's consent to this provision by deceiving them. His subterfuge would haunt Creeks. McGillivray misled other delegates to believe that the new boundary line ran along the Oconee's north fork, yet he conceded the Apalachee to Americans.[24] He considered this a great "Sacrifice" and worried that Creeks might reject the entire treaty, so he concealed his consent.[25]

Both George Washington and Alexander McGillivray perceived trade to be the thorniest issue. Both men understood that Creeks would be dependent on whoever provided their goods.[26] They resolved the issue with a secret article deferring any trade talks for two years. This left all trade to McGillivray's partners, Panton, Leslie & Company, a Scottish firm operating out of Spanish Pensacola since being ousted from Savannah as loyalists during the American Revolution. The secret article allowed McGillivray to control trade in Creek country even if his relationship with Panton, Leslie ended. He would be allowed to import sixty thousand dollars' worth of goods duty free in case of any "obstructions."[27] McGillivray understood that these compromises on sovereignty, territory, and trade were not ideal. He expected some resistance from talwa leaders and young hunters, but he apparently believed he had acquired enough authority as a national leader to secure Creeks' compliance.

Reasserting Talwa Autonomy, Renewing Border Patrols

Talwa leaders and common hunters soon reasserted talwa autonomy, turning the Treaty of New York into a failed nation-building exercise. Representatives from a few prominent towns had sent delegates to negotiate an agreement with a foreign power that was of great importance to all. Shortly after the treaty's completion in August 1790, however, it became clear the signers did not represent consensus. The majority of Creeks still resented Georgians' occupation of the Oconee's east bank and their encroachment west of the river. Many rejected Alexander McGillivray's claim to executive leadership of a unified nation. The border patrols of the 1790s were similar to those of the 1780s in that raiders took action as members of autonomous talwas, yet their behavior reflected popular sentiment.[28] One American observer noted in 1791 that "the Interests of the Indians & that of the Citizens of the adjacent States are so opposite & irreconcilable, and both Parties are so vindictive, licentious & ungovernable, that their inherent animosity, must soon burst forth in mutual aggression."[29] The prediction proved accurate. Between 1790 and 1793, some Creek leaders struggled to assert monopoly control of violence

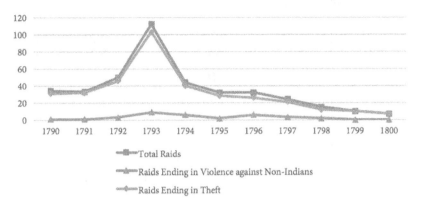

FIGURE 3. Creek Raids in Georgia, 1790–1800

through long-standing talwa leadership networks rather than relying on a figurehead executive. Common Creeks exercised their autonomy by trading, hunting, stealing, and killing on their own terms.

The search for alternate sources of trade goods inhibited consensus in the early 1790s and undercut Alexander McGillivray's influence. Common Creeks rejected McGillivray's claim to leadership in part because he often put his own wealth first. He controlled Creek trade, according to Spanish agent Carlos Howard, by protecting "the interests of his close friends and protectors, Panton, Leslie, and Co." and by seizing the goods of any traders operating without a license issued on his authority.[30] He used his kin network at the growing Tensaw settlement to further anchor his control of trade with the Spanish Gulf Coast.[31] Yet, like any micco, McGillivray distributed presents to win public support. He regularly sent couriers to Pensacola to pick up gifts to be given out as "little bountys . . . to the deserving people."[32] Such little bounties, however, proved inadequate.

In 1791, a cadre of Upper and Lower Town headmen hatched an ambitious attempt to circumvent McGillivray and restore British trade on the Gulf coast. Muskogee speakers in the Lower Towns of Coweta, Cussita, and Ooseechee joined forces with Koasati speakers from the Lower Town of Cheaha and Muskogee speakers in the prominent Upper Town of Okfuskee. They collaborated with the American adventurer William Augustus Bowles. Bowles had fought in the British army during the Revolutionary War and was living in Ooseechee by 1791. Together, the Creek leaders and the spirited American hoped to establish a British

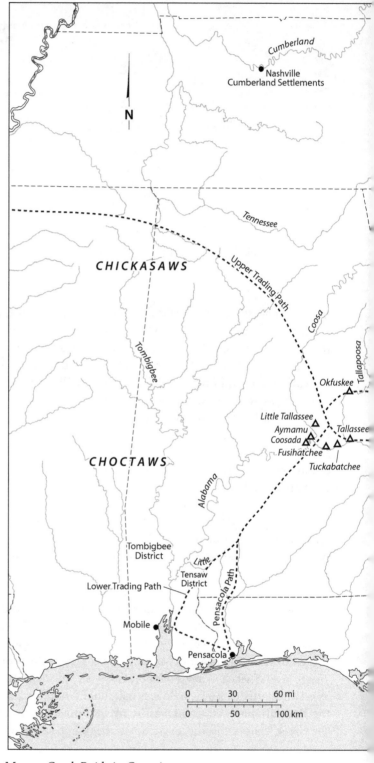

MAP 9. Creek Raids in Georgia, 1790–1792

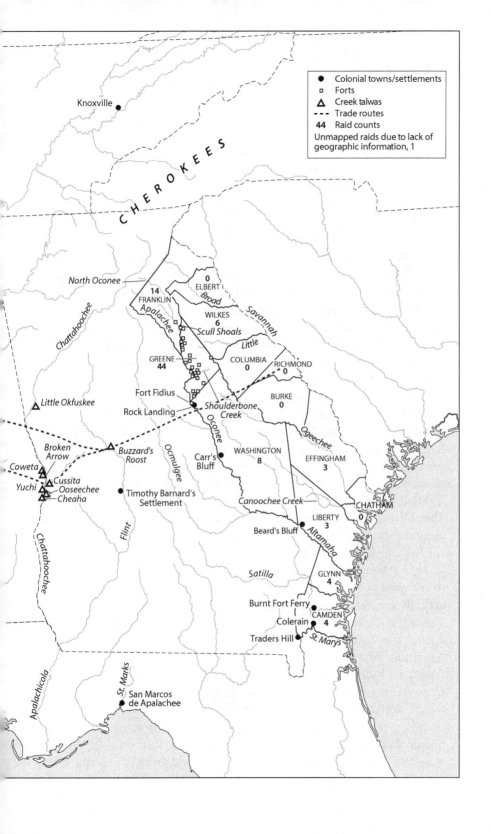

Legend:
● Colonial towns/settlements
□ Forts
△ Creek talwas
--- Trade routes
44 Raid counts
Unmapped raids due to lack of geographic information, 1

Knoxville

C H E R O K E E S

North Oconee

Chattahoochee

Apalachee

FRANKLIN
14

ELBERT
0

Broad

Savannah

WILKES
6
Scull Shoals

Little

GREENE
44

COLUMBIA
0

RICHMOND
0

Fort Fidius

Rock Landing

Shoulderbone Creek

BURKE
0

Little Okfuskee

Oconee

Ogeechee

Buzzard's Roost

Carr's Bluff

WASHINGTON
8

EFFINGHAM
3

Broken Arrow

Ocmulgee

Coweta

Cussita

Yuchi
Ooseechee
Cheaha

Timothy Barnard's Settlement

Canoochee Creek

CHATHAM
0

LIBERTY
3

Beard's Bluff

Altamaha

Flint

Chattahoochee

Satilla

GLYNN
4

Burnt Fort Ferry

CAMDEN
4

Colerain

Traders Hill

St. Marys

Apalachicola

St. Marks

San Marcos de Apalachee

trade depot in East Florida at the mouth of the Apalachicola River.[33] This reasonable expression of local self-interest threatened Alexander McGillivray's national leadership by undermining his control of trade and his efforts to maintain Spanish alliance.[34] The promise of more generous trade led one hundred Cussitas, Cowetas, Okfuskees, and others to join Bowles in the seizure of a Panton, Leslie & Company store at San Marcos de Apalache.[35] Some observers believed that leaders from every Lower Creek town participated in the raid and that a majority of Creeks supported the effort to establish an alternative trade—not just a few renegade towns, as McGillivray reported.[36]

Bowles argued that the raid benefited Creeks by helping break William Panton's effective trade monopoly as well as Spain's diplomatic monopoly.[37] The new Spanish governor of Louisiana, Francisco Luis Hector de Carondelet, responded energetically. Like his predecessor, Carondelet hoped to use exclusive alliances with southeastern Indians to secure Spain's Gulf Coast colonies against British and American threats. Carondelet aggressively pursued Bowles and appointed new Spanish agents in Creek country. Concerned that marking the Creek-Georgia border line pursuant to the Treaty of New York would "bring forth commercial relations" with the United States, Carondelet and his agents encouraged Creek headmen to avoid running the line. Creek trade with Americans or the British would deprive both Spain and Panton of an advantageous relationship.[38] In the fall of 1792, Carondelet's agents captured Bowles and imprisoned him in New Orleans. Undeterred, Cowetas traveled to the Bahamas to negotiate a British trade deal on their own. They ultimately failed, but the attempt concerned McGillivray enough to request that Governor Carondelet patrol the Florida coast to prevent any further Creek contact with British vessels.[39]

Throughout the 1780s, Creeks had asserted their hunting rights to the Oconee's east bank in treaties with Georgia. In 1791 and 1792, men actually increased their hunting on the east bank. They believed that U.S. agent Colonel Marinus Willet had confirmed their right to do so during the summer of 1790, when he was in Creek country to escort Alexander McGillivray to New York. Trader and Indian countryman Abraham Mordecai confirmed that Creeks were crossing the border more frequently because of Willet's purported assent, and he worried that it would be "a continual cause of quarrels and disputes."[40] As the deerskin trade continued its long-term decline, every acre of viable deer habitat became more important to commercial hunters. McGillivray reported that, by the end of 1791, Cheahas and Ooseechees, like most

Creek hunters, could no longer supply themselves through commercial hunting.[41] By August 1792, there had been a handful of murders in the Oconee valley, yet Cussita and Coweta headmen cautioned U.S. Indian agent and trader James Seagrove that, as fall approached, desperate Creeks "will be over the Oconee a hunting."[42]

Theft raids spiked from a low of 32 in 1790 to a high of 112 in 1793. Like the quest for alternate trade sources and continued hunting on the east bank, border patrol raids signified a combination of self-interest and political resistance to Georgia settlement. As in previous periods of heavy raiding, some leaders opposed the practice. Creeks accompanied Cherokees on a few raids in Cumberland, reportedly killing settlers, taking captives, and stealing property.[43] Creeks, however, most frequently targeted the upper Oconee valley, the region about which they were most sensitive.[44] With Spanish encouragement, Alexander McGillivray himself soon began advocating raids to forestall the running of boundary lines pursuant to the Treaty of New York. He claimed to have ordered Lower Town warriors to seize the cattle and burn the huts of Georgians on the Apalachee River.[45] Georgians knew the Oconee-Apalachee forks were contested despite the Treaty of New York, yet they continued moving large cattle herds there knowing the practice would "exasperate the Indians."[46]

Men stole livestock to hamper non-Indian settlement in the Oconee strip, but they also had more basic motives including hunger and the scarcity of horses. Lower Towns were experiencing famine in late 1792, so the prospect of rustling beef on the hoof appealed to them. Autonomous talwas pursued other ways to alleviate hunger. Lower Towns accepted a gift of five thousand bushels of corn from James Seagrove, though they did so against Alexander McGillivray's better judgment.[47] Also, a virulent horse distemper ravaged Creek country in the fall of 1792, destroying countless animals. This left just "ten in a hundred Indians" with enough horses to "pack out his provisions to the hunting grounds."[48] If Creeks wanted a productive winter hunt, they needed to replenish their horse herds quickly, and that meant raiding.

Despite having good reason to steal horses, some Lower Town leaders tried to mitigate the diplomatic tension by punishing rustlers and returning contraband.[49] In July 1792, the Cussita King, also known as Kiskilikaski, urged several towns to round up all the stolen horses they could find to be returned.[50] If rustlers refused to cooperate, Cussita King ordered them beaten.[51] With the help of the Yuchi King and Indian countryman Timothy Barnard, the Cussita King promised to return six horses to Captain Benjamin Harrison at Carr's Bluff, a name and place that would soon become synonymous with the savagery of white Georgians.[52] Yuchis recently had robbed Harrison, and Barnard convinced James Seagrove to compensate Harrison for the theft.[53] By August, Cussitas and Cowetas had returned three more stolen horses and were rounding up others.[54] A prominent Creek man of mixed ancestry named John Kinnard assisted in the return of a dozen more horses. He argued that "the bad people" who stole horses did so without the sanction of talwa leaders. Kinnard also requested rewards of rum for those who returned animals—a dubious method of discouraging future theft.[55]

As in previous years, theft raids could turn deadly when Georgians pursued Creeks. In June 1792, a group of Georgia militiamen pursued rustlers dozens of miles into Creek country all the way to the Ocmulgee River. Creeks ambushed the militiamen as they crossed the river, killing one. In response, the commander of the federal garrison at Rock Landing on the Oconee requested that a Georgia light horse troop regularly patrol the border. He also ordered construction of another fort near the Oconee-Apalachee confluence.[56] Frontier settlers began building forts of their own and sending unauthorized "spyes" into Creek country.[57] This was but one stage of a long-term American military buildup in the Oconee valley.[58]

Increased raiding led to many anxious encounters. At least eighteen of them resulted in bloodshed, and some of those ended in the deaths of Creeks. As ever, when Creek men were killed, sacred duty required satisfaction killings to restore cosmic balance apart from any national interest. Though not exclusively politically motivated, satisfaction killings suited the agenda of leaders who wished to forestall running the Oconee line. Alexander McGillivray, William Augustus Bowles, Governor Carondelet, and the Cussita King all rejected the border defined in the Treaty of New York, yet none could claim to lead a unified Creek Nation whose warriors followed orders.

A satisfaction killing committed in 1792 illustrates the complex motives and consequences involved. Georgians killed a Coweta man in June 1791, and, a year later, the state still had not provided justice.[59] Taking satisfaction, Cowetas travelled to the upper Oconee valley, crossed the river into Greene County, and tomahawked two white men.[60] Georgians were outraged, yet they had expected retaliation, so the killings did not cause "the usual alarm."[61] Creeks considered balance restored and calmly noted that "We waited twelve months before we took Satisfaction," perhaps expecting that Georgians would behave with equal restraint.[62]

The Coweta men acted as members of an autonomous talwa, yet several leaders beyond Coweta responded to the satisfaction killings with greater assertions of authority. Alexander McGillivray exerted national leadership by delaying the running of the Oconee boundary, avowedly from fear of Georgians' vengeance.[63] McGillivray condemned raiding in general, and he blamed William Augustus Bowles for exciting Coweta, Cheaha, and Ooseechee raiders who were dragging the Creek Nation toward "unavoidable" war.[64] Bowles, however, reportedly begged Creeks to refrain from any border raids while he sought restoration of the Oconee lands diplomatically.[65] McGillivray vowed to remove Georgians from the Oconee's east bank peacefully by September 1792, though he received a pledge from Governor Carondelet in Louisiana to provide weapons if removal by force became necessary.[66] The Cussita King also declined to run the Oconee boundary following Cowetas' satisfaction killings. Instead, he ventured to Mobile and New Orleans, where he promised to restrain Creek raiding and accepted Spanish presents. He also discussed the merits of a "permanent congress," or confederacy, of all southeastern Indians with Governor Carondelet and diplomats from the Cherokees, Chickasaws, and Choctaws. He also agreed to meet with U.S. agent James Seagrove later that fall.[67] The Cussita King, Yahola Micco of Coweta, and other headmen urged young men to refrain from expelling white trespassers from the Oconee strip. The Treaty of New York explicitly confirmed their rights to do so, but headmen worried that zealous border patrollers could "over do the thing" and provoke retaliation.[68]

In August 1792, the White Lieutenant of Okfuskee observed that Creeks were "confused" by the various national, regional, talwa, and individual interests involved in the Oconee boundary dispute. He simplified things by placing the interests of his own talwa first.[69] He disagreed with the many disparate parties who resisted running the Oconee line. Despite evidence to the contrary, the White Lieutenant assured James Seagrove that "the greatest part of our nation" accepted the Treaty of New York and would help run the boundary line. He hinted that well-regulated American trade in Creek country, perhaps a U.S. commissary in Okfuskee, might help Creeks resolve their confusion. The White Lieutenant's position confirms the prevalence of talwa autonomy. Rather than following McGillivray's lead or attempting multilateral talks like the Cussita King, the White Lieutenant announced that, as a talwa leader, he was "as good as any" and wanted U.S. alliance. He stressed, however, that while he spoke for "the greatist part of the head men," Seagrove should not mistake him as a representative "for all the nations."[70]

Talwas by Choice, Nation by Necessity

Alexander McGillivray passed away in February 1793 after years of chronic ailments, and his death ushered in a new period of instability in Creek politics. Creeks had struggled for decades to create a dynamic, if tense, balance between governance based on talwa autonomy and the need for a highly skilled executive who could represent Creeks as a nation when necessary. McGillivray's role in Creek politics was not always positive, but he frequently had proven useful, as had Emistisiguo in the 1770s and Brims and Malatchi earlier in the century.[71] The struggle continued as ambitious leaders put themselves forward either through diplomacy or border raiding. Each one hoped to stem the tide of Georgia's encroachment. Spanish, British, and U.S. agents each hoped to facilitate the rise of a new executive figurehead who would favor their interests.[72] William Panton urged the Spanish to summon all Creek leaders to Pensacola at once to establish new executives and provide them with Spanish titles and pensions. Panton suggested John Kinnard, the Little Prince of Broken Arrow, or Alexander Cornel of Tuckabatchee. All three men were influential, but they lacked the crucial skill of literacy.[73] Panton expected that most towns in the Alabama, Abika, and Okfuskee provinces would choose their own representatives.[74] The White Lieutenant of Okfuskee, upon whom McGillivray reportedly relied to sway Abika and Okfuskee towns, also lacked McGillivray's bicultural skills.[75] Louis le Clerc Milfort, an Indian countryman and the late McGillivray's brother-in-law, put himself forward as a leader of three Alabama towns and their 1,200 warriors. Milfort also warned about the rise of John Galphin. Once a courier and translator trusted by Georgians, Galphin had begun raiding Spanish subjects as well as Americans along the St. Marys River, stealing cattle, horses, slaves, and killing.[76]

While Creek politics underwent a period of uncertainty, Georgians strengthened their grip on the Oconee valley by grazing ever-larger cattle herds between the Oconee and the Apalachee.[77] Creeks remained especially sensitive about the area, and in February 1793, some reportedly threatened to drive away all the livestock and "kill those that oppose them."[78] Timothy Barnard, the Indian countryman and frequent go-between, stated clearly what residents of the region surely knew. Although the terms of the Treaty of New York set the border at the Apalachee River, the area was very much "in dispute."[79] Barnard warned that Creeks "seem much agitated" about the "gangs of cattle being drove into the fork."[80] He chastised settlers, writing that "they have no right" to graze cattle there, and he was disappointed that Georgia's leaders failed to "oppose such measures."[81] Barnard fully expected cattle rustling to end in bloodshed and believed that settlers "must abide by the consequence."[82]

Georgians' provocations could not have come at a worse time.[83] Adding to the political uncertainty caused by McGillivray's death, a small delegation of militant Shawnees arrived in Creek country in February 1793. Shawnees and a broad coalition of Ohio valley Indians had achieved astonishing victories against American armies in 1790 and 1791. U.S. agent James Seagrove worried they would inspire Creeks to resume a hard-line stance against Georgia's expansion.[84] The Cussita King and Efau Hadjo of Tuckabatchee avowed that their towns were not "deluded by the Shawanese talks," nor were their people involved in livestock rustling.[85] Instead, they begged Georgians to leave Tuckabatchee and Cussita hunters to their business as they harvested deer on the Oconee lands.[86]

Other Lower Creeks, however, despised Georgians' encroachment, and the Shawnee message appealed to them. John Galphin had become especially "rascally."[87] He led the most vigorous attacks against Georgians in years. On March 11, 1793, a party of thirty Cheahas and other Lower Creeks attacked the store of Robert Seagrove, brother of James Seagrove, at Traders Hill on the St. Marys River, the border between Georgia and East Florida. During the attack, they killed two white men "in a most brutal and Savage manner."[88] They also robbed the store of goods valued at two thousand pounds sterling. As they left, they torched the buildings at Traders Hill and a nearby timber-cutting operation.[89]

Two days after the attack at Traders Hill, John Galphin's band raided a wagon train bound for East Florida.[90] The Green family suffered the brunt of the attack. The extended family was driving seventy-five head of cattle and five horses ahead of a wagon loaded with household furniture. Shortly after they crossed the Satilla River at Burnt Fort ferry about twenty miles north of Traders Hill, Galphin's men ambushed them. They killed and scalped the family patriarch, James Green, as well as two other men and James's daughter, Polly.[91] James's wife, Elizabeth, escaped along with her remaining children and two other women.[92] Galphin and his men then emptied the wagon and drove off the cattle.[93] The raiders attacked a second party in the wagon train, took seven black slaves, and later sold them to Spanish buyers in Pensacola. After securing captives, they methodically emptied the wagons, slashed the settlers' feather beds, and stole the ticking.[94]

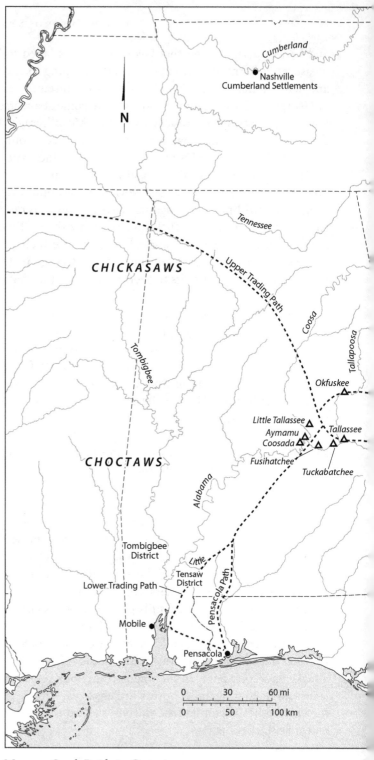

MAP 10. Creek Raids in Georgia, 1793–1795

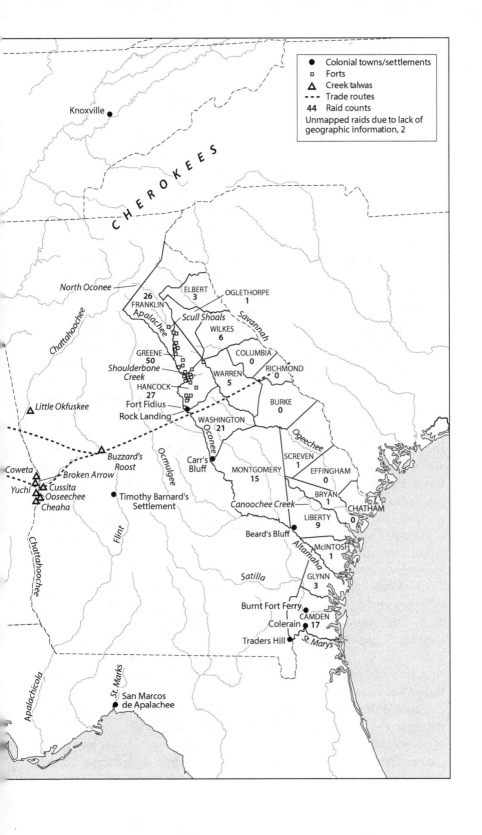

Legend

- ● Colonial towns/settlements
- ▫ Forts
- △ Creek talwas
- - - - Trade routes
- **44** Raid counts

Unmapped raids due to lack of geographic information, 2

Knoxville ●

C H E R O K E E S

North Oconee

Chattahoochee

FRANKLIN
26

Apalachee

Scull Shoals

ELBERT
3

OGLETHORPE
1

WILKES
6

Savannah

GREENE
50

Shoulderbone Creek

COLUMBIA
0

HANCOCK
27

WARREN
5

RICHMOND
0

Fort Fidius

Rock Landing

BURKE
0

WASHINGTON
21

Oconee

Ocmulgee

△ Little Okfuskee

Buzzard's Roost

Carr's Bluff

MONTGOMERY
15

Ogeechee

SCREVEN
1

EFFINGHAM
0

Coweta △
Broken Arrow
Yuchi △ △ Cussita
△ Ooseechee
Cheaha

● Timothy Barnard's Settlement

BRYAN
1

CHATHAM
0

Canoochee Creek

LIBERTY
9

Flint

Beard's Bluff

Altamaha

McINTOSH
1

Chattahoochee

Satilla

GLYNN
3

Burnt Fort Ferry ●

Colerain ●

CAMDEN
17

Traders Hill ●

St. Marys

Apalachicola

St. Marks

St. Marks

San Marcos de Apalachee ●

In April, Timothy Barnard concluded that three-quarters of Creeks renounced the attacks and would leave Galphin's men to Georgians.[95] James Seagrove was shocked by the attack on his brother's store and the killing of settlers. "I cannot believe that the Creek Nation are Acquainted with it," he wrote. "The Source of the Evil is from another quarter."[96] Cussitas and Alexander Cornel of Tuckabatchee spearheaded an effort to give satisfaction by capturing and executing the raiders.[97] In light of some towns disavowing the attacks, one may be tempted to dismiss them as the anomalous actions of a few renegades with no political significance. Galphin's band struck lucrative targets more than two hundred miles south of the Apalachee-Oconee confluence, the most contested space along the border. However, a similar attack near the Apalachee and wide participation among Lower Towns suggest Galphin's raids were part of a pattern of resistance.

Creeks attacked the upper Oconee valley within weeks of Galphin's raids on Traders Hill and Burnt Fort ferry. Near the end of April, thirty raiders attacked and robbed the Thrasher family near Scull Shoals, a few miles upriver from the Oconee-Apalachee confluence near present-day Athens. They killed Richard Thrasher, two of his children, and one enslaved woman. Searchers initially believed that Thrasher's wife and infant child had escaped, but they soon found the infant drowned in the Oconee. Mrs. Thrasher was badly wounded—scalped, shot twice, stabbed, and tomahawked.[98] Compared with this violence, the theft seems insignificant. Creeks stole blankets, clothes, and a hat.[99] Timothy Barnard's brooding response drew attention to the attack's political implications. The Thrasher family had settled between the Oconee's north fork and the Apalachee River. "After all the warning I sent down," wrote Barnard, "they could have expected no better as they well know the Indians still desputed giving up their rights to that land."[100]

Creeks also resumed raiding the Cumberland and Tennessee River valleys with Cherokees and Shawnees in 1792 and 1793. Creeks even aided Cherokees in ambitious raids against Nashville and Knoxville, the biggest settlements in the region. General John Sevier retaliated by burning the Cherokee town of Etowah and killing one hundred people. A second party of Cumberland settlers invaded Creek country, killing three Okfuskees and likely others.[101]

None of these attacks—Traders Hill, Burnt Fort ferry, the Thrasher family, or the Cumberland raids—were merely the opportunistic raiding of a few mad young men. As had been the case for decades, some young men exercised their autonomy by lashing out against white encroachment without the approval of miccos or nationalist leaders.[102] Upper Creeks from Tallassee and Fusihatchee and Lower Creeks from Coweta, its daughter town Broken Arrow, Cheaha, and Ooseechee participated in the various attacks.[103] Many of the participating towns, especially Coweta, had a history of active resistance to Oconee valley encroachment dating back at least to the 1760s, when Escotchaby threatened to burn squatters' houses.[104] The raids alarmed the U.S. War Department, and Secretary Knox ordered James Seagrove to redouble his efforts to convince headmen that "the existence of the Creeks as a nation must depend upon their being at peace with us."[105] For many Creeks, however, a unified national policy on anything more than a temporary basis was not desirable. When Seagrove demanded an explanation for the attacks, Creeks confirmed the political motives. The attackers had been inspired by militant Shawnees' talks, rallied by John Galphin's anti–United States talks, and supported by William Panton's offer of weapons.[106]

The violence of the spring of 1793 tends to overshadow a larger trend. Raids reached a peak for the decade at 112. While 103 included theft, just 10 of them ended in bloodshed. Theft raids hit both the upper Oconee valley and the southern counties between the Altamaha and the St. Marys Rivers. Creeks captured dozens of horses, hundreds of cattle and hogs, dozens of black slaves, and myriad home furnishings.[107] They robbed James Cashen's store at Burnt Fort ferry on the Satilla River of goods and livestock valued at more than three thousand dollars, then they destroyed the buildings.[108] Cowetas raided the upper Oconee valley and retreated through Buzzard's Roost, a Cussita daughter town. They intended to provoke Georgians into attacking the village, dragging Cussitas into the conflict.[109] A large party of Tallassees raided at will for most of April in the upper Oconee valley.[110] Timothy Barnard judged that there were too many warriors involved to end the conflict without a significant American military strike.[111]

Georgians responded to this spike in raiding by expanding the military buildup they already had begun. They built more forts, requested more federal military aid, and sent large militia patrols into Creek country. The state commissioned the construction of nearly a dozen new blockhouses. Garrisons returned to forts that had been abandoned since the Treaty of New York.[112] Settlers deluged state, local, and national leaders with requests for weapons and the construction of still more frontier forts.[113] In his capacity as U.S. Indian agent, James Seagrove asked for two companies of federal horsemen to be stationed on the St. Marys River and at Burnt Fort ferry.[114] Governor Edward Telfair petitioned for federal arms and ammunition. The secretary of war sent the weapons and authorized Telfair to call up one hundred horsemen and one hundred infantrymen at U.S. expense. Secretary Knox, however, clarified that President Washington's administration intended them for "defensive purposes only."[115] Georgia senator James Jackson scorned the "trifling assistance" offered his state and insisted the federal government do more.[116] By June, Georgia's militia had mustered nine hundred men, convened a war council, and penetrated deep into Creek country to the Ocmulgee River.[117]

Faced with this intensifying American threat, a cadre of Creek leaders made a resolute move toward coalescence when they sent out the broken days calling for a "full meeting" at Tuckabatchee on May 10, 1793. The Tuckabatchee council drew delegates from thirty-two talwas—twenty-four Upper Towns and eight Lower Towns—greater representation than any other recorded joint council of the period.[118] During the meeting, Peter Olivier, the French-born Spanish commissary in Creek country, intended to deliver a talk from Governor Carondelet encouraging more raids. The headmen, however, renounced the recent violence, rendering Olivier "Afrade to give the talk out."[119] The Big Warrior of Cussita explained that raiders had succumbed to unrealistic dreams of regaining the Oconee strip. William Panton and the Spanish, he noted, had promised weapons and encouraged Creeks to force white settlers to move "off the Oconee land."[120] The Big Warrior of Cussita felt that Panton's ulterior motive was merely to prevent Georgia traders from undercutting his business. The "mutinous" towns took Panton's advice because he "is a master of so much goods" and bought their stolen horses.[121]

The looming threat of American military buildup made Creek consensus on borders more important than ever, leading to a shocking attempt at nationalist coercion. At the Tuckabatchee council, leaders from aggressive towns agreed to cease raiding, but they soon reversed that position. The remaining towns of the joint council then adopted a risky, two-pronged solution.[122] They would execute John Galphin's men and invite Georgia to attack the towns that supported raiding. They identified the aggressive towns as Coweta, Broken Arrow, Cheaha, and Ooseechee. The Big Warrior of Cussita delivered instructions to James Seagrove on behalf of the joint council. He declared that they had failed to persuade aggressive towns to make amends, so he authorized Georgia's militia to "burn, kill, and destroy all they can find in them four towns."[123] Timothy Barnard urged the Cussita King to attack the wayward Lower Towns himself, essentially promoting civil war, but the micco refused.[124] The Big Warrior explained this reticence in terms of talwa autonomy and the customary tension between older leaders and young warriors. "The red people have not laws to restrain their people," the Big Warrior said, "neither is it in their power to command each other to take up arms to suppress such conduct."[125]

Attempts to execute John Galphin also revealed the enduring importance of talwa autonomy, and they echoed the 1774 joint council's difficulties in executing Ochtullkee for the White-Sherrill killings. Alexander Cornel of Tuckabatchee blamed all the recent raiding solely on John Galphin and urged the Lower Towns to bring him to heel by force. He claimed that the Upper Towns would never tolerate such "mad people."[126] The council agreed and sent Cussita warriors to assassinate five of Galphin's followers. Even Cornel recognized, however, that this depended on guile rather than national authority. The planned assassinations "must be Kept a great Secret for they aren't like White people that can do a thing directly."[127] Indeed, the aggressive towns learned of the plan and protected Galphin's men.[128]

Inviting Georgians to attack the aggressive towns was a hazardous, ill-advised strategy that undermined Creek sovereignty rather than promoting the multitown council's national authority. The fact that Creeks proposed it speaks to desperation among some leaders to consolidate power to govern young men. If the Big Warrior of Cussita and his peers could direct a surgical strike executed by the Georgia militia, it might intimidate independent talwas into submitting to a national council government. The Big Warrior gave militia leaders detailed directions to the "mutinous towns" to ensure that Georgians attacked only them.[129] Timothy Barnard warned repeatedly that militia commanders must strictly control their troops; otherwise the "up-country people" would kill indiscriminately and alienate all Creeks.[130] Rumors held that veteran Indian fighter Elijah Clarke raised 2,500 men to invade Creek country, and Barnard begged James Seagrove to restrain him especially, or "he will kill all, without distinction."[131]

Georgia's "Mad Men"

Like Creeks, many Georgians disliked the Treaty of New York, and they, too, resisted it with politics and violence.[132] Mere months after its ratification in August 1790, the state legislature issued a formal protest against the treaty, citing its restoration of some Creek lands ceded in the 1780s and its failure to provide adequately for the return of confiscated property.[133] In the following years, Georgians—sometimes in official militia actions and sometimes merely as gangs—committed numerous acts of theft and violence against Creeks. By 1793, settlers habitually grazed cattle west of the Oconee-Apalachee confluence in undisputed Creek country and busily expanded plantations in the southern counties between the Altamaha and the St. Marys. Some accepted a Spanish invitation to settle East Florida, further expanding slave-based agriculture. They nursed their bitterness against what they considered Creeks' unprovoked thefts, savage attacks, and the failure of U.S. troops to protect them. One settler complained that he needed an "independent Company" of cavalry to wage war against Creeks because, when they stole property, they were "protected by the laws" under the Treaty of New York.[134] Essentially, the man recommended that Georgians break their constitutional bonds with the federal government and exercise independent military powers. That is exactly what they did.[135] From 1793 to 1795, Georgians exercised their own brand of local autonomy, committing a series of brutal assaults on Creek people without the permission of federal or state governments. Georgians may have seen these attacks as legitimate retaliation and possibly even as self-defense, yet the victims were rarely guilty of anything beyond being Indians. In this sense, Georgia's ungovernable mad men refused to be bound by the rule of law.[136]

The murder of David Cornel illustrated Georgians' contempt for both Creek people and the federal government. Cornel was a prominent, politically connected young Tuckabatchee warrior who had raided Cumberland and scalped Americans in 1793.[137] He was the son of a Creek woman and Joseph Cornel, a longtime Indian countryman, trader, and translator for Alexander McGillivray. During the spring of 1793, the Big Warrior of Cussita and the unprecedented joint council he represented were struggling to repair relations with Georgia. They selected David Cornel to deliver their talks to Colerain, U.S. agent James Seagrove's headquarters on the St. Marys River. Cornel presented Creeks as a nation that governed its people by force. "The upper Creeks," he informed Timothy Barnard, "are determined to make the whole nation take one peace talk & give up all the plundered property."[138] Since Cussita assassins had failed to execute John Galphin's raiders, Upper Towns threatened to send their own warriors to do the deed.[139]

In mid-May, the joint Creek council sent David Cornel and three Cussitas to Colerain escorted by a white express courier named McDonald. They were to notify James Seagrove of the plan to assassinate Galphin's men and return stolen property. Cornel was also to invite Seagrove and General James Jackson of Georgia to Creek country to verify that the perpetrators had been executed and to convince them that, since McGillivray's death, Creeks had rejected Spanish alliance. Just weeks after the council meetings, however, the aggressive towns of Coweta, Broken Arrow, Ooseechee, and Cheaha, balked.[140] They ridiculed Cussitas for slavish compliance with American commands.[141]

Before departing for Colerain, David Cornel sent white wampum and a white wing as customary tokens of peace and friendship "to keep the path White" between Creeks and Americans.[142] Cornel spoke some English but was illiterate, so on his way, he visited Timothy Barnard and asked the trader to write letters explaining his intentions. He feared there would be no reliable interpreter at Seagrove's headquarters.[143] Barnard advised the U.S. agent by letter that "If Cornell is well used and comes back full handed, it will be of great service to the United States."[144] He counseled Seagrove to send trustworthy guards to protect Cornel because "if any accident should happen to him we are done in this quarter."[145]

A Georgia militia officer later reported that, as Cornel's party neared Colerain, their white escort absconded "in a very Curious and Clandestine manner."[146] The following day, Cornel and his companions sighted a dozen armed white men. Unarmed himself, Cornel rode up to the troop with his teenage porter and signaled peaceful intentions by presenting a white wing. He then announced the purpose of his visit in English. One of the white men called out, dismounted his horse, and carefully braced his weapon against a tree for steadier aim. Cornel raced toward the gunman crying, "NO NO NO," but the man "poured a load of Buck Shot" into him.[147] As the wounded Cornel wheeled his mount and galloped for the safety of a nearby thicket, a second gun blast tore him from his saddle. He rose to his knees declaring again that he was a friend of Georgia and bore letters for Seagrove. Cornel begged for his life as white men surrounded him. They shot him again, "Cut him in pieces," and "mock[ed] him in his dying Groanes."[148]

In the weeks following this brutality, it became clear that the murder was premeditated. Cornel's white escort had abandoned the party in order to alert the killers. Not only was the United States unable to control Georgians' exercise of violence, state militia commanders could not restrain individual units. Cornel and his porter were killed and scalped, but his two other companions narrowly escaped as militiamen chased them, slashing at them with swords as they ran. The Cussitas made for Timothy Barnard's settlement on the Flint River over the course of six days without stopping for food or rest. There they recounted what they had witnessed.[149] The militiamen at Colerain justified their actions by portraying David Cornel as a ferocious villain who had raided white set-tlements in Georgia and Cumberland, killing and scalping white people. Barnard, after hearing the reports of the Cussita survivors, excoriated the militiamen as "inhumane cowardly and savage like."[150] With such compelling evidence, it seemed unlikely the militiamen would escape punishment. One of the soldiers later testified that their leader, Captain John F. Randolph, had explicitly ordered them to kill all the Indians they found.[151] Even other county militia officers considered Captain Randolph's unit to be "a bandity" who were "mutineers disobeying the laws of this state."[152] Despite all this, a Court of Inquiry found "the Indians were to blame for sending so desperate & obnoxious a Character" as David Cornel, and the militiamen were "justly to be applauded" for their actions.[153]

The murder of David Cornel could not have been better calculated to shatter Creek goodwill.[154] Timothy Barnard and James Seagrove believed they could salvage the diplomatic relationship if they acted quickly. Seagrove scheduled a congress with Creek leaders for September 10. He planned to send lavish gifts to the White Lieutenant of Okfuskee and Efau Hadjo of Tuckabatchee, and he hoped to isolate the aggressive towns of Coweta, Broken Arrow, Ooseechee, and Cheaha by withhold-ing presents from these "ungrateful" Indians.[155]

By contrast, many Georgians hoped for a final, decisive war. Militia commanders advocated a full-scale invasion, but President Washington forbade it.[156] Instead, Georgians conducted a campaign of harassment and terror. As James Seagrove prepared for his congress with Creeks, outraged Georgians intimidated him so much that he required a federal escort.[157] Militias patrolled the Oconee River's west bank searching for Creeks.[158] White settlers in the lower Oconee valley stole horses from their neighbors, secretly led them across the river into Creek country, and accused Creeks of the theft. Then they formed a company of two hundred men to invade and, purportedly, reclaim the animals.[159] One of the men responsible for this scheme, a Captain Stokes, accused four Creeks of the sham horse theft and then chased them to the Ocmulgee River where he robbed and murdered them.[160] Militiamen in the upper Oconee valley fired on Creeks between the Apalachee and Oconee Rivers without provocation.[161]

These several examples of harassment and murder, however strik-ing, paled in comparison with the razing of Little Okfuskee in Septem-ber 1793. A band of Georgia settlers ostensibly pursuing Coweta horse rustlers attacked the town on the Chattahoochee River deep in Creek country. Georgia raiders burned the town, killed and scalped six men, and took eight women and girls captive.[162] The White Lieutenant of Okfuskee was enraged and demanded the immediate return of the captives, one of whom was a relative. By March 1794, the captives still had not been returned, so President Washington ordered Governor George Mathews to see it done.[163] Timothy Barnard expected Okfuskees to commit satisfaction killings and warned whites to stay well back from the Oconee River.[164] He urged Okfuskees to execute the Coweta rustlers instead.[165]

The murder of David Cornel, the razing of Little Okfuskee, and the broader campaign of harassment and terror combined with other factors to bring Creeks closer to compromising talwa autonomy for national leadership in this moment of crisis. Georgians' violence frightened Creek leaders. As winter neared, Creek hunters needed to focus on the upcoming hunting season rather than avoiding indiscriminate frontiersmen scouring Creek country. They moved to accept the lost Creek lives as satisfaction for Americans killed at Traders Hill, Burnt Fort ferry, the Oconee-Apalachee fork, and Cumberland. Still, it remained unclear how, or if, they could constrain the actions of young warriors.[166]

8 /   "Like Pulling Out Their Hearts and Throwing Them Away": State Control, 1793–1796

Georgia unleashed a widespread campaign of violent harassment in the early 1790s that was only partially a response to Creek raiding. The murder of David Cornel, the razing of Little Okfuskee, and many other actions represented the latest phase of a decades-long drive to take the Oconee valley. U.S. government support for Georgia's military buildup on the Oconee's east bank encouraged greater violence in 1793, but Georgians misread federal action. Following a few violent Creek raids in the spring of 1793, the United States promised Georgia more funding, more troops, and a new Indian factory, or trading post. Emboldened by this apparent approval, Georgia's militias and citizens attacked Creeks repeatedly. Federal authorities, angered by Georgians' reckless lawlessness, redoubled their efforts to control Indian affairs by regulating the Oconee border, protecting Creek leaders, and restraining Georgians.

Beginning in 1793, conflicts first with France and later with Great Britain overwhelmed Spain, depriving Creeks and other southeastern Indians of their Spanish allies. In 1795, Spain and the United States signed the Treaty of San Lorenzo in which Spain ceded the rights of free navigation on the Mississippi River and its claims to lands north of the thirty-first parallel, present-day Florida's northern border. Spain also agreed to end its military alliances with southeastern Indians. The treaty thus blasted a decade of Native-Spanish diplomacy and placed virtually all of Creek, Choctaw, and Chickasaw country, including the Creeks' Tensaw district, within U.S.-claimed territory. Creeks had used

Spanish support to resist Georgia expansion for more than a decade, but the Treaty of San Lorenzo left Creeks to face Georgia alone.[1]

Creek leaders in the mid-1790s built on the previous decades' coalescence when multitown councils had attempted to force truculent talwas to provide satisfaction to Georgians following deadly attacks. They labored to create a national consensus to end all border raids and accept the Oconee River as a permanent boundary. The keys to this consensus were incorporating young men into the political process and reconciling talwa autonomy with national authority.[2] The drive toward national control of violence culminated in the 1796 Treaty of Colerain. Creek leaders successfully created consensus by embracing talwa autonomy rather than relying on a charismatic, skilled executive. Creeks incorporated young men into the political process directly. This gave them an alternative path to leadership and prestige outside of battlefield valor and largely persuaded them to forego the spiritual duty of crying blood killings. Once a robust cadre of talwa leaders and young men arrived at consensus, they presented themselves as a unified Creek Nation with a single foreign policy. Paradoxically, Creeks fully recognized the value of presenting themselves as a nation, yet they were able to do so only by embracing the long-standing system of autonomous talwas. In the Treaty of Colerain, Creeks won peace and nation-to-nation relations with the United States by capitulating once and for all to the Oconee boundary. They accepted U.S. commissioners' claims that federal troops would police white border jumpers. Creeks yielded to the federal government's demands as the price of an alliance they hoped would thwart Georgians, their most vexing enemies for decades. After 1796, however, Creek border security would depend on U.S. soldiers rather than Creek warriors.[3]

"Unruly Whites" Break Constitutional Bonds

Georgians intensified their campaign of violent harassment throughout 1794 and 1795, notwithstanding Creek efforts to restrain border raids and execute John Galphin. Despite the vicious murder of their emissary David Cornel, Creeks still desired to end the long-running border dispute. Georgians, however, launched a series of vigorous attacks inside Creek country and ceaselessly trespassed on Creek lands in defiance of both federal and state authority.[4] This lawlessness put unruly Georgians on a collision course with their elected leaders. Ultimately, the federal government responded with a forceful assertion of dominance in Indian Affairs with the 1796 Treaty of Colerain.

Georgia militiamen murdered two Cussitas in December 1793, propelling frontier communities into a confrontation with federal and state officials. While patrolling deep in Creek country, Captain Jon Adams and three militiamen, all from Greene County on the Oconee River, encountered a Cussita hunting camp near the Ocmulgee. Cussitas welcomed the white men and offered them food and drink. Adams and his men enjoyed the hospitality and departed, but they soon returned, crept into the camp, and murdered two of the Cussita hunters. Creeks demanded justice from federal troops at Fort Fidius below the Oconee-Apalachee confluence near present-day Milledgeville. War Department agent Constant Freeman promised the White Bird Tail King of Cussita, also known as Fusihatchee Micco, that he would pressure Georgia's governor to arrest the killers. In turn, Fusihatchee Micco pledged to prevent young Creek warriors from taking satisfaction through crying blood killings. Freeman, though, had few illusions about Governor George Mathews's ability to control militia violence. He warned Mathews that Major David Adams, a relation of the accused, planned to attack Fusihatchee Micco as the headman traveled to Augusta for diplomatic talks. Governor Mathews met with Fusihatchee Micco and agreed to get satisfaction for the victims, but it is unclear how far he was willing or able to go.[5]

Over time, Georgians' harassment of Creeks became more systematic and more defiant of elected authorities. This lawlessness culminated in 1794, when some Georgians severed their constitutional bonds with the United States, invaded Creek country, and founded an independent nation that historians have called the Trans-Oconee Republic. This episode appears infrequently in historiography, yet it stands as an astonishing example of the tension between local and national interests in the early republic, similar to the better-known Whiskey Rebellion.[6] As early as February 1794, Elijah Clarke led a small but significant number of Georgians to colonize the Oconee River's west bank in undisputed Creek country. They intended to create permanent settlements, and by fall, they had built forts, declared themselves an independent nation, and adopted a constitution.[7] A year earlier, French ambassador Edmond Genêt had recruited Clarke to invade Spanish East Florida. Clarke perhaps intended the Trans-Oconee Republic as a step toward executing the scheme, though France had recalled Genêt.[8] Creek warriors were eager to attack Clarke's people and drive them from Creek country. This was their right under the Treaty of New York, but older Creek leaders appealed to state and federal authorities to remove the brazenly illegal settlements. Georgia's leaders hesitated to prosecute the white lawbreakers even as some frontiersmen denounced this breakdown of civil authority.[9] The "greatest number" of the Trans-Oconee Republic adventurers, wrote one Greene County man, "are men under bad caractors."[10] A group of Greene County settlers described Clarke's scheme as a "Riotous and unlawful assembly of armed men" that had formed "to the Terror of the good Citizens of this County."[11] They were right to be afraid. In March, an armed company of Trans-Oconee men invaded the home of one white settler and threatened the residents with whipping or death if they refused to join the venture.

Creeks resumed border raids after Captain Adams's murder of Cussitas and Elijah Clarke's blatant violations of their territory and sovereignty. Those raids precipitated a confrontation between the militia and the U.S. Army that instilled little confidence in federal authorities' ability to control Georgians. A band of thirty Cussitas stole horses from disputed territory on the Apalachee River in May 1794, and a series of attacks and counterattacks followed. A Georgia militia officer named Lieutenant Hay and eighteen men pursued the Cussita rustlers fifteen miles across the Apalachee River into Creek country. The rustlers left the contraband horses in a clearing to attract Hay's party. When the militiamen came near, Cussitas ambushed them, killing Lieutenant Hay and a second man and wounding a third. Creeks then scalped, stripped, and mutilated the bodies of the deceased, reportedly severing their genitals. On a tree near the corpses, they allegedly fixed a letter authored by U.S. Indian agent Timothy Barnard permitting them to hunt in the Oconee-Apalachee forks. Cussita warriors understood the ambush as a defense of their territorial rights protected by the Treaty of New York, and federal authorities suggested that Georgians may have exaggerated the attack's ferocity.[12]

Following Creeks' ambush of Lieutenant Hay, Georgia militiamen intensified their violence, and federal officials did little to restrain them. Major David Adams pursued Hay's killers. His earlier threats against Fusihatchee Micco of Cussita indicated that Creeks could expect no quarter.[13] Elijah Clarke soon killed two Creeks purportedly involved in Hay's death.[14] Another party of ten militiamen patrolling Little River, a western tributary of the Oconee well inside Creek country, shot and wounded the Dog King of Cussita while he and his brother were hunting. Major Richard Brooke Roberts, a frustrated federal officer, complained that he lacked the manpower "to keep the people from molesting the Indians."[15]

David Adams proved himself as devoted to local interests as Elijah Clarke when he threatened to storm a federal fort and kill U.S. soldiers for allegedly harboring Creeks. The reasons for his attack point up the intensely local nature of the conflict, the gravity of the breach between Georgians and the United States, and the base opportunism of some Georgians. After Lieutenant Hay's death, Adams gathered 150 militiamen and attacked a large group of Creeks under U.S. protection beneath the very walls of a federal installation, Fort Fidius. Creeks were there visiting U.S. Indian agent James Seagrove and awaiting the return of leaders then engaged in peace talks with Governor Mathews at Augusta. Federal troops dared not venture out of Fort Fidius to protect Creeks as required by the Treaty of New York. During Adams's attack, however, more than a dozen Creeks sought refuge inside the fort. Adams demanded that federals send out the Creeks, and if they refused, he promised to take the Indians by force. Constant Freeman reacted by simply sending the Creeks away in the hope that they could "make their escape, if possible."[16] Unsatisfied with this passive response, Adams threatened to murder the Creek leaders then returning from Augusta.

When U.S. officer Dr. Frederick Dalcho demanded an explanation for Major Adams's shocking behavior, the militiaman replied that he intended to kill and scalp all the Indians he could find in revenge for the ambush of Lieutenant Hay. In fact, only one Georgian and one Creek died in the Fort Fidius fight. Adams's militiamen, however, illustrated their economic opportunism when they stole Creeks' horses, rifles, and deerskins. Adams also boasted with evident approval that Elijah Clarke was then marching against Creek towns. Surprisingly, he later declined an invitation to join Clarke's Trans-Oconee Republic.[17]

The Fort Fidius fight exasperated both Creeks and federal officials. The episode irritated federals weary of having their efforts thwarted by renegade Georgians. Creeks' frustration deepened because U.S. troops failed to enforce the Treaty of New York. "The connexion" between the United States and Georgia, Constant Freeman wrote, was an idea "too complex for their comprehension."[18] Creeks could be forgiven for their confusion. Federal officials often had insisted that Creeks exert state control of violence, as the United States claimed to do. When put to the test, however, federal authorities seemed incapable of forcing Georgians to obey. Federals pressured Governor Mathews to control renegades lest they bring on war with Creeks. They demanded that David Adams be punished, but Governor Mathews insisted that Adams's attack was a legitimate response to Lieutenant Hay's ambush. Adams testified before a court of enquiry that the assault on Creeks was a regrettable lapse in discipline. He entered the camp to arrest one of the Creeks who had ambushed Hay. One of his own men disobeyed orders by opening fire, and chaotic plundering ensued. Adams claimed that he even offered to give his own horse and saddle to his renegade volunteers if they would desist.[19]

Shortly after the Fort Fidius fight, Elijah Clarke constructed several new posts in his Trans-Oconee Republic, including one strategically located at the Oconee-Apalachee confluence. While David Adams declined Clarke's invitation to join the Trans-Oconee Republic, it is likely that some of Adams's militiamen accepted. By midsummer, Clarke's aggressive border jumpers had appointed an agent of Indian affairs.[20] Governor Mathews assured Creeks that any forts west of the Oconee and Apalachee Rivers were unauthorized, and he pledged that federal forces would remove them.[21]

The United States lost patience with Georgia's backcountry defectors, resulting in a strong exercise of federal government power that endorsed Creek rights. President Washington insisted that the state government deal with the lawbreakers, and Secretary of War Henry Knox ordered federal troops to oversee the state militia. Knox declared that the Trans-Oconee Republic was "offending against the laws of the United States" and must be "repelled by military force."[22] When Governor Mathews finally deployed state troops to remove the Trans-Oconee forts, Elijah Clarke bluffed that he would fight to the death.[23] Clarke agreed, however, to appear before a Wilkes County grand jury, knowing the people of his home county would exonerate him.[24]

Clarke rejected the authority of both the United States and the State of Georgia. He ordered his subordinates to arrest anyone who attempted to detain Trans-Oconee settlers or confiscate their property.[25] As General Jared Irwin's Georgia militia approached the Oconee, however, Clarke's bravado vanished. The Trans-Oconee settlers accepted amnesty and abandoned their forts under General Irwin's scrutiny.[26] As Clarke abandoned his last station, Fort Defiance, Irwin unceremoniously burned it.[27] Irwin's behavior persuaded Creeks that he was "a friend to the red people," and this made them more amenable to working with him when he became governor in January 1796.[28] Federal agents and some of Georgia's leaders hoped that evicting the Trans-Oconee settlers by force would demonstrate their control over unruly citizens. They expected, in turn, that Creeks would exert similar state control over raiders.

In the early months of 1795 following the conclusion of the tense Trans-Oconee Republic episode, Efau Hadjo of Tuckabatchee and James

Seagrove asserted themselves as representatives of their nations. Both men quickly discovered the limits of state control. Efau Hadjo travelled to Augusta to meet with Governor Mathews, and, upon his return, he summoned leaders of the Lower Towns to arrange the return of all captives and recently taken property. This restoration, Efau Hadjo hoped, would console Georgians and put an end to Trans-Oconee encroachment. If establishing a firm, safe border meant coercing Creeks into returning captives and property, Efau Hadjo was willing to do so for the nation's good. He threatened to send Tuckabatchee and Cussita warriors to confiscate some contraband black slaves being held in Cheaha, home talwa of some of the Traders Hill raiders. Efau Hadjo also complained to Governor Mathews about Georgians' cattle grazing across the Oconee River on Creek land. He prodded federal agents to increase pressure on Mathews to restrain white settlers. Some Creek warriors ignored Efau Hadjo's threats of force and attempts at diplomacy, however. When one party killed some members of a white family, Efau Hadjo found himself unable to provide satisfaction. Timothy Barnard expected the survivors to take revenge on their own.[29]

James Seagrove worked to assert federal government supremacy in Indian affairs throughout 1795 while Georgians renewed their vociferous demands for Creek lands. They petitioned the state legislature to open the Oconee's west bank for immediate settlement.[30] When Seagrove called for a congress with Creeks on the Altamaha River so they could return more property and captives, he demanded that Governor Mathews provide an armed escort to protect Indians from "the smallest insult."[31] By the end of June, the agent had met with Creeks and distributed a boatload of presents. He wrote to Governor Mathews that, in doing so, he had established "a firm peace."[32]

Reports from the Oconee valley confirmed the peace, though escalating Creek conflict with Chickasaws allied to Cumberland threatened fragile Creek-U.S. relations. In July 1795, Georgia militia Captain Jonas Fauche reported that Creeks made frequent, friendly visits to Fort Philips near the confluence of the Oconee and Apalachee Rivers. However, he also reported a rumor that Creeks had planned a full council meeting at which they expected to raise warriors to wipe out white settlements on the Tennessee River.[33] That fall, Chickasaws killed five Creeks reportedly on their way to raid Cumberlanders, likely at Muscle Shoals on the Tennessee River. Chickasaws delivered the Creek scalps to Nashville, where they collected a bounty offered by Governor William Blount. Creeks retaliated by sending a large force against Chickasaw towns, but they found that James Robertson, Cumberland land speculator and U.S. Indian agent to the Chickasaws, had provided them with weapons and fifty militiamen. Together, Chickasaws and their Cumberland allies drove off the Creek warriors, reportedly killing twenty-six over the course of several engagements. Creeks protested, insisting that Americans had intervened unjustly in a war between Indians. Such protests rang hollow, however, considering earlier Creek raids on Cumberlanders trading with Chickasaws at Muscle Shoals.[34]

The number of Creek warriors and Georgia settlers who defied their national leaders declined in 1795. One final, stunning act of violence led to an unprecedented exertion of U.S. authority. It also led Creeks to accept an alliance with the United States based on the federal government's guarantee to protect Creeks from Georgians, though Creeks reserved the right to commit crying blood killings if U.S. justice failed them. Perhaps Georgians yielded to federal authority because the Carr's Bluff massacre appalled even other frontiersmen.

In September 1795, a group of five Creeks visited the boatyard of Captain Benjamin Harrison at Carr's Bluff on the lower Oconee River near present-day Dublin, Georgia. Harrison and his followers reported that the Creeks behaved like ruffians. They brandished guns and knives at two white men and a black slave, assaulted one of the men, and demanded gifts of a kettle and rum.[35] Unsubstantiated rumors held that a gang of Yuchis had been stealing corn and pumpkins and setting boats adrift nearby.[36] Yuchis spoke a language isolate, and, though other Creeks sometimes derided them as "stinkards," the Yuchi talwa had associated with Cussita at least since the 1720s.[37] Shortly after their visit to Harrison's boatyard, all five Creek men were found murdered, floating in the Oconee near Carr's Bluff. Their killers had decapitated them before casting the bodies into the river.[38] A few days later, five more men, all Yuchis, were found murdered near Harrison's station.[39]

Almost immediately, other white Georgians and Indians refuted the perpetrators' version of events in ways that revealed the limits of Creek coalescence. Testimony suggested that Benjamin Harrison and his men intentionally murdered the Indians to reignite border conflict and provide a pretext for more land taking. The first five victims—one Yuchi, two Cussitas, one Hitchiti, and one unidentified—were frequent visitors to Montgomery County. Many white people knew them and considered them "honest innocent fellows."[40] According to one survivor from the second group of victims, Benjamin Harrison lured them to his station with promises of rum. Hesitant to approach, the Yuchi man watched from a short distance as his friends entered Harrison's house and were gunned down. The observer escaped, but Harrison's men shot him in the leg as he fled.[41] Reports differed, but ultimately Harrison and his accomplices stood accused of killing as many as seventeen Creeks from at least six different clans and three separate talwas. At least five of the victims appeared utterly innocent of any offense, real or rumored.[42] The preponderance of Yuchi victims and the anemic response of avowedly national leaders challenged the very idea of a Creek Nation. As Timothy Barnard's nephew, John, explained, "Yuchis reside within the bounds of the lower Creeks are not deemed a part of the Nation—Speaking a different language."[43]

Aspiring Creek national leaders from Cussita and Tuckabatchee declared their intention to leave Benjamin Harrison to American justice. They supported Timothy Barnard's desperate effort as a deputy U.S. Indian agent to prevent the victims' clans and home talwas from committing crying blood satisfaction killings. This impossible task revealed the limits of coalescence.[44] Yuchis openly declared their intention to attack Harrison. Alexander Cornel of Tuckabatchee notified James Seagrove that a council of Upper Creeks had met and resolved to defer to U.S. law.[45] Cussitas representing themselves as the "Heads of the Nation" wanted to know whether any of the Creek victims had "brought trouble on themselves" before they took any action.[46] Ultimately, Cussitas declared they would attempt to persuade Yuchis to await American justice.[47]

Federal officials and some Georgians quickly condemned the Carr's Bluff massacre. One Georgia man touring the Oconee valley visited the neighborhood just days after the discovery of Benjamin Harrison's victims. He observed that the murdered Indians had been killed "without offense to the citizens of the United States," and that the violence "was a violation of the existing Treaty."[48] Secretary of War Timothy Pickering was outraged and flatly asserted federal supremacy. "Several Creek men some of them known to be great friends of the white people and all coming to that frontier with peaceable purposes," he wrote, "have been basely and cruelly murdered."[49] Pickering instructed the commander of two hundred federal troops bound for Colerain on the St. Marys River to prevent any further violence against Indians even if it meant using force against Georgians. He demanded that Governor Mathews use all the powers of his office to punish the guilty.[50] James Seagrove urged the governor to prosecute the killers quickly before Creeks took satisfaction themselves.[51] One Georgia citizen later testified against Benjamin Harrison, claiming that Harrison had sworn to attack any Creeks who participated in peace talks.[52]

James Seagrove used federal resources to indemnify the victims' families in the hope of preventing satisfaction killings. Seagrove lacked the power to arrest and punish the culprits, but he gave presents to compensate the victims' families for several horses and rifles plundered by Benjamin Harrison's followers.[53] Neither Seagrove's presents nor the persuasions of nationalist headmen satisfied Yuchis. As Lower Creeks turned out for winter hunts, some went to fetch the property that belonged to their murdered relatives. When they neared Carr's Bluff, they encountered a herd of Georgians' livestock foraging on the Oconee's west bank. This appears to have been the final indignity. Four miles upriver from Carr's Bluff, they murdered a white couple and two black slaves, reportedly beheading a woman and placing her head on a stake.[54] Some weeks later, Yuchis attacked another settler's home on the Altamaha River, killing one man and wounding four more.[55]

Following these killings, headmen from Yuchi, Ooseechee, Coweta, and Cussita gathered and tried again to persuade young warriors to join a national consensus against border raids, sometimes at great emotional cost. Despite impassioned pleas for unity, local interests and the sacred duty to maintain balance again proved more important to common Creeks. A Yuchi headman called Old Yuchi Will who had lost a son in the Carr's Bluff massacre shed tears but resolved to swallow his own grief. He devoted himself to Creek national interests by urging warriors bent on retribution to desist. He reportedly declared that crying blood killings "would not bring his lost son back."[56] Three months earlier, two nephews of Tussekee Micco, the Warrior King of Cussita, had gone missing on the Apalachee River and were feared dead. Despite this personal loss, Tussekee Micco also urged Creeks to be patient, and allow Georgians time to provide satisfaction. He insisted that if his own nephews were proven murdered, he too would forbid any crying blood killings.[57]

Timothy Barnard placed blame squarely on Georgians for the Carr's Bluff massacre and all the theft and violence that followed. He wrote that until the United States controlled "the unruly Whites," there could be no peace.[58] State control, he believed, would require a thousand federal troops in Georgia to protect Creeks, and, perhaps, to contain them. Events seemed to confirm his assessment. In February 1796, Creeks attacked and burned Fort Habersham north of the Oconee-Apalachee confluence and stole a large number of cattle.[59] In March, Georgians debated evacuating Fort Republick on the Apalachee, but one settler warned Governor Jared Irwin that Creeks would burn it within days if it were abandoned.[60] That same month, a party of seven Georgians pursued

Creek horse thieves to the Oconee River two miles above Carr's Bluff. A firefight ensued in which Creeks killed four white people.[61] Creeks scalped one of the victims, and another was stripped naked and had "his head and private parts skinned and his Intestines cut out."[62] Indeed, the Carr's Bluff massacre would reverberate in Creek-Georgia relations for years to come. When Creeks killed a white settler in March 1798, Brigadier General Jared Irwin believed they still were avenging those murdered by Benjamin Harrison three years earlier.[63] Harrison and several of his comrades were arrested and bound for trial in April 1796, but considering the acquittal of David Cornel's killers, Creeks had little reason to expect a satisfactory outcome.[64]

"Binding on Our Nation": The Treaty of Colerain

In the mid-1790s, Creeks endured renewed violence with Georgians, a conspicuous lack of Spanish support, and increased tension between talwa autonomy and Creek national interests.[65] Americans also experienced growing conflict between local and national agendas. President Washington used the power of the central government to impose order on this unstable situation. He directed James Seagrove and a cohort of U.S. commissioners to establish peace.[66] In April 1796, Seagrove dutifully invited Creeks to new treaty talks. Deprived of their Spanish allies after the 1795 Treaty of San Lorenzo and suffering intense, random violence, Creeks quickly agreed to meet at Colerain station on the St. Marys River without the usual series of delays.[67] Creeks had been holding larger, more frequent multitown councils since the 1770s, and the recent 1793 council had favored working with the U.S. government in the hope that the centralized state could contain Georgians' violence. Creeks were prepared and motivated to move quickly. By the end of June, they had signed the Treaty of Colerain.

The Treaty of Colerain was different from its predecessors because each party—the Creek Nation and the United States—exercised state control in unprecedented ways. A full complement of some four hundred Creek leaders represented at least twenty-four talwas. They conducted negotiations as a unified nation by achieving consensus and incorporating young men into the decision-making process rather than relying on executive figureheads such as Alexander McGillivray or small cohorts of town leaders such as Yahola Micco, Hitcheta Micco, Neha Micco, and Hoboithle Micco. The United States exercised unprecedented federal authority by policing Georgia's aggressive citizens. These differences facilitated real problem solving that dramatically reduced the politically motivated theft and violence that had characterized Creek-Georgia relations since the American Revolution.[68]

Several factors pushed Creeks toward tighter coalescence and brought them to the negotiating table. Their primary concerns remained political sovereignty and territorial integrity, just as they had been for decades. The Creek economy was also in dire straits. The deerskin trade had declined steadily since the Revolution. Georgians' constant pressure on Creek hunting lands and violence against Creek people reduced income from both the deerskin trade and theft. After Spain ceded its claims to most southeastern lands in the Treaty of San Lorenzo, Spanish officials ceased giving presents to Creek leaders, reducing income from that quarter. By 1796, many common Creeks were destitute and famine had struck several communities. Timothy Barnard expected that as many as two thousand Creeks might attend the Colerain talks because a "numerous set of them are very poor and of course nearly naked, therefore will flock to a treaty in expectation of gitting a blanket."[69]

As negotiations neared, Creeks pushed Governor Jared Irwin to contain Georgians east of the Oconee River because any disturbance could derail the talks. Barnard hoped that Benjamin Harrison's arrest would persuade grieving Creeks to suppress any further violence.[70] For their part, some Georgians continued to portray themselves as victims and defend belligerent militia officers like Elijah Clarke and David Adams. They condemned the federal government for its failure to provide robust military aid that "Georgia, as a common member of the union may claim."[71]

The Treaty of Colerain was an unlikely turning point in Creek-American relations. Border patrols did not entirely cease following Coleraine, but they declined steadily between 1796 and 1800. The breadth of talwa representation, Creek consensus that included young men, and the efforts of federal agents to restrain Georgians led to unique new treaty terms. First, the treaty did not require a new land cession. Second, it promised Creek hunters a reliable source of trade under federal control via new posts to be built closer to the talwas than the U.S. factory at Colerain.

At the outset of talks in June 1796, Creeks and federal commissioners scrupulously confirmed that delegates fully represented the Creek Nation. Attending were 22 "kings," 75 "principal chiefs," 152 warriors, and an additional 200 Creeks.[72] The 435 Creek attendees met in council and selected Fusihatchee Micco, the White Bird Tail King of Cussita, as

their "chief speaker."[73] He confidently claimed that the delegation represented all Creeks. Any agreement, he declared, "shall be binding on our
nation."[74] More than 120 leaders from at least twenty-four towns signed
the final treaty representing roughly half of all the talwas in Creek country and double the number represented at earlier treaties. Signers came
from every province and every language group. Indeed, signers came
from nine of the twelve Lower Towns profiled by U.S. Superintendent
of Indian Affairs Benjamin Hawkins during his tours of Creek country
in 1798 and 1799. Signers represented twelve of the twenty-five Upper
Towns Hawkins profiled.[75] Particularly large delegations represented the
Tallapoosa province Upper Towns of Atasi, Tallassee, and Tuckabatchee.
Five Abika towns and two Alabama towns also signed. Only one Okfuskee
man signed, a conspicuous absence for "the largest town in the nation."[76]
Large delegations represented the Muskogee-speaking Lower Towns of
Cussita and Coweta, and smaller groups consented for the Lower Towns
of Ooseechee, Cheaha, Yuchi, and Hitchiti. It is especially noteworthy
that the most aggressive towns of the 1790s accepted the treaty—Yuchi,
Tallassee, Coweta and its daughter town, Broken Arrow, and the Point
Towns of Ooseechee and Cheaha.[77] While this cadre of consenting talwas did not constitute unanimity, it displayed an astonishingly high level
of consensus that was rare in Creek country. Even so, Benjamin Hawkins
later complained that "a spirit of party or opposition" to "the will of the
nation" was common in each talwa as well as the broader nation.[78]

In a strong display of federal government supremacy, U.S. commissioners and troops limited the actions of Georgia's representatives during the Colerain talks. One historian described Colerain as a "theatre of
humiliation" for Georgians.[79] Commissioners adopted a series of camp
regulations, including one that prevented Georgians from communicating directly with Creeks without supervision. They refused to allow a
militia escorting Georgia's representatives to disembark from its ship on
the St. Marys River. Instead, federal troops exercised complete authority
over camp security, including the right to eject any citizen who misbe-
haved. Federal commissioners even forced Georgia's commissioners to
edit their inflammatory opening statement to the Creek delegation. Federal agents deemed the final version of the Georgians' talk to be merely
counterproductive rather than openly hostile.[80]

Creeks repeatedly expressed their preference for dealing with federal
commissioners over Georgians. After hearing the Georgia commissioners' talk demanding remuneration for property stolen or destroyed since
the 1780s, Creeks replied to federal commissioners rather than speaking

to Georgians. Creeks invited U.S. commissioners to a private council square in their encampment for a confidential conversation on property issues. Fusihatchee Micco spoke for the whole nation when he declared that he had come to talk with the "beloved men from our Great Father, General Washington." "Had we been invited to meet the Georgians only," he continued, "there would not have been one attending."[81] Fusihatchee Micco expected federal authority to constrain Georgia's bellicosity, and he castigated earlier failures to do so. Invoking the U.S. government's claims to centralized authority, he reminded commissioners that, when he was in New York in 1790, President Washington had promised to remove white trespassers and urged Creeks to ignore Georgia's demands for land.[82]

Still, federal commissioners provided their Georgia counterparts with an opportunity to present their demands for land cessions and the return of all property and captives. Georgians continued to define the confiscation of border jumpers' property as simple theft, and they demanded compensation. Creeks held that Georgians had no legitimate grievances because they had already returned all white captives. They also had returned all the horses they could, but the same distemper that reduced Creek herds had killed contraband animals. Creeks argued that they also had returned as many black slaves as possible, but some had been exchanged too often to be located. More importantly, they argued that there had never been the amount of theft represented in Georgians' "pretended claims."[83] Fusihatchee Micco also dismissed claims on the grounds that Georgians had not compensated Creeks adequately for thousands of acres of land already ceded. On those lands, white people harvested a fortune in timber, made tar and turpentine, raised fortunes in tobacco and cattle, and even used the rivers as assets by building mills. Creeks had been compensated at a fraction of the land's real value, and in light of that incongruity, it was miserly of Georgians to insist on recompense for a few horses and slaves. Moreover, citing the razing of Little Okfuskee, Fusihatchee Micco declared that Georgians had no right to compensation for the squatters' homes that border patrols had burned.[84]

Creeks adamantly refused to cede any more land and then issued their own claims of depredations committed by white hunters and livestock. White hunters and cattle routinely trespassed dozens of miles into Creek country. Trespassers harvested deer, and their cattle destroyed the habitat on which whitetails depended. Creeks also reported that their population was growing, so they could not possibly cede any more land.[85] Instead, they must plan for the future when "every fork of a creek where there is a little good land, will be of use to them."[86] Creeks were simply uninterested in Georgia's proposal to trade land for a shipload of goods. Alexander Cornel of Tuckabatchee put it bluntly: "As for talking any more about the land, it is needless to talk any more."[87]

Perhaps concerned that Georgians' insistence on additional land cessions would derail the talks, Benjamin Hawkins, then serving as U.S. treaty commissioner, reminded Creeks that Georgia had no authority to use force. The federal government guaranteed Creek land rights under the Treaty of New York. Hawkins confirmed that the treaties of the 1780s were nonbinding, since, under the Articles of Confederation, the power to make treaties with Indians was "vested in the confederation of Congress" rather than the states.[88] He informed delegates that Congress had passed a new Indian Trade and Intercourse Act earlier in 1796 authorizing the deployment of federal troops to keep peace in the Oconee valley, but only with Creek consent.[89] Hawkins also chastised the mad young men on both sides of the border. "The young and ambitious must be taught to respect the decisions of their wise and old chiefs," he admonished. "They must be taught to respect the law, to acquiesce to its decisions, and not attempt to be judges in their own case."[90] In sum, he demanded that both nations exercise monopoly control over violence, though he surely understood this as aspirational.

Assured of U.S. support, Creeks refused Georgia's demands and moved to the core issues: the precise location of the Oconee boundary and the theft and violence engendered by that disagreement. Creek consensus on the matter was clear: the boundary ran along the Oconee River's north fork. Fusihatchee Micco stated flatly, "We are not satisfied; we must, and do, insist on the line as we understand it."[91] Creek understanding of the boundary, however, rested on Alexander McGillivray's subterfuge. McGillivray conducted most of the negotiations at New York in 1790, and he told Creek delegates that President Washington had confirmed to them the lands between the Oconee's north fork and the Apalachee. McGillivray, however, promised the same land to the United States in the treaty's final text.[92]

Fusihatchee Micco insisted that Creeks had the right to defend the border as they defined it while Georgians interpreted border patrols as unprovoked warfare. Fusihatchee Micco explained border raids by citing both Creek sovereignty and U.S. government authority. He claimed that President Washington had encouraged Creek warriors to take the property of any white intruders in Creek country and deport the trespassers.[93]

This argument implicitly justified the deaths of several white militiamen killed while patrolling west of the Oconee without U.S. approval. Creeks worried that, if they accepted the Apalachee border, Georgia cattle would overrun Creek country because the branch was shallow enough for the animals to ford at will. No federal authorities would be able to restrain the livestock, and Creeks and Georgians would constantly bicker over errant animals lost or confiscated.[94] Creeks understood that they lacked the military capability to remove all Georgians, so they wanted U.S. commissioners to understand that, by insisting on the Apalachee border, they were taking Creek property without consent.

Federal negotiators insisted that the Treaty of New York set the boundary at the Apalachee, and Creeks gathered at Colerain slowly accepted that raw power would carry the day. U.S. commissioners blamed Alexander McGillivray's duplicity for any misunderstanding about the boundary's location. Alexander Cornel claimed that McGillivray had "called the nation together" and described the boundary as the Oconee's north fork.[95] James Seagrove bristled at this, arguing that he had explained the Apalachee border to Creeks himself. After more than a week of talks, Creeks continued to insist that the Oconee's north fork was the only acceptable boundary while Americans remained equally adamant that only the Apalachee would suffice.[96] An unnamed Coweta warrior infuriated by the lengthy, unproductive debate, burst out with "violent emotions."[97] He demanded that Creeks withdraw to deliberate privately and "determine the public good," that is, establish national consensus, before answering U.S. commissioners further.[98]

Ultimately, Creeks conceded the Apalachee border with much regret. Yahola Micco of Coweta openly wept.[99] After the entire delegation privately reached consensus, Alexander Cornel delivered their decision in English and Muskogee. "It was with the utmost reluctance they consented to give the land away," he lamented; "It was like pulling out their hearts, and throwing them away."[100] Though a bitter loss, delegates arrived at the difficult decision by reaching consensus through deliberation in a large council where many talwas were represented.

The terrible grief and anger that resulted from surrendering the Oconee-Apalachee fork made Creeks all the more determined to protect the Oconee's west bank. They demanded that Georgians remove all cattle, horses, and pigs then ranging in large numbers west of the river. Older leaders and young hunters displayed national unity in presenting this ultimatum. Removing the livestock, they argued, would be proof that the United States intended to abide by its promise to control Georgians.

Creeks complained again about white hunters constantly taking deer and fish everywhere between the Oconee and Ocmulgee Rivers.[101]

Old and young alike demanded an immediate end to "this trespass of our rights."[102] This assertion of Native rights represented a critical element of national unity. Leaders acknowledged that young men were most aggrieved by the presence of white hunters. For perhaps the first time in negotiations with Americans and Georgians, the interests of common young men were presented directly to treaty commissioners, without deferring exclusively to older leaders and economic elites.[103] Alexander Cornel presented a talk particularly from "our young men who are present." They acquiesced to the Apalachee boundary because they understood this "sacrifice" was necessary. They also proclaimed that the west bank was Creek property, that the new boundary must be "perpetual," and that "whites have no right to go there."[104] Any property found on the Creek side of the river would be confiscated without hesitation. The participation of common young men signified that the normal, generational tension in Creek society had yielded to consensus.[105] After the violence and theft committed by young Creeks in the previous twenty years, older leaders likely recognized that if peace with the United States were to prevail, they must take young men's concerns seriously.

With the border finally settled, Americans desired to negotiate two remaining issues. First, the parties must agree on the location of new federal factories. Second, they must settle all unresolved killings. Creeks suggested a site near Beard's Bluff on the Altamaha for a new federal post, roughly a dozen miles below the Ocmulgee-Oconee confluence. They also agreed to allow a post in the upper Oconee valley, with the site to be selected during the running of the border line.

Creeks expressed much greater interest in balancing unresolved killings. They wanted to see the executions of those responsible for the Carr's Hill massacre and the murder of David Cornel before they left Colerain. U.S. commissioners demurred, assuring Creeks that the accused would be tried according to federal and state law. All other white people accused of killing Creeks would receive amnesty. Americans forbade any future revenge attacks on Creeks, essentially granting the same amnesty to any Creeks who had killed Georgians.[106] U.S. commissioners insisted that Creeks should be content with this offer because Creeks had murdered twice as many Georgians. Creeks reluctantly accepted U.S. terms, yet they remained "not quite satisfied of the justice of the act."[107] Some Creeks believed that Georgia never would punish the guilty.[108] Nevertheless, they agreed to wait at least four months for justice. If they received none, Creeks planned to appeal to President Washington rather than conduct crying blood killings.

Imperfect Peace

Creek and U.S. leaders signed the Treaty of Colerain on June 29, 1796. The 435 Creeks who had participated in the talks prepared to return to their talwas and persuade others to abide by the terms. To overcome anticipated objections, Creek leaders requested that a federal agent accompany them. They intended to escort the agent "through the whole nation" and promised to treat him "as if he was the President himself."[109] Creeks left Colerain content with their relationship with the United States and hopeful that the young republic would control Georgians. The plan to establish federal factories inside Creek country independent of Georgia authorities satisfied both Creeks and federal treaty commissioners. Creeks grew anxious to see the posts built.[110] As Creeks left Colerain, U.S. commissioners learned that they had stashed a thousand pounds of smoked beef along an escape route in case Georgians attacked them. This palpable expression of fear suggests that Creeks had every reason to wish for federal government intervention. They left Colerain "with a degree of confidence" in the United States.[111]

The Treaty of Colerain brought peace that had eluded the Oconee valley for two decades, but the peace was neither perfect nor permanent. The region between the Altamaha and the St. Marys Rivers enjoyed tranquility and a bustling Indian trade at the U.S. factory at Colerain. Edward Price, the American factor, constantly worried about attacks like those that had struck William Panton's San Marcos de Apalache store in 1792 and Traders Hill in 1793. Creeks loitered near the Colerain factory demanding presents, indicating that, after the treaty, Creeks expected regular gift giving would remain part of Creek-U.S. relations. James Seagrove had been generous with presents, but Price saw his role as that of merchant, not diplomat. He provided only a few presents to be taken into the nation to Alexander Cornel and another man, both of whom were acting as deputy Indian agents.[112] Georgians occasionally took advantage of Indian visitors by stealing their horses, leaving U.S. agents to provide compensation.[113] Slave thefts nearly disappeared, and some evidence suggests that the thefts Georgians reported were not thefts at all, but enslaved people escaping to Creek country.[114]

Georgians persisted in risky, provocative behaviors in the upper Oconee valley such as frequent trespassing, hunting, grazing their cattle,

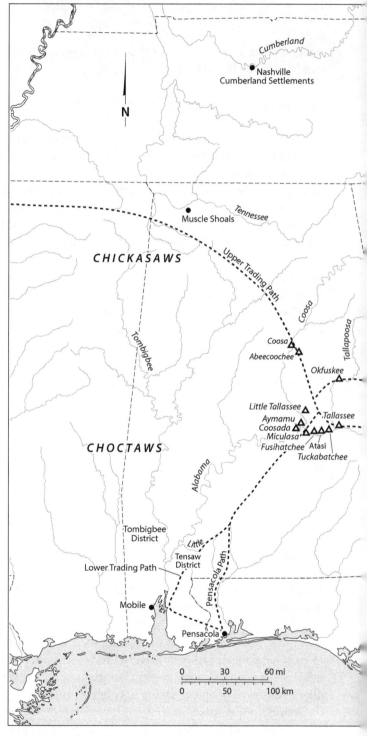

MAP 11. Creek Raids in Georgia, 1796–1800

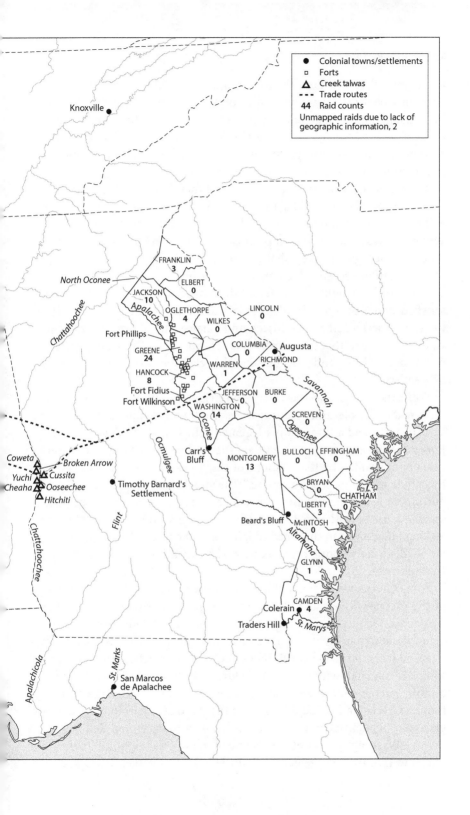

Knoxville ●

● Colonial towns/settlements
□ Forts
△ Creek talwas
--- Trade routes
44 Raid counts
Unmapped raids due to lack of
geographic information, 2

North Oconee

Chattahoochee

Apalachee

FRANKLIN
3

ELBERT
0

JACKSON
10

OGLETHORPE
4

LINCOLN
0

WILKES
0

Fort Phillips

COLUMBIA
0

Augusta ●

GREENE
24

WARREN
1

RICHMOND
1

HANCOCK
8

Savannah

Fort Fidius
Fort Wilkinson

JEFFERSON
0

BURKE
0

WASHINGTON
14

Oconee

Ogeechee

SCREEN
0

Ocmulgee

Carr's
Bluff ●

MONTGOMERY
13

BULLOCH
0

EFFINGHAM
0

Coweta
△ ●Broken Arrow
Yuchi △ △Cussita
Cheaha △ △Ooseechee
△ Hitchiti

● Timothy Barnard's
Settlement

BRYAN
0

CHATHAM
0

LIBERTY
3

McINTOSH
0

Beard's Bluff ●

Altamaha

Flint

Chattahoochee

GLYNN
1

CAMDEN
4
Colerain ●

Traders Hill ●

St. Marys

Apalachicola

St. Marks

San Marcos
de Apalachee ●

and planting cornfields on the west bank. A few Georgians continued to lash out violently. In late 1797, for example, five Creeks travelled to Fort Wilkinson, the new federal fort and trading factory on the Oconee River at present-day Milledgeville. The Creeks were to guide U.S. surveyors running a boundary line pursuant to the Treaty of Colerain. Georgians attacked the men, killing one and wounding two more.[115]

As in preceding years, Creeks defended their lives and property, and they occasionally restored balance with crying blood killings against the will of talwa and nationalist leaders.[116] Just a month after the treaty, Cussitas grew weary of waiting on promised satisfaction for two young men killed by Georgians. They shot a Georgia settler near the Apalachee-Oconee confluence, stole his horses, and burned both the victim's house and that of his neighbor.[117] Afterward, they announced that they were satisfied and that white border settlers had nothing more to fear. The Cussita leaders Fusihatchee Micco and Chalee Matla, uncle of the two youths, explained that the murder was committed by "impatient" young people acting independently, but that the relations of the deceased were now satisfied.[118]

From the Cussita perspective, this retributive killing did not negate the Treaty of Colerain. Instead, it resolved a final, outstanding issue that the talks had addressed inadequately. The Cussita leaders entreated James Seagrove to see the assault as "the Action of men who were continually upbraided by the relations of the deceased, and were forced to this affair to live in peace at home." The attack was not meant "to spoil our talks"; it was simply an unavoidable sacred duty.[119] James Seagrove scolded Cussita leaders for their failure to control their young men, as he long had done. On this occasion, however, he warned that the behavior of "disorderly young men" jeopardized Creeks' relationship with the United States.[120]

Some Creeks were reluctant to give up use of land and resources east of the Oconee River, and they remained particularly attached to the Apalachee-Oconee fork. Paradoxically, this suited some white Georgians while irritating others. Late in 1796, a group of Creeks reportedly attacked white hunters near Barber's Creek, an Apalachee tributary, and wounded one man with a musket.[121] During the winter of 1797–98, Creek hunting parties continued to harvest animals on the Oconee's east bank, though Creeks had ceded all rights to that land at Colerain. One Georgian cautioned a party of five Creeks led by a man named Red Mouth to leave Washington County, or "some of the whites might kill them."[122] The new U.S. Indian agent, Benjamin Hawkins, however, had issued a passport to Red Mouth for cross-border travel. Though some Georgians frowned on this, others encouraged it by purchasing stolen horses from Indians.[123]

After the Treaty of Colerain, theft and violence on the Creek-Georgia frontier declined but did not disappear. The two young states remained unable to control completely their people's hostility, yet theft and violence as overtly political acts subsided. At Colerain, the Creek Nation and the United States had built a tense but stable relationship. In the 1770s and 1780s, Creeks had experimented with presenting themselves as a unified nation that vested authority in a highly skilled executive. Leaders of autonomous talwas usually rejected such leadership claims. Those leaders, and young men striving to improve their status, asserted autonomy and territorial rights through border patrols. They overwhelmingly preferred to confiscate property from unauthorized settlers, but border patrols occasionally turned violent. By the 1790s, a series of factors, most importantly Georgians' own violence, pushed Creeks toward greater unity. Rather than constructing themselves as a nation modeled after those of Europe or the United States, Creeks made their indigenous form of governance serve their needs. They founded national unity on talwa consensus, yet in so doing, they sacrificed other long-held practices. Young men could no longer expect to gain prestige through military valor, livestock rustling, slave theft, or defending Creek country from trespassers. The families of murder victims could no longer urge young men to commit retribution killings without endangering the entire nation. Young men's full participation at the Colerain talks, however, suggested that relations with the United States might afford other ways to distinguish themselves. Diversity in the multilingual, coalescent society continued to influence cultural practices, but the larger polity increasingly engrossed regionally specific territorial claims. Creeks preserved their sovereignty by embracing talwa autonomy. The price of that sovereignty was beloved ground, yet the sacrifice promised to secure a future for the Creek Nation separated from Georgia by a firm border. The security of that border, however, would no longer depend on Creek border patrols. Instead, it would depend on Americans.

Epilogue: "All the Apprehensions of Savage Ferocity"

In the late eighteenth century, Creek people experienced greater coalescence while preserving the privileges of talwa autonomy. In the first decade of the nineteenth century, a minority of nationalist leaders consolidated wealth and power and increasingly ignored the interests of a majority still devoted to local independence. Ceaseless American pressure helped widen rifts in Creek society until they became unbridgeable, resulting in a Creek civil war. The Redstick War from 1813 to 1814 pitted Redstick dissidents against supporters of the Creek National Council. However, the struggle between local and national leaders to control border patrols between 1770 and 1796 shows that rancorous disagreement between various interest groups long had been a feature of Creek society. Border patrols emerged from a spirit of unity around the need to defend Creek country, but they also reflected complicated tensions between local and national authority, age and youth, and diverse linguistic groups with regional territorial claims and disparate economic interests. Creeks agreed that their territory and sovereignty must be protected, but they frequently found themselves divided over how best to do so. After the Treaty of Colerain in 1796, several factors deepened existing tensions and caused new ones between Creeks who embraced centralized governance, ranching, and slave plantation agriculture, and those who resisted such innovation. The combined impact of all those stressors led to civil war. During and after the Redstick War, Americans continued to exaggerate Creek ferocity and use that political narrative to justify violence and punitive land-taking.[1]

Raiding along Creek country's borders, and, increasingly, on roads through Creek country, continued between the Treaty of Colerain and the Redstick War. Young men possessed a range of motives similar to those of raiders in the 1780s and 1790s. Generational tension between older leaders and ambitious young men manifested itself in raiding. Raiders asserted territorial sovereignty. Confiscating property from outsiders became an essential economic pursuit after the deerskin trade evaporated. Nationalist leaders frequently appealed to federal authorities to remove American squatters and livestock from Creek lands and govern ever-growing white traffic through the Creek Nation bound for Mississippi Territory. This, they believed, would reduce young men's opportunities and reasons for theft and violence.[2]

Raiding briefly halted after the Treaty of Colerain as Creeks waited breathlessly to see whether the U.S. government could meet its commitment to restrain hostile Georgians. Benjamin Hawkins reported in December 1796 that "Since the treaty at Colerain the Indians have manifested a disposition for peace, unknown before, it is almost universal."[3] He expected no trouble creating a national council, which he believed Creeks desperately needed because, in his estimation, they possessed no government or law.[4] That near-universal disposition for peace changed as federal authorities failed to protect Creek land and sovereignty. In January 1797, some young Coweta hunters complained to Benjamin Hawkins of "the stocks of white people ranging on their lands, and requested that measures might be taken to cause them to be removed."[5] Cowetas and Cussitas requested U.S. military protection from belligerent Georgians squatting on Creek lands. Federal forces promised to "destroy the plantations" on the Oconee's west bank, "collect such stock as remains on the Indian lands," and drive them across the river into Georgia.[6] Federal forces, however, proved unable or unwilling to fulfill those pledges. Young Cussitas and Cowetas continued asserting their own authority by confiscating Georgians' horses and other livestock left to range freely on the Creek side of the Oconee as well as from settlements between the St. Marys and the Altamaha. At Hawkins's urging, older headmen like Cussita Micco had such young men whipped and the horses confiscated.[7] Cowetas also promised to do more to govern "disorderly young men."[8]

Benjamin Hawkins worried in 1797 that generational tension was especially severe at Cussita, the biggest of the Lower Towns. In town council meetings throughout the nation, young men were confined to seating at the back of the warriors' cabin, denoting their low status. Creek culture still required young men to achieve status through war honors, yet there were ever-fewer opportunities to do so without incurring the wrath of nationalist leaders and hostile Americans.[9] Such pressures resulted in periodic murders, such as when "giddy hotheaded mad young men" from Coweta killed a black woman on the Apalachee River in January 1797.[10] A few months later, Creeks warriors killed, beheaded, and scalped Isaac Brown, wounded his wife, and burned his house at Long Bluff, some eighty miles down the Oconee River from the Apalachee.[11]

Combining political and economic motives, young Creeks raided surveyors in the late 1790s and early 1800s when they attempted to mark borders or plot roads. They robbed and extorted non-Indian travelers in Creek country as the numbers of migrants and mail couriers steadily increased. Such actions should not be dismissed as mere opportunism. Like the border patrols of the late eighteenth century, they should be recognized as politically motivated "resistance to American intrusions" that reflected popular opinion in Creek country.[12] A federal road-widening project through Creek country authorized in 1811 became a particular target for Creeks irritated by U.S. expansion. Resistance to the road united Creeks regardless of age, linguistic division, economic pursuit, or political persuasion.[13]

When the Redstick War began in 1813, attacks on post riders along the Federal Road and slave plantations on the lower Alabama River resembled late eighteenth-century border patrols because they targeted emblems of U.S. encroachment including American travelers, livestock, and plantations themselves. Like Creek efforts to clear the Oconee lands of Georgia settlers, Redsticks fought "to reclaim lands for Indians alone."[14] Redsticks routinely slaughtered livestock owned by wealthy, nationalist Creeks because they represented the intrusion of American culture and economic practices. Road building, cattle ranching, slaveholding, and centralizing government strangled local autonomy and stymied common Creeks who lived by older agricultural and hunting practices. Slave plantations owned by Creeks such as those at Tensaw posed a threat to common Creeks because the wealth they represented underpinned the power of a domineering National Council that monopolized Creek resources.[15]

Tension between those who preferred talwa autonomy and those who preferred national authority deepened as families associated with the Creek National Council consolidated power, wealth, and influence in the first decade of the nineteenth century. The tension between factions no longer centered on command of warriors patrolling Creek borders. Instead, tension centered on the command of Creek country's resources. The National Council advanced the interests of Creeks who embraced ranching, dispersed settlement, slaveholding, commercial agriculture, private property, and U.S. alliance. It largely ignored the desires of common Creeks. Council members controlled a key source of capital— annuity payments that flowed from existing treaties. They also made new treaties that ceded still more Creek land to the United States, and they monopolized the proceeds from those new agreements, as well.[16]

Generational tension contributed to the economic and political divisions. United States policy as implemented by Superintendent of Indian Affairs Benjamin Hawkins focused on civilizing purportedly savage Creeks by creating and nurturing a new, stronger National Council in the 1790s and the first decade of the new century. Hawkins was never entirely satisfied with his creation. In the late 1790s, the National Council remained unable to overcome the resistance of some talwa leaders. It often failed to rigidly enforce laws on disorderly young men. Hawkins believed that each talwa retained a "spirit of party or opposition" to "the will of the nation."[17]

In the first decade of the nineteenth century, however, the Creek National Council's police force was ruthless in whipping and even killing dissidents who defied the Council's will. They did this in large part to protect the financial interests of elite Creek families, frequently but not always those with mixed European and Native American ancestry who had accumulated slaves and livestock. Those families, especially the extended family of the late Alexander McGillivray in the Tensaw district, claimed Creek land as privately owned property and increasingly pursued slave-based plantation agriculture. Other Creeks, including some with mixed European, African, and Indian ancestry, from Hitchiti, Koasati, and Muskogee-speaking Lower Towns continued stealing or rescuing slaves from Georgia plantations in border raids between the Altamaha and St. Marys Rivers. Raiders brought those people to Lower Towns and Seminole towns on the lower Chattahoochee River and northern Florida where they lived as mostly free men and women.[18] Such behavior further widened the gulf between nationalists and localists.

Despite an increasingly dispersed settlement pattern that accommodated ranching and slave plantations, many Creeks remained bound to talwas that continued to function as political and ritual centers fostering group identity. For example, in 1796, Benjamin Hawkins visited Hill-aubee, an Abika province Upper Town. He reported there was only "one house in the town," but noted that "here is the town house and here they have their husks and dances." There were a total of 170 gun men "belonging to the town," but they were settled in four separate villages where several Creeks, mestizos, and white Indian countrymen kept cattle, hogs, and horses.[19]

Creek Redstick prophets fought against the abuses of the National Council's police force. The vast majority of Creeks were sympathetic to an older form of decentralized governance where power was vested in autonomous talwas with greater control over communal resources. When Redstick prophets targeted the "old chiefs" of the National Council, it may have reflected generational tension.[20] However, aging leaders including Hoboithle Micco, a perennial voice in favor of talwa autonomy, claimed a leadership role in the Redstick movement. Despite such diversity of opinions, by war's end, some 1,500 Creeks had been killed and another 8,000 made refugees.[21]

Linguistic diversity and disparate provincial interests continued throughout the early nineteenth century and beyond. In the first decade of the century, however, the National Council engrossed provincial territorial priorities. This process paralleled and facilitated the growing tendency among some Creeks to develop slave plantations and claim them as private property, subverting long-standing beliefs in communal land ownership. Benjamin Hawkins noted linguistic diversity in Creek country in the late 1790s, but he believed such differences would matter little as National Council rule matured and more Creeks adopted Euro-American culture. For example, he wrote that the people of Coosada town in the Alabama province of the Upper Towns "are not Creeks, although they conform to their ceremonies."[22] He found the Alabama towns themselves even more distinct, noting that the people "do not conform to the customs of the Creeks, and the Creek law for the punishment of adultery is not known among them."[23] The people of Tuskegee town in the Alabama province likely derived from the Koasati-speaking, precontact chiefdom of Coste in the Tennessee River valley. Hawkins observed that they had "lost their language, and speak Creek, and have adopted the customs and manners of the Creeks."[24] Hawkins also delineated differences between Yuchis and Creeks. He wrote that they "speak a tongue different from the Creeks," "they retain all their original customs and laws, and have adopted none of the Creeks."[25] Ignoring Yuchi involvement in the border violence in the 1790s, however, Hawkins commented approvingly that Yuchis "are more civil and orderly than their neighbors; their women are more chaste, and the men better hunters."[26]

The Redstick War was a civil war, and the tensions between Creeks were more complicated than linguistic or geographic divisions. Each faction drew members from several provinces. The provinces continued to assert superior claims to particular territories in opposition to the National Council's land policies. For example, Coosadas demanded that Creek planters operating a ferry across the Alabama River in the Tensaw district pay a fee for the privilege. When they refused, Coosadas attacked the ferry operator and burned the boat.[27] Some Yuchis aided Americans in their attacks on Redsticks, yet hundreds of other Yuchis sided with Shawnee and Creek relatives among the Redsticks. Several Alabama, Abika, and Tallapoosa province towns joined the Redstick movement while the Natchez supported the National Council. At least nine talwas endured internal schisms. The divisions that led to the Redstick War were many, and, as with the raids of the late eighteenth century, patterns of behavior reflected in violence provide perspective on multiple issues.[28]

Georgians and other Americans continued using the narrative of exaggerated Creek ferocity to justify overwhelming violence, land taking, and ultimately, removal. In his classic analysis of the Redstick War, *Sacred Revolt*, Joel Martin argued that Americans eagerly provoked Creek violence to create "a pretext to crush the Muskogees and absorb greater portions of their land."[29] The 1813 Redstick attack on Fort Mims, a fortified plantation on the lower Alabama River, became a cause célèbre that Americans used to justify total war against Creeks. While Redstick forces attacked Fort Mims largely to punish the many slaveholding Creeks there, they also killed many white people. News reports depicted the "Fort Mims Massacre" as "the butchery of hundreds of 'white settlers' by 'hostile Creek Indians.'" The late Robert G. Thrower, Tribal Historic Preservation Officer for the Poarch Band of Creek Indians, noted that the event is still misinterpreted on "the various historical markers at the present Fort Mims site."[30] Just as in the late eighteenth century, Americans used the trope of Creek ferocity unleashed on blameless white victims to justify punitive land taking. The 23 million acres General Andrew Jackson demanded as the price of peace at the 1814 Treaty of Fort Jackson dwarfed the size of previous land cessions.[31]

The exaggerated narrative of Creek ferocity cast a long shadow. In 1783, the family of future Georgia governor Wilson Lumpkin moved to the newly created Wilkes County in the Ceded Lands just east of the Oconee River. Throughout the late eighteenth century, Wilkes was one of the most raided counties in Georgia. Lumpkin spent his early childhood in that environment, where he imbibed visceral fear and hatred of Native Americans. As an adult, Lumpkin served as a member of the U.S. House of Representatives from 1827 to 1831, governor of Georgia from 1831 to 1835, and U.S. commissioner to the Cherokees in 1836–37. Few politicians of the era were as instrumental in advocating for Indian Removal. Lumpkin never forgot his experiences on the Creek-Georgia frontier. In the opening pages of his massive, two-volume memoir, *The Removal of the Cherokee Indians from Georgia*, Lumpkin recalled that his childhood home was exposed to "frequent depredations from hostile and savage Indian neighbors, so far as to force them and their frontier neighbors to erect and live within the enclosed walls of a rough but strong built fort."[32] He even claimed to be present at Tuckabatchee in 1811 when Tecumseh spoke to a council of Creeks, fueling the broader Redstick movement. Traveling in Creek country, he felt, was a great hazard because the paths were "infested with bands of the most bloody robbers."[33] Lumpkin expanded his assumption of Creek ferocity and the dismissal of Creek sovereignty to Cherokees. Among his many arguments in favor of removal, he declared that "unoffending citizens" must be protected from "all the apprehensions of savage ferocity." In the end, Lumpkin concluded that "such an enemy as this ought not to be permitted to repose in the bosom of the State."[34]

NOTES

Introduction

1. James P. Preston to John C. Calhoun, 15 March 1822, Indian Depredations, 1787–1825, ed. Louise F. [Mrs. J. E.] Hays, vol. 2, pt. 1:4, Georgia Archives (hereafter cited as DEPS).

2. *Georgia Gazette*, 26 April 1787.

3. Walter Lowrie and Matthew St. Clair Clarke, eds., *American State Papers, Documents, Legislative and Executive, of the Congress of the United States, from the First Session of the First to the Third Session of the Thirteenth Congress, Inclusive: Commencing March 3, 1789, and Ending March 3, 1815, Indian Affairs*, vol. 1 (Washington, DC: Gales and Seaton, 1832), 15 (hereafter cited as *ASPIA*).

4. Deposition of Thomas Wilder, 12 June 1812, DEPS, vol. 2, pt. 1:102-e.

5. Absalom H. Chappell, *Miscellanies of Georgia, Historical, Biographical, Descriptive, etc.* (Atlanta: Meegan, 1874), 7.

6. Ibid., 7; Louise Frederick Hays, *Hero of the Hornet's Nest: A Biography of Elijah Clark, 1733 to 1799* (New York: Stratford House, 1946), 147–216.

7. Michael D. Green, *The Politics of Indian Removal: Creek Government and Society in Crisis* (Lincoln: University of Nebraska Press, 1982), 4–15, 33–43, 149–52; Kathryn E. Holland Braund, *Deerskins and Duffels: The Creek Indian Trade with Anglo-America, 1685–1815*, 2nd ed. (1993; Lincoln: University of Nebraska Press, 2008), 3, 5–8, 15–22; Claudio Saunt, *A New Order of Things: Property, Power, and the Transformation of the Creek Indians, 1733–1816* (Cambridge: Cambridge University Press, 1999), 19–26, 34–36, 179; Robbie Ethridge, *Creek Country: The Creek Indians and Their World* (Chapel Hill: University of North Carolina, 2003), 28–30, 92–103, 107–8; Joshua A. Piker, "'White & Clean' & Contested: Creek Towns and Trading Paths in the Aftermath of the Seven Years' War," *Ethnohistory* 50, no. 2 (Spring 2003): 315–47; Joshua A. Piker, *Okfuskee: A Creek Indian Town in Colonial America* (Cambridge: Harvard University Press, 2004), 1–10, 115–18, 154–57, 178–82; Angela Pulley Hudson, *Creek Paths and*

Federal Roads: Indians, Settlers, and Slaves and the Making of the American South (Chapel Hill: University of North Carolina Press, 2010), 2–3, 12–13.

8. Fabian Hilfrich, "The Corruption of Civic Virtue by Emotion: Anti-Imperialist Fears in the Debate on the Philippine-American War (1899–1902)," in *Emotions in American History: An International Assessment*, ed. Jessica C. E. Gienow-Hect, 51–65 (New York: Berghahn, 2010); Lisa Ford, *Settler Sovereignty: Jurisdiction and Indigenous People in America and Australia, 1788–1836* (Cambridge: Harvard University Press, 2010), 85–97, 101–3; Peter Silver, *Our Savage Neighbors: How Indian War Transformed Early America* (New York: Norton, 2008).

9. "Coalescent societies" has become the generally preferred term for eighteenth-century southeastern Indian polities. See Robbie Ethridge, "The Making of a Militaristic Slaving Society: The Chickasaws and the Colonial Indian Slave Trade," in *Indian Slavery in Colonial America*, ed. Allan Gallay (Lincoln: University of Nebraska Press, 2009), 252, 268n1; Robbie Ethridge, *From Chicaza to Chickasaw: The European Invasion and the Transformation of the Mississippian World, 1540–1715* (Chapel Hill: University of North Carolina Press, 2010), 2, 250–51, 257n1, 302n40.

10. Louis le Clerc Milfort, *Memoirs, or a Quick Glance at My Various Travels and My Sojourn in the Creek Nation*, trans. and ed. Ben C. McCary (1959; Savannah: Beehive, 1972), 37, 97, 102–22; Cameron Wesson, *Households and Hegemony: Early Creek Prestige Goods, Symbolic Capital, and Social Power* (Lincoln: University of Nebraska Press, 2008), xx–xxiv, 126–36; Alan Gallay, *The Indian Slave Trade: The Rise of the English Empire in the American South, 1670–1717* (New Haven: Yale University Press, 2002); Eric E. Bowne, *The Westo Indians: Slave Traders of the Early Colonial South* (Tuscaloosa: University of Alabama Press, 2005); Robbie Ethridge and Sheri M. Shuck-Hall, eds., *Mapping the Mississippian Shatter Zone: The Colonial Indian Slave Trade and Regional Instability in the American South* (Lincoln: University of Nebraska Press, 2009); Joseph M. Hall, *Zamumo's Gifts: Indian-European Exchange in the Colonial Southeast* (Philadelphia: University of Pennsylvania Press, 2009); Christina Snyder, *Slavery in Indian Country: The Changing Face of Captivity in Early America* (Cambridge: Harvard University Press, 2010); Ethridge, *From Chicaza to Chickasaw*, 35, 112–15, 162, 166, 212–15, 239–40, 245–46, 251.

11. H. Thomas Foster II, *Archaeology of the Lower Muskogee Creek Indians, 1715–1836* (Tuscaloosa: University of Alabama Press, 2007); H. Thomas Foster II, "The Yuchi Indians along the Chattahoochee and Flint Rivers (1715–1836): A Synthesis," in *Yuchi Indian Histories before the Removal Era*, ed. Jason Baird Jackson, 101–22 (Lincoln: University of Nebraska Press, 2012).

12. John R. Swanton, "Social Organization and Social Usages of the Indians of the Creek Confederacy," in *Forty-Second Annual Report of the Bureau of American Ethnology to the Secretary of the Smithsonian Institution, 1924–1925* (Washington, DC: U.S. Government Printing Office, 1928), 242, 305.

13. Green, *The Politics of Indian Removal*, 4; Piker, *Okfuskee*, 9.

14. Ethridge, *From Chicaza to Chickasaw*; Robin Beck, *Chiefdoms, Collapse, and Coalescence in the Early American South* (Cambridge: Cambridge University Press, 2013); James Taylor Carson, *Searching for the Bright Path: The Mississippi Choctaws from Prehistory to Removal* (Lincoln: University of Nebraska Press, 1999); Bonnie G. McEwan, "The Apalachee Indians of Northwest Florida," in *Indians of the Greater*

Southeast: Historical Archaeology and Ethnohistory, ed. McEwan (Gainesville: University Press of Florida, 2000), 62–63.

15. Green, *The Politics of Indian Removal*, 8–10; Jack B. Martin and Margaret McKane Mauldin, *A Dictionary of Creek/Muskogee with Notes on the Florida and Oklahoma Seminole Dialects of Creek* (Lincoln: University of Nebraska Press, 2000), 49.

16. Swanton, "Social Organization and Social Usages," 113, 156–57; George Stiggins, *Creek Indian History: A Historical Narrative of the Genealogy, Traditions and Downfall of the Ispocoga or Creek Indian Tribe of Indians* (Birmingham: University of Alabama Press, 1989), 29–30, 150n35; Marvin T. Smith, *Coosa: The Rise and Fall of a Southeastern Mississippian Chiefdom* (Gainesville: University Press of Florida, 2000), 55; Green, *The Politics of Indian Removal*, 7; William Bartram, *William Bartram on the Southeastern Indians*, ed. Gregory A. Waselkov and Kathryn E. Holland Braund (Lincoln: University of Nebraska Press, 1995), 108–10, 156, 260n144; Snyder, *Slavery in Indian Country*, 116-17.

17. Ethridge, *Creek Country*, 92–94, 102–3; Green, *Politics of Indian Removal*, 8–10, 33; Smith, *Coosa*, 55–56; John T. Juricek, *Endgame for Empire: British-Creek Relations in Georgia and Vicinity, 1763–1776* (Gainesville: University Press of Florida, 2015), 54–55, 76; Steven C. Hahn, *The Invention of the Creek Nation, 1670–1763* (Lincoln: University of Nebraska Press, 2004), 33–35; Tyler Boulware, *Deconstructing the Cherokee Nation: Town, Region, and Nation among Eighteenth-Century Cherokees* (Gainesville: University Press of Florida, 2011), 11–13; Ethridge, *From Chicaza to Chickasaw*, 191–192, 222-31, 247; Patricia Galloway, *Practicing Ethnohistory: Mining Archives, Hearing Testimony, Constructing Narrative* (Lincoln: University of Nebraska Press, 2006), 217, 337, 341-54, 358-63, 366-70; John Phillip Reid, *A Law of Blood: The Primitive Law of the Cherokee Nation* (1970; DeKalb: Northern Illinois University Press, 2006), 21.

18. Milfort, *Memoirs*, 27, 33, 90-109, 114, 121; James Adair, *The History of the American Indians*, ed. Kathryn E. Holland Braund (Tuscaloosa: University of Alabama Press, 2005), 190–91; Swanton, "Social Organization and Social Usages," 276–306; Green, *The Politics of Indian Removal*, 4–16, 21–22, 25, 27, 34; Braund, *Deerskins and Duffels*, 15–23; Ethridge, *Creek Country*, 95–97, 102-8; Saunt, *A New Order of Things*, 17, 19, 22–27, 31–37; Piker, *Okfuskee*, 7–9, 17, 22–24, 30, 40–42; Wesson, *Households and Hegemony*, xix-xx, 27–32, 40–41, 51, 71–73; Boulware, *Deconstructing the Cherokee Nation*, 11–12, 52–53, 157, 167, 174; Ethridge, *From Chicaza to Chickasaw*, 14, 23–24, 45–50, 68, 82, 103, 106, 108, 135–36, 186; Galloway, *Practicing Ethnohistory*, 292–94, 337-54, 362-63, 366–67, 370; Carson, *Searching for the Bright Path*, 14–15, 62–64; Reid, *A Law of Blood*, 51; Greg O'Brien, *Choctaws in a Revolutionary Age, 1750–1830* (Lincoln: University of Nebraska Press, 2002), 33–48, 83–84, 92; Beck, *Chiefdoms, Collapse, and Coalescence*, 67–68, 123, 138, 156–59, 177–78, 196–97, 207–10, 236; Tiya Miles, *Ties That Bind: The Story of an Afro-Cherokee Family in Slavery and Freedom*, 2nd ed. (Oakland: University of California Press, 2015), 103.

19. Ethridge, *From Chicaza to Chickasaw*, 15, 47–48; Adam King, "The Historic Period Transformation of Mississippian Societies," in *Light on the Path: The Anthropology and History of the Southeastern Indians*, ed. Thomas J. Pluckhahn and Robbie Ethridge (Tuscaloosa: University of Alabama Press, 2006), 186–87, 191–95; Smith, *Coosa*, 58–59; Wesson, *Households and Hegemony*, 146–47.

20. Swanton, "Social Organization and Social Usages," 276.

21. Ibid., 284, 276.

22. Ethridge, *Creek Country*, 93.

23. Benjamin Hawkins, *The Collected Works of Benjamin Hawkins, 1796–1810*, ed. Thomas Foster (Tuscaloosa: University of Alabama Press, 2003), 67s; Foster, *Archaeology of the Lower Muskogee Creek Indians*, 7; Wesson, *Households and Hegemony*, 25–26; Steven C. Hahn, "'They Look upon the Yuchis as Their Vassals': An Early History of Yuchi-Creek Political Relations," in *Yuchi Indian Histories*, ed. Jason Baird Jackson, 123–26, 129–31, 140–41, 143–45.

24. Green, *Politics of Indian Removal*, 12–13; Ethridge, *Creek Country*, 105–7; Juricek, *Endgame for Empire*, 40–41, 53–56, 133, 197–98.

25. Piker, *Okfuskee*, 1–4, 7–8, 209n13; Green, *The Politics of Indian Removal*; Ethridge, *Creek Country*; Saunt, *A New Order of Thing*; Wesson, *Households and Hegemony*; Carson, *Searching for the Bright Path*; O'Brien, *Choctaws in a Revolutionary Age*; Ethridge, *From Chicaza to Chickasaw*; Galloway, *Practicing Ethnohistory*, 311–12, 329–30; Boulware, *Deconstructing the Cherokee Nation*; Beck, *Chiefdoms, Collapse, and Coalescence*; Stephen Warren, *The Worlds the Shawnees Made: Migration and Violence in Early America* (Chapel Hill: University of North Carolina Press, 2014); Sami Lakomäki, *Gathering Together: The Shawnee People through Diaspora and Nationhood, 1600–1870* (New Haven: Yale University Press, 2014).

26. Green, *The Politics of Indian Removal*, 4–16; Piker, *Okfuskee*, 7–10, 117–18, 162–64; Braund, *Deerskins and Duffels*, 21, 24; Ethridge, *Creek Country*, 95, 147, 228–32; Saunt, *A New Order of Things*, 22, 43; Hahn, "They Look upon the Yuchis as Their Vassals," 145–46.

27. Green, *The Politics of Indian Removal*, 4–7; Braund, *Deerskins and Duffels*, 11–12; Piker, *Okfuskee*, 9–10, 23, 56, 59–62; Ethridge, *Creek Country*, 25, 92–93, 109–11, 228–32; Saunt, *A New Order of Things*, 19–21, 81–82, 91–97, 101–3, 106–8; Reid, *A Law of Blood*, 73–84, 99–103, 108, 153–62, 168–70; Denise Bossy, "Indian Slavery in Southeastern Indian and British Societies, 1670–1730," in *Indian Slavery in Colonial America*, ed. Alan Gallay (Lincoln: University of Nebraska Press, 2009), 210–13; Snyder, *Slavery in Indian Country*, 80–100; Boulware, *Deconstructing the Cherokee Nation*, 2, 29, 60, 105–9.

28. *Return of the Whole Number of Persons within the Several Districts of the United States, According to "An Act Providing for the Enumeration of the Inhabitants of the United States," Passed March First, One Thousand Seven Hundred and Ninety One* (Philadelphia Printed: London Reprinted, and Sold by J. Phillips, George-Yard, Lombard-Street, 1793), 3; Peter H. Wood, "The Changing Population of the Colonial South: An Overview by Race and Region, 1685–1790," in *Powhatan's Mantle: Indians in the Colonial Southeast*, ed. Gregory A. Waselkov, Peter H. Wood, and Tom Hatley (1989; Lincoln: University of Nebraska Press, 2006), 86.

29. DEPS, 5 vols. All tallies of Creek raids and their geographic distribution presented in this volume come primarily from my analysis of the five-volume collection of depredations claims held in the Georgia Archives. I have confirmed and elaborated on the trends identified by using a variety of other sources.

30. Carson, *Searching for the Bright Path*, 65; O'Brien, *Choctaws in a Revolutionary Age*, 27, 30–33, 35–40, 42–44, 99–100; Saunt, *A New Order of Things*, 257.

31. Matthew Jennings, *New Worlds of Violence: Cultures and Conquests in the Early American Southeast* (Knoxville: University of Tennessee Press, 2011), 95; James Taylor

Carson, "Horses and the Economy and Culture of the Choctaw Indians, 1690–1840," *Ethnohistory* 42, no. 3 (Summer 1995): 495–502.

32. Braund, *Deerskins and Duffels*, 14; Stephen Aron, *American Confluence: The Missouri Frontier from Borderland to Border State* (Bloomington: Indiana University Press, 2006), xix; Lakomäki, *Gathering Together*.

33. Hahn, *The Invention of the Creek Nation*, 5, 124–39, 145–48, 151–76; Saunt, *A New Order of Things*, 67–185; Michael D. Green, "Alexander McGillivray," in *American Indian Leaders: Studies in Diversity*, ed. R. David Edmunds, 41–63 (Lincoln: University of Nebraska Press, 1980); Green, *The Politics of Indian Removal*, 4–14, 20–43; Braund, *Deerskins and Duffels*, 140–42; Wesson, *Households and Hegemony*, 7–21, 27–32, 39–46, 51–53, 71–81, 86–87, 126–32, 146–51; Cameron B. Wesson, "Creek and Pre-Creek Revisited," in *The Archaeology of Traditions: Agency and History Before and After Columbus*, ed. Timothy Pauketat (Gainesville: University Press of Florida, 2001), 101–5; Cameron B. Wesson, "Prestige Goods, Symbolic Capital, and Social Power in the Protohistoric Southeast," in *Between Contacts and Colonies: Archaeological Perspectives on the Protohistoric Southeast*, ed. Wesson and Mark A. Rees (Tuscaloosa: University of Alabama Press, 2002), 114–19, 121–23; Cameron B. Wesson, "When Moral Economies and Capitalism Meet: Creek Factionalism and the Colonial Southeastern Frontier," in *Across a Great Divide: Continuity and Change in Native North American Societies, 1400–1900*, ed. Laura L. Scheiber and Mark D. Mitchell, 61–78 (Tucson: University of Arizona Press, 2010).

34. Jennings, *New Worlds of Violence*, 166–75; Hahn, *The Invention of the Creek Nation*, 2, 8, 15, 43, 102, 108–9, 119, 157–63, 179–210, 220–25, 230, 250–58; Alexandra Minna Stern, *Eugenic Nation: Faults and Frontiers of Better Breeding in Modern America* (Berkeley: University of California Press, 2005), 24, 72–81.

35. Jonathan Haas, *The Evolution of the Prehistoric State* (New York: Columbia University Press, 1982), 1–33; Keith H. Basso, *Wisdom Sits in Places: Landscape and Language among the Western Apache* (Albuquerque: University of New Mexico Press, 1996); James Taylor Carson, "Ethnogeography and the Native American Past," *Ethnohistory* 49, no. 4 (Fall 2002): 769–88; James H. Merrell, *The Indians' New World: Catawbas and Their Neighbors from European Contact through the Era of Removal* (Chapel Hill: University of North Carolina Press, 1989), 23–24, 26–27; William Cronon, *Changes in the Land: Indians, Colonists, and the Ecology of New England* (New York: Hill and Wang, 1983); Warren, *The Worlds the Shawnees Made*; Ronald Cohen and Elman R. Service, eds., *Origins of the State: The Anthropology of Political Evolution* (Philadelphia: Institute for the Study of Human Issues, 1978), 1–12; Henri J. M. Claesson and Peter Skalnik, eds., *The Early State* (The Hague: Mouton, 1978), 5–16; Hastings Donnan and Thomas M. Wilson, eds., *Border Approaches: Anthropological Perspectives on Frontiers* (Lanham, MD: University Press of America, 1994), 1–11; Henri J. M. Claesson and Jarich G. Oosten, eds., *Ideology and the Formation of Early States* (Leiden: Brill, 1996), 1–24, 116–35; R. Brian Ferguson and Neil L. Whitehead, eds., *War in the Tribal Zone: Expanding States and Indigenous Warfare* (Santa Fe: School of American Research, 2001), xi–xxxv, 1–28, 83–102, 127–74; Neil L. Whitehead, ed., *Violence* (Santa Fe: School of American Research Press, 2004), 3–24, 55–77, 107–24; Christian Krohn-Hansen and Knut G. Nustad, eds., *State Formation: Anthropological Perspectives* (London: Pluto, 2005), vii–52; Ford, *Settler Sovereignty*.

36. Green, *The Politics of Indian Removal*, 21–23; Braund, *Deerskins and Duffels*, 132–36; Hahn, *The Invention of the Creek Nation*, 54–62, 78–123, 145–48, 229–70; Jennings, *New Worlds of Violence*, xix, 16–27, 65–81, 88–95, 109–12, 130–31, 166–77; Juricek, *Endgame for Empire*.

37. Juricek, *Endgame for Empire*; Kevin T. Harrell, "The Terrain of Factionalism: How Upper Creek Communities Negotiated the Recourse of Gulf Coast Trade, 1763–1780," *Alabama Review* 68, no. 1 (January 2015): 74–113; Kevin Thomas Harrell, "Creek Corridors of Commerce: Converging Empires, Cultural Arbitration, and the Recourse of Gulf Coast Trade" (Ph.D. diss., University of Mississippi, 2013).

38. Braund, *Deerskins and Duffels*, 144, 166; Piker, "'White & Clean' and Contested," 317.

39. Chappell, *Miscellanies of Georgia*, 5–22; Hays, *Hero of the Hornet's Nest*, 160–238; Randolph C. Downes, "Creek-American Relations, 1782–1790," *Georgia Historical Quarterly* 21, no. 2 (June 1937): 142–84; Randolph C. Downes, "Creek American Relations, 1790–1795," *Journal of Southern History* 8, no. 3 (August 1942): 350–73; Angie Debo, *The Road to Disappearance: A History of the Creek Indians* (1941; 5th reprinting, Norman: University of Oklahoma Press, 1988, 35–83; Green, *The Politics of Indian Removal*, 21–40; Joel W. Martin, *Sacred Revolt: The Muskogees' Struggle for a New World* (Boston: Beacon, 1991), 80–101; Braund, *Deerskins and Duffels*, 148–89; Saunt, *A New Order of Things*, 78–89, 97–110, 126–29 177–79, 192–98; Edward J. Cashin, *Lachlan McGillivray, Indian Trader: The Shaping of the Southern Colonial Frontier* (Athens: University of Georgia Press, 1992), 271–89, 302–3; Gregory A. Waselkov, *A Conquering Spirit: Fort Mims and the Redstick War of 1813–1814* (Tuscaloosa: University of Alabama Press, 2006), 11–12, 20–23, 43; A. Hudson, *Creek Paths and Federal Roads*, 17–56; Theda Perdue, *Cherokee Women: Gender and Culture Change, 1700–1835* (Lincoln: University of Nebraska Press, 1998); Thomas M. Hatley, *The Dividing Paths: Cherokees and South Carolinians through the Era of Revolution* (New York: Oxford University Press, 1993); Carson, *Searching for the Bright Path*; O'Brien, *Choctaws in a Revolutionary Age*; J. Hall, *Zamumo's Gifts*; Ethridge, *From Chicaza to Chickasaw*; Gallay, *The Indian Slave Trade*; Bowne, *The Westo Indians*; Snyder, *Slavery in Indian Country*; Boulware, *Deconstructing the Cherokee Nation*; Kathryn E. Holland Braund, ed., *Tohopeka: Rethinking the Creek War and War of 1812* (Tuscaloosa: University of Alabama Press, 2012); Robert Paulett, *An Empire of Small Places: Mapping the Southeastern Anglo-Indian Trade, 1732–1795* (Athens: University of Georgia Press, 2012); Juricek, *Endgame for Empire*; Harrell, "The Terrain of Factionalism"; Kevin Kokomoor, "'Let Us Try to Make Each Other Happy, and Not Wretched:' The Creek-Georgian Frontier, 1776–1796" (Ph.D. diss., Florida State University, 2013).

40. Claudio Saunt, "The Native South: An Account of Recent Historiography," *Native South* 1 (2008): 45–60; Richard White, *The Middle Ground: Indians, Empires, and Republics in the Great Lakes Region, 1650–1815* (Cambridge: Cambridge University Press, 1991); Merrell, *The Indians' New World*; Daniel H. Usner, *Indians, Settlers and Slaves in a Frontier Exchange Economy: The Lower Mississippi Valley before 1783* (Chapel Hill: University of North Carolina Press, 1992); Andrew R. L. Cayton and Fredrika J. Teute, eds., *Contact Points: American Frontiers from the Mohawk Valley to the Mississippi, 1750–1830* (Chapel Hill: University of North Carolina Press, 1998); James F. Brooks, *Captives and Cousins: Slavery, Kinship, and Community in the Southwest Borderlands* (Chapel Hill: University of North Carolina Press, 2002); Piker, *Okfuskee*;

Andrew Frank, *Creeks and Southerners: Biculturalism on the Early American Frontier* (Lincoln: University of Nebraska Press, 2005); Julie Anne Sweet, *Negotiating for Georgia: British-Creek Relations in the Trustee Era, 1733–1752* (Athens: University of Georgia Press, 2005); Kathleen DuVal, *The Native Ground: Indians and Colonists in the Heart of the Continent* (Philadelphia: University of Pennsylvania Press, 2006); Aron, *American Confluence*; Juliana Barr, *Peace Came in the Form of a Woman: Indians and Spaniards in the Texas Borderlands* (Chapel Hill: University of North Carolina Press, 2007); J. Hall, *Zamumo's Gifts*; Warren, *The Worlds the Shawnees Made.*

41. Joshua Piker, "Colonists and Creeks: Rethinking the Pre-Revolutionary Southern Backcountry," *Journal of Southern History* 70, no. 3 (August 2004): 503–40; Piker, *Okfuskee*; Sweet, *Negotiating for Georgia*; Saunt, *A New Order of Things*, 79–83, 104–8, 249–72; A. Hudson, *Creek Paths and Federal Roads*, 26–120; Martin, *Sacred Revolt.*

42. Green, *The Politics of Indian Removal*; Piker, *Okfuskee*; Martin, *Sacred Revolt*; Braund, *Deerskins and Duffels*; Saunt, *A New Order of Things*; Hahn, *Inventing the Creek Nation.*

43. A. Hudson, *Creek Paths and Federal Roads*, 32; Samuel Edward Butler diary, 1784–1786, Hargrett Rare Book and Manuscript Library, University of Georgia (hereafter cited as HAR).

44. Whitehead, "On the Poetics of Violence," in *Violence*, ed. Whitehead, esp. 58–68.

45. Chappell, *Miscellanies of Georgia*, 8.

46. Amanda Blackhorse, "Blackhorse: Do You Prefer 'Native American' or 'American Indian'? 6 Prominent Voices Respond," *Indian Country Today Media Network*, May 21, 2015, http://indiancountrytodaymedianetwork.com; Amanda Blackhorse, "Blackhorse: 'Native American' or 'American Indian'? 5 More Native Voices Respond," *Indian Country Today Media Network*, July 2, 2015, http://indiancountrytodaymedianetwork.com; Juricek, *Endgame for Empire*, 33, 266n41; Lakomäki, *Gathering Together*, 7–12, 225–29, 241n12; Beck, *Chiefdoms, Collapse, and Coalescence*, 232; Kathleen DuVal, *Independence Lost: Lives on the Edge of the American Revolution* (New York: Random House, 2015), xxii, 358n10; Ethridge, "The Making of a Militaristic Slaving Society," 252; Ethridge, *From Chicaza to Chickasaw*, 2, 257n1.

1 / "The Whole Nation in Common"

The chapter title is taken from Proceedings of a Congress at Pensacola, 16 February 1772, Gage Papers, American Series, vol. 137, folio 13, William L. Clements Library, University of Michigan (hereafter cited as Gage Papers).

1. Green, *The Politics of Indian Removal*, 4; Braund, *Deerskins and Duffels*, 8–18; Piker, *Okfuskee*, 7–10, 127–29; A. Hudson, *Creek Paths and Federal Roads*, 4; Wood, "The Changing Population of the Colonial South," 86; Newton D. Mereness, ed., "David Taitt's Journal of a Journey through the Creek Country, 1772," in *Travels in the American Colonies* (New York: Macmillan, 1916), 528.

2. Ned J. Jenkins, "Tracing the Origins of the Early Creeks, 1050–1700 CE," in *Shatter Zone*, ed. Ethridge and Shuck-Hall, 193, 200–203, 207–8, 218; Adam King, *Etowah: The Political History of a Chiefdom Capital* (Tuscaloosa: University of Alabama Press, 2003), 78–81; Ethridge, *From Chicaza to Chickasaw*, 62, 69–71; Wesson, *Households and Hegemony*, 63, 108; Gregory A. Waselkov and Marvin T. Smith, "Upper Creek Archaeology," in *Indians of the Greater Southeast: Historical Archaeology and Ethnohistory*, ed. Bonnie

G. McEwan, 242–64 (Gainesville: University Press of Florida, 2000); Smith, *Coosa*; John Worth, "The Lower Creeks: Origins and Early History," in *Indians of the Greater Southeast*, ed. McEwan, 265–98; Sheri M. Shuck-Hall, "Alabama and Coushatta Diaspora and Coalescence in the Mississippian Shatter Zone," in *Shatter Zone*, ed. Ethridge and Shuck-Hall, 250–71; J. Hall, *Zamumo's Gifts*, 102–3; Warren, *The Worlds the Shawnees Made*, 105–6, 192, 206, 208–12; Lakomäki, *Gathering Together*, 56–59; Cameron B. Wesson, J. A. Wall, and D. W. Chase, "A Spaghetti Style Gorget from the Jere Shine Site (1MT6), Montgomery County, Alabama," *Journal of Alabama Archaeology* 47, no. 2 (2001): 144–46; Amanda L. Regnier, *Reconstructing Tascalusa's Chiefdom: Pottery Styles and the Social Composition of Late Mississippian Communities along the Alabama River* (Tuscaloosa: University of Alabama Press, 2014), 27–31.

3. Regnier, *Reconstructing Tascalusa's Chiefdom*, 6–7, 16–49, 135–37.

4. Jenkins, "Tracing the Origins of the Early Creeks," 211–16, 226, 231–25; Ethridge, *From Chicaza to Chickasaw*, 68–69; Shuck-Hall, "Alabama and Coushatta Diaspora," 254, 257–63; Worth, "The Lower Creeks," 271–72; J. Hall, *Zamumo's Gifts*, 163; Waselkov and Smith, "Upper Creek Archaeology," 248–49; Warren, *The Worlds the Shawnees Made*, 66, 105–6, 192, 206, 208–12; Lakomäki, *Gathering Together*, 56–59.

5. Jenkins, "Tracing the Origins of the Early Creeks," 218–19, 235; Waselkov and Smith, "Upper Creek Archaeology," 244–47, 255–56; Ethridge, *From Chicaza to Chickasaw*, 62–66, 166–67; Wesson, *Households and Hegemony*, 30; J. Hall, *Zamumo's Gifts*, 146; Warren, *The Worlds the Shawnees Made*, 211–12; Piker, *Okfuskee*, 7, 180; Green, *The Politics of Indian Removal*, 14; A. Hudson, *Creek Paths and Federal Roads*, 3–4; Smith, *Coosa*, 60, 74, 77, 100–117; George Edward Milne, *Natchez Country: Indians, Colonists, and the Landscapes of Race in French Louisiana* (Athens: University of Georgia Press, 2015), 204, 207–8.

6. Wesson, Wall, and Chase, "A Spaghetti Style Gorget from the Jere Shine Site," 144–46; Jenkins, "Tracing the Origins of the Early Creeks," 207, 211, 215; David J. Hally, "Mississippian Shell Gorgets in Regional Perspective," in *Southeastern Ceremonial Complex: Chronology, Content, Context*, ed. Adam King (Tuscaloosa: University of Alabama Press, 2007), 185, 195, 197–99, 205, 208, 213, 216, 218–21, 226–29; Galloway, *Practicing Ethnohistory*, 294–96; O'Brien, *Choctaws in a Revolutionary Age*, 1–3.

7. John H. Blitz and Karl G. Lorenz, *The Chattahoochee Chiefdoms* (Tuscaloosa: University of Alabama Press, 2006), 74–75, 79–87, 94, 100, 102, 108–21, 125, 133–34, 137, 185, 243.

8. Jenkins, "Tracing the Origins of the Early Creeks," 189, 199, 210–11, 217–21, 233–35; Worth, "The Lower Creeks," 267–73, 280–86; Regnier, *Reconstructing Tascalusa's Chiefdom*, 21, 40; Blitz and Lorenz, *The Chattahoochee Chiefdoms*, 137, 193–95; Steven C. Hahn, "The Cussita Migration Legend: History, Ideology, and the Politics of Mythmaking," in *Light on the Path*, ed. Pluckhahn and Ethridge, 75–77; J. Hall, *Zamumo's Gifts*, 78; Ethridge, *From Chicaza to Chickasaw*, 62, 69–70; Foster, *Archaeology of the Lower Muskogee Creek Indians*, 57–60, 70–71, 90–94, 134; Jackson, ed., *Yuchi Indian Histories*, 36–39, 43–48, 55–56, 106, 124–32, 160–61.

9. Ethridge, *Creek Country*, 26–30; Hahn, *The Invention of the Creek Nation*, 5–8; J. Hall, *Zamumo's Gifts*, 137; Martin and Mauldin, *A Dictionary of Creek/Muskogee*, xiii–xvii; T. Dale Nicklas, "Linguistic Provinces of the Southeast at the Time of Columbus," in *Perspectives on the Southeast: Linguistics, Archaeology, and Ethnohistory*, ed. Patricia B. Kwachka (Athens: University of Georgia Press, 1994), 8–9; Jack Martin, "Modeling Language Contact in the Prehistory of the Southeastern United States," ibid., 16–19.

10. Green, *The Politics of Indian Removal*, 4–16; Braund, *Deerskins and Duffels*, 3, 6, 8, 11–12, 15–24; Saunt, *A New Order of Things*, 14, 19–28, 34–37; Ethridge, *Creek Country*, 29–30, 93–108; Piker, *Okfuskee*, 7–10; Hahn, *The Invention of the Creek Nation*, 2–8, 18–26.

11. Wood, "The Changing Population of the Colonial South," 86.

12. Jennings, *New Worlds of Violence*, 95.

13. Proceedings of a Congress of the Chiefs of the Creek Nation held at Pensacola, West Florida and John Stuart, Enclosure in Stuart to Gage, 16 February 1772, Gage Papers, vol. 137, folio 13; Thomas Gage to John Stuart, 22 June 1772, Gage Papers, vol. 112.

14. Captain Musgrave's 164th Regiment Intelligence about a Road from South Carolina to Pensacola, 1771, Gage Papers, vol. 108.

15. Ibid.

16. Piker, "'White & Clean' & Contested," 317; Wood, "The Changing Population of the Colonial South," 60, 84–87.

17. Extract from the Address of the Council of West Florida to the Earl of Hillsborough transmitted by Lieutenant Governor Elias Durnford, July 1770, Gage Papers, vol. 108.

18. Abstract of a Letter from Lieutenant Governor Elias Durnford of West Florida to the Earl of Hillsborough, Abstract no. 171, 8 July 1770, Gage Papers, vol. 108; O'Brien, *Choctaws in a Revolutionary Age*, 27–28, 35, 39, 48, 51, 61, 84–85; Juricek, *Endgame for Empire*, 112–15, 122, 140–46, 196; Greg O'Brien, "Protecting Trade through War: Choctaw Elites and the British Occupation of the Floridas," in *Pre-Removal Choctaw History: Exploring New Paths*, ed. O'Brien (Norman: University of Oklahoma Press, 2008), 102–22; *Early American Indian Documents: Treaties and Laws, 1607–1789*, ed. John T. Juricek, vol. 12, *Georgia and Florida Treaties, 1763–1776* (Bethesda: University Publications of America, 2002), 284–88, 325–32, 361–63 (hereafter cited as *EAID*); Harrell, "The Terrain of Factionalism," 89–91, 98, 102, 105.

19. Abstract of a Letter from Lieutenant Governor Elias Durnford of West Florida to the Earl of Hillsborough, Abstract no. 171, 8 July 1770, Gage Papers, vol. 108; Lieutenant Governor Durnford's Reply to the Upper Creeks, 13 March 1770, *EAID*, 12:354; Upper Creeks to Charles Stuart, September 1770, ibid., 12:372.

20. Abstract of a Letter from Lieutenant Governor Elias Durnford of West Florida to the Earl of Hillsborough, Abstract no. 171, 8 July 1770, Gage Papers, vol. 108; John Stuart to Escotchaby, Sempoyasse, & the White King, Chiefs of The Cowetas, Capt Aleck of the Cussitaws and Tallechi Great medal Chief & Head of Ten Lower Towns, 16 October 1771, Gage Papers, vol. 108.

21. Abstract of a Letter from Lieutenant Governor Elias Durnford to the Earl of Hillsborough, Abstract no. 22, 14 July 1770, Gage Papers, vol. 108.

22. Proceedings of a Congress of the Chiefs of the Creek Nation held at Pensacola, West Florida and John Stuart. cy. made and signed by William Ogilvy, 32 pp., n.d., enclosure in John Stuart to Thomas Gage, 16 February 1772, Gage Papers, vol. 137, folio 13; Ethridge, *Creek Country*, 27, 82–87, 136–37.

23. Thomas Gage to John Stuart, 20 January 1771, Gage Papers, vol. 109.

24. J. Leitch Wright Jr., *Creeks and Seminoles: The Destruction and Regeneration of the Muscogulge People* (Lincoln: University of Nebraska Press, 1986), 102; Wood, "The Changing Population of the Colonial South," 60, 80.

25. Qtd. from Upper Creek "Great Talk" to Superintendent [John] Stuart and Governor [James] Wright, 10 April 1764, *EAID*, 12:212. See also Emistisiguo and Other

Upper Creek Headmen to Superintendent [John] Stuart, 15 July 1764, ibid., 12:216; The Mortar and Other Upper Creek Headmen to Superintendent [John] Stuart, Rejecting Trade from West Florida, 22 July 1764, ibid., 12:218; Congress at Pensacola: Proceedings Following the Treaty, 30 May 1765, ibid., 12:271–72; Upper Creek Headmen to Superintendent [John] Stuart, Declaring Issue of Oconee Murders Settled and Complaining of Encroachments, 1 May 1771, ibid., 12:97, 519n64; Proceedings of the Second Pensacola Congress with the Upper Creeks, 31 October 1771, ibid., 12:398; Upper Creeks to Superintendent [John] Stuart, Rejecting any Further Cession, 19 April 1772, ibid., 12:427; Deposition of William Smith and William Gregory, November 1770, ibid., 12:378–79; Emistisiguo to Superintendent [John] Stuart, 19 April 1772, ibid., 12:428.

26. The Royal Proclamation, 7 October 1763, Avalon Project: Documents in Law, History, and Diplomacy, Lillian Goldman Law Library, Yale Law School, http://avalon.law.yale.edu; Louis De Vorsey Jr., *The Indian Boundary in the Southern Colonies, 1763–1775* (1961; Chapel Hill: University of North Carolina Press, 1966), 34–36; Alan Gallay, *The Formation of a Planter Elite: Jonathan Bryan and the Southern Colonial Frontier* (Athens: University of Georgia Press, 1989), 110.

27. John Stuart to Peter Chester, 30 August 1771, Gage Papers, vol. 108.

28. Ibid.

29. Ibid.; White, *The Middle Ground*, 351–54.

30. John Stuart to Peter Chester, 30 August 1771, Gage Papers, vol. 108.

31. John Stuart to Thomas Gage, 28 September 1771, Gage Papers, vol. 108.

32. Ibid.

33. Ibid.

34. O'Brien, *Choctaws in a Revolutionary Age*, 27–28, 35, 39, 48, 51, 61, 84–85; Juricek, *Endgame for Empire*, 112–15, 122, 140–46, 196; O'Brien, "Protecting Trade through War," 102–22; *EAID*, 12:284–88, 325–32, 361–63; Harrell, "The Terrain of Factionalism," 89–91, 98, 102, 105.

35. Peter Chester to John Stuart, 10 September 1771, Gage Papers, vol. 108.

36. Ibid.

37. Ibid.

38. Ibid.

39. Proceedings of a Congress of the Chiefs of the Creek Nation held at Pensacola, West Florida and John Stuart, Enclosure in Stuart to Gage 16 February 1772, Gage Papers, vol. 137, folio 13.

40. Peter Chester to John Stuart, 10 September 1771, Gage Papers, vol. 108.

41. Ibid.

42. The declaration of John Stuart Esqr Superintendent of Indian Affairs in the southern district Entered on the Minutes of the Council of West Florida October 1771, Gage Papers, vol. 108.

43. John Stuart to Escotchaby Sempoyasse & the White King, Chiefs of The Cowetas, Capt Aleck of the Cussitaws and Tallechi Great medal Chief & Head of Ten Lower Towns, 16 October 1771, Gage Papers, vol. 108. David Taitt later insisted that the perpetrators were Eufaulas and Oconees, rather than Yuchis and Chiscalaloos. Mereness, ed., "David Taitt's Journal of a Journey through the Creek Country, 1772," 551.

44. John E. Worth, "Enigmatic Origins: On the Yuchi of the Contact Era," in *Yuchi Indian Histories*, ed. Jackson, 37–39; Ethridge, *From Chicaza to Chickasaw*, 85, 209; Saunt, *A New Order of Things*, 182.

45. Mereness, ed., "David Taitt's Journal of a Journey through the Creek Country, 1772," 547, 554, 558–59.

46. Ibid., 551–57.

47. Worth, "The Lower Creeks," 287; Wesson, *Households and Hegemony*, 102; J. Hall, *Zamumo's Gifts*, 87, 146, 148; Ethridge, *From Chicaza to Chickasaw*, 86, 100; Foster, *Archaeology of the Lower Muskogee Creek Indians*, 68–69.

48. Foster, *Archaeology of the Lower Muskogee Creek Indians*, 60–62.

49. The declaration of John Stuart Esqr Superintendent of Indian Affairs in the southern district Entered on the Minutes of the Council of West Florida October 1771, Gage Papers, vol. 108; John Stuart to Escotchaby Sempoyasse & the White King, Chiefs of The Cowetas, Capt Aleck of the Cussitaws and Tallechi Great medal Chief & Head of Ten Lower Towns, 16 October 1771, Gage Papers, vol. 108. For a different interpretation, see Harrell, "The Terrain of Factionalism."

50. Emistisiguo to Superintendent [John] Stuart, Postponing Marking the Boundary, 12 July 1769, *EAID*, 12:348; Upper Creeks to Charles Stuart, September 1770, *EAID*, 12:372; Congress at Pensacola with the Upper and Lower Creeks: Proceeding before the Treaty, 27–28 May 1765, ibid., 12:262, 264, 541n100; Juricek, *Endgame for Empire*, 76; Saunt, *A New Order of Things*, 15–21, 42; Wesson, *Households and Hegemony*, 24–25; Ethridge, *From Chicaza to Chickasaw*, 23; Braund, *Deerskins and Duffels*, 142, 252n12; Bryan C. Rindfleisch, "The 'Owner of the Town Ground, Who Overrules All When on the Spot': Escotchaby of Coweta and the Politics of Personal Networking in Creek Country, 1740–1780," *Native South* 9 (2016): 58; Harrell, "The Terrain of Factionalism."

51. John Stuart to Thomas Gage, 23 May 1772, Gage Papers, vol. 111; Mereness, ed., "David Taitt's Journal of a Journey through the Creek Country, 1772," 507, 523–24.

52. Congress at Pensacola with the Upper and Lower Creeks: Proceeding before the Treaty, 27–28 May 1765, *EAID*, 12:262; Braund, *Deerskins and Duffels*, 162; Saunt, *A New Order of Things*, 19–21, 81–82, 96.

53. Juricek, *Endgame for Empire*, 80–81, 95–96.

54. Wesson, *Households and Hegemony*, 25–26, 39–42, 51–53, 71–73, 80–81, 86–87, 109–11, 126, 129–31; Wesson, "Prestige Goods, Symbolic Capital, and Social Power in the Protohistoric Southeast"; Wesson, "Creek and Pre-Creek Revisited," 101–5; Wesson, "When Moral Economies and Capitalism Meet"; Adam King, "Creek Chiefdoms at the Temporal Edge of the Mississippian World," *Southeastern Archaeology* 21, no. 2 (Winter 2002): 221–26; Jenkins, "Tracing the Origins of the Early Creeks," 119; David G. Anderson, *The Savannah River Chiefdoms: Political Change in the Late Prehistoric Southeast* (Tuscaloosa: University of Alabama Press, 1994), 1–48; Galloway, *Practicing Ethnohistory*, 292–97, 302–8, 324; Piker, *Okfuskee*, 66; Piker, "'White & Clean' & Contested," 315–20; Paulette, *An Empire of Small Places*, 118, 220n11; Ethridge, *Creek Country*, 2, 253n10, 9–10, 23–26; Immanuel Wallerstein, *The Modern World System: Capitalist Agriculture and the Origin of the European World Economy in the Sixteenth Century* (New York: Academic Press, 1974); Harrell, "The Terrain of Factionalism," 88, 91–92.

55. Proceedings of the Second Pensacola Congress with the Upper Creeks, 29 October 1771, *EAID*, 12:387–88; Juricek, *Endgame for Empire*, 80–81.

56. Carson, "Ethnogeography and the Native American Past," 769–88.

57. Proceedings of a Congress at Pensacola, 16 February 1772, Gage Papers, vol. 137, folio 13; Braund, *Deerskins and Duffels*, 149; Kathryn E. Holland Braund, "'Like a

Stone Wall Never to Be Broke': The British-Indian Boundary Line with Creek Indians, 1763–1773," in *Britain and the American South from Colonialism to Rock and Roll*, ed. Franklin T. Lambert and Joseph P. Ward (Jackson: University Press of Mississippi, 2003), 70–72.

58. Proceedings of a Congress at Pensacola, 16 February 1772, Gage Papers, vol. 137, folio 13.

59. Upper Creek Chiefs to Superintendent [John] Stuart, Replying to His December 17 Talk, 20 April 1767, *EAID*, 12:335.

60. Provincial Council: Talks with Emistisiguo, 3 September 1768, *EAID*, 12:51.

61. Upper Creeks to Charles Stuart, September 1770, *EAID*, 12:372; Emistisiguo to Charles Stuart, Explaining Accompanying Peace Belt to the Choctaws, 13 December 1770, ibid., 12:373; Emistisiguo and the Mortar to the Choctaws, Explaining Peace Tokens, 13 December 1770, ibid., 12:375.

62. Martin and Mauldin, *A Dictionary of Creek/Muskogee*, 41, 276; R. M. Loughridge and David M. Hodge, *English and Muskokee Dictionary* (St. Louis: Printing House of J. T. Smith, 1890), 52, 201.

63. Proceedings of a Congress at Pensacola, 16 February 1772, Gage Papers, vol. 137, folio 13.

64. Ibid.

65. Ibid.

66. Ibid.

67. Ibid.

68. Ibid.

69. Ibid.

70. Charles Stuart to Superintendent [John] Stuart, Reporting Council Meeting with Emistisiguo and Apparent Peace, 17 June 1770, *EAID*, 12:358.

71. Hahn, *The Invention of the Creek Nation*, 226; Rindfleisch, "The 'Owner of the Town Ground,'" 55, 60; Bryan Rindfleisch, "'Our Lands Are Our Life and Breath': Coweta, Cusseta, and the Struggle for Creek Territory and Sovereignty during the American Revolution," *Ethnohistory* 60, no. 4 (Fall 2013): 588, 601n25; Harrell, "The Terrain of Factionalism," 80–97, 110–11; Edward J. Cashin, *William Bartram and the American Revolution on the Southern Frontier* (Columbia: University of South Carolina Press, 2000), 73.

72. *EAID*, 12:5–6; Deposition of William Frazier, 2 July 1768, *EAID*, 12:41–43; Commissary [Roderick] McIntosh to Superintendent [John] Stuart, 18 April 1768, *EAID*, 12:43–44; Commissary [Roderick] McIntosh to Superintendent [John] Stuart, on Emistisiguo's "Authorized" Raid, 29 May 1768, *EAID*, 12:44–46.

73. Saunt, *A New Order of Things*, 17, 23–24, 31–34, 144–48; Braund, *Deerskins and Duffels*, 68–69, 100–101, 105–6, 131, 146, 158; Piker, *Okfuskee*, 52–63, 100–101, 152–55, 163–65, 176–95.

74. Proceedings of a Congress at Pensacola, 16 February 1772, Gage Papers, vol. 137, folio 13.

75. Thomas Gage to Lord Viscount Barrington, Secretary at War, 4 March 1772, Gage Papers, English Series, vol. 21.

76. Thomas Gage to John Stuart, 22 June 1772, Gage Papers, vol. 112.

77. Treaty of Pensacola, 2 November 1771, Gage Papers, vol. 108; Proceedings of a Congress at Pensacola, 16 February 1772, Gage Papers, vol. 137, folio 13. Thirteen

leaders are named in the treaty, but the text states that representatives from "Sixteen Towns of the Alibamus, Abekas, and Tallipouses" were present. See also *EAID*, 12:365, 561n26, 403, 565–66n76.

78. John Stuart to Thomas Gage, 14 December 1771, Gage Papers, vol. 108.

79. Ibid.; Proceedings of a Congress at Pensacola, 16 February 1772, Gage Papers, vol. 137, folio 13.

80. To William Ogilvy Dr. for Sundry goods bought by order of the Honorable John Stuart . . . for the use of the Congress Held at Mobile November 1771 to 1 January 1772, report dated 6 February 1772, Gage Papers, vol. 109. See J. Hall, *Zamumo's Gifts*, 7–11.

81. Proceedings of a Congress at Pensacola, 16 February 1772, Gage Papers, vol. 137, folio 13.

82. Braund, "Like a Stone Wall Never to Be Broke," 69; J. Hall, *Zamumo's Gifts*, 62–64.

83. Mereness, ed., "David Taitt's Journal of a Journey through the Creek Country, 1772," 509, 536.

84. Proceedings of a Congress at Pensacola, 16 February 1772, Gage Papers, vol. 137, folio 13.

85. Ibid.; Mereness, ed., "David Taitt's Journal of a Journey through the Creek Country, 1772," 508, 539.

86. Ibid.

87. Ibid.

88. *EAID*, 12:80; Hahn, *Inventing the Creek Nation*, 70, 124, 170, 200, 259, 272; Hahn, "They Look upon the Yuchis as Their Vassals," 143–44; Foster, *Archaeology of the Lower Muskogee Creek Indians*, 6, 15; Smith, *Coosa*, 62.

89. Mereness, ed., "David Taitt's Journal of a Journey through the Creek Country, 1772," 511–16, 518–20; Ethridge, *Creek Country*, 84; Green, *Politics of Indian Removal*, 26–27; Piker, *Okfuskee*, 49–50, 86–87, 115, 179–80; A. Hudson, *Creek Paths and Federal Roads*, 3–4.

90. "Congress at Pensacola with the Upper and Lower Creeks: Proceedings before the Treaty," *EAID*, 12:262; Harrell, "The Terrain of Factionalism," 91–102.

91. A Talk from Emistisigo and other Chiefs of the Upper Creek Nation to Governor James Wright, 1 May 1771, Allen D. Candler, ed., *The Colonial Records of the State of Georgia*, vol. 28, pt. 2 (Atlanta: Franklin Printing and Publishing Co., 1904–16; New York: AMS, 1970), 365–69. Citations refer to the AMS edition (hereafter cited as *CRG*).

92. Saunt, *A New Order of Things*, 15–17.

93. A Talk from Emistisigo and other Chiefs of the Upper Creek Nation to Governor James Wright, 1 May 1771, *CRG*, vol. 28, pt. 2:366.

94. Ibid.; De Vorsey, *The Indian Boundary in the Southern Colonies*, 34–36; Braund, "Like a Stone Wall Never to Be Broke," 70–72.

95. A Talk from Emistisigo and other Chiefs of the Upper Creek Nation to Governor James Wright, 1 May 1771, *CRG*, vol. 28, pt. 2:366.

96. Ibid., 367.

97. Ibid.

98. Mereness, ed., "David Taitt's Journal of a Journey through the Creek Country, 1772," 508.

99. A Talk from Emistisigo and other Chiefs of the Upper Creek Nation to Governor James Wright, 1 May 1771, *CRG*, vol. 28, pt. 2:367.

100. Braund, "Like a Stone Wall Never to Be Broke," 55–59; Jennings, *New Worlds of Violence*, 1, 15–18, 23, 26–27, 65, 69–71, 81–83, 95; Hahn, *The Invention of the Creek Nation*, 15; J. Hall, *Zamumo's Gifts*, 1–2, 17–20, 24, 78; Snyder, *Slavery in Indian Country*, 13–45.

101. A Talk from Emistisigo and other Chiefs of the Upper Creek Nation to Governor James Wright, 1 May 1771, *CRG*, vol. 28, pt. 2:367.

102. Journal of the Congress of the Four Southern Governors, and the Superintendent of that District, with the Five Nations of Indians, at Augusta, 1763 (Charles Town, South Carolina: Printed by Peter Timothy, 1764), Early American Imprints, Series 1, Evans, 1639–1800, no. 9706, 38–42; A Talk from Emistisigo and other Chiefs of the Upper Creek Nation to Governor James Wright, 1 May 1771, *CRG*, vol. 28, pt. 2:367; Proceedings of a Congress at Pensacola, 16 February 1772, Gage papers, vol. 137, folio 13; Mereness, ed., "David Taitt's Journal of a Journey through the Creek Country, 1772," 509, 536.

103. A Talk from Emistisigo and other Chiefs of the Upper Creek Nation to Governor James Wright, 1 May 1771, *CRG*, vol. 28, pt. 2:368.

104. Ibid.

105. Ibid.

106. Memorial of James Wright to the Earl of Hillsborough, with several enclosures, 12 December 1771, *CRG*, vol. 28, pt. 2:350.

107. Ibid., 351.

108. Ibid.

109. Ibid.

110. Quote from Governor Wright's Reply to Upper Creek Talk of May 1, 25 June 1771, *EAID*, 12:105; *EAID*, 12:80; Lower Creek Headmen to Governor Wright, 5 September 1770, ibid., 12:92–93; Governor Wright to Lower Creeks, Protesting Murders near Oconee River, 2 October 1770, ibid., 12:93–94; Lower Creek Reply to Governor Wright's Protest, November 1770, ibid., 12:94; George Galphin to Superintendent [John] Stuart, 19 February 1771, ibid., 12:95; Upper Creek Headmen to Superintendent Stuart, Declaring Issue of Oconee Murders Settled and Complaining of Encroachments, 1 May 1771, ibid., 12:96–98.

111. Memorial of James Wright to the Earl of Hillsborough, with several enclosures, 12 December 1771, *CRG*, vol. 28, pt. 2:350, 353; A Talk from Governor James Wright to Emistisigo and the Gun Merchant, 25 June 1771, ibid., vol. 28, pt. 2:370.

112. Memorial of James Wright to the Earl of Hillsborough, with several enclosures, 12 December 1771, *CRG*, vol. 28, pt. 2:357.

113. Ibid., 354.

114. William Bartram, *The Travels of William Bartram: Naturalist's Edition by William Bartram*, ed. Francis Harper (editorial material copyright, New Haven: Yale University Press, 1958; Athens: University of Georgia Press, 1998), 379.

115. Ibid., 380.

116. Earl of Hillsborough to James Habersham, 1 April 1772, Marquis of Wills Hill Downshire, Hargrett Rare Book and Manuscript Library, University of Georgia Libraries, presented in the Digital Library of Georgia (hereafter cited as HAR DLG).

117. Ibid.

118. Mereness, ed., "David Taitt's Journal of a Journey through the Creek Country, 1772," 526–27, 539.

119. Journal of the Upper House of Assembly, 22 April 1772, *CRG*, 17:657; John Stuart to Thomas Gage, 23 May 1772, Gage Papers, vol. 111.

120. Worth, "The Lower Creeks," 282; Ethridge, *From Chicaza to Chickasaw*, 112, 166; Foster, *Archaeology of the Lower Muskogee Creek Indians*, 54–57; Worth, "Enigmatic Origins," 33, 36–37; Ethridge, *Creek Country*, 50, 62; Hahn, *The Invention of the Creek Nation*, 168; Smith, *Coosa*, 35, 47–48, 60–62, 81, 87; Robin A. Beck Jr., "Catawba Coalescence and the Shattering of the Carolina Piedmont, 1540–1675," in *Shatter Zone*, ed. Ethridge and Shuck-Hall, 124–26, 129.

121. Braund, *Deerskins and Duffels*, 155–56; Hahn, *The Invention of the Creek Nation*, 212–17; Piker, *Okfuskee*, 59–60; Joshua Piker, "Lying Together: The Imperial Implications of Cross-Cultural Untruths," *American Historical Review* 116, no. 4 (October 2011): 964–86; Joshua Piker, *The Four Deaths of Acorn Whistler: Telling Stories in Colonial America* (Cambridge: Harvard University Press, 2013).

122. John Stuart to Thomas Gage, 22 April 1773, Gage Papers, vol. 118.

123. Mereness, ed., "David Taitt's Journal of a Journey through the Creek Country, 1772," 509–10.

124. Ibid.

125. Stephen Forrester to John Stuart, 7 September 1772, Gage Papers, vol. 114.

126. Thomas Gage to John Stuart, 21 June 1772, Gage Papers, vol. 112.

127. John Stuart to Thomas Gage, 7 September 1772, Gage Papers, vol. 114.

128. Stephen Forrester to John Stuart, 7 September 1772, Gage Papers, vol. 114; Mereness, ed., "David Taitt's Journal of a Journey through the Creek Country, 1772," 524–25.

129. Mereness, ed., "David Taitt's Journal of a Journey through the Creek Country, 1772," 507, 513–14, 518–20, 524–25, 543–44.

130. Protest from Emistisiguo and Lower Creek Headmen over Proposed Cherokee Cession, 20 August 1771, *EAID*, 12:106.

131. *EAID*, 12:82–87; Protest from Emistisiguo and Lower Creek Headmen over Proposed Cherokee Cession, 20 August 1771, ibid., 12:106; Commissary [David] Taitt to Superintendent [John] Stuart, 21 September 1772, ibid., 12:114–15.

132. Deposition of Joseph Dawes, 4 August 1772, Gage Papers, vol. 114.

133. Conference between Sir James Wright and Upper Creek Indians, 14 April 1774, in *Documents of the American Revolution, 1770–1783 (Colonial Office Series)*, ed. K. G. Davies, vol. 8, *Transcripts, 1773* (Dublin: Irish University Press, 1975), 93 (hereafter cited as *DAR*).

134. Ibid.; Mereness, ed., "David Taitt's Journal of a Journey through the Creek Country, 1772," 515.

135. Deposition of Joseph Dawes, 4 August 1772, Gage Papers, vol. 114.

136. Ibid.

137. Ibid.

138. Ibid.

139. Ibid.

140. Snyder, *Slavery in Indian Country*, 134–45.

141. Braund, *Deerskins and Duffels*, 62–63, 133; Ethridge, *Creek Country*, 28, 135–37; A. Hudson, *Creek Paths and Federal Roads*, 4; Hahn, *The Invention of the Creek Nation*, 10–13, 26–29, 34–39, 157–63, 180, 186–210; Ethridge, *From Chicaza to Chickasaw*, 71–74; Proceedings of a Congress at Pensacola, 16 February 1772, Gage Papers,

vol. 137, folio 13; A Talk from the Lower Creeks to John Stuart Esqr dated at Pallachicola 19 September 1772 delivered to Mr. David Taitt, Gage Papers, vol. 115; Saunt, *A New Order of Things*, 40–42.

142. Deposition of Joseph Dawes, 4 August 1772, Gage Papers, vol. 114.

143. A Talk from the Lower Creeks to John Stuart Esqr dated at Pallachicola 19 September 1772 delivered to Mr. David Taitt, Gage Papers, vol. 115.

144. Jenkins, "Tracing the Origins of the Early Creeks," 189, 200, 217–21, 228; Worth, "The Lower Creeks," 270–72, 281; J. Hall, *Zamumo's Gifts*, 78–80; Foster, *Archaeology of the Lower Muskogee Creek Indians*, 90–92.

145. Rindfleisch, "The 'Owner of the Town Ground.'"

146. A Talk from the Lower Creeks to John Stuart Esqr dated at Pallachicola 19 September 1772 delivered to Mr. David Taitt, Gage Papers, vol. 115; Braund, *Deerskins and Duffels*, 133, 150–51.

147. Hahn, *The Invention of the Creek Nation*, 220–25; Braund, *Deerskins and Duffels*, 133; Boulware, *Deconstructing the Cherokee Nation*, 57–74.

148. A Talk from the Lower Creeks to John Stuart Esqr dated at Pallachicola 19 September 1772 delivered to Mr. David Taitt, Gage Papers, vol. 115; John Stuart to Thomas Gage, 24 November 1772, Gage Papers, vol. 115.

149. A Talk from the Lower Creeks to John Stuart Esqr dated at Pallachicola 19 September 1772 delivered to Mr. David Taitt, Gage Papers, vol. 115; Saunt, *A New Order of Things*, 143–50.

150. A Talk from the Lower Creeks to John Stuart Esqr dated at Pallachicola 19 September 1772 delivered to Mr. David Taitt, Gage Papers, vol. 115.

151. Ibid.; John Stuart to Thomas Gage, 24 November 1772, Gage Papers, vol. 115.

152. A Talk from the Lower Creeks to John Stuart Esqr dated at Pallachicola 19 September 1772 delivered to Mr. David Taitt, Gage Papers, vol. 115; Mereness, ed., "David Taitt's Journal of a Journey through the Creek Country, 1772," 548–49; Worth, "The Lower Creeks," 272–73.

153. Mereness, ed., "David Taitt's Journal of a Journey through the Creek Country, 1772," 520; Piker, *Okfuskee*, 87–88.

154. David Taitt to John Stuart, 19 October 1772, Gage Papers, vol. 115.

155. Mereness, ed., "David Taitt's Journal of a Journey through the Creek Country, 1772," 552.

156. Cashin, *William Bartram*, 54.

157. John Stuart to Thomas Gage, 24 November 1772, Gage Papers, vol. 115.

158. Thomas Gage to John Stuart, 20 December 1772, Gage Papers, vol. 116.

159. Abstract of a letter from Alexander Cameron Esq Deputy Superintendent of Indian Affairs dated Lochaber near Keowee, 30 December 1772, Gage Papers, vol. 116; Cashin, *William Bartram*, 20–21.

160. Journal of Commons House, 12 March 1773, *CRG*, 15:425; John Stuart to Thomas Gage, 22 April 1773, Gage Papers, vol. 118.

161. Abstract of a Letter from Charles Stuart Esqr dated Mobile 17th March 1773, Gage Papers, vol. 118; John Stuart to Thomas Gage, 22 April 1773, Gage Papers, vol. 118.

162. Bartram, *The Travels of William Bartram*, 307; 1773 Treaty of Augusta, in Indian Treaties, Cessions of Land in Georgia, 1705-1837, ed. Louise F. [Mrs. J. E.] Hays, Georgia Archives, 70–74 (hereafter cited as ITCL); 1773 Treaty of Augusta, *CRG*,

39:496–499; *EAID*, 12:86; David Taitt to Patrick Tonyn, 3 May 1776, vol. 16, folio 40, Henry Clinton Papers, William L. Clements Library, University of Michigan (hereafter cited as Clinton Papers).

163. Bartram, *The Travels of William Bartram*, 22.

164. Ibid.; Cashin, *William Bartram*, 53–54; John Stuart to Thomas Gage, 8 August 1774, Gage Papers, vol. 122.

165. Treaty at Augusta, ITCL, 72.

166. Cashin, *William Bartram*, 63–65, 70.

167. Bartram, *The Travels of William Bartram*, 28.

168. Ibid., 23.

169. Ibid., 30.

170. Cashin, *William Bartram*, 66.

2 / "Neither the Abicas, Tallapuses, nor Alibamas Desire to Have Any Thing to Say to the Cowetas but Desire Peace"

The chapter title comes from A Talk Delivered by the Creeks at Augusta 23 August 1774, Gage Papers, vol. 123.

1. Governor Sir James Wright to Earl of Dartmouth (No. 3), 17 June 1773, *DAR*, 6:156; Juricek, *Endgame for Empire*, 183.

2. Governor Sir James Wright to Earl of Dartmouth (No. 3), 17 June 1773, *DAR*, 6:158.

3. Ibid., 157.

4. Piker, *Okfuskee*, 63–74, quotes from 72, 73, and 74; Braund, *Deerskins and Duffels*, 163.

5. Braund, *Deerskins and Duffels*, 158–63; Cashin, *William Bartram*, 71–75; *EAID*, 12:123–26, 368–70; Wesson, "Creek and Pre-Creek Revisited," 96; Juricek, *Endgame for Empire*, 178–81, 186–203, 215–16; Rindfleisch, "Our Lands Are Our Life and Breath," 586–88.

6. Snyder, *Slavery in Indian Country*, 84–87, 91–98, 165–68; Stephen Ellis, "Interpreting Violence: Reflections on West African War," in *Violence*, ed. Whitehead, 107–24; Hahn, *Inventing the Creek Nation*, 139–41, 173–84, 195–200, 210–16, 234–35, 247, 253–60; Sweet, *Negotiating for Georgia*, 140–58; Piker, *Okfuskee*, 45–63, 77–78, 82–86, 100–102, 163–65, 176–91; J. Hall, *Zamumo's Gifts*, 146–51; Adair, *History of the American Indians*, 171, 297; Saunt, *A New Order of Things*, 16–17, 23–24, 31–34; John R. Swanton, *Creek Religion and Medicine* (Lincoln: University of Nebraska Press, 2000), 484–85, 518, 536–39, 542, 544, 549, 570, 570–73, 583, 585, 609–10; John R. Swanton, *Myths and Tales of the Southeastern Indians* (Norman: University of Oklahoma Press, 1995), 8–9, 21, 57–58, 115, 147–48, 155–57; Whitehead, "On the Poetics of Violence," 55–77.

7. Juricek, *Endgame for Empire*, 187–89; Rindfleisch, "The 'Owner of the Town Ground, Who Overrules All When on the Spot,'" 64, 66.

8. David Taitt to John Stuart, 24 January 1774, *DAR*, 7:43; *South Carolina Gazette*, 31 January 1774; James Wright to Earl of Dartmouth, 31 January 1774, ibid., 8:30–32; James Wright to the Head Men and Warriours in the Upper and Lower Creek Countrys, 1 February 1774, ITCL, 75; *Georgia Gazette*, 2 February 1774; John Stuart to Frederick Haldimand, 3 February 1774, *DAR*, 8:34–37; *South Carolina Gazette*, 14 February 1774; John Stuart to Earl of Dartmouth, 13 February 1774, ibid., 8:48–49;

Georgia Gazette, 16 March 1774; Conference between Sir James Wright and Upper Creek Indians, 14 April 1774, *DAR*, 8:90–95; Braund, *Deerskins and Duffels*, 158–63; *EAID*, 12:123–26; Cashin, *William Bartram*, 71–75; Piker, *Okfuskee*, 63–74.

9. *Georgia Gazette*, 2 February 1774; *South Carolina Gazette*, 14 February 1774; Adair, *History of the American Indian*, 91, 182–189; Saunt, *New Order*, 91–94; Snyder, *Slavery in Indian Country*, 80–100; Charles Hudson, *Conversations with the High Priest of Coosa* (Chapel Hill: University of North Carolina Press, 2003), 145–51; Reid, *A Law of Blood*, 99, 103, 108, 153–62, 168–70.

10. Cashin, *William Bartram*, 71; *EAID*, 12:123; John Stuart to Frederick Haldimand, 3 February 1774, *DAR*, 8:34–36; James Wright to Frederick Haldimand, 18 April 1774, Gage Papers, vol. 119; John Stuart to Frederick Haldimand, 5 July 1774, ibid., vol. 121.

11. John Stuart to Frederick Haldimand, 5 July 1774, Gage Papers, vol. 121; David Taitt to John Stuart, 18 July 1774, ibid., vol. 122; Cashin, *William Bartram*, 73; Piker, *Okfuskee*, 68.

12. David Taitt to John Stuart, 24 January 1774, *DAR*, 8:43.

13. John Stuart to Earl of Dartmouth, 13 February 1774, *DAR*, 8:48.

14. James Wright to Earl of Dartmouth, 31 January 1774, *DAR*, 8:32; Conference between Sir James Wright and Upper Creek Indians, 14 April 1774, ibid., 8:94; *EAID*, 12:142; Braund, *Deerskins and Duffels*, 158–63. Governor Wright later came to believe that Ochtullkee murdered his companion and blamed William White to conceal his guilt. Braund endorses that interpretation.

15. *EAID*, 12:5, 36–39, 510n28.

16. Braund, *Deerskins and Duffels*, 158–63.

17. John Stuart to Frederick Haldimand, 3 February 1774, *DAR*, 8:35.

18. Ibid., 8:34.

19. *Georgia Gazette*, 2 February 1774.

20. *South Carolina Gazette*, 31 January 1774; James Wright to Earl of Dartmouth, 31 January 1774, *DAR*, 8:30; Governor James Wright to the Head Men and Warriours in the Upper and Lower Creek Countrys, 1 February 1774, ITCL, 75; *Georgia Gazette*, 2 February 1774; John Stuart to Frederick Haldimand, 3 February 1774, *DAR*, 8:34; *South Carolina Gazette*, 14 February 1774; *Georgia Gazette*, 16 March 1774; Braund, *Deerskins and Duffels*, 159.

21. James Wright to Earl of Dartmouth, 31 January 1774, *DAR*, 8:30; John Stuart to Frederick Haldimand, 3 February 1774, ibid., 8:34.

22. Braund, *Deerskins and Duffels*, 159–160; Cashin, *William Bartram*, 72–73; *Georgia Gazette*, 2 February 1774.

23. *South Carolina Gazette*, 14 February 1774; John Stuart to Frederick Haldimand, 3 February 1774, *DAR*, 8:34.

24. James Wright to Earl of Dartmouth, 31 January 1774, *DAR*, 8:30.

25. *South Carolina Gazette*, 31 January 1774; James Wright to Earl of Dartmouth, 31 January 1774, *DAR*, 8:30.

26. James Wright to Earl of Dartmouth, 31 January 1774, *DAR*, 8:30.

27. *South Carolina Gazette*, 14 February 1774; John Stuart to Earl of Dartmouth, 13 February 1774, *DAR*, 8:48.

28. J. Hall, *Zamumo's Gifts*, 107; Jennings, *New Worlds of Violence*, 134–35.

29. James Wright to Earl of Dartmouth, 31 January 1774, *DAR*, 8:31.

30. Ibid., 32.

31. Ibid., 31.

32. John Stuart to Frederick Haldimand, 3 February 1774, *DAR*, 8:36.

33. Ibid.

34. James Wright to Earl of Dartmouth, 31 January 1774, *DAR*, 8:31; Braund, *Deerskins and Duffels*, 163.

35. James Wright to Frederick Haldimand, 18 April 1774, Gage Papers, vol. 119; James Wright to the Head Men and Warriours in the Upper and Lower Creek Countrys, 1 February 1774, ITCL, 75.

36. James Brown and David H. Dye, "Severed Heads and Sacred Scalplocks: Mississippian Iconographic Trophies," in *The Taking and Displaying of Human Body Parts as Trophies by Amerindians*, ed. Richard J. Chacon and Dye (New York: Springer Science+Business Media, 2007), 278–98, esp. 293–94; Keith P. Jacobi, "Disabling the Dead: Human Trophy Taking in the Prehistoric Southeast," ibid., 299–338, esp. 299–306, 332–34.

37. Governor Sir James Wright to Earl of Dartmouth, No. 11, 31 January 1774, *DAR*, 7:31.

38. Conference between Sir James Wright and Upper Creek Indians, 14 April 1774, *DAR*, 8:90–95. In this conference, both Captain Aleck of Cussita and Emistisiguo of Little Tallassee repudiated the White-Sherrill affair.

39. *South Carolina Gazette*, 14 February 1774; *EAID*, 12:35, 136–41; Juricek, *Endgame for Empire*, 189; Rindfleisch, "The 'Owner of the Town Ground Who Overrules All When on the Spot,'" 70; Braund, *Deerskins and Duffels*, 159.

40. *Georgia Gazette*, 2 February 1774; *South Carolina Gazette*, 14 February 1774; *Georgia Gazette*, 16 March 1774.

41. Snyder, *Slavery in Indian Country*, 85–86; Wayne E. Lee, "Fortify, Fight, or Flee: Tuscarora and Cherokee Defensive Warfare and Military Culture Adaptation," *Journal of Military History* 86 (2004): 718–23, 752–56, 763–68.

42. Captain Allick, *EAID*, 12:140; *South Carolina Gazette*, 14 February 1774.

43. *Georgia Gazette*, 2 February 1774; *Georgia Gazette*, 16 March 1774.

44. Friedrich Peter Hamer, "Indian Traders, Land and Power: Comparative Study of George Galphin on the Southern Frontier and Three Northern Traders" (master's thesis, University of South Carolina, 1982), 48; Hahn, *The Invention of the Creek Nation*, 225–28; Juricek, *Endgame for Empire*, 128.

45. Piker, *Okfuskee*, 67.

46. Rindfleisch, "The 'Owner of the Town Ground Who Overrules All When on the Spot,'" 70–71; Claudio Saunt, *West of the Revolution: An Uncommon History of 1776* (New York: Norton, 2014), 196–99.

47. *South Carolina Gazette*, 14 February 1774.

48. Extract of a letter from Augusta, dated March 9, *Georgia Gazette*, 16 March 1774.

49. James Wright to Frederick Haldimand, 18 April 1774, Gage Papers, vol. 119.

50. Ibid.

51. *Georgia Gazette*, 16 March 1774.

52. Journal of Commons House, Speaker William Young, The Humble Address of the Commons House of Assembly of your Majesty's Province of Georgia to the King's Most Excellent Majesty, 8 March 1774, *CRG*, 15:542–43.

53. Journal of the Upper House of Assembly, President James Habersham to His Excellency Sir James Wright, the Humble Address of the Upper House of Assembly, 9 March 1774, *CRG*, 17:771–72.

54. Ibid.

55. James Wright to Frederick Haldimand, 10 March 1774, Gage Papers, vol. 119.

56. Alexander Macullagh to Thomas Hutchins, 26 March 1774, Gage Papers, vol. 120.

57. Peter Chester to the Officer Commanding the Troops in the Garrison of Pensacola, 26 March 1774, Gage Papers, vol. 120.

58. Extract of a letter from Augusta dated March 9, *Georgia Gazette*, 16 March 1774; ibid., 23 March 1774; *EAID*, 12:144; Juricek, *Endgame for Empire*, 193.

59. James Wright to Frederick Haldimand, 18 April 1774, Gage Papers, vol. 119.

60. *EAID*, 12:136–37, 141, 144.

61. John Stuart to Frederick Haldimand, 23 April 1774, Gage Papers, vol. 119.

62. Conference between Sir James Wright and Upper Creek Indians, 14 April 1774, *DAR*, 8:93; Saunt, *A New Order of Things*, 48–49; Piker, *Okfuskee*, 102.

63. Conference between Sir James Wright and Upper Creek Indians, 14 April 1774, *DAR*, 8:92.

64. Ibid., 93–94.

65. Ibid., 94.

66. Ibid., 93.

67. James Wright to Frederick Haldimand, 18 April 1774, Gage Papers, vol. 119.

68. John Stuart to Earl of Dartmouth, 6 May 1774, *DAR*, 8:109.

69. John Stuart to Frederick Haldimand, 23 April 1774, Gage Papers, vol. 119, second of two of this date; Piker, *Okfuskee*, 67; Juricek, *Endgame for Empire*, 191, 193–94.

70. Abstract of a Letter from Andrew McLean esq., Merchant at Augusta to William Ogilvy, 13 May 1774, Gage Papers, vol. 119.

71. Ibid.; Piker, *Okfuskee*, 68.

72. Extract of a letter from Major Dickson 16th Regiment to Frederick Haldimand, 9 May 1774, Gage Papers, vol. 120.

73. Ibid.

74. John Stuart to Thomas Gage, 3 July 1774, Gage Papers, vol. 120; John Stuart to Frederick Haldimand, 23 April 1774, Gage Papers, vol. 119; *EAID*, 12:146, 148.

75. John Stuart to Frederick Haldimand, 23 April 1774, Gage Papers, vol. 119, second of two of this date.

76. Juricek, *Endgame for Empire*, 196.

77. Ibid.; Extract of a Letter from Peter Chester to Frederick Haldimand, 12 May 1774, *EAID*, 12:442; Braund, *Deerskins and Duffels*, 163; Piker, *Okfuskee*, 71.

78. Harrell, "The Terrain of Factionalism," 110–11.

79. Frederick Haldimand to James Wright, 4 May 1774, Gage Papers, vol. 119.

80. David Taitt to John Stuart, 3 June 1774, Gage Papers, vol. 121.

81. James Wright to John Stuart, 13 June 1774, Gage Papers, vol. 121; Abstract of a letter from Andrew McLean to John Stuart, 29 May 1774, Gage Papers, vol. 119.

82. James Wright to John Stuart, 13 June 1774, Gage Papers, vol. 121; Juricek, *Endgame for Empire*, 197–98.

83. Frederick Haldimand to John Stuart, 14 May 1774, Gage Papers, vol. 119.

84. Abstract of a Letter from Andrew McLean esq., Merchant at Augusta to William Ogilvy dated 13 May 1774, Gage Papers, vol. 119.

85. John Stuart to Frederick Haldimand, 25 June 1774, Gage Papers, vol. 120.

86. Abstract of a letter from Andrew McLean to John Stuart, 29 May 1774, Gage Papers, vol. 119. To their credit, on 20 June 1774, the Georgia Assembly responded to the situation by passing "An Act Declaring that to Murder any free Indian in Amity with this Province is equally penal with the Murdering of any white person and that to rescue a prisoner Committed for such Offence is Felony." Still, the damage was done. *CRG*, vol. 19, pt. 2:36–37.

87. David Taitt to John Stuart, 3 June 1774, Gage Papers, vol. 121.

88. William Ogilvy to Frederick Haldimand, 13 June 1774, Gage Papers, vol. 120.

89. A Talk from the Pumpkin King, The Headmen of the Hitchitaws, Pallachicolas, Oconies & Oakmulgies, 23 June 1774, Gage Papers, vol. 122; John Stuart to Thomas Gage, 3 July 1774, ibid., vol. 120; David Taitt to John Stuart, 7 July 1774, ibid., vol. 121; John Stuart to Emistisiguo Warriour of the Little Tallasies and Neothlacko Second Man, July 1774, ibid., vol. 122; Cashin, *William Bartram*, 73.

90. David Taitt to John Stuart, 7 July 1774, Gage Papers, vol. 121.

91. James Wright to Thomas Gage, 9 September 1774, Gage Papers, vol. 123; Piker, *Okfuskee*, 184.

92. Kathryn E. Holland Braund, "'Like to Have Made a War among Ourselves': The Creek Indians and the Coming of the War of Revolution," in *Nexus of Empire: Negotiating Loyalty and Identity in the Revolutionary Borderlands, 1760s-1820s*, ed. Gene Allen Smith and Sylvia L. Hilton (Gainesville: University Press of Florida, 2010), 41–44.

93. David Taitt to John Stuart, 7 July 1774, Gage Papers, vol. 121; David Taitt to John Stuart, 18 July 1774, ibid., vol. 122.

94. David Taitt to John Stuart, 18 July 1774, Gage Papers, vol. 122; *EAID*, 12:151.

95. *EAID*, 12:563n42.

96. A Talk from the Pumpkin King, The Headmen of the Hitchitaws, Pallachicolas, Oconies & Oakmulgies, 23 June 1774, Gage Papers, vol. 122.

97. Ibid.

98. David Taitt to John Stuart, 29 August 1774, Gage Papers, vol. 123.

99. A Talk Delivered by the Creeks at Augusta 23 August 1774, Gage Papers, vol. 123; Piker, *Okfuskee*, 64–70.

100. Piker, *Okfuskee*, 63–70, 189.

101. A Talk Delivered by the Creeks at Augusta 23 August 1774, Gage Papers, vol. 123; David Taitt to John Stuart, 26 August 1774, ibid., vol. 123.

102. David Taitt to John Stuart, 26 August 1774, Gage Papers, vol. 123; Memorial of James Wright to the Earl of Hillsborough, with several enclosures, 12 December 1771, *CRG*, vol. 28, pt. 2:351.

103. A Talk Delivered by the Creeks at Augusta 23 August 1774, Gage Papers, vol. 123.

104. Ibid.

105. Ibid.

106. David Taitt to John Stuart, 26 August 1774, Gage Papers, vol. 123.

107. To Emistisiguo Warriour of the Little Tallasies and to Neothlacko Second Man from John Stuart, July 1774, Gage Papers, vol. 122.

108. John Stuart to Frederick Haldiman, 5 July 1774, Gage Papers, vol. 121.

109. Ibid.; John Stuart to Frederick Haldimand, 8 August 1774, Gage Papers, vol. 122.

110. John Stuart to Thomas Gage, 8 August 1774, Gage Papers, vol. 122.

111. James Wright to Thomas Gage, 29 June 1774, Gage Papers, vol. 120.

112. Ibid.

113. Ibid.

114. David Taitt to John Stuart, 26 August 1774, Gage Papers, vol. 123; James Wright to Thomas Gage, 9 September 1774, Gage Papers, vol. 123.

115. James Wright to Thomas Gage, 9 September 1774, Gage Papers, vol. 123.

116. John Stuart to Thomas Gage, 14 September 1774, Gage Papers, vol. 123.

117. Ibid.

118. *EAID*, 12:123.

119. James Wright to Thomas Gage, 9 September 1774, Gage Papers, vol. 123.

120. Ibid.

121. Ibid.

122. *EAID*, 12:123.

123. James Wright to Thomas Gage, 9 September 1774, Gage Papers, vol. 123.

124. John Stuart to Thomas Gage, 14 September 1774, Gage Papers, vol. 123.

125. John Stuart to Thomas Gage, 6 October 1774, Gage Papers, vol. 123; Treaty at Savannah, Georgia, 20 October 1774, ibid., vol. 137, folio 15.

126. Treaty at Savannah, Georgia, 20 October 1774, Gage Papers, vol. 137, folio 15; *EAID*, 12:126. The signers from Upper Towns included Emistisiguo of Little Tallassee, Tuckabatche Mala of Tuckabatchee, and Fushatchee of Fusihatchee, all Tallapoosa province towns. Mucklasses Testonake of the Alabama province town of Mucclassee also signed. Hillibe Testonake of Hillaubee signed for Okfuskee province towns. The signers from the Lower Towns included Talleachie of Ocmulgee and Pumpkin King of Hitchiti, both Apalachicola province Hitchiti-speaking towns. Cusseta King of Cussita and Le Cuffee of Coweta also signed, representing Apalachicola province Muskogee speakers. Cheehaw King and Cheehaw Warrior of Cheaha also signed, representing their Koasati-speaking Apalachicola province town.

127. Treaty at Savannah, Georgia, 20 October 1774, Gage Papers, vol. 137, folio 15.

128. Ibid.; James Wright to John Stuart, 6 July 1775, Gage Papers, vol. 132.

129. John Stuart to Thomas Gage, 6 October 1774, Gage Papers, vol. 123.

130. Treaty at Savannah, Georgia, 20 October 1774, Gage Papers, vol. 137, folio 15.

131. Ibid.

132. John Stuart to Thomas Gage, 19 November 1774, Gage Papers, vol. 124.

133. Treaty at Savannah, Georgia, 20 October 1774, Gage Papers, vol. 137, folio 15.

134. Ibid.

135. Ibid.

136. James Wright to Thomas Gage, 21 October 1774, Gage Papers, vol. 124; John Stuart to Thomas Gage, 19 November 1774, ibid., vol. 124.

137. Samuel Thomas to David Taitt, 10 December 1774, Gage Papers, vol. 125.

138. Ibid.; John Stuart to Thomas Gage, 18 January 1775, ibid., vol. 125.

139. Samuel Thomas to David Taitt, 10 December 1774, Gage Papers, vol. 125.

140. John Stuart to Thomas Gage, 18 January 1775, second letter of that date, Gage Papers, vol. 125.

3 / "Settle the Matter Yourselves"

The chapter title comes from A Talk an Answer to the Great Beloved Man John Stuart Esqr from the Lower Creeks, 29 September 1775, Clinton Papers, vol. 11, folio 14.

1. Colin G. Calloway, *The American Revolution in Indian Country: Crisis and Diversity in Native Americans Communities* (Cambridge: Cambridge University Press, 1995), 26–32, 43–47; Frank, *Creeks and Southerners*, 24; Ford, *Settler Sovereignty*, 20.

2. John Stuart to Thomas Gage, 27 March 1774, Gage Papers, vol. 127; Calloway, *The American Revolution in Indian Country*, 31.

3. John Stuart to Thomas Gage, 26 May 1775, Gage Papers, vol. 129.

4. Ibid.

5. John Stuart to Edward Howarth, 15 June 1775, Gage Papers, vol. 132; John Stuart to Thomas Gage, 9 July 1775, ibid., vol. 131; John Stuart to William Henry Drayton, 18 July 1775, ibid., vol. 132.

6. William Campbell to Thomas Gage, 1 July 1775, Gage Papers, vol. 131; John Stuart to Thomas Gage, 9 July 1775, ibid., vol. 131.

7. James Wright to John Stuart, 6 July 1775, Gage Papers, vol. 132; Jim Piecuch, *Three Peoples, One King: Loyalists, Indians, and Slaves in the Revolutionary South, 1775–1782* (Columbia: University of South Carolina Press, 2008), 67, 73; Braund, "Like to Have Made a War among Ourselves," 41; Juricek, *Endgame for Empire*, 215–18.

8. Rindfleisch, "Our Lands Are Our Life and Breath," 588, 601n25; Hahn, *The Invention of the Creek Nation*, 226.

9. David Taitt to John Stuart, 20 September 1775, Clinton Papers, vol. 11, folio 11; Braund, *Deerskins and Duffels*, 54–55, 174; Saunt, *A New Order of Things*, 100–101; Frank, *Creeks and Southerners*, 83–84; Debo, *Road to Disappearance*, 56–59; Martin, *Sacred Revolt*, 71–72; Braund, "Like to Have Made a War among Ourselves," 43; Juricek, *Endgame for Empire*, 164–87, 215–18.

10. John Stuart to Thomas Gage, 20 July 1775, Gage Papers, vol. 132.

11. Ibid.

12. Ibid.; Leslie Hall, *Land and Allegiance in Revolutionary Georgia* (Athens: University of Georgia Press, 2001), 26; Juricek, *Endgame for Empire*, 218–20.

13. David Taitt to John Stuart, 20 September 1775, Clinton Papers, vol. 11, folio 11.

14. Ibid.

15. A Talk from John Stuart to Ouconnastotah & the Principal Chiefs and Warriours of the Upper & Lower Cherokee Nation given at St. Augustine, January 1776, Clinton Papers, vol. 13, folio 28; Thomas Gage to John Stuart, 12 September 1775, Gage Papers, vol. 135.

16. Charles Hudson, *The Southeastern Indians* (Knoxville: University of Tennessee Press, 1976), 120–48; C. Hudson, *Conversations with the High Priest of Coosa*, 38–51; F. Kent Reilly III, "People of the Earth, People of the Sky: Visualizing the Sacred in Native American Art of the Mississippian Period," in *Hero, Hawk, and Open Hand: American Indian Art of the Ancient Midwest and South*, ed. Richard F. Townsend and Robert V. Sharp (Chicago: Art Institute of Chicago, 2004), 125–31.

17. A Talk Given by Emistisiguo at Little Tallassee, 20 September 1775, Clinton Papers, vol. 11, folio 10.

18. A Talk Given by Jesse Micco in Answer to His Excellency Sir James Wright Talk to the Lower Creeks, 25 July 1775, Clinton Papers, vol. 11, folio 5.

19. Ibid.

20. Ibid.

21. Ibid.

22. Ibid.

23. A Talk an Answer to the Great Beloved Mans John Stuart Esqr from the Lower Creeks, 29 September 1775, Clinton Papers, vol. 11, folio 14.

24. Ibid.

25. Interpreter Samuel Thomas to John Stuart, 2 October 1775, Clinton Papers, vol. 11, folio 21.

26. Calloway, *The American Revolution in Indian Country*, 196–97, 201. Cherokees experienced similar generational conflict during the American Revolution. Generational tension was normal and accommodated in both Creek and Cherokee society, but the pressures of the American Revolution rendered that tension insoluble.

27. A Talk an Answer to the Great Beloved Man John Stuart Esqr from the Lower Creeks, 29 September 1775, Clinton Papers, vol. 11, folio 14.

28. A Talk by John Stuart to a pt.y of Creeks at St. Augustine, November 1775, Clinton Papers, vol. 12, folio 17.

29. Ibid.

30. Ibid.

31. Thomas Brown to Patrick Tonyn, 2 May 1776, second of two of that date, Clinton Papers, vol. 16, folio 36.

32. David Taitt to Patrick Tonyn, 3 May 1776, Clinton Papers, vol. 16, folio 40.

33. Journal of the Council of Safety, meeting, 15 May 1776, Allen D. Candler, *The Revolutionary Records of the State of Georgia* (Atlanta: Franklin-Turner, 1908), 1:125 (hereafter cited as *RRG*); Cashin, *The King's Ranger*, 46–49.

34. Juricek, *Endgame for Empire*, 221–35.

35. Watson W. Jennison, *Cultivating Race: The Expansion of Slavery in Georgia, 1750–1860* (Lexington: University Press of Kentucky, 2012), 42–44; L. Hall, *Land and Allegiance in Revolutionary Georgia*, xi–xiv.

36. Patrick Tonyn to Sir Henry Clinton, 8 June 1776, Clinton Papers, vol. 16, folio 35.

37. By His Honour John Adam Treutlen Esquire, Captain General & Commander in Chief in and over the Said State of Georgia, A Proclamation, 4 June 1777, *RRG*, 1:311.

38. Journal of the Council of Safety, meeting, 17 May 1776, *RRG*, 1:129.

39. Ibid., 5 July 1776, *RRG*, 1:152.

40. Ibid., 1:152–53; ibid., 19 August 1776, *RRG*, 1:181; Jennison, *Cultivating Race*, 43. Jennison argues that the threat of potential black-Creek alliances made Georgians apathetic about the patriot cause.

41. Journal of the Council of Safety, meeting, 5 July 1776, *RRG*, 1:153; ibid., 19 August 1776, *RRG*, 1:181.

42. Saunt, *A New Order of Things*, 111–35.

43. Lachlan McIntosh to unknown recipient, July 1775, Keith Read Collection, HAR DLG.

44. Ibid.

45. Braund, "Like to Have Made a War among Ourselves," 42–49.

46. Braund, *Deerskins and Duffels*, 168; Braund, "Like to Have Made a War among Ourselves"; DuVal, *Independence Lost*, 76–89, 165–94, 205–16, 228–38; Kokomoor, "Let Us Try to Make Each Other Happy, and Not Wretched," 77–107.

47. Deposition of Malaciah Culpepper, 3 September 1821, DEPS, vol. 4:238–39.

48. L. Hall, *Land and Allegiance in Revolutionary Georgia*, 61–62.

49. Piker, "'White & Clean' & Contested," 330; Piker, *Okfuskee*, 70; Cashin, *The King's Ranger*, 55–56; Braund, "Like to Have Made a War among Ourselves," 48.

50. Braund, *Deerskins and Duffels*, 167.

51. Lord George Sackville Germain to John Stuart, 6 November 1776, George Sackville Germain Papers, vol. 5, William L. Clements Library, University of Michigan (hereafter cited as Germain Papers).

52. Ibid.

53. Piecuch, *Three Peoples, One King*, 70–73; Calloway, *The American Revolution in Indian Country*, 43–44, 49–50, 197–99.

54. John Stuart to Sir William Howe, 4 February 1778, Clinton Papers, vol. 31, folio 4.

55. Cashin, *The King's Ranger*, 67–72; Piecuch, *Three Peoples, One King*, 111–13, 116–17; Braund, "Like to Have Made a War among Ourselves," 50–53; DuVal, *Independence Lost*, 80–81; Kokomoor, "Let Us Try to Make Each Other Happy and Not Wretched," 89–91.

56. Talk to the Handsome Man and others from Samuel Elbert, 13 August 1777, Keith Read Collection, HAR DLG.

57. Ibid.

58. Cashin, *The King's Ranger*, 69; Braund, "Like to Have Made a War among Ourselves," 52–53.

59. Talk to the Handsome Man and others from Samuel Elbert, 13 August 1777, Keith Read Collection, HAR DLG.

60. Ibid.

61. Ibid.

62. Braund, "Like to Have Made a War among Ourselves," 53.

63. Cashin, *The King's Ranger*, 66–67.

64. J. H. O'Donnell, "Alexander McGillivray: Training for Leadership, 1777–1783," *Georgia Historical Quarterly* 49, no. 2 (June 1965): 173; DuVal, *Independence Lost*, 89.

65. Waselkov, *A Conquering Spirit*, 41–42.

66. Cashin, *The King's Ranger*, 71–72; John Stuart to Sir William Howe, 4 February 1778, Clinton Papers, vol. 31, folio 4.

67. John Stuart to Sir William Howe, 4 February 1778, Clinton Papers, vol. 31, folio 4.

68. John Stuart to Sir William Howe, 22 March 1778, Clinton Papers, vol. 32, folio 29; DuVal, *Independence Lost*, 81–82.

69. L. Hall, *Land and Allegiance in Revolutionary Georgia*, 72–74.

70. George Sackville Germain to Henry Clinton, 8 March 1778, Germain Papers, vol. 7; Braund, "Like to Have Made a War among Ourselves," 53–57.

71. Minutes of the Executive Council, 26 August 1778, *RRG*, 2:90.

72. Ibid., 18 September 1778, *RRG*, 2:103.

73. Ibid., 26 August 1778, *RRG*, 2:91.

74. Ibid., 18 September 1778, *RRG*, 2:103.

75. Ibid., 24 September 1778, *RRG*, 2:104; Cashin, *The King's Ranger*, 52.

76. George Galphin to Henry Laurens, 26 October 1778, in *The Papers of Henry Laurens*, ed. Philip M. Hamer, George C. Rogers, and David T. Chesnutt (Columbia: University of South Carolina Press, 1968), 14:452–54 (hereafter cited as *LP*); Piecuch, *Three Peoples, One King*, 117.

77. Deposition of Richard Story, 13 August 1821, DEPS, vol. 2, pt. 3:869–70.

78. Deposition of Martha Stevens, 14 October 1822, DEPS, vol. 2, pt. 2:399.

79. Deposition of Sarah Jordan, 14 October 1822, DEPS, vol. 2, pt. 2:398.

80. Ibid.

81. Braund, "Like to Have Made a War among Ourselves," 57; DuVal, *Independence Lost*, 83–85, 89.

82. David Taitt to Henry Clinton, 11 June 1779, Clinton Papers, vol. 60, folio 39.

83. Augustine Prevost to David Taitt, 14 March 1779, Clinton Papers, vol. 60, folio 40.

84. David Taitt to Henry Clinton, 11 June 1779, Clinton Papers, vol. 60, folio 39.

85. Ibid.

86. Ibid.

87. Ibid.

88. Ibid; Cashin, *King's Ranger*, 96–98.

89. DuVal, *Independence Lost*, 85–88.

90. Cashin, *The King's Ranger*, 94–96, 102.

91. Minutes of the Executive Council, 16 August 1779, *RRG*, 2:155–57.

92. George Galphin to Henry Laurens, 26 October 1778, *LP*, 14:453.

93. Ibid.

94. Qtd. in Braund, "Like to Have Made a War among Ourselves," 51, 47.

95. Deposition of Noah Cloud, 18 January 1822, DEPS, vol. 2, pt. 3:787.

96. L. Hall, *Land and Allegiance in Revolutionary Georgia*, 104; Cashin, *King's Ranger*, 106. Brown claimed to have 360 Creeks "in service" as he moved into Augusta.

97. Stephen Heard to unnamed correspondent in Henry County, Virginia, 2 March 1781, Keith Read Collection, HAR DLG.

98. Ibid.

99. Cashin, *King's Ranger*, 118.

100. Lilla M. Hawes, "Miscellaneous Papers of James Jackson, 1781–1798, pt. 1," *Georgia Historical Quarterly* 37, no. 1 (March 1953): 70.

101. Stephen Heard to unnamed correspondent in Henry County, Virginia, 2 March 1781, Keith Read Collection, HAR DLG.

102. Cashin, *King's Ranger*, 120.

103. Thomas Brown to Charles Cornwallis, 17 December 1780, Clinton Papers, vol. 134, folio 10.

104. Stephen Heard to unnamed correspondent in Henry County, Virginia, 2 March 1781, Keith Read Collection, HAR DLG.

105. Ibid.; L. Hall, *Land and Allegiance in Revolutionary Georgia*, 104–5.

106. Cashin, *King's Ranger*, 106–14; L. Hall, *Land and Allegiance in Revolutionary Georgia*, 97–98, 105–6; Hawes, "Miscellaneous Papers of James Jackson, 1781–1798, pt. 1," 73.

107. Cashin, *King's Ranger*, 106–20; L. Hall, *Land and Allegiance in Revolutionary Georgia*, 104–5.

108. DuVal, *Independence Lost*, 165–66.

109. Charles Shaw to Lord George Sackville Germain, 19 June 1780, Germain Papers, vol. 12.

110. Ibid.; DuVal, *Independence Lost*, 178.

111. Michael D. Green, "The Creek Confederacy in the American Revolution: Cautious Participants," in *Anglo-Spanish Confrontation on the Gulf Coast during the American Revolution*, Proceedings of the Gulf Coast History and Humanities Conference, ed. William S. Coker and Robert Right Rea (Pensacola, FL: Gulf Coast History and Humanities Conference, 1982), 54–75, see esp. 69–72; Kathryn Holland, "The Anglo-Spanish Contest for the Gulf Coast as Viewed from the Townsquare," in *Anglo-Spanish Confrontation*, ed. Coker and Rea, 90–105, see esp. 100–102; DuVal, *Independence Lost*, 177–82, 194–95, 205–6, 215–17.

112. Cashin, *King's Ranger*, 127–30, 141.

113. Piecuch, *Three Peoples, One King*, 255.

114. Cashin, *King's Ranger*, 130–33.

115. Qtd. ibid., 137.

116. To the Great Warriors and the Beloved Men of the Creek Nation the talk of Nathan Brownson Governor, and the beloved men the Council of Georgia, undated, ITCL, 158.

117. Ibid.

118. Hugh M'Call, *The History of Georgia: Containing Brief Sketches of the Most Remarkable Events up to the Present Day* (1784), vol. 2 (Savannah: William T. Williams, 1816), 380–97.

119. Cashin, *King's Ranger*, 145; L. Hall, *Land and Allegiance in Revolutionary Georgia*, 123–24; DuVal, *Independence Lost*, 228–29.

120. Minutes of the Executive Council, 10 January 1782, *RRG*, 2:299.

121. A Talk to Creek Indians, undated, ITCL, 95–97.

122. Isaac Jackson to the Governor and Council, 6 January 1782, Creek Indian Letters, Talks, and Treaties, 1705–1839, ed. Louise F. [Mrs. J. E.] Hays, pt. 1:19, Georgia Archives (hereafter cited as CILTT).

123. Minutes of the Executive Council, 30 November 1781, *RRG*, 2:288.

124. Depositions of Deserters Mark King and William Henson, 5 January 1782, Telamon Cuyler Collection, HAR DLG.

125. A Talk to Creek Indians, undated, ITCL, 96.

126. Cashin, *King's Ranger*, 150; Piecuch, *Three Peoples, One King*, 304.

127. Elijah Clarke to John Martin, 21 May 1782, CILTT, pt. 1:22–23.

128. Ibid.

129. Micajah Williamson to Governor John Martin, 24 May 1782, CILTT, pt. 1:24.

130. A Talk Given by the Tallassee King and Sundry Head Men of the Upper and Lower Creek Nation, 28 May 1782, Telamon Cuyler Collection, HAR DLG. The Lower Towns presenting white beads were Cussita, Hitchiti, Parachocolau [Pallachicola], Hoconey [Oconee], Savoucolo [Sauwoogelo], Savocolouchess [Sauwoogelooche]. The list apparently includes only two Upper Towns—Usshatcee [Fusihatchee] and Hoboithle Micco's own Tallassee.

131. Jonathan Martin to Andrew Pickens, 27 May 1782, CILTT, pt. 1:25.

132. Ibid.

133. Cashin, *King's Ranger*, 154–55.

134. Piecuch, *Three Peoples, One King*, 305–6; Cashin, *King's Ranger*, 151–54, 156; DuVal, *Independence Lost*, 229.

135. A Talk to Indians Asking for a Treaty to be Signed at Old Town on Ogeechee on 1 May 1782, ITCL, 100; manuscript in File II, Box 74, Folder 5, Georgia Archives.

136. Cashin, *King's Ranger*, 155–58.

4 / "We Mean to Have the Consent of Every Headman in the Whole Nation"

The chapter title comes from Talk from the Kings and Beloved Men of the Lower Creeks at Cussita, 5 May 1785, ITCL, 169.

1. Adam Rothman, *Slave Country: American Expansion and the Origins of the Deep South* (Cambridge: Harvard University Press, 2005), 56.

2. DuVal, *Independence Lost*, 262–68.

3. David J. Weber, *The Spanish Frontier in North America* (New Haven: Yale University Press, 1992), 258, 274–82; Waselkov, *A Conquering Spirit*, 17–27; DuVal, *Independence Lost*, 313–26.

4. DuVal, *Independence Lost*, 313–26.

5. Richard Gildrie, "Tennessee in the American Revolution: A Reconsideration," in *Before the Volunteer State: New Thoughts on Early Tennessee History, 1540–1800*, ed. Kristofer Ray (Knoxville: University of Tennessee Press, 2014), 117–19.

6. Don Luis Chacheré to Don Francisco Bouligny, 1785, in "Papers from the Spanish Archives Relating to Tennessee and the Old Southwest, 1783–1800," trans. and ed. D. C. Corbitt and Roberta Corbitt, *The East Tennessee Historical Society's Publications* 9 (1937): 140 (hereafter cited as *ETHSP*); Kristofer Ray, *Middle Tennessee, 1775–1825* (Knoxville: University of Tennessee Press, 2007), 14.

7. DuVal, *Independence Lost*, 313–14; Ray, *Middle Tennessee*, xix, 1–24; Ray, ed., *Before the Volunteer State*, xv; Gildrie, "Tennessee in the American Revolution," 123–24; Natalie Inman, "Military Families: Kinship in the American Revolution," in *Before the Volunteer State*, ed. Ray, 142–43; Kevin Barksdale, "The State of Franklin: Separatism, Competition, and the Legacy of Tennessee's First State, 1783–1789," in *Before the Volunteer State*, ed. Ray, 158, 165–66, 173–76; David Britton, "John Montgomery and the Perils of American Identity in the Mero District, 1780–1795," in *Before the Volunteer State*, ed. Ray, 188.

8. Green, *The Politics of Indian Removal*, 4–12; Piker, *Okfuskee*, 3–4, 7–10. Hoboithle Micco was also known as the Tallassee King, the Tame King, the Good Child King, or the Halfway House King. Neha Micco was also known as the Fat King.

9. A Talk Delivered by the Second Man of the Cussetaws and Two Other Creek Indians at Augusta in Georgia, 14 July 1784, ITCL, 146; Tallassee King's Talk delivered to the Governor and Council 22 September 1784, File II, Box 74, Folder 5, Georgia Archives; Alexander McGillivray to Arturo O'Neill, 18 April 1787, in *McGillivray of the Creeks*, ed. John Walton Caughey (Norman: University of Oklahoma Press, 1938), 150–51; Green, "Alexander McGillivray," 41–63; Saunt, *A New Order of Things*, 77–83, 104–8; Braund, *Deerskins and Duffels*, 171–173; Downes, "Creek-American Relations, 1782–1790," 142–84.

10. Hahn, *The Invention of the Creek Nation*, 173–225.

11. Piker, "'White & Clean' & Contested," 315–47; Robbie Ethridge, *From Chicaza to Chickasaw*, 72–82; A. Hudson, *Creek Paths and Federal Roads*, 4.

12. Braund, *Deerskins and Duffels*, 164–70; Paulett, *An Empire of Small Places*, 175–76.

13. Timothy Barnard to Major Patrick Carr, 13 April 1784, in Unpublished Letters of Timothy Barnard, 1784–1820, ed. Louise F. [Mrs. J. E.] Hays, 29–31, Georgia Archives (hereafter cited as LTB); Frank, *Creeks and Southerners*, 39–41.

14. A Talk Given by the Tallassee King and Sundry Head Men of the Upper and Lower Creek Nation, 28 May 1782, Telamon Cuyler Collection, HAR DLG.

15. Quote from A Talk Given by the Tallassee King and Sundry Head Men of the Upper and Lower Creek Nation, 28 May 1782, Telamon Cuyler Collection, HAR DLG. See also Superintendent of Indian Affairs Richard Henderson to Governor John Martin from Augusta, 1782 December 23, CILTT, pt. 1:42–44; Patrick Carr to Governor John Martin, 1782 December 28, CILTT, pt. 1:45–46; James Rae to Governor Lyman Hall, 1783 January 29, CILTT, pt. 1:47. The Lower Towns presenting white beads were Cussita, Hitchiti, Parachocolau [Pallachicola], Hoconey [Oconee], Savoucolo

[Sauwoogelo], Savocolouchess [Sauwoogelooche]. The list includes only two Upper Towns—Usshatcee [Fusihatchee] and Hoboithle Micco's own Tallassee.

16. Daniel McMurphy to John Martin, 22 September 1782, CILTT, pt. 1:30. The delegation represented several Upper Towns (Okfuskee, Holawaga/Hoithlewaule, Tallassee, Tuckabatchee, and Songahatchey/Soughohatche) and some Lower Towns (Cussita, Hitticks/Hitchiti, Oconey/Oconee). Many of the towns represented later signed the 1783 Treaty of Augusta. Signers included Hoboithle Micco of Tallassee, Neha Micco of Cussita, Songa Hatchey/Sugahacho of Soughohatche, Oconey/Okoney of Oconee town, and possibly Hitcheto Warrior/Hicott of Hitticks from Hitchiti town.

17. Daniel McMurphy to John Martin, 22 September 1782, CILTT, pt. 1:30.

18. Richard Henderson to John Martin, 23 September 1782, CILTT, pt. 1:33.

19. Ibid.; DuVal, *Independence Lost*, 250–51.

20. Patrick Carr to Governor John Martin, 13 December 1782, CILTT, pt. 1:40.

21. Ibid., 41; Tallassee King's Talk delivered to the Governor and Council 22 September 1784, File II, Box 74, Folder 5, Georgia Archives.

22. Richard Henderson to John Martin, 23 December 1782, CILTT, pt. 1:43; Patrick Carr to Governor John Martin, 13 December 1782, ibid., pt. 1:41.

23. Richard Henderson to John Martin, 23 December 1782, CILTT, pt. 1:42–44.

24. Saunt, *A New Order of Things*, 55.

25. Ibid., 55–57.

26. The Treaty of Augusta, 1783—With the Cherokee Indians, ITCL, 100–110; Downes, "Creek-American Relations, 1782–1790," 143.

27. Andrew McLean, Secretary to Georgia's Board of Commissioners on Indian Affairs to the Creek Traders, 6 June 1783, ITCL, 116.

28. A Talk Sent by His Honor the Governor and beloved men of Georgia by William Cousins to the Tallassee King, the Fat King and the rest of the Kings, Head Warriors, and beloved men of the upper and lower towns of the Creek Nation, 1783 Treaty of Augusta with Cherokees, Indian Claims (Treaties and Spoliations), 001-01-025, RG 1-1-25, Georgia Archives.

29. Treaty at Augusta with the Creek Indians in 1783, ITCL, 129–31. In all, fourteen Creek men signed the 1783 Treaty of Augusta. They were Tallassee King aka Hoboithle Micco, Tallassee Warrior, Fat King aka Neha Micco, Mad Fish, Topwar King, Alachago, Hitcheto Warrior, Okolege, Cowetaw, Cuse King, Second Man, Inomatuhata, Inomatawtusnigua, and Sugahacho. Okoney and Head Warrior are listed as representatives but do not appear as signers.

30. Treaty at Augusta with the Creek Indians in 1783, ITCL, 129.

31. Ibid., ITCL, 130. See also Treaty of Augusta with the Creeks, Nov. 1, 1783, *EAID*, 18:372.

32. A Talk Delivered by the Go. & council to Tallassee and Fat Kings at Augusta on Friday 24 September 1784, ITCL, 167.

33. *Georgia Gazette*, 6 February 1783.

34. Ibid., 27 March 1783; An Act to Amend and Alter Some pt.s, and Repeal Other pt.s of the Several Land Acts in this State, 22 February 1785, *CRG*, vol. 19, pt. 2:440.

35. Patrick Carr to Governor John Martin, 28 December 1782, CILTT, pt. 1:45.

36. *Georgia Gazette*, 25 December 1783.

37. Ibid., 20 November 1783.

38. Ibid., 1 April 1784.

39. DuVal, *Independence Lost*, 236–38, 246–48, 250–55; C. Hudson, *Southeastern Indians*, 234–39.

40. *Georgia Gazette*, 24 June 1784.

41. Debo, *Road to Disappearance*, 40–43; Downes, "Creek-American Relations, 1782–1790," 145–51; Green, *The Politics of Indian Removal*, 34–35; Martin, *Sacred Revolt*, 81–83, 101; Braund, *Deerskins and Duffels*, 171–75; Saunt, *A New Order of Things*, 79–83, 104–8.

42. Milfort, *Memoirs*, 28–29, 67–68, 95–96.

43. Alexander McGillivray to Governor Vizente Manuel de Zéspedes of Spanish East Florida, 1 January 1784, CILTT, pt. 1:52b–52c.

44. Ibid.; Green, "Alexander McGillivray," 42, 46–48; Saunt, *A New Order of Things*, 75–78; DuVal, *Independence Lost*, 256–62.

45. Harrell, "Creek Corridors of Commerce," 223–40.

46. Patrick Carr to Governor John Houston, 22 August 1784, CILTT, pt. 1:63; Saunt, *A New Order of Things*, 62, 99, 196, 260–61. Joseph Cornels also owned a plantation next to Alexander McGillivray's.

47. Patrick Carr to Governor John Houston, 22 August 1784, CILTT, pt. 1:63.

48. Ibid.

49. Memo. of the Kings Proposals and Complaints, 1 March 1784, ITCL, 117.

50. Ibid.

51. A Talk delivered by the Fat King, 5 April 1784, ITCL, 132.

52. A Talk delivered by the Second Man of the Cussetaws, 14 July 1784, ITCL, 146.

53. J. Hall, *Zamumo's Gifts*, 35.

54. Memo. of the Kings Proposals and Complaints, 1 March 1784, ITCL, 117–18.

55. Ibid.

56. Wesson, *Households and Hegemony*, 109–11, 131; Wesson, "When Moral Economies and Capitalism Meet," 68, 70; Galloway, *Practicing Ethnohistory*, 293–97, 302, 308, 324.

57. Memo. of the Kings Proposals and Complaints, 1 March 1784, ITCL, 118.

58. Patrick Carr to Governor John Houston, 22 August 1784, CILTT, pt. 1:63.

59. Memo. of the Kings Proposals and Complaints, 1 March 1784, ITCL, 119; emphasis in original.

60. Tallassee King's Talk delivered to the Governor and Council, 22 September 1784, File II, Box 74, Folder 5, Georgia Archives.

61. Ibid.

62. Ibid.

63. Ibid.

64. Ibid.

65. Ibid.

66. Ibid.; A. Hudson, *Creek Paths, Federal Roads*, 32, 186n118.

67. Tallassee King's Talk delivered to the Governor and Council, 22 September 1784, File II, Box 74, Folder 5, Georgia Archives.

68. Timothy Barnard to Governor John Houstoun, 8 October 1784, LTB, 35.

69. Talk from the Kings and Beloved Men of the Lower Creeks at Cussita, 5 May 1785, ITCL, 169.

70. John Carr at Coweta to Mr. William Clark Merchant at Beard's Bluff, 7 April 1785, CILTT, pt. 1:70.

71. DuVal, *Independence Lost*, 262–68, 313–20; Alan Taylor, *American Revolutions: A Continental History, 1750–1804* (New York: Norton, 2016), 344–50.

72. Walter Lowrie and Matthew St. Clair Clarke, eds., *American State Papers, Documents, Legislative and Executive, of the Congress of the United States, from the First Session of the First to the Second Session of the Twenty-Second Congress, Inclusive: Commencing March 3, 1789, and Ending March 3, 1833, Foreign Affairs*, vol. 1 (Washington, DC: Gales and Seaton, 1833), 278–79; DuVal, *Independence Lost*, 257–59, 264–65.

73. Alexander McGillivray to William Clarke from Tuckabatche, 24 April 1785, CILTT, pt. 1:89.

74. Ibid., 90.

75. Alexander McGillivray to Estevan Míro, 1 May 1786, Caughey, *McGillivray of the Creeks*, 107; Patrick Carr to Governor John Houstoun, 8 October 1784, LTB, 35.

76. James Durouzeaux to Mr. William Clark at Beard's Bluff, 8 May 1785, CILTT, pt. 1:72.

77. William Clark to Governor Samuel Elbert, 15 May 1785, CILTT, pt. 1:74–75.

78. Talk from the Kings and Beloved Men of the Lower Creeks at Cussita, 5 May 1785, ITCL, 170.

79. Ibid.

80. Ibid.

81. James Durouzeaux in Coweta to William Clark at Beard's Bluff, 25 May 1785, CILTT, pt. 1:76–77.

82. William Clark to Samuel Elbert, 15 May 1785, CILTT, pt. 1:74–75.

83. For a different interpretation, see Kokomoor, "Let Us Try to Make Each Other Happy and Not Wretched," 121–31.

84. James Durouzeaux to Samuel Elbert, 14 July 1785, CILTT, pt. 1:79.

85. Ibid., 81; Timothy Barnard to Governor John Houstoun, 8 October 1784, LTB, 35.

86. Ibid., 81.

87. Deposition of John King, 3 February 1821, DEPS, vol. 2, pt. 2:489; Deposition of Joseph McCutchen, 3 February 1821, DEPS, vol. 2, pt. 2:489.

88. Deposition of Robert Flournoy, 3 September 1821, DEPS, vol. 2, pt. 2:434; Deposition of Robert Flournoy, 11 November 1802, ibid., vol. 4:200.

89. Alexander McGillivray to Andrew Pickens, 1785 September 5, *ASPIA*, 1:18.

90. Braund, *Deerskins and Duffels*, 173–74; Downes, "Creek-American Relations, 1782–1790," 147–51.

91. Alexander McGillivray to Arturo O'Neill, 24 July 1785, in Caughey, *McGillivray of the Creeks*, 94; Alexander McGillivray to Arturo O'Neill, 6 July 1785, ibid., 90.

92. Alexander McGillivray to Estevan Miró, 25 August 1785, in Caughey, *McGillivray of the Creeks*, 95; James Durouzeaux to Samuel Elbert, 20 July 1785, CILTT, pt. 1:82.

93. James Durouzeaux to Samuel Elbert, 20 July 1785, CILTT, pt. 1:82.

94. Ibid.

95. Alexander McGillivray to Charles McLatchy, 4 October 1784, in Caughey, *McGillivray of the Creeks*, 82; Alexander McGillivray to William Panton, 19 December 1785, ibid., 100.

96. Headmen of Cowerther [Coweta] to Samuel Elbert, 17 August 1785, CILTT, pt. 1:83–84.

97. Ibid., 84.
98. Ibid., 83–84.
99. Ibid.
100. Ibid., 83.
101. Milfort, *Memoirs*, 65–67; DuVal, *Independence Lost*, 297–99.
102. Alexander McGillivray to James Durouzeaux, 2 September 1785, CILTT, pt. 1:86–88.
103. Swanton, "Social Organization and Social Usages," 193, 295–97; Swanton, *Creek Religion and Medicine*, 610–14; Green, *The Politics of Indian Removal*, 9. It is possible that McGillivray was following appropriate channels of leadership by calling on another man to deliver his talk. Formal oratory required specialized skills, so miccos delegated the task to one of two classes of professional speakers, *yatika* or *hothlibonaya*. This is, however, unlikely because each town had its own micco and yatika, though not all had a hothlibonaya. McGillivray would have had no authority to ask the yatika or hothlibonaya of Coweta to speak for him. Moreover, there is no clear evidence that Yahola Micco was such a professional speaker.
104. Alexander McGillivray to James Durouzeaux, 2 September 1785, CILTT, pt. 1:86–88.
105. Green, *Politics of Indian Removal*, 12–13; Ethridge, *Creek Country*, 105–7; Juricek, *Endgame for Empire*, 40–41, 53–56, 133, 197–98.
106. Alexander McGillivray to Andrew Pickens, 5 September 1785, ASPIA, 1:18.
107. Ibid.
108. Alexander McGillivray to James Durouzeaux, 12 September 1785, CILTT, pt. 1:94.
109. Luke Mann to Governor Samuel Elbert, 4 November 1785, CILTT, pt. 1:100.
110. Downes, "Creek-American Relations, 1782–1790," 151; James Durouzeaux to Governor Samuel Elbert, 21 September 1785, CILTT, pt. 1: 96–98; Luke Mann to Governor Samuel Elbert, 4 November 1785, ibid., pt. 1:100.
111. Alexander McGillivray to James White, 8 April 1787, ASPIA, 1:18; Downes, "Creek-American Relations, 1782–1790," 152–53, 160.
112. Saunt, *A New Order of Things*, 77–83, 104–8.
113. Report from H. Knox, Secretary of War, to the President of the United States, 6 July 1789, ASPIA, 1:15.
114. Treaty at Galphinton with the Creek Indians, 12 November 1785, Article 11, ITCL, 173; Treaty at Augusta with the Creek Indians in 1783, ITCL, 130.
115. Treaty at Galphinton with the Creek Indians, 12 November 1785, Article 11, ITCL, 173.
116. Taylor, *American Revolutions*, 346.
117. Treaty at Galphinton with the Creek Indians, 12 November 1785, Article 2, ITCL, 171.
118. Ibid., 171–72.
119. Ibid., 171. Signers apparently represented five Upper Towns as follows: (1) Pohilthe Oakfuskies for Okfuskee; (2) Abeco Tuskanucky for Abecooche; (3) Hoboithle Micco and Dickson Tallicee for Tallassee; (4) Tuskia Micko for Tuskegee; and (5) Coso Micko and Cuso Micko for Coosa. Signers representing Lower Towns included (1) Inneha Micko (Neha Micco) for Cussita; (2) Yaholo Micko for Coweta; and (3) O'Kemalguy Tustanagee for Ocmulgee.
120. *Georgia Gazette*, 23 February 1786.

121. Alexander McGillivray to Arturo O'Neill, 10 February 1786, in Caughey, *McGillivray of the Creeks*, 102–3.

122. Ibid.

123. Ibid., 102.

124. Ibid., 103.

125. Downes, "Creek-American Relations, 1782–1790," 152; *ASPIA*, 1:17.

126. Randolph Roth, *American Homicide* (Cambridge: Belknap Press of Harvard University Press, 2009), 161–71.

5 / "Always in Defense of Our Rights"

The chapter title comes from Alexander McGillivray to Arturo O'Neill, 3 December 1786, in Caughey, *McGillivray of the Creeks*, 140.

1. Britton, "John Montgomery and the Perils of American Identity in the Mero District, 1780–1795," 185.

2. Weber, *The Spanish Frontier in North America*, 258, 274–82; Waselkov, *A Conquering Spirit*, 17–27; DuVal, *Independence Lost*, 313–26; Ray, *Middle Tennessee*, xix, 1–24; Ray, ed., *Before the Volunteer State*, xv; Gildrie, "Tennessee in the American Revolution," 123–24; Inman, "Military Families," 142–43; Barksdale, "The State of Franklin," 158, 165–66, 173–76; Britton, "John Montgomery and the Perils of American Identity in the Mero District, 1780–1795," 188.

3. Georgians themselves reported the total casualties as six in the Journal of the Treaty of Shoulderbone Creek, but killings in the Cumberland region attributed to Creeks bring the total to nine. According to Arturo O'Neill, Efau Hadjo of Tuckabatchee claimed that raids under his leadership claimed the lives of ten Georgians (Arturo O'Neill to Bernardo de Gálvez, May 30, 1786, *ETHSP*, 10:139).

4. Timothy Barnard to Edward Telfair, 1786, LTB, 55; James Durouzeaux to Timothy Barnard, Talk to the Upper & Lower Creek Nation by the Commissioners, 13 June 1786, CILTT, pt. 1:116–17.

5. Ibid., 104; DuVal, *Independence Lost*, 300–302.

6. Alexander McGillivray to Arturo O'Neill, 28 March 1786, in Caughey, *McGillivray of the Creeks*, 104; Alexander McGillivray to Estevan Miró, 1 May 1786, ibid., 107–10.

7. Alexander McGillivray to Arturo O'Neill, 28 March 1786, in Caughey, *McGillivray of the Creeks*, 104; Talk that Zéspedes the Governor of Florida had with Yntipaya Masla, principal warrior of the Lower Creek Indians, called Toclatoche, 29 May 1786, ibid., 115–16.

8. John Stuart to Thomas Gage, 3 July 1774, Gage Papers, vol. 120; John Stuart to Frederick Haldimand, 23 April 1774, ibid., vol. 119.

9. Alexander McGillivray to Estevan Miró, 1 May 1786, in Caughey, *McGillivray of the Creeks*, 109.

10. Saunt, *A New Order of Things*, 122, 158, 174, 180, 199, 217.

11. Green, *Politics of Indian Removal*, 38; Saunt, *A New Order of Things*, 47–48, 87, 99–100, 105, 107–10, 122, 132, 146, 155–56, 180–81, 190–91, 198–99, 206–7, 222, 261.

12. Alexander McGillivray to Hallowing King, 14 April 1786, CILTT, pt. 1:101.

13. Deposition of Thomas Page, 1 November 1803, DEPS, vol. 2, pt. 3:745; Talk from Head Men Cussetaus & Buzzard Roost Indians to Edward Telfair, 2 May 1786, LTB, 51.

14. Alexander McGillivray to Arturo O'Neill, 28 March 1786, in Caughey, *McGillivray of the Creeks*, 104; Alexander McGillivray to Hallowing King, 14 April 1786, CILTT, pt. 1:101.

15. Talk from Head Men Cussetaus & Buzzard Roost Indians to Edward Telfair, 2 May 1786, LTB, 51.

16. Ibid.

17. Ibid.

18. Ibid., 52.

19. Ibid.

20. Ibid.

21. Braund, *Deerskins and Duffels*, 157–58.

22. Commissioner John A. Cuthbert's Approval of the Claim of the Estate of John Trice, 28 May 1835, DEPS, vol. 2, pt. 1:30–31.

23. Depositions of Francis Moran and Tabitha Hoskins, 3 November 1821, DEPS, vol. 2, pt. 1:29.

24. Talk from Head Men Cussetaus & Buzzard Roost Indians to Edward Telfair, 2 May 1786, LTB, 52.

25. Ibid.

26. J. Hall, *Zamumo's Gifts*, 1–2, 11–14.

27. Talk from Head Men Cussetaus & Buzzard Roost Indians to Edward Telfair, 2 May 1786, LTB, 53.

28. J. Hall, *Zamumo's Gifts*, 1–3, 29–31, 95–96, 100–105, 137–42.

29. Jonathan Clements to Edward Telfair, 6 May 1786, CILTT, pt. 1:103; Daniel McMurphy to Arturo O'Neill, 11 July 1786, in Caughey, *McGillivray of the Creeks*, 119.

30. Ibid.

31. Jonathan Clements to Edward Telfair, 14 May 1786, CILTT, pt. 1:106.

32. Deposition of John Galphin sworn before Jonathan Clements, 6 May 1786, CILTT, pt. 1:104; Jonathan Clements to Edward Telfair, 6 May 1786, ibid., pt. 1:103; Daniel McMurphy to Arturo O'Neill, 11 July 1786, in Caughey, *McGillivray of the Creeks*, 119.

33. Alexander McGillivray to Hallowing King, 14 April 1786, CILTT, pt. 1:101.

34. Treaty of Galphinton with the Creek Indians, 12 November 1785, ITCL, 173. Ineehana Ufollies signed the Treaty of Galphinton.

35. Deposition of John Galphin sworn before Jonathan Clements, 6 May 1786, CILTT, pt. 1:104.

36. Arthur Fort to Edward Telfair, 14 May 1786, CILTT, pt. 1:105.

37. Ibid.

38. Evan Nooe, "Common Justice: Vengeance and Retribution in Creek Country," *Ethnohistory* 62, no. 2 (April 2015): 241–61.

39. Timothy Barnard to Edward Telfair, undated, 1786–1787, LTB, 55.

40. Talk from Head Men of Cussetaus & Buzzard Roost to Governor of Ga., T. Barnard Interpreter, 27 May 1786, LTB, 56.

41. Ibid.

42. Ibid.

43. Ibid.

44. Daniel McMurphy to unnamed correspondent, likely Edward Telfair, 30 May 1786, CILTT, pt. 1:113.

45. Daniel McMurphy to Arturo O'Neill, 11 July 1786, in Caughey, *McGillivray of the Creeks*, 119.

46. Gov. of Ga. to Joshua Inman, 23 May 1786, Letters from Georgia Settlers Regarding Indian Depredations, 1786–1838, C. Mildred Thompson Papers, Box 1, Folder 2, HAR.

47. Elijah Clarke to Edward Telfair, 23 May 1786, CILTT, pt. 1:112.

48. *Georgia Gazette*, 25 May 1786.

49. Elijah Clarke to Edward Telfair, 23 May 1786, CILTT, pt. 1:112.

50. *Georgia Gazette*, 1 June 1786; Gov. of Ga. to Joshua Inman, 23 May 1786, Letters from Georgia Settlers Regarding Indian Depredations, 1786–1838, C. Mildred Thompson Papers, Box 1, Folder 2, HAR.

51. John Sevier to George Matthews, 3 March 1787, CILTT, pt. 1:147.

52. Timothy Barnard to Edward Telfair, undated, LTB, 55.

53. James Durouzeaux to Edward Telfair, 5 June 1786, CILTT, pt. 1:114.

54. Alexander McGillivray to Andrew Pickens, 5 September 1785, *ASPIA*, 1:17–18; Benjamin Hawkins to Alexander McGillivray, 11 January 1786, *ETHSP*, 10:128; Arturo O'Neill to Bernardo de Gálvez, 20 May 1786, ibid., 10:137; Alexander McGillivray to Arturo O'Neill, 10 July 1787, in Caughey, *McGillivray of the Creeks*, 155; Alexander McGillivray to Estevan Miró, 4 October 1787, ibid., 160–61; Henry Knox, Instructions to the Commissioners for Treating with the Southern Indians, 29 August 1789, *ASPIA*, 1:67; Braund, *Deerskins and Duffels*, 172–73; David Andrew Nichols, *Red Gentlemen and White Savages: Indians Federalists and the Search for Order on the American Frontier* (Charlottesville: University of Virginia Press, 2008), 52–55, 58, 66, 69; Kevin T. Barksdale, *The Lost State of Franklin: America's First Secession* (Lexington: University Press of Kentucky, 2009), 43–44, 72, 77–78, 83–90, 148, 151–53, 158–59; Ray, *Middle Tennessee*, 10, 16–20.

55. James Durouzeaux to Timothy Barnard, Talk to the Upper & Lower Creek Nation by the Commissioners, 13 June 1786, CILTT, pt. 1:116.

56. Wood, "The Changing Population of the Colonial South," 84–86.

57. James Durouzeaux to Timothy Barnard, Talk to the Upper & Lower Creek Nation by the Commissioners, 13 June 1786, CILTT, pt. 1:116.

58. Ibid.

59. Letter from the Cheehaw, Oakmulgey, Ouseechee, & Hitcheta Towns of the Creek nation signed John Harvard, 28 June 1786, CILTT, pt. 1:124.

60. Ibid.

61. Ibid.; Saunt, *A New Order of Things*, 100–101.

62. Patrick Carr to Governor John Houston, 22 August 1784, CILTT, pt. 1:63; Daniel McMurphy to unidentified correspondent, 13 June 1786, ibid., pt. 1:118; Daniel McMurphy to unidentified correspondent, likely Alexander McGillivray, 29 June 1786, ibid., pt. 1:125.

63. A Talk Delivered by the King, Headmen, and Warriors of the Creek Nation, to the Commissioners for Holding a Conference Treaty with the said Indians by the General Assembly of the State of Georgia near the Mouth of Shoulderbone Creek on the Oconee River, 22 October 1786, Journal of the Treaty of Shoulderbone, Indian Claims (Treaties and Spoliations), RG 1-1-25, Location RMSS #4, Georgia Archives, 70–71 (hereafter cited as Shoulderbone Journal).

64. Daniel McMurphy to Edward Telfair, 30 July 1786, CILTT, pt. 1:129.

65. Ibid., 130.

66. Ibid.

67. Ibid.

68. Ibid., 129–32.

69. Ibid.

70. Ibid.

71. Timothy Barnard to Edward Telfair, 14 August 1786, LTB, 59.

72. Arturo O'Neill to Estevan Miró, 18 September 1786, *ETHSP*, 10:146–47; Alexander McGillivray to Vizente Manuel de Zéspedes, 3 August 1786, in Caughey, *McGillivray of the Creeks*, 125.

73. DuVal, *Independence Lost*, 295–98, 304–9; Nichols, *Red Gentlemen and White Savages*, 70–72; Chickasaw Nation to John Sevier, 28 July 1786, Telamon Cuyler Collection, HAR DLG; Tuskiatapa Mingo to William Davenport, 11 October 1786, Telamon Cuyler Collection, HAR DLG.

74. Alexander McGillivray to Vizente Manuel de Zéspedes, 3 August 1786, in Caughey, *McGillivray of the Creeks*, 124–25; Alexander McGillivray to William Panton, 3 August 1786, ibid., 123; Alexander McGillivray to Arturo O'Neill, 8 October 1786, ibid., 134.

75. Talk of Part of the Creek Indians to the Georgia Legislature, 3 August 1786, in Caughey, *McGillivray of the Creeks*, 123.

76. Timothy Barnard to His Honor Edward Telfair Governor, 14 August 1786, LTB, 60.

77. Ibid.

78. Ibid.

79. Ibid.; Weber, *The Spanish Frontier in North America*, 282–85; DuVal, *Independence Lost*, 341.

80. Report of the Committee on Indian Affairs, 3 August 1786, Shoulderbone Journal, 1.

81. Ibid., 2.

82. Ibid., 3.

83. Ibid., 4.

84. Barksdale, *The Lost State of Franklin*, 53–66, 79, 85, 89; Ray, *Middle Tennessee*, 2–3.

85. Arturo O'Neill to Sonora, 10 August 1786, in Caughey, *McGillivray of the Creeks*, 125.

86. *Georgia Gazette*, 26 April 1787.

87. Milfort, *Memoirs*, 86–89.

88. Nichols, *Red Gentlemen and White Savages*, 13, 22, 43, 54, 56, 82, 84–85.

89. Report of the Committee on Indian Affairs, 3 August 1786, Shoulderbone Journal, 9.

90. Robert Middleton to Governor Edward Telfair, 1 May 1786, DEPS, vol. 1, pt. 1:46.

91. Benjamin Cleveland, Jesse Walton, and John Cleveland to Edward Telfair, 15 May 1786, CILTT, pt. 1:107.

92. Ibid.

93. Daniel McMurphy to Arturo O'Neill, 11 July 1786, in Caughey, *McGillivray of the Creeks*, 119.

94. Ibid.

95. Joshua Inman to the Gov. of Ga., 23 May 1786, Letters from Georgia Settlers Regarding Indian Depredations, 1786–1838, C. Mildred Thompson Papers, Box 1, Folder 1, HAR.

96. Edward Telfair to Benjamin Cleveland, Jesse Walton, and John Cleveland, 19 May 1786, CILTT, pt. 1:109.

97. William Thompson to Edward Telfair, 17 May 1786, CILTT, pt. 1:108.

98. Joseph Martin to Edward Telfair, 3 July 1786, CILTT, pt. 1:127.

99. Barksdale, *The Lost State of Franklin*, 77–78, 83–90.

100. Arturo O'Neill to Bernardo de Gálvez, 11 October 1786, *ETHSP*, 10:149; Alexander McGillivray to Arturo O'Neill, 8 October 1786, ibid., 10:152.

101. Alexander McGillivray to Estevan Miró, 1 May 1786, in Caughey, *McGillivray of the Creeks*, 110.

102. *Georgia Gazette*, 14 September 1786.

103. Ibid., 28 September 1786.

104. Ibid.

105. Ibid.

106. Ibid.

107. Jennison, *Cultivating Race*, 3–4, 92–99.

108. Gregory Evans Dowd, "The Panic of 1751: The Significance of Rumors on the South Carolina-Cherokee Frontier," *William and Mary Quarterly*, 3rd ser., 53, no. 3 (July 1996): 527–60, see esp. 528–31, 547–56. Dowd analyzes a similar situation in which rumors led Cherokees and South Carolinians to the brink of war. For a more thorough analysis of frontier rumors, see Gregory Evans Dowd, *Groundless: Rumors, Legends, and Hoaxes on the Early American Frontier* (Baltimore: Johns Hopkins University Press, 2015).

109. Joseph Martin to Edward Telfair, 7 September 1786, CILTT, pt. 1:137–38.

110. Ibid.

111. Ibid.

112. Alexander McGillivray to Vizente Manuel de Zéspedes, 3 August 1786, in Caughey, *McGillivray of the Creeks*, 125; Alexander McGillivray to Arturo O'Neill, 8 October 1786, ibid., 134.

113. *Georgia Gazette*, 5 April 1787.

114. John Sevier to George Matthews, 3 March 1787, CILTT, pt. 1:147; *Georgia Gazette*, 5 April 1787.

115. James Durouzeaux to John Habersham, 23 September 1786, CILTT, pt. 1:139.

116. Ibid.; James Durouzeaux to John Habersham, 23 September 1786, Shoulderbone Journal, 46; *Georgia Gazette*, 12 October 1786.

117. James Durouzeaux to John Habersham, 23 September 1786, CILTT, pt. 1:139.

118. Qtd. from Alexander McGillivray to Arturo O'Neill, 3 December 1786, in Caughey, *McGillivray of the Creeks*, 140; Alexander McGillivray to His Honor the Governor and the other beloved men of the state of Georgia, 3 August 1786, Shoulderbone Journal, 38–40; Alexander McGillivray to John Habersham, 16 September 1786 (Tuckabatchee), Shoulderbone Journal, 43–45.

119. Alexander McGillivray to John Habersham, 16 September 1786, *Georgia Gazette*, 12 October 1786.

120. *Georgia Gazette*, 26 October 1786.

121. Ibid.; James Durouzeaux to John Habersham, 23 September 1786, *Georgia Gazette*, 12 October 1786.

122. Alexander McGillivray to Vizente Manuel de Zéspedes, 15 November 1786, in Caughey, *McGillivray of the Creeks*, 138–140.

123. Report of a Committee of the Georgia House of Assembly on Relations with the Creek Indians, 23 October 1787, *ASPIA*, 1:24.

124. Edward Telfair to James Durouzeaux, 20 May 1786, CILTT, pt. 1:111.

125. Alexander McGillivray, 10 January 1787, *Georgia Gazette*, 26 April 1787.

126. Edward Telfair to James Durouzeaux, 20 May 1786, CILTT, pt. 1:111; By the Honourable Lyman Hall, Governor . . . A Proclamation, *Georgia Gazette*, 26 June 1783; House of Assembly, 19 July 1783, ibid., 22 April 1784; By the Honourable John Houstoun, Governor . . . A Proclamation, ibid., 24 June 1784; A Talk Delivered by the Governor and Council to Tallassee and Fat Kings at Augusta, 24 September 1784, File II, Box 76, Folder 8, Georgia Archives.

127. Treaty at Shoulder-bone, ITCL, 183–88.

128. Ibid., 183.

129. Treaty of Shoulderbone, 3 November 1786, Shoulderbone Journal, 92a, 93b.

130. Treaty at Shoulder-bone, ITCL, 186.

131. A Talk delivered by the Commissioners appointed by the General Assembly of the State of Georgia to the Kings, Head Men, and Warriors of the Creek Nation on Shoulder Bone Creek near the Oconee River, the 21st October 1786, Shoulderbone Journal, 67; A Talk Delivered by the King, Headmen, and Warriors of the Creek Nation, to the Commissioners for Holding a Conference Treaty with the said Indians by the General Assembly of the State of Georgia near the Mouth of Shoulderbone Creek on the Oconee River, 22 October 1786, Shoulderbone Journal, 70–71; A Talk Delivered by the Commissioners appointed by the General Assembly of the State of Georgia to the Kings, Head men, and Warriors of the Creek nation, On Shoulder Bone, near the Oconee River, 23 October 1786, Shoulderbone Journal, 77; Resolution of the Board of Commissioners on Shoulder Bone Creek, 2 November 1786, Shoulderbone Journal, 91.

132. Board of Commissioners of Shoulderbone Creek Treaty to Daniel McMurphy, 3 November 1786, Shoulderbone Journal, 102.

133. Treaty of Shoulderbone, 3 November 1786, Shoulderbone Journal, 93b.

134. Ibid., 92a–101; Report from H. Knox, Secretary of War, to the President of the United States, 6 July 1789, *ASPIA*, 1:15.

135. Edward Telfair to James Durouzeaux, 20 May 1786, CILTT, pt. 1:111.

136. Alexander McGillivray to Thomas Pinckney, 26 February 1789, *ASPIA*, 1:20.

137. Timothy Barnard to the Georgia Board of Commissioners of Indian Affairs at Shoulderbone Creek, 17 October 1786, Shoulderbone Journal, 61–64; James Durouzeaux to John Habersham, 23 September 1786, ibid., 45–46; A Talk delivered by the Commissioners appointed by the General Assembly of the State of Georgia to the Kings, Head Men, and Warriors of the Creek Nation on Shoulder Bone Creek near the Oconee River, the 21st October 1786, ibid., 68–69.

138. A Talk Delivered by the King, Headmen, and Warriors of the Creek Nation, to the Commissioners for Holding a Conference Treaty with the said Indians by the General Assembly of the State of Georgia near the Mouth of Shoulderbone Creek on the Oconee River, 22 October 1786, Shoulderbone Journal, 71.

139. Ibid.

140. Ibid.

141. Treaty of Shoulderbone, 3 November 1786, Shoulderbone Journal, 92, 93a–101. Lower Towns included (1) Coweta represented by Yaholo Micko; (2) Cussita represented by Cussitas Mico and Enea Mico also known as the Fat King; (3) Eufaula

represented by Eufalla Tustonoky; (4) Hitchiti represented by Hitcheta Mico; and (5) Ousichee represented by Osuchee Mathla. Upper Towns included (1) Tallassee led by Hoboithle Micco; (2) Fusihatchee led by Fousachee Mico; (3) Coosa led by Cousa Tustonoke and two additional men, both of whom signed as "Cusa mico"; and (4) Atasi led by Hottesy Mico.

142. John Habersham to Edward Telfair, 8 November 1786, Shoulderbone Journal, 110–11.

143. *Georgia Gazette*, 13 September 1787.

144. COPY of a Letter from Gen. CLARKE to his Honour the GOVERNOR. Long Creek, 24 September 1787, *Georgia Gazette*, 4 October 1787.

145. Saunt, *A New Order of Things*, 77–83, 104–8; Braund, *Deerskins and Duffels*, 171–73; Downes, "Creek-American Relations, 1782–1790," 142–84.

146. Tallassee King's Talk delivered to the Governor and Council, 22 September 1784, File II, Box 74, Folder 5, Georgia Archives.

6 / "An Uncommon Degree of Ferocity"

1. James P. Preston to John C. Calhoun, 15 March 1822, DEPS, vol. 2, pt. 1:4.

2. *Return of the Whole Number of Persons within the Several Districts of the United States*, 55.

3. J. Meriwether, Secretary of the Executive Department, "A Return of Persons killed Wounded and taken prisoners together with Property taken and distroyed by the Creek Indians from the 1st Jany 1787 untill 1789—Inclusively," File II, Box 74, Folder 5, Georgia Archives; *Return of the Whole Number of Persons within the Several Districts of the United States*, 3, 55; Wood, "The Changing Population of the Colonial South," 60.

4. Boulware, *Deconstructing the Cherokee Nation*, 110–29, 166–77; Beck, *Chiefdoms, Collapse, and Coalescence*, 210, 231–33, 240–41, 259–60.

5. J. Meriwether, Secretary of the Executive Department, "A Return of Persons killed Wounded and taken prisoners together with Property taken and distroyed by the Creek Indians from the 1st Jany 1787 untill 1789—Inclusively," File II, Box 74, Folder 5, Georgia Archives; *Return of the Whole Number of Persons within the Several Districts of the United States*, 3, 55; Wood, "The Changing Population of the Colonial South," 60.

6. Qtd. in Downes, "Creek-American Relations, 1782–1790," 170.

7. Wood, "The Changing Population of the Colonial South," 86.

8. Nichols, *Red Gentlemen and White Savages*, 55, 66, 69–72; John Anthony Caruso, *The Appalachian Frontier: America's First Surge Westward* (Indianapolis: Bobbs-Merrill, 1959), 271–79; Barksdale, *The Lost State of Franklin*, 148–60; DuVal, *Independence Lost*, 295–98, 304–9, 313–25; Ray, *Middle Tennessee*, 1–14; James Robertson to John Sevier, 7 August 1787, CILTT, pt. 1:157; James Robertson to Governor George Mathews, 3 October 1787, Telamon Cuyler Collection, HAR DLG; James Robertson to Alexander McGillivray 3 August 1788, Tennessee Historical Society, Tennessee State Library and Archives, Nashville, HAR DLG; Anthony Bledsoe to John Sevier, 5 August 1787, Telamon Cuyler Collection, HAR DLG.

9. DuVal, *Independence Lost*, 323–24; Waselkov, *A Conquering Spirit*, 30–31; Harrell, "Creek Corridors of Commerce," 236–37, 245–49, 260, 264–65; Alexander McGillivray to William Panton, 20 May 1789, in "Papers Relating to the Georgia-Florida

Frontier, 1784–1800," IV, ed. and trans. D. C. Corbitt, *Georgia Historical Quarterly* 21, no. 3 (September 1937): 283–86; William Panton to Alexander McGillivray, 6 June 1789, ibid., V, 373–74; William Panton to Alexander McGillivray, 7 June 1789, ibid., V, 375–76; William Panton to Estevan Miró, 9 June 1789, ibid., V, 377.

10. *Georgia Gazette*, 24 May 1787, Nichols, *Red Gentlemen and White Savages*, 54, 67, 76, 80, 94–95; DuVal, *Independence Lost*, 333–34.

11. Report of a Committee of the Georgia House of Assembly on Relations with the Creek Indians, 23 October 1787, *ASPIA*, 1:24.

12. Ibid.; Ford, *Settler Sovereignty*, 96.

13. Carson, "Horses and the Economy and Culture of the Choctaw Indians, 1690–1840," 500–502.

14. Adair, *History of the American Indians*, 90.

15. Foster, *Archaeology of the Lower Muskogee Creek Indians*, 30, 114–16.

16. A Talk from the head men of the Buzzard roust and Cussetas to the Governor of Georgia, 1 May 1787, CILTT, pt. 1:155.

17. Ibid.

18. Ibid.

19. DuVal, *Independence Lost*, 302–4.

20. James White to Henry Knox, 24 May 1787, *ASPIA*, 1:21.

21. James White to George Matthews, 23 April 1787, CILTT, pt. 1:153.

22. James White to Henry Knox, 24 May 1787, *ASPIA*, 1:21.

23. Alexander McGillivray to Vizente Manuel de Zéspedes, 10 April 1787, in Caughey, *McGillivray of the Creeks*, 148.

24. Alexander McGillivray to Arturo O'Neill, 18 April 1787, in Caughey, *McGillivray of the Creeks*, 149–51; Green, "Alexander McGillivray," 53; Nichols, *Red Gentlemen and White Savages*, 67.

25. Alexander McGillivray to Arturo O'Neill, 18 April 1787, in Caughey, *McGillivray of the Creeks*, 149–51; DuVal, *Independence Lost*, 312.

26. The Memorial of a Large Number of the Principle Planters and Other Inhabitants of Liberty County, DEPS, vol. 1, pt. 1:250–54; Colonel James Maxwell, A Return of the Killed wounded & the losses sustained by the Ravages of the Indians in Liberty County, 8 August 1788, DEPS, vol. 1, pt. 1:256; Kokomoor, "Let Us Make Each Other Happy and Not Wretched," 155, 159–60.

27. Adair, *History of the American Indians*, 185–90, 218–20.

28. *Georgia Gazette*, 4 October 1787.

29. Deposition of John McMichael, 2 July 1787, DEPS, vol. 1, pt. 1:104.

30. Ibid.

31. Ibid., 104–5.

32. Ibid., 105; Snyder, *Slavery in Indian Country*, 182, 194.

33. Wayne E. Lee, "Peace Chiefs and Blood Revenge: Patterns of Restraint in Native American Warfare, 1500–1800," *Journal of Military History* 71 (July 2007): 718–26.

34. *Georgia Gazette*, 14 June 1787.

35. Ibid.; John Habersham to Lachlan McIntosh, 30 June 1787, Felix Hargrett Papers, HAR DLG.

36. James Seagrove to the Governor of Georgia, *ASPIA*, 1:306.

37. Talk of the Fat King to his Honour Governor Mathews and the Council, &c., In a Meeting of the Lower Creeks held in the Cussetahs 27th July 1787, *Georgia Gazette*, 16 August 1787.

38. *Georgia Gazette*, 14 June 1787; ibid., 5 July 1787.

39. Ibid., 28 June 1787.

40. Deposition of David McMichael, 2 July 1787, DEPS, vol. 1, pt. 1:105.

41. Ibid.

42. Snyder, *Slavery in Indian Country*, 82–83; Adair, *History of the American Indians*, 185–90, 196, 382–85.

43. Grantham, *Creation Myths and Legends of the Creek Indians*, 38–41; Brown and Dye, "Severed Heads and Sacred Scalplocks," 278–98, esp. 293; Jacobi, "Disabling the Dead," 299–338, esp. 300–301, 312–13; Nancy A. Ross-Stallings, "Trophy Taking in the Central and Lower Mississippi Valley," in Chacon and Dye, *The Taking and Displaying of Human Body Parts*, 339–76, esp. 357–58.

44. Saunt, *A New Order of Things*, 100; Snyder, *Slavery in Indian Country*, 84–85, 87, 91, 97–98.

45. Saunt, *A New Order of Things*, 98–101; C. Hudson, *The Southeastern Indians*, 225, 325–27; Green, *The Politics of Indian Removal*, 7–8; Adair, *History of the American Indians*, 90–193, 218–20, 375–76, 390–92.

46. Deposition of Richard Bradley, 3 August 1802, DEPS, vol. 1, pt. 1:77.

47. Deposition of Samuel Knox, 3 September 1821, DEPS, vol. 2, pt. 3:708–9.

48. Snyder, *Slavery in Indian Country*, 85–86; Adair, *History of the American Indians*, 378, 380.

49. Deposition of James Woods, 20 September 1821, DEPS, vol. 2, pt. 1:304.

50. Deposition of John Chandler, 24 January 1803, DEPS, vol. 2, pt. 1:192b.

51. Deposition of Joel Mabry, 26 October 1802, DEPS, vol. 2, pt. 1:193–94.

52. Martin, *Sacred Revolt*, 8; Kathryn Holland Braund, "Reflections on 'Shee Coocys' and the Motherless Child: Creek Women in a Time of War," *Alabama Review* 64, no. 4 (October 2011): 272, 267–72; Ray, *Middle Tennessee*, 1–24; Chappell, "Chapter I. The Oconee War," "Chapter II. The Oconee War Continued," *Miscellanies of Georgia*, 5–14. See also John Grenier, *The First Way of War: American War Making on the Frontier, 1607–1814* (Cambridge: Cambridge University Press, 2005).

53. Martin, *Sacred Revolt*, 89–92; Rothman, *Slave Country*.

54. Deposition of William Ramsey, 3 September 1821, DEPS, vol. 1, pt. 1:63; Deposition of William Melton, 3 September 1821, DEPS, vol. 1, pt. 1:64.

55. Deposition of William Ramsey, 3 September 1821, DEPS, vol. 1, pt. 1:63; Deposition of William Melton, 3 September 1821, DEPS, vol. 1, pt. 1:64.

56. A Talk of the Fat King to his Honor Governor Matthews and the Council, 27 July 1787, *ASPIA*, 1:33.

57. Georgia Governor George Matthews to the Commissioners of the United States for Indian Affairs, in the Southern Department, 9 August 1787, *ASPIA*, 1:31.

58. Talk of the Fat King to his Honour Governor Mathews and the Council, &c., 27 July 1787, *Georgia Gazette*, 16 August 1787.

59. Ibid.

60. Hallowing King and Fat King to Governor George Matthews, 14 June 1787, *ASPIA*, 1:32; DuVal, *Independence Lost*, 303–4.

61. Ibid.

62. Treaty of Shoulderbone, 3 November 1786, Shoulderbone Journal, 93b, 94.

63. Hallowing King and Fat King to Governor George Matthews, 14 June 1787, *ASPIA*, 1:32.

64. Ford, *Settler Sovereignty*, 115–17.

65. A Talk from Georgia to the Head-men and Warriors of the Lower Creeks, 29 June 1787, *ASPIA*, 1:32.

66. Ibid., 33.

67. "HIS Honour the Governor . . . To the Fat King, and other head men of the Lower Creek Nation," *Georgia Gazette*, 16 August 1787.

68. Downes, "Creek-American Relations, 1782–1790," 162; DuVal, *Independence Lost*, 303–4.

69. James White to Alexander McGillivray, 4 April 1787, *ASPIA*, 1:21.

70. *ASPIA*, 1:31–33.

71. DuVal, *Independence Lost*, 309.

72. *Georgia Gazette*, 13 September 1787.

73. General Elijah Clarke to his Honour the Governor, 24 September 1787, *Georgia Gazette*, 4 October 1787.

74. *Georgia Gazette*, 4 October 1787.

75. General Elijah Clarke to his Honour the Governor, 24 September 1787, *Georgia Gazette*, 4 October 1787.

76. Ibid.

77. Downes, "Creek-American Relations, 1782–1790," 163.

78. General Elijah Clarke to his Honour the Governor, 24 September 1787, *Georgia Gazette*, 4 October 1787.

79. Ibid.; Alexander McGillivray to Arturo O'Neill, 20 November 1787, in Caughey, *McGillivray of the Creeks*, 164. McGillivray indicates that Creeks led by men from the Tallapoosa province town of Atasi and Afro-Creek Seminoles defeated Clarke's militia.

80. *Georgia Gazette*, 4 October 1787.

81. Deposition of David and Charles Furlow, 3 September 1821, DEPS, vol. 1, pt. 1:56–57.

82. *Georgia Gazette*, 25 October 1787.

83. Ibid.

84. Ibid., 4 October 1787.

85. Ibid.

86. *Georgia Gazette*, 25 October 1787.

87. Ibid.

88. Ibid., 11 October 1787.

89. George Matthews to James White, 15 November 1787, *ASPIA*, 1:23; Downes, "Creek-American Relations, 1782–1790," 163; Thaddeus Brokett Rice, *History of Greene County, Georgia, 1786–1886* (Macon, GA: Burke, 1961), 6, 23.

90. Deposition of Robert Corry, 3 September 1821, DEPS, vol. 1, pt. 1:52.

91. Alexander McGillivray to Arturo O'Neill, 20 November 1787, in Caughey, *McGillivray of the Creeks*, 164.

92. *Georgia Gazette*, 8 November 1787; George Matthews to James White, 15 November 1787, *ASPIA*, 1:23.

93. *Georgia Gazette*, 25 October 1787.

94. Ibid.; Roscoe R. Hill, ed., *Journals of the Continental Congress, 1774–1789*, vol. 33 (Washington, DC: U.S. Government Printing Office, 1936), 531.

95. *Georgia Gazette*, 29 November 1787; Nichols, *Red Gentlemen and White Savages*, 93–95.

96. Report of the Secretary at War [Henry Knox] relative to the Southern Indians, 18 July 1787, in *Journals of the Continental Congress, 1774–1789*, ed. Hill, 33:365–69.

97. *Georgia Gazette*, 14 September 1786; Articles of Confederation, Article IX.

98. James White to Henry Knox, 24 May 1787, *ASPIA*, 1:21.

99. DuVal, *Independence Lost*, 313–20; Barksdale, *The Lost State of Franklin*, 145–60; Ray, *Middle Tennessee*, 12.

100. *ASPIA*, 1:16.

101. Richard Winn, Andrew Pickens, and George Matthews to Alexander McGillivray, 28 November 1788, *ASPIA*, 1:30.

102. George Matthews to James White, 15 November 1787, *ASPIA*, 1:23.

103. Elijah Clarke to George Handley, 8 February 1788, CILTT, pt. 1:166.

104. Israel Bird to James Jackson, 14 February 1788, CILTT, pt. 1:168.

105. Elijah Clarke to George Handley, 2 February 1788, CILTT, pt. 1:164.

106. *Georgia Gazette*, 6 March 1788; Elijah Clarke to George Handley, 8 February 1788, CILTT, pt. 1:166.

107. *Georgia Gazette*, 10 April 1788; Robert McLeod to Colonel James Armstrong, 5 April 1788, CILTT, pt. 1:177–78.

108. *Georgia Gazette*, 10 April 1788.

109. Deposition of David Ray, 21 July 1823, DEPS, vol. 2, pt. 3:849; Deposition of John Fielder, 1 September 1821, ibid., vol. 2, pt. 2:385; Deposition of John Fielder, 7 August 1802, ibid., vol. 2, pt. 2:386; Robert M. Echols to Wilson Lumpkin, 22 May 1835, ibid., vol. 2, pt. 2:387; Deposition of John Fielder, 4 October 1821, ibid., vol. 2, pt. 2: 671; Deposition of Sarah Fielder, 4 October 1821, ibid., vol. 2, pt. 2:671; Commissioner John A. Cuthbert's Approval of the Claim of John Fielder, 27 March 1835, ibid., vol. 2, pt. 2:672; Deposition of John Fielder, 25 July 1823, ibid., vol. 4:33–34.

110. Deposition of John Fielder, 1 September 1821, DEPS, vol. 2, pt. 2:385; Deposition of John Fielder, 7 August 1802, ibid., vol. 2, pt. 2:386; Robert M. Echols to Wilson Lumpkin, 22 May 1835, ibid., vol. 2, pt. 2:387; Deposition of John Fielder, 4 October 1821, ibid., vol. 2, pt. 2: 671; Deposition of Sarah Fielder, 4 October 1821, ibid., vol. 2, pt. 2:671; Commissioner John A. Cuthbert's Approval of the Claim of John Fielder, 27 March 1835, ibid., vol. 2, pt. 2:672; Deposition of John Fielder, 25 July 1823, ibid., vol. 4:33–34.

111. Deposition of Diocletian Davis and Moses Sinquefield, 3 September 1821, DEPS, vol. 1, pt. 2:363–64; *Georgia Gazette*, 10 April 1788. The *Georgia Gazette* reported the incident somewhat differently, holding that "they killed Mr. David Jackson's family, consisting of his wife and four children, his brother and two negroes, and scalped another young girl."

112. Caruso, *Appalachian Frontier*, 271–79; *Georgia Gazette*, 4 October 1787.

113. DuVal, *Independence Lost*, 305–9; Ray, *Middle Tennessee*, 21; T. Mingo to William Davenport, 11 October 1786, Telamon Cuyler Collection, HAR DLG; Alexander McGillivray to Estevan Miró, 8 June 1791, in Caughey, *McGillivray of the Creeks*, 291–92; Alexander McGillivray to Francisco Luis Hector de Carondelet, 3 September 1792, ibid., 336.

114. Barksdale, *The Lost State of Franklin*, 148–153; *Georgia Gazette*, 4 December 1788.

115. Nichols, *Red Gentlemen and White Savages*, 55, 66; DuVal, *Independence Lost*, 319–20, 325–26; Alexander McGillivray to Arturo O'Neill, 25 April 1788, in Caughey,

McGillivray of the Creeks, 178; Alexander McGillivray to Arturo O'Neill, 12 August 1788, ibid., 192.

116. *Georgia Gazette*, 7 February 1788.

117. Ibid., 10 April 1788; By the United States in Congress Assembled, 15 July 1788, ibid., 16 April 1789.

118. Report of the Secretary at War [Henry Knox] on Protection of the Georgia Frontier, 26 July 1788, in *Journals of the Continental Congress, 1774–1789*, ed. Hill, 34:362–66.

119. By the Honorable GEORGE HANDLEY . . . A PROCLAMATION, *Georgia Gazette*, 17 June 1788; *Georgia Gazette*, 19 June 1788; ibid., 26 June 1788.

120. Alexander McGillivray to George Whitefield, 12 August 1788, *Georgia Gazette*, 25 September 1788.

121. *Georgia Gazette*, 14 August 1788.

122. Ibid., 4 September 1788.

123. Ibid.

124. Qtd. in Braund, "Reflections on 'Shee Coocys,'" 272; Snyder, *Slavery in Indian Country*, 170.

125. *Georgia Gazette*, 25 September 1788; Richard Winn, Andrew Pickens, and George Matthews to Alexander McGillivray, 28 August 1788, *Georgia Gazette*, 4 December 1788.

126. Report from H. Knox, Secretary of War, to the President of the United States, 6 July 1789, *ASPIA*, 1:16.

127. Nichols, *Red Gentlemen and White Savages*, 107–8; Ray, *Middle Tennessee*, 20–21.

128. *Georgia Gazette*, 4 September 1788.

129. Ibid., 25 September 1788.

130. Ibid., 4 September 1788.

131. Ibid.; *Georgia Gazette*, 25 September 1788.

132. The Memorial of a Large Number of the Principal Planters and other Inhabitants of Liberty County to Governor George Handley and the Executive Council, 12 October 1788, DEPS, vol. 1, pt. 1:251–55.

133. Alexander McGillivray to Richard Winn, Andrew Pickens, and George Mathews, 15 September 1788, *Georgia Gazette*, 4 December 1788.

134. TALKS delivered to Mr. George Whitefield by the Hollowing King of the Cowetaws and the Mad Dog of the Tuckabatchies, *Georgia Gazette*, 2 October 1788.

135. George Whitefield, Esq. to his Honour the Governor, *Georgia Gazette*, 2 October 1788.

136. Ibid.

137. Ibid.

138. TALKS delivered to Mr. George Whitefield by the Hollowing King of the Cowetaws and the Mad Dog of the Tuckabatchies, *Georgia Gazette*, 2 October 1788; Hollowing King, Worseter Square, 26 May 1788, *Georgia Gazette*, 2 October 1788; Mad Dog, Tuckabatchee, 31 May 1788, *Georgia Gazette*, 2 October 1788.

139. Downes, "Creek-American Relations, 1782–1790," 168–69.

140. Alexander McGillivray to Estevan Miró, 26 May 1789, in Caughey, *McGillivray of the Creeks*, 235; Alexander McGillivray to William Panton, 10 August 1789, ibid., 246.

141. A Proclamation Notifying the 8th June 1789 the times for holding a treaty with the Creek Indians, File II, Box 74, Folder 1, Georgia Archives; Alexander McGillivray to Estevan Miró, 9 June 1789, in Caughey, *McGillivray of the Creeks*, 236.

142. *Georgia Gazette*, 30 April 1789; Extract of a letter from Col. Maxwell to Lieut. Col. Fishbourn, 24 May 1789, *Georgia Gazette*, 28 May 1789; Deposition of John Chandler, 24 January 1803, DEPS, vol. 2, pt. 1:192b; *Georgia Gazette*, 4 June 1789; Alexander McGillivray to Estevan Miró, 24 June 1789, in Caughey, *McGillivray of the Creeks*, 238.

143. Copy of a Letter from Brigadier General Clarke to his Honour the Governour, 29 May 1789, *Georgia Gazette*, 4 June 1789.

144. Alexander McGillivray to Estevan Miró, 9 June 1789, in Caughey, *McGillivray of the Creeks*, 236.

145. Alexander McGillivray to William Panton, 10 August 1789, in Caughey, *McGillivray of the Creeks*, 246; *Georgia Gazette*, 11 June 1789; Elijah Clarke to Benjamin Cleveland, 24 June 1789, HAR DLG; *Georgia Gazette*, 2 July 1789.

146. Alexander McGillivray to Estevan Miró, 24 June 1789, in Caughey, *McGillivray of the Creeks*, 238.

147. *Georgia Gazette*, 9 July 1789; Andrew Pickens and H. Osborne to George Walton, 23 June 1789, *Georgia Gazette*; John Galphin to George Walton, 16 June 1789, ibid.

148. Alexander McGillivray to Estevan Miró, 10 August 1789, in Caughey, *McGillivray of the Creeks*, 245; Alexander McGillivray to Estevan Miró, 15 August 1789, ibid., 250.

149. Extract of a letter from one of the Commissioners to his friend in Augusta, 6 August 1789, *Georgia Gazette*, 20 August 1789; *Georgia Gazette*, 27 August 1789.

150. Estevan Miró to Alexander McGillivray, 22 July 1789, in Caughey, *McGillivray of the Creeks*, 243; Alexander McGillivray to William Panton, 10 August 1789, ibid., 246; Downes, "Creek-American Relations, 1782–1790," 178–79.

151. *Georgia Gazette*, 1 October 1789.

152. Alexander McGillivray to Estevan Miró, 24 June 1789, in Caughey, *McGillivray of the Creeks*, 238; *Georgia Gazette*, 8 October 1789.

153. Alexander McGillivray to William Panton, 8 October 1789, in Caughey, *McGillivray of the Creeks*, 251–54.

154. *Georgia Gazette*, 3 December 1789.

155. Caleb Howell to George Walton, 4 October 1789, Letters from Georgia Settlers Regarding Indian Depredations, 1786–1838, C. Mildred Thompson Papers, Box 1, Folder 4, HAR; Jared Irwin to George Walton, Augusta, 12 October 1789, ibid.

156. George Walton to Jacob Irwin, 13 October 1789, Letters from Georgia Settlers Regarding Indian Depredations, 1786–1838, C. Mildred Thompson Papers, Box 1, Folder 6, HAR; *Georgia Gazette*, 19 November 1789.

157. *Georgia Gazette*, 3 December 1789; Nichols, *Red Gentlemen and White Savages*, 106–13.

158. *Georgia Gazette*, 15 July 1790; ibid., 22 July 1790; ibid., 29 July 1790; A Proclamation by His Excellency Edward Telfair, Governor, and Commander in Chief in and over the State aforesaid, 19 July 1790, CILTT, pt. 1:222.

159. *Georgia Gazette*, 6 May 1790; ibid., 17 June 1790.

160. Ibid., 17 June 1790.

161. Ibid.

162. Benjamin Hawkins to Alexander McGillivray, 6 March 1790, in Caughey, *McGillivray of the Creeks*, 257.
163. Ibid.
164. Ibid.
165. Martin, *Sacred Revolt*, 84.

7 / "The Indians Still Disputed Giving up Their Rights to That Land"

The chapter title comes from Timothy Barnard to Edward Telfair, 7 July 1793, LTB, 203.

1. Downes, "Creek-American Relations, 1782–1790," 174–75; *Georgia Gazette*, 16 April 1789; Stephen Johnson to George Walton, 20 April 1789, CILTT, pt. 1:196–97; Jno. Clarke to George Walton, 25 April 1789, ibid., pt. 1:201; Elijah Clarke to George Walton, 4 May 1789, ibid., pt. 1:202; *Georgia Gazette*, 28 May 1789; Timothy Barnard to George Walton, 27 May 1789, LTB, 96; *Georgia Gazette*, 4 June 1789; John Twiggs to George Walton, 31 May 1789, C. Mildred Thompson Papers, Box 1, Folder 3, HAR; Benjamin Lanier to His Honour the Governor of Georgia, 4 June 1789, Hays, CILTT, pt. 1:207; *Georgia Gazette*, 11 June 1789; Elijah Clarke to Benjamin Cleveland, 24 June 1789, HAR DLG; Caleb Howell to George Walton, 4 October 1789, Letters from Georgia Settlers Regarding Indian Depredations, 1786–1838, C. Mildred Thompson Papers, Box 1, Folder 4, HAR; Jared Irwin to George Walton, Augusta, 12 October 1789, ibid., Box 1, Folder 5, HAR; George Walton to Jacob Irwin, 13 October 1789, ibid., Box 1, Folder 6, HAR; Timothy Barnard to George Walton, 6 November 1789, LTB, 98–99; Colonel H. Karr to Hallowing King of the Cowetas, 6 June 1790, CILTT, pt. 1:220–21.

2. Timothy Barnard to Edward Telfair, 23 June 1790, LTB, 104–5; *Georgia Gazette*, 22 July 1790; Talk from the Principle Chiefs of the Lower Creeks Hallowing King, Smoking King, Dog Warrior AKA Efau Tustanagee, Second Man, Mad Warrior AKA Tustanagee Hadjo, Red Shoes to Governor Edward Telfair, 17 July 1790, CILTT, pt.1: 221b–221c; Jared Irwin to Edward Telfair, 29 July 1790, CILTT, pt. 1:234.

3. Alexander McGillivray to Estevan Miró, 9 June 1789, in Caughey, *McGillivray of the Creeks*, 236; Timothy Barnard to Edward Telfair, 23 June 1790, LTB, 104–5.

4. Cherokees [Bloody Fellow, The Glass, Charles of Chickamauga, Waterhunter, Spider of Lookout Mountain, Richard Justice, Badger's Mother Warriors, William Shorey] (By John McDonald) to Francisco Luis Hector de Carondelet, 5 April 1793, *ETHSP*, 32:72–73.

5. John Forbes to Francisco Luis Hector de Carondelet, 1 November 1792, *ETHSP*, 28:121–32; Manuel Gayoso de Lemos to Francisco Luis Hector de Carondelet, 8 January 1793, ibid., 29:141–42; Juan de la Villebeuvre to Francisco Luis Hector de Carondelet, 4 February 1793, ibid., 29:147–49; Piomingo and others to Francisco Luis Hector de Carondelet, 11 February 1793, ibid., 29:154–155; Juan de la Villebeuvre to Francisco Luis Hector de Carondelet, [28?] February 1793, ibid., 29:158–60; [Ogoulayacabe] to Manuel [Gayoso] de Lemos, 22 March 1793, ibid., 31:68–69; Barksdale, *The Lost State of Franklin*, 158–59; DuVal, *Independence Lost*, 337; Ray, *Middle Tennessee*, 20–32; Kokomoor, "Let Us Try to Make Each Other Happy, and Not Wretched," 220–22, 312–13, 317; Wendy St. Jean, "How the Chickasaws Saved the Cumberland Settlement in the 1790s," *Tennessee Historical Quarterly* 68, no. 1 (2009): 2–14.

6. DuVal, *Independence Lost*, 323–24; Estevan Miró, "A Proclamation, New Orleans, September 2, 1789," *ETHSP*, 21:89–90; Estevan Miró, "Proclamation Setting Forth the Privileges and Benefits Granted by the King to Immigrants to the Province of Louisiana, New Orleans, September 6, 1789," ibid., 21:90–91; James Robertson to Estevan Miró, 13 January 1790, ibid., 22:131.

7. Alexander McGillivray to Estevan Miró, 10 August 1789, *ETHSP*, 21:86.

8. Alexander McGillivray to Vizente Folch, 22 April 1789, in Caughey, *McGillivray of the Creeks*, 227; Alexander McGillivray to Estevan Miró, 26 May 1789, ibid., Caughey, 234.

9. Bartram, *William Bartram on the Southeastern Indians*, 108–10, 156, 260n144; Snyder, *Slavery in Indian Country*, 116-117.

10. Alexander McGillivray to Vizente Folch, 22 April 1789, in Caughey, *McGillivray of the Creeks*, 227.

11. Alexander McGillivray to Francisco Luis Hector de Carondelet, 22 July 1792, in *McGillivray of the Creeks*, 333; Alexander McGillivray to Benjamin James, 10 August 1792, ibid., 333–34; Carson, *Searching for the Bright Path*, 63–65.

12. A Talk from the Kings, Chiefs & Warriors of the Lower Creek Nation to Captain Pedro Olivier Comisario Espanol, 3 July 1792, in Caughey, *McGillivray of the Creeks*, 314.

13. Alexander McGillivray to William Panton, 8 October 1789, in Caughey, *McGillivray of the Creeks*, 251–54.

14. Alexander McGillivray to William Panton, 8 May 1790, in Caughey, *McGillivray of the Creeks*, 261.

15. *Georgia Gazette*, 6 May 1790; ibid., 27 May 1790; ibid., 17 June 1790; Nichols, *Red Gentlemen and White Savages*, 118–25; Milfort, *Memoirs*, 69–72.

16. "Treaty with Creeks, 1790," Charles J. Kappler, ed., *Indian Affairs: Laws and Treaties*, vol. 2 (Washington, DC: U.S. Government Printing Office, 1904), 25–29.

17. Alexander McGillivray to Carlos Howard, 11 August 1790, in Caughey, *McGillivray of the Creeks*, 274–75, 275n252; *ASPIA*, 1:127; Josef Ygnacio de Viar to Juan Nepomuceno de Quesada, 13 August 1790, in Caughey, *McGillivray of the Creeks*, 276; Caughey, *McGillivray of the Creeks*, 278n256; Downes, "Creek-American Relations, 1782-1790," 181–84; *Georgia Gazette*, 26 August 1790; *Pennsylvania Packet and Daily Advertiser*, 18 August 1790, Early American Newspapers Series 1, 1690–1876; *Gazette of the United States* (New York), 24 July 1790. The signers were as follows (1) Alexander McGillivray of Little Tallassee, (2) Opa Mico aka the Singer of Little Tallassee, (3) Totkeshajou aka Sam Moniac of Little Tallassee, (4) Sohotessee aka Young Second Man of Tuckabatchee, (5) Ochehajou aka Aleck Cornel of Tuckabatchee, (6) Hapothe Mico aka Tallisee King of Big Tallassee, (7) Opetotache aka the Long Side of Big Tallassee, (8) Chinabie aka the Great Natches Warrior, (9) Natsowachehe aka the Great Natches Warriors Brother, (10) Thakoteehee aka the Mole of Natches, (11) Oquakabee of Natches, (12) Mumagechee aka David Francis of Oaksoys, (13) Choosades Hopoy aka the Measurer of Coosada, (14) Muthtee aka the Misser of Coosada, (15) Stimafutchkee aka Good Humour of Coosada, (16) Stilmaleeje aka Disputer of Alabama, (17) Fuskatche Mico aka Birdtail King of Cussita, (18) Neathlock aka Second Man of Cussita, (19) Halietem Ithle aka Blue Giver of Cussita, (20) Tuskenaah aka Big Lieutenant of Coweta, (21) Homatch aka Leader of Coweta, (22) Chinnabie, aka Matthews of Coweta, (23) Juleetaulemat ha aka Dry

Pine of Coweta, (24) Chawockly Mico of Broken Arrow. Eight other Creeks were present but did not sign the treaty. They were: two unnamed men of Coosada, Holatah aka The Blue and an unnamed warrior of Tallassee, David Tate (McGillivray's nephew), Mico Nomathle of Coweta, Fusikiah Mico aka Warrior King of Cussita, and Tuskeegie Tustunegie aka Big Fear of Cussita.

18. Alexander McGillivray to Estevan Miró, 2 June 1790, in Caughey, *McGillivray of the Creeks*, 265.

19. Downes, "Creek-American Relations, 1782–1790," 181–84.

20. Alexander McGillivray to Carlos Howard, 11 August 1790, in Caughey, *McGillivray of the Creeks*, 274; *ASPIA*, 1:81.

21. Alexander McGillivray to Estevan Miró, 26 February 1791, in Caughey, *McGillivray of the Creeks*, 289; Nichols, *Red Gentlemen and White Savages*, 122.

22. *ASPIA*, 1:81–82; Alexander McGillivray to Carlos Howard, 11 August 1790, in Caughey, *McGillivray of the Creeks*, 274.

23. *ASPIA*, 1:81–82.

24. Saunt, *A New Order of Things*, 194–98; *ASPIA*, 1:586–616.

25. Alexander McGillivray to Estevan Miró, 26 February 1791, in Caughey, *McGillivray of the Creeks*, 289.

26. *ASPIA*, 1:80.

27. Ibid.; Downes, "Creek-American Relations, 1782–1790," 181–84.

28. Deposition of David Shaw, 2 June 1792, DEPS, vol. 2, pt. 1:281; Pedro Olivier to Francisco Luis Hector de Carondelet, 29 May 1792, in Caughey, *McGillivray of the Creeks*, 326; Carondelet-McGillivray Treaty, 6 July 1792, ibid., 329.

29. James Wilkinson to Estevan Miró, 14 February 1791, *ETSHP*, 25:82; qtd. in Caughey, *McGillivray of the Creeks*, 291n266.

30. Carlos Howard to Juan Nepomuceno de Quesada, 24 September 1790, in Caughey, *McGillivray of the Creeks*, 283.

31. Harrell, "Creek Corridors of Commerce," 258–59.

32. Alexander McGillivray to Arturo O'Neill, 2 November 1790, in Caughey, *McGillivray of the Creeks*, 286; Alexander McGillivray to Arturo O'Neill, 13 January 1791, ibid., 288; Alexander McGillivray to Arturo O'Neill, 22 May 1792, ibid., 323.

33. William Panton to the Kings, Warriors, & Headmen of the Cussitaws, Cowetas, Broken Arrow my Friend John Kennard & all the rest of the Lower Towns, 19 February 1792, in Caughey, *McGillivray of the Creeks*, 308; Debo, *Road to Disappearance*, 52, 56; Wright, *Creeks and Seminoles*, 43, 87, 92, 115, 118, 141; Saunt, *A New Order of Things*, 86, 104–5, 132; J. Leitch Wright Jr., *William Augustus Bowles, Director General of the Creek Nation* (Athens: University of Georgia Press, 1967); Nichols, *Red Gentlemen and White Savages*, 155–56.

34. Alexander McGillivray to William Panton, 28 October 1791, in Caughey, *McGillivray of the Creeks*, 298.

35. William Panton to the Kings, Warriors, & Headmen of the Cussitaws, Cowetas, Broken Arrow my Friend John Kennard & all the rest of the Lower Towns, 19 February 1792, in Caughey, *McGillivray of the Creeks*, 308; Robert Leslie to William Panton, 30 January 1792, ibid., 305–6.

36. Timothy Barnard to James Seagrove, 10 May 1792, LTB, 116; Deposition of David Shaw, 2 June 1792, DEPS, vol. 2, pt. 1:281; Timothy Barnard to James Seagrove, 13 July 1792, ibid., 121.

37. Robert Leslie to William Panton, 30 January 1792, in Caughey, *McGillivray of the Creeks*, 305–6.

38. Francisco Luis Hector de Carondelet to William Panton, 24 March 1792, in Caughey, *McGillivray of the Creeks*, 316; Francisco Luis Hector de Carondelet to Las Casas, 22 March 1792, ibid., 313–14; Alexander McGillivray to Enrique White, 6 May 1792, ibid., 321; James Leonard to James Seagrove, 24 July 1792, *ASPIA*, 1:308.

39. Alexander McGillivray to Francisco Luis Hector de Carondelet, 15 November 1792, in Caughey, *McGillivray of the Creeks*, 345–46.

40. Affidavit of Abraham Mordecai, 20 July 1790, CILTT, pt. 1:223.

41. Alexander McGillivray to Estevan Miró, 30 December 1791, in Caughey, *McGillivray of the Creeks*, 301.

42. A Talk from the Kings, Chief Warriors and Head Men of the Cussatahs and Cowetahs to James Seagrove, 23 August 1792, CILTT, pt. 1:255.

43. *ASPIA*, 1:316, 329, 375, 384, 432; John Forbes to Francisco Luis Hector de Carondelet, 1 November 1792, *ETHSP*, 28:121–32; Ray, *Middle Tennessee*, 24–32.

44. Henry Karr to Edward Telfair, 28 May 1792, CILTT, pt. 1:249; Henry Karr to Joseph Phillips, 28 May 1792, CILTT, pt. 1:249–50; Elijah Clark to Edward Telfair, 15 October 1792, ibid., pt. 1:261; A. Hudson, *Creek Paths and Federal Roads*, 186n118. Hudson suggests that the lands between the Oconee and Apalachee Rivers may have had particular "historic and spiritual" significance to Creeks.

45. Alexander McGillivray to Francisco Luis Hector de Carondelet, 15 November 1792, in Caughey, *McGillivray of the Creeks*, 345; Alexander McGillivray to William Panton, 28 November 1792, ibid., 347; Richard Call to Edward Telfair, 17 September 1791, CILTT, pt. 1:240.

46. Samuel Alexander to Adjutant General Elholm, 25 January 1793, CILTT, pt. 1:264.

47. Francisco Luis Hector de Carondelet to Alexander McGillivray, 14 September 1792, in Caughey, *McGillivray of the Creeks*, 338; Alexander McGillivray to Francisco Luis Hector de Carondelet, 15 November 1792, ibid., 345; Alexander McGillivray to William Panton, 28 November 1792, ibid., 346–47; Louis le Clerc Milfort to Francisco Luis Hector de Carondelet, 9 April 1793, *ETHSP*, 31:79–80.

48. Alexander McGillivray to William Panton, 28 November 1792, in Caughey, *McGillivray of the Creeks*, 348; Timothy Barnard to James Seagrove, 13 July 1792, LTB, 120; *ASPIA*, 1:603; Ethridge, *Creek Country*, 135, 163.

49. Deposition of James Espey, 23 July 1821, DEPS, vol. 2, pt. 1:137.

50. Francisco Luis Hector de Carondelet to Prime Minister Pedro Pablo Abarca de Bolea, Conde de Aranda, 28 November 1792, *ETHSP*, 28:139–40.

51. Timothy Barnard to James Seagrove, 13 July 1792, LTB, 122.

52. Ibid.

53. Ibid.

54. A Talk from the Kings, Chief Warriors and Head Men of the Cussatahs and Cowetahs to James Seagrove, 23 August 1792, CILTT, pt. 1:255–56.

55. John Kinnard to Indian Affairs Agent James Seagrove, 28 August 1792, CILTT, pt. 1:257.

56. Henry Karr to Edward Telfair, 16 June 1792, CILLT, pt. 1:250–53.

57. Elijah Clark to Edward Telfair, 15 October 1792, CILTT, pt. 1:261; Samuel Alexander to Adjutant General Elholm, 25 January 1793, ibid., pt. 1:264.

58. Henry Karr to Edward Telfair, 16 June 1792, CILLT, pt. 1:250–53.

59. Alexander McGillivray to Estevan Miró, 8 June 1791, in Caughey, *McGillivray of the Creeks*, 292; Henry Karr to Edward Telfair, 14 June 1791, Telamon Cuyler Collection, HAR DLG.

60. Henry Karr to Elijah Clarke, 16 April 1792, CILLT, pt. 1:244; Timothy Barnard to James Seagrove, 10 May 1792, LTB, 116.

61. Richard Call to Edward Telfair, 29 April 1792, CILLT, pt. 1:246.

62. A Talk from the Kings, Chief Warriors, and Head Men of the Cussatahs and Cowetahs to James Seagrove, 23 August 1792, CILLT, pt. 1:255.

63. Timothy Barnard to James Seagrove, 10 May 1792, LTB, 116.

64. Alexander McGillivray to William Panton, 28 October 1791, in Caughey, *McGillivray of the Creeks*, 300.

65. Statement by Middleton, 21 December 1791, in Caughey, *McGillivray of the Creeks*, 300.

66. Carondelet-McGillivray Treaty, 6 July 1792, in Caughey, *McGillivray of the Creeks*, 330; Alexander McGillivray to Francisco Luis Hector de Carondelet, 15 November 1792, ibid., 344; Alexander McGillivray to William Panton, 28 November 1792, ibid., 346.

67. Timothy Barnard to James Seagrove, 13 July 1792, LTB, 121; quotes from Francisco Luis Hector de Carondelet to Prime Minister Pedro Pablo Abarca de Bolea, Conde de Aranda, 28 November 1792, *ETHSP*, 28:139–40.

68. A Talk from the Kings, Chief Warriors and Head Men of the Cussatahs and Cowetahs to James Seagrove, 23 August 1792, CILTT, pt. 1:256.

69. Talk from the White Lieutenant of the Oakfurkeys to James Seagrove, 15 August 1792, CILTT, pt. 1:254.

70. Ibid.

71. On the careers of Brims and Malatchi, see Hahn, *The Invention of the Creek Nation*; Piker, *The Four Deaths of Acorn Whistler*.

72. William Panton to Francisco Luis Hector de Carondelet, 20 February 1793, in Caughey, *McGillivray of the Creeks*, 354.

73. Declaration of James Dearment, 18 April 1793, in Caughey, *McGillivray of the Creeks*, 357. Kinnard and Cornel both spoke English but could not write.

74. William Panton to Francisco Luis Hector de Carondelet, undated, likely late February 1793, in Caughey, *McGillivray of the Creeks*, 355–356.

75. A Talk from the White Lieut. of the Ofuskees to his Friend & Brother, and also his Father the Governor of New Orleans, 9 November 1793, in Caughey, *McGillivray of the Creeks*, 360–61; Timothy Barnard to James Seagrove, 2 July 1793, LTB, 189.

76. Louis Milfort to Francisco Luis Hector de Carondelet, 26 May 1793, Caughey, *McGillivray of the Creeks*, 358–59; James Jackson to Edward Telfair, 27 May 1793, CILTT, pt. 1:314. For a different interpretation of this period, see Kokomoor, "Let Us Try to Make Each Other Happy and Not Wretched," 293–331.

77. Timothy Barnard to Henry Gaither, 18 February 1793, LTB, 125.

78. Ibid.

79. Timothy Barnard to Henry Gaither, 4 March 1793, LTB, 130.

80. Ibid.

81. Timothy Barnard to Henry Gaither, 18 February 1793, LTB, 125.

82. Ibid.; Timothy Barnard to Henry Gaither, 4 March 1793, LTB, 130.

83. Saunt, *A New Order of Things*, 104–7.

84. James Seagrove to Timothy Barnard, 24 February 1793, LTB, 127–128; Debo *The Road to Disappearance*, 55–56; Reginald Horsman, *Expansion and American Indian Policy, 1783–1812* (Lansing: Michigan State University Press, 1967), 86–96; Nichols, *Red Gentlemen and White Savages*, 113–18, 137–40; Colin Calloway, *The Victory with No Name: The Native American Defeat of the First American Army* (Oxford: Oxford University Press, 2014).

85. Timothy Barnard to Major Henry Gaither, 4 March 1793, LTB, 130.

86. Ibid.

87. James Seagrove to Timothy Barnard, 24 February 1793, LTB, 127–28; Debo, *Road to Disappearance*, 55–57.

88. James Seagrove to Edward Telfair, 17 March 1793, CILTT, pt. 1:272; William Panton to Francisco Luis Hector de Carondelet, 10 April 1793, *ETHSP*, 31:80.

89. Financial Claim and deposition pertaining to the estate of James Green, 23 April 1835, sworn to by Isaac Green, C. Mildred Thompson Papers, Box 1, Folder 17, HAR DLG; Deposition of Samuel Smith, 21 July 1835, DEPS, vol. 2, pt. 1:112–13.

90. Deposition of John Hardee, 28 April 1835, DEPS, vol. 2, pt. 1:81; Deposition of John Crews, 20 March 1824, DEPS, vol. 2, pt. 1:123.

91. Financial Claim and deposition pertaining to the estate of James Green, 23 April 1835, sworn to by Isaac Green, C. Mildred Thompson Papers, Box 1, Folder 17, HAR DLG; Deposition of John W. Hunter, 22 April 1835, DEPS, vol. 2, pt. 1:23–24.

92. James Seagrove to Edward Telfair, 17 March 1793, CILTT, pt. 1:272; Financial Claim and deposition pertaining to the estate of James Green, 23 April 1835, sworn to by Isaac Green, C. Mildred Thompson Papers, Box 1, Folder 17, HAR DLG.

93. Deposition of John Hardee, 28 April 1835, DEPS, vol. 2, pt. 1:81.

94. Deposition of John W. Hunter, 22 April 1835, DEPS, vol. 2, pt. 1:23–24.

95. James Seagrove to Edward Telfair, 17 March 1793, CILTT, pt. 1:273; Timothy Barnard to Major Henry Gaither, 20 April 1793, LTB, 154.

96. James Seagrove to Edward Telfair, 17 March 1793, CILTT, pt. 1:273.

97. Timothy Barnard to Major Henry Gaither, 20 April 1793, LTB, 154; A Talk of Alick Cornells to James Seagrove, 14 June 1793, CILTT, pt. 1:323.

98. Deposition of Michael Cupp, 23 April 1793, File II, Box 76, Folder 7, Georgia Archives; Depositions of Joseph C. Thrasher and Payton Smith, 15 March 1803, DEPS, vol. 4:139.

99. Deposition of Duncan Cameron, 3 October 1795, DEPS, vol. 2, pt. 2:324.

100. Timothy Barnard to Edward Telfair, 7 July 1793, LTB, 203.

101. Debo, *Road to Disappearance*, 59–60; Nichols, *Red Gentlemen and White Savages*, 151–59; Ray, *Middle Tennessee*, 24–32; John Forbes to Francisco Luis Hector de Carondelet, 1 November 1792, *ETHSP*, 28:121–32; Manuel Gayoso de Lemos to Francisco Luis Hector de Carondelet, 8 January 1793, ibid., 29:141–42.

102. Timothy Barnard to Henry Gaither, 20 April 1793, LTB, 155.

103. Ibid., 154–55; Timothy Barnard to Henry Gaither, undated, ca. 30 April 1793, LTB, 157; Copy of a Talk from the Big Warrior of the Cassetahs, and Two of the Chiefs from the Same Town, 2 May 1793, ibid., 160; Deposition of James Akins, 3 May 1793, File II, Box 76, Folder 1, Georgia Archives; Timothy Barnard to James Seagrove, 12 May 1793, LTB, 165.

104. Braund, *Deerskins and Duffels*, 158.

105. War Department to James Seagrove, 10 June 1793, File II, Box 74, Folder 5, Georgia Archives.

106. Deposition of James Akins, 3 May 1793, File II, Folder 1, Box 76, Georgia Archives.

107. Daniel J. Stewart to James Jackson, 18 March 1793, DEPS, vol. 2 pt. 1:230; James Houstoun to Edward Telfair, 18 March 1793, CILTT, pt. 1:275; Deposition of James Akins, 3 May 1793, File II, Box 76, Folder 1, Georgia Archives; James Jackson to Edward Telfair, 9 May 1793, CILTT, pt. 1:309.

108. Deposition of James Cashen, undated, and deposition of Susan Murphy, 3 July 1835, DEPS, vol. 2, pt. 1:79–80; Extract of a letter from Major William McIntosh to his Father, General Lachlan McIntosh, 18 March 1793, addressed to James Jackson, CILTT, pt. 1:276.

109. Timothy Barnard to Henry Gaither, 20 April 1793, LTB, 155.

110. Timothy Barnard to Henry Gaither, undated, ca. 30 April 1793, LTB, 158.

111. Ibid., 157.

112. General Orders from Governor Edward Telfair to Georgia Militia Commanders, 15 March 1793, 6 April 1793, 11 April 1793, 20 April 1793, 26 April 1793, 1 May 1793, CILTT, pt. 1:269–70, 284, 299; Augustus C. G. Elholm to The Inhabitants adjacent in the presence of David Dickson, 22 April 1793, ibid., pt. 1:286; Deposition of Michael Cupp, 26 April 1793, ibid., pt. 1:289–90.

113. Nathan Barnett to Major General Twiggs, 28 April 1793, CILTT, pt. 1:291; Petition of Nathan Barnett, et al., to Major General Twiggs, 28 April 1793, ibid., pt. 1:292, 295; Petition of George W. Foster, et al., to Governor Edward Telfair and Major General John Twiggs, 29 April 1793, ibid., pt. 1:294–95; Petition of Thomas Houghton et al. to Governor Edward Telfair, 29 April 1793, ibid., pt. 1:296–97; James Jackson to Governor Edward Telfair, 5 May 1793, ibid., pt. 1:304–5; James Jackson to Edward Telfair, 9 May 1793, ibid., pt. 1:309–10; An Inspection of Fort Clark Greene County 15 July 1793, ibid., pt. 1:331; A List of Men Who Served As Guard at the Building of Fort Twiggs, 23 July 1793, ibid., pt. 1:340; Garrison at Colerain, 26 February 1794, ibid., pt. 2:356–58; Deposition of Martin Palmer, et al., 8 March 1794, ibid., pt. 2:363; Jonathan Clark to George Matthews, 5 July 1794, ibid., pt. 2:391; Certificate of Brigadier General Jared Irwin, 12 August 1794, ibid., pt. 2:399; Petition of the Inhabitants of Montgomery County, 5 November 1794, ibid., pt. 2:421; E. Wamberg to George Mathews, 10 December 1794, ibid., pt. 2:424; John Burnett to George Mathews, 22 April 1795, ibid., pt. 2:434–35; Michael Cupp to George Mathews, 18 July 1795, ibid., pt. 2:441; Extract of a Letter from the Secretary of War, undated, ca. 30 October 1795, ibid., pt. 2:452–53; Deposition of James and John Kirkpatrick, 13 February 1796, ibid., pt. 2:355c.

114. James Seagrove to Edward Telfair, 17 March 1793, CILTT, pt. 1:247.

115. Henry Knox to Edward Telfair, 29 April 1793, CILTT, pt. 1:293; Henry Knox to Edward Telfair, 30 May 1793, ASPIA, 1:364.

116. James Jackson to Edward Telfair, 8 July 1793, CILTT, pt. 1:329–30.

117. Extract from the Journal of the Adjutant General's Office, Augustus C. G. Elholm, to Edward Telfair, 11–14 June 1793, CILTT, pt. 1:317–20; Jennison, *Cultivating Race*, 102.

118. Copy of a Talk from the Big Warrior of the Cassetahs, and Two of the Chiefs from the Same Town, 2 May 1793, LTB, 160; A Talk of the White Lieutenant, Alec

Cornell, and Charles Weatherford to Major General James Jackson, 14 July 1793, CILTT, pt. 1:321.

119. A Talk of the White Lieutenant, Alec Cornell, and Charles Weatherford to Major General James Jackson, 14 July 1793, CILTT, pt. 1:321; Caughey, *McGillivray of the Creeks*, 51.

120. Copy of a Talk from the Big Warrior of the Cassetahs, and Two of the Chiefs from the Same Town, 2 May 1793, LTB, 163.

121. Ibid., 163–64.

122. Timothy Barnard to James Seagrove, 2 July 1793, LTB, 188; A Talk of the White Lieutenant, Alec Cornell, and Charles Weatherford to Major General James Jackson, 14 July 1793, CILTT, pt. 1:321.

123. Timothy Barnard to James Seagrove, 12 May 1793, LTB, 166.

124. Ibid., 167.

125. Copy of a Talk from the Big Warrior of the Cassetahs, and Two of the Chiefs from the Same Town, 2 May 1793, LTB, 163.

126. Alick Cornel to James Seagrove, 14 June 1793, LTB, 169.

127. A Talk of the White Lieutenant, Alec Cornell, and Charles Weatherford to James Jackson, 14 July 1793, CILTT, pt. 1:321.

128. Timothy Barnard to James Jackson, 20 June 1793, LTB, 171–73; Timothy Barnard to James Seagrove, 20 June 1793, LTB, 174–76; Timothy Barnard to James Seagrove, 2 July 1793, LTB, 189.

129. Copy of a Talk from the Big Warrior of the Cassetahs, and Two of the Chiefs from the Same Town, 2 May 1793, LTB, 161.

130. Timothy Barnard to James Seagrove, 12 May 1793, LTB, 166; Timothy Barnard to James Seagrove, 2 July 1793, LTB, 192.

131. Timothy Barnard to James Seagrove, 12 May 1793, LTB, 166.

132. The quote in the subhead comes from White Lieutenant to James Seagrove, 23 June 1793, *ASPIA*, 1:401.

133. Protest of the Legislature of the State of Georgia against the Treaty of New York, *ASPIA*, 2:790–791.

134. Samuel Alexander to Adjutant General Elholm, 25 January 1793, CILTT, pt. 1:264.

135. Henry Gaither to Edward Telfair, 15 February 1793, CILTT, pt. 1:267; Elijah Clarke to Augustus Christian George Elholm, 19 February 1793, ibid., pt. 1:268.

136. Jennison, *Cultivating Race*, 90; Gordon S. Wood, *Empire of Liberty: A History of the Early Republic, 1789–1815* (Oxford: Oxford University Press, 2009), 132. See also Nichols, *Red Gentlemen and White Savages*.

137. David Cornell to James Seagrove using a "linguister," 6 January 1793, *ASPIA*, 1:375.

138. Timothy Barnard to James Jackson, 20 June 1793, LTB, 171.

139. Ibid., 171–73; Timothy Barnard to James Seagrove, 20 June 1793, LTB, 174–76; Timothy Barnard to James Seagrove, 20 June 1793, ibid., 177–81; Timothy Barnard to Henry Gaither, 21 June 1793, ibid., 183–86.

140. Timothy Barnard to James Jackson, 20 June 1793, LTB, 171–73; Timothy Barnard to James Seagrove, 20 June 1793, ibid., 174–76; Timothy Barnard to James Seagrove, 20 June 1793, ibid., 177–81; Timothy Barnard to Henry Gaither, 21 June 1793, ibid., 183–86; Timothy Barnard to James Seagrove, 2 July 1793, ibid., 188–92; Timothy Barnard to Henry Gaither, 7 July 1793, ibid., 197–99; Jacob Townsend to

James Jackson, undated, ca. 7 July 1793, ibid., 200–201; James Jackson to Edward Telfair, 8 July 1793, CILTT, pt. 1:329–30; A Talk of the White Lieutenant, Alec Cornell, and Charles Weatherford to Major General James Jackson, 14 July 1793, CILTT, 321–322.

141. Timothy Barnard to James Seagrove, 2 July 1793, LTB, 192.

142. Timothy Barnard to James Jackson, 20 June 1793, LTB, 172; Timothy Barnard to James Seagrove, 20 June 1793, ibid., 179.

143. Timothy Barnard to James Jackson, 20 June 1793, LTB, 171–73; Timothy Barnard to James Seagrove, 20 June 1793, ibid., 174–76; Timothy Barnard to James Seagrove, 20 June 1793, ibid., 177–81.

144. Timothy Barnard to James Seagrove, 20 June 1793, LTB, 176.

145. Extract of a letter from T. Barnard to Jas. Seagrove esqr. dated 20th June 1793, LTB, 182.

146. Jacob Townshend to James Jackson, June 1793, CILTT, pt. 1:327; Extract of a letter from T. Barnard to Jas. Seagrove esqr. dated 20th June 1793, LTB, 182; Timothy Barnard to James Seagrove, 3 July 1793, CILTT, pt. 1:326c.

147. Deposition of James Kirby, 22 July 1793, CILTT, pt. 1:338–39; Jacob Townshend to James Jackson, June 1793, ibid., pt. 1:327.

148. Jacob Townshend to James Jackson, June 1793, CILTT, pt. 1:327–28; Timothy Barnard to James Seagrove, 3 July 1793, ibid., pt. 1:326b-326e; James Seagrove to Timothy Barnard, 5 July 1793, LTB, 193–196; Timothy Barnard to Henry Gaither, 7 July 1793, ibid., 197–99; Jacob Townsend to General James Jackson, undated, ca. 7 July 1793, ibid., 200–1.

149. Jacob Townshend to James Jackson, June 1793, CILTT, pt. 1:327–28; Timothy Barnard to James Seagrove, 3 July 1793, ibid., pt. 1:326b-326e; Jacob Townsend to General James Jackson, undated, ca. 7 July 1793, LTB, 200–201.

150. James Seagrove to Timothy Barnard, 5 July 1793, LTB, 193–96.

151. James Jackson to Edward Telfair, 8 July 1793, CILTT, pt. 1:329–30; Deposition of James Kirby, 22 July 1793, CILTT, pt. 1:338–39.

152. A. Hammond, etc., to Thomas Carr, 21 September 1793, CILTT, pt. 1:342; Proceedings of a Court of Inquiry, 26 October 1793, ibid., pt. 1:344–48.

153. Proceedings of a Court of Inquiry, 26 October 1793, CILTT, pt. 1:344–48.

154. James Jackson to Edward Telfair, 8 July 1793, CILTT, pt. 1:329–30.

155. James Seagrove to Timothy Barnard, 29 July 1793, LTB, 208–11; Timothy Barnard to James Seagrove, 3 July 1793, CILTT, pt. 1:326e; James Seagrove to Timothy Barnard, 5 July 1793, LTB, 193–96; Timothy Barnard to Edward Telfair, 7 July 1793, ibid., 202–4; Debo, *Road to Disappearance*, 58.

156. Unsigned letter to unknown correspondent, likely James Jackson to Edward Telfair, 21 July 1793, CILTT, 334–37.

157. Debo, *Road to Disappearance*, 58.

158. Timothy Barnard to James Seagrove, 17 October 1793, LTB, 215–16; Timothy Barnard to James Seagrove, 18 October 1793, ibid., 220–22.

159. Extract of a Letter from Lieutenant van Allen to Colonel Henry Gaither, 18 October 1793, CILTT, pt. 1:343.

160. Affadavit of Henry Carrel, 6 September 1793, C. Mildred Thompson Papers, HAR DLG; John Twiggs to Edward Telfair, 8 September 1793, C. Mildred Thompson Papers, HAR DLG.

161. Jonas Fauche to Augustus Christian George Elholm, 20 July 1793, CILTT, pt. 1:332–33.

162. Debo, *Road to Disappearance*, 58; Saunt, *A New Order of Things*, 99–100; Jennison, *Cultivating Race*, 105; Timothy Barnard to James Seagrove, 17 October 1793, LTB, 217–19.

163. Henry Knox to George Mathews, 6 March 1794, CILTT, pt. 2:362.

164. Timothy Barnard to Henry Gaither, 5 October 1793, LTB, 214.

165. Timothy Barnard to James Seagrove, 1 October 1793, LTB, 212–13; Timothy Barnard to Henry Gaither, 5 October 1793, ibid., 214; Timothy Barnard to James Seagrove, 17 October 1793, ibid., 218.

166. Timothy Barnard to James Seagrove, 17 October 1793, LTB, 215–16; Timothy Barnard to James Seagrove, 18 October 1793, ibid., 220–22; Saunt, *A New Order of Things*, 158, 160, 172–73, 218.

8 / "Like Pulling out Their Hearts and Throwing Them Away"

The chapter title comes from Alexander Cornel, 1796, *ASPIA*, 1:607.

1. Weber, *Spanish Frontier in North America*, 280, 289–90; Carson, *Searching for the Bright Path*, 47–48; Ray, *Middle Tennessee*, 32–33; Nichols, *Red Gentlemen and White Savages*, 172; Waselkov, *A Conquering Spirit*, 17–27; Harrell, "Creek Corridors of Commerce," 271.

2. Calloway, *The American Revolution in Indian Country*, 188. Cherokees adopted a similar strategy of incorporating young men "into the political decision-making process to restrain them."

3. A. Hudson, *Creek Paths and Federal Roads*, 123; Nichols, *Red Gentlemen and White Savages*, 183, 188.

4. The quote in the subheading comes from Timothy Barnard to James Seagrove, 22 December 1795, LTB, 262.

5. Constant Freeman to George Mathews, 1 January 1794, CILTT, pt. 1:352–54; A Talk from the Bird Tail King, undated, ca. 1 January 1794, ibid., pt. 2:354b; George Mathews to James Seagrove, 3 February 1794, ibid., pt. 2:355b; Timothy Barnard to George Matthews, 25 February 1794, LTB, 230.

6. Jennison, *Cultivating Race*, 89–125; Nichols, *Red Gentlemen and White Savages*, 160–63, 170–71.

7. Elijah Clarke to Gentlemen, 5 September 1794, CILTT, pt. 2:426–27; Timothy Barnard to George Matthews, 25 February 1794, LTB, 229; Copy of a letter from Constant Freeman, Agent for the War Department, in Georgia, to the Secretary of War, 29 September 1794, *ASPIA*, 1:500.

8. Nichols, *Red Gentlemen and White Savages*, 162.

9. Timothy Barnard to Governor George Matthews, 25 February 1794, LTB, 229–31.

10. Thomas Houghton to George Mathews, 20 May 1794, "An Elijah Clarke Document," *Georgia Historical Quarterly* 14, no. 3 (September 1930): 254–55.

11. Thomas Houghton et al., Inhabitants of Greene County, to George Mathews, 16 March 1794, CILTT, pt. 2:366.

12. The Report of Dr. Frederick Dalcho, Surgeon's Mate and Paymaster to the Troops of the United States in Georgia, 10 May 1794, LTB, 236–37; Deposition of Archer Norris, 1 August 1794, CILTT, pt. 2:396–97; George Mathews to Timothy

Barnard, 11 August 1794, LTB, 240+ through 240++; Constant Freeman to George Mathews, 9 May 1794, CILTT, pt. 2:375.

13. Constant Freeman to George Mathews, 1 January 1794, CILTT, pt. 2:353–54.

14. Deposition of Jesse Thompson and Charles Clay, 14 May 1794, CILTT, pt. 2:379; James Seagrove to George Mathews, 26 May 1794, LTB, 239.

15. Affidavit of James Adams, 3 May 1794, CILTT, pt. 2:374b; Constant Freeman to George Mathews, 9 May 1794, ibid., pt. 2:375–77; Richard Brooke Roberts to Henry Knox, 10 May 1794, LTB, 232–33; Deposition of Archibald Norris, 6 August 1821, DEPS, vol. 1, pt. 1:27–29.

16. Constant Freeman to Henry Knox, 10 May 1794, LTB, 234–35.

17. Ibid.; Report of Dr. Frederick Dalcho, Surgeon's Mate and Paymaster to the Troops of the United States in Georgia, 10 May 1794, LTB, 236–37; Constant Freeman to George Mathews, 10 May 1794, CILTT, pt. 2:378; James Seagrove to George Mathews, 26 May 1794, LTB, 239; Elijah Clarke to Major David Adams, 17 May 1794, CILTT, pt. 2:380.

18. Constant Freeman to Henry Knox, 10 May 1794, LTB, 234–35.

19. James Seagrove to George Mathews, 26 May 1794, CILTT, pt. 2:384–85; George Mathews to Timothy Barnard, 27 May 1794, LTB, 239b; Proceedings of the Court of Enquiry respecting the Conduct of Major David Adams on 10 May 1794, 22 July 1794, CILTT, pt. 2:387–90.

20. James Seagrove to George Mathews, 7 December 1795, CILTT, pt. 2:461.

21. George Mathews to Timothy Barnard, 11 August 1794, LTB, 240+ through 240++.

22. Copy of a Letter from the Secretary of War to his Excellency the Governor of Georgia, 28 July 1794, ASPIA, 1:501–2.

23. Jared Irwin to George Mathews, 3 October 1794, CILTT, pt. 2:413–15.

24. Discharge of General Clarke by the Justices of Wilkes County, 28 July 1794, ASPIA, 1:496.

25. Elijah Clarke to Gentlemen, 5 September 1794, CILTT, pt. 2:426–27.

26. Elijah Clarke to Jared Irwin, 24 September 1794, CILTT, pt. 2:407.

27. Elijah Clarke to Jared Irwin, 26 September 1794, CILLT, pt. 2:408–10; John Twiggs to George Mathews, 2 October 1794, ibid., pt. 2:411; Jared Irwin to George Mathews, 3 October 1794, ibid., pt. 2:413–15; Jonas Fauche to George Mathews, 19 October 1794, ibid., pt. 2:418–19.

28. Timothy Barnard to Jared Irwin, 7 May 1796, LTB, 265–66.

29. Extract of a letter from Timothy Barnard, deputy agent of Indian affairs, to James Seagrove, Esq., 18 December 1794, LTB, 241a; Timothy Barnard to George Matthews, 21 January 1795, ibid., 242; Timothy Barnard to unknown correspondent, 2 February 1795, ibid., 243–44; James Seagrove to George Mathews, 11 May 1795, CILTT, pt. 2:436.

30. Copy of a Petition for Opening an Office for the Lands South of the Oconee, Which Is to be Presented to the legislature of Georgia, 29 September 1794, ASPIA, 1:500.

31. James Seagrove to George Mathews, 11 May 1795, CILTT, pt. 2:436.

32. James Seagrove to George Mathews, 29 June 1795, CILTT, pt. 2:440.

33. Jonas Fauche to George Mathews, 28 July 1795, CILTT, pt. 2:442; Nichols, *Red Gentlemen and White Savages*, 169.

34. St. Jean, "How the Chickasaws Saved the Cumberland Settlement in the 1790s," 14–15; DuVal, *Independence Lost*, 309; General James Robertson to Colonel David Henley, War Department, 24 October 1795, Telamon Cuyler Collection, HAR DLG; Piomingo to General James Robertson, 29 September 1795, Telamon Cuyler Collection, HAR DLG.

35. Deposition of Daniel Currie, 17 September 1795, CILTT, pt. 2:443–44; Jared Irwin to George Mathews, 2 October 1795, ibid., pt. 2:445.

36. Timothy Barnard to an unnamed resident of the Carr's Bluff neighborhood, 14 October 1795, LTB, 248.

37. Bartram, *William Bartram and the Southeastern Indians*, 108–10, 156, 260n144; Jackson, ed., *Yuchi Indian Histories*, 36–39, 43–48, 55–56, 106, 124–32, 140–45, 160–61; Snyder, *Slavery in Indian Country*, 116-117.

38. Timothy Barnard to James Seagrove, 18 December 1795, LTB, 257.

39. Jared Irwin to George Mathews, 2 October 1795, CILTT, pt. 2:445; Deposition of David Culpepper, 27 September 1795, ibid., pt. 2:444; Hawkins, *Collected Works*, 62s–63s; Snyder, *Slavery in Indian Country*, 170; Ethridge, *Creek Country*, 217-218.

40. Timothy Barnard to George Mathews, 9 October 1795, LTB, 246–47; Timothy Barnard to an unnamed resident of the Carr's Bluff neighborhood, 14 October 1795, ibid., 248; James Seagrove to Different Euchees, undated, ca. December 1795, Record Group 75, Records of the Bureau of Indian Affairs, Records of the Creek Agency East, 1794–1818, The National Archives and Records Service, General Services Administration, Washington: 1966, Microfilm held by Georgia Archives (hereafter cited as Records of the Creek Agency East); Examination of Mr. John Barnard, 22 October 1795, LTB, 251.

41. Timothy Barnard to an unnamed resident of the Carr's Bluff neighborhood, 14 October 1795, LTB, 248.

42. Timothy Pickering to Governor George Matthews, 12 November 1795, File II, Box 76, Folder 8, Georgia Archives; Timothy Barnard to James Seagrove, 22 December 1795, LTB, 260.

43. Examination of Mr. John Barnard, 22 October 1795, LTB, 251; Hawkins, *Collected Works*, 61s–63s.

44. Hawkins, *Collected Works*, 74s–75s.

45. Ibid.; Alexander Cornel to James Seagrove, 28 November 1795, CILTT, pt. 2:458–59.

46. Timothy Barnard to an unnamed resident of the Carr's Bluff neighborhood, 14 October 1795, LTB, 248.

47. Timothy Barnard to James Seagrove, 18 December 1795, LTB, 256–59.

48. H. Hampton to George Mathews, 5 October 1795, CILTT, pt. 2:446.

49. Timothy Pickering, War Office, Instructions to Captain William Eaton, Commander at Fort Pickering [Colerain, St. Mary's River], 26 November 1795, Record Group 75, Records of the Creek Trading House, Letter Book, 1795–1816, File Microcopies of Records in The National Archives, microfilm in Georgia Archives (hereafter cited as Records of the Creek Trading House).

50. Ibid.; Timothy Pickering to George Matthews, 12 November 1795, File II, Box 76, Folder 8, Georgia Archives.

51. James Seagrove to George Mathews, 5 November 1795, CILTT, pt. 2:455; James Seagrove to George Mathews, 7 December 1795, ibid., pt. 2:460–61.

52. Deposition of William Scarbrough, 9 January 1796, CILTT, pt. 2:62.

53. James Seagrove to Different Euchees, undated, ca. December 1795, Records of the Creek Agency East; Timothy Barnard to James Seagrove, 22 December 1795, LTB, 260–63.

54. Timothy Barnard to James Seagrove, 18 December 1795, LTB, 256–59.

55. Edward Price to Tench Francis, 11 January 1796, Records of the Creek Trading House; Deposition of George Tarvin, 27 December 1795, CILTT, pt. 2:469.

56. Timothy Barnard to James Seagrove, 18 December 1795, LTB, 256–59; Joshua Piker, "To the Backcountry and Back Again: The Yuchi's Search for Stability in the Eighteenth-Century Southeast," in Jackson, ed., *Yuchi Indian Histories*, 195.

57. Timothy Barnard to James Seagrove, 22 December 1795, LTB, 260–63.

58. Ibid., 262.

59. Roderick Easley to Jared Irwin, 1 February 1796, CILTT, pt. 2:463.

60. Davis Grasham to Jared Irwin, 4 March 1796, CILTT, pt. 2:467.

61. Deposition of Isum Carr, 11 February 1796, CILTT, pt. 2:464b-464c; Deposition of David Blackshear, 11 February 1796, DEPS, vol. 3, 70–71.

62. Deposition of David Blackshear, 11 February 1796, DEPS, vol. 3, 70.

63. Jared Irwin to James Jackson, 20 March 1798, CILTT, pt. 2:520.

64. James Seagrove to Jared Irwin, 9 April 1796, CILTT, pt. 2:470.

65. The quote in the subheading comes from *ASPIA*, 1:597.

66. James Seagrove to Jared Irwin, 9 April 1796, CILTT, pt. 2:470.

67. A Talk from James Seagrove to the Kings, Chiefs, Headmen & Warriors of the Upper and Lower Creeks, Simanolias, and all other Tribes Living in the Creek Land, undated, ca. 18 April 1796, CILTT, pt. 2:472–73.

68. Debo, *The Road to Disappearance*, 62–66; Nichols, *Red Gentlemen and White Savages*, 182–83, 186.

69. Timothy Barnard to Jared Irwin, 7 May 1796, LTB, 265; Hawkins, *Collected Works*, 24s.

70. Timothy Barnard to Jared Irwin, 7 May 1796, LTB, 266.

71. The Following Gentlemen Address the President and the Secretary of War, 11 June 1796, CILTT, pt. 2:478.

72. *ASPIA*, 1:597.

73. Ibid.

74. Ibid.

75. Hawkins, *Collected Works*, 25s.

76. Ibid., 45s.

77. "Treaty with the Creeks, 1796," Kappler, *Indian Affairs*, vol. 2:46–50.

78. Hawkins, *Collected Works*, 27s, 72s.

79. Nichols, *Red Gentlemen and White Savages*, 182.

80. *ASPIA*, 1:590–97.

81. Ibid. 1:599.

82. Ibid.

83. Ibid., 1:608.

84. Ibid.

85. Ibid., 1:603–4.

86. *ASPIA*, 1:604.

87. Ibid.

88. *ASPIA*, 1:605.

89. Nichols, *Red Gentlemen and White Savages*, 160, 176.

90. *ASPIA*, 1:605.

91. Ibid., 1:606.

92. Ibid., 1:586–616; Alexander McGillivray to Estevan Miró, 26 February 1791, in Caughey, *McGillivray of the Creeks*, 289.

93. *ASPIA*, 1:599.

94. Ibid., 1:606.

95. Ibid., 1:604.

96. Ibid., 1:606.

97. Ibid.

98. Ibid.

99. Ibid., 1:605.

100. Ibid., 1:607.

101. Ibid.

102. Ibid.

103. Hawkins, *Collected Works*, 70–71; Nichols, *Red Gentlemen and White Savages*, 179.

104. *ASPIA*, 1:607.

105. Saunt, *A New Order of Things*, 23–24.

106. *ASPIA*, 1:608–9, 611, 615.

107. Ibid., 1:610.

108. Ford, *Settler Sovereignty*, 90–97.

109. *ASPIA*, 1:610.

110. Ibid.

111. Ibid., 1:611.

112. Edward Price to Benjamin Hawkins, 14 January 1797, Records of the Creek Trading House; Edward Price to Timothy Pickering, 24 January 1797, ibid.; Edward Price to Constant Freeman, 5 January 1797, ibid.; Edward Price to Henry Gaither, 9 January 1797, ibid.

113. Henry Gaither to David Blackshear, receipt for horses, Fort Wilkinson, 7 January 1798, CILTT, pt. 2:505; James Ford to James Jackson, 16 February 1799, DEPS, vol. 2, pt. 3:817.

114. Edward Price to Timothy Barnard, 17 January 1797, Records of the Creek Trading House.

115. Edward Price to Jared Irwin, 5 January 1798, CILTT, pt. 2:504.

116. James Seagrove to Jared Irwin, 18 September 1796, CILTT, pt. 2:494.

117. Deposition of John Hamlen, 10 August 1796, CILTT, pt. 1:485; Deposition of John Lamar, 10 August 1796, DEPS, vol. 2, pt. 2:439; Deposition of Henry Butts, 10 August 1796, CILTT, pt. 2:484; A Message from James Seagrove . . . to the Kings, Chief, Headmen, and Warriors of the Creek Nation, in reply to a Talk received . . . from the White Bird King, and Chalee Mathla, two Cusseta Chiefs, 18 August 1796, ibid., pt. 2:489–93; James Seagrove to Jared Irwin, 18 September 1796, ibid., pt. 2:494.

118. A Talk from Chalee Matla (Uncle to the two young men killed by the Georgians when Mr. Seagrove was in the Nation), and the Bird King, to James, 18 August 1796, LTB, 269.

119. Ibid.

120. A Message from James Seagrove . . . to the Kings, Chief, Headmen, and Warriors of the Creek Nation, in reply to a Talk received . . . from the White Bird King, and Chalee Mathla, two Cusseta Chiefs, 18 August 1796, CILTT, pt. 2:489.
121. Deposition of John Barnett, 11 January 1797, DEPS, vol. 3:59.
122. Affidavit of Jessee Embree, 15 January 1798, CILTT, pt. 2:508.
123. Deposition of Solomon Wood, 20 July 1798, DEPS, vol. 2, pt. 2:578; Deposition of George Spann, 1 October 1800, ibid., vol. 2, pt. 2:580; Hawkins, *Collected Works*, 35.

Epilogue

Wilson Lumpkin, *The Removal of the Cherokee Indians from Georgia*, vol. 1 (New York: Dodd, Mead, 1907), 149.

1. Robert G. Thrower, "Causalities and Consequences of the Creek War: A Modern Creek Perspective," in *Tohopeka*, ed. Braund, 10–29; Saunt, *A New Order of Things*, 205–72.
2. A. Hudson, *Creek Paths and Federal Roads*, 39–90.
3. Hawkins, *Collected Works*, 35.
4. Ibid., 56–57, 59, 77.
5. Ibid., 63.
6. Ibid., 65, 71.
7. Ibid., 64–65, 73–74.
8. Ibid., 76.
9. Ibid., 59s, 70s–71s.
10. Ibid., 52–53, 58.
11. Lieutenant Colonel John Watts on behalf of Isaac Brown and family, 10 April 1797, DEPS, vol. 3: 2, 77; Petition of Mary Brown to the Speaker and Representatives in General Assembly, undated, Telamon Cuyler Collection, HAR-DLG.
12. A. Hudson, *Creek Paths and Federal Roads*, 83.
13. Ibid., 44, 55–56, 69–72, 79–80, 83–87.
14. Gregory A. Waselkov, "Fort Jackson and the Aftermath," in *Tohopeka*, ed., Braund, 158.
15. Martin, *Sacred Revolt*, 142–43, 151–55; Saunt, *A New Order of Things*, 254–59; A. Hudson, *Creek Paths and Federal Roads*, 91–120; Thrower, "Causalities and Consequences of the Creek War," 15, 18; Robert P. Collins, "'A Packet from Canada': Telling Conspiracy Stories on the 1813 Creek Frontier," in *Tohopeka*, ed. Braund, 63.
16. Saunt, *A New Order of Things*, 205–29; Ethridge, *Creek Country*, 195–214.
17. Hawkins, *Collected Works*, 27s; Waselkov, *A Conquering Spirit*, 89–90; Nichols, *Red Gentlemen and White Savages*, 178; Ethridge, *Creek Country*, 232–36.
18. Saunt, *A New Order of Things*, 116–35, 164–85, 205–29; Green, *Politics of Indian Removal*, 37–41; Martin, *Sacred Revolt*, 102–8, 110–11, 120–22, 125; Collins, "Conspiracy Stories on the 1813 Creek Frontier," 59.
19. Hawkins, *Collected Works*, 30, 43s–45s; Ethridge, *Creek Country*, 158–74.
20. Collins, "Conspiracy Stories on the 1813 Creek Frontier," 62, 69.
21. Saunt, *A New Order of Things*, 251–54, 270; Martin, *Sacred Revolt*, 133–35; Green, *Politics of Indian Removal*, 41; Collins, "Conspiracy Stories on the 1813 Creek Frontier," 69–70; Waselkov, *A Conquering Spirit*, 89–90; Waselkov, "Fort Jackson and the Aftermath," 158, 165.

22. Hawkins, *Collected Works*, 35s.

23. Ibid., 37s.

24. Hawkins, *Collected Works*, 39s; Shuck-Hall, "Alabama and Coushatta Diaspora," 261.

25. Hawkins, *Collected Works*, 61s–62s.

26. Ibid.

27. Thrower, "Causalities and Consequences of the Creek War," 21; Waselkov, *A Conquering Spirit*, 54.

28. Collins, "Conspiracy Stories on the 1813 Creek Frontier," 69; Braund, ed., *Tohopeka*, 5–6; Martin, *Sacred Revolt*, 133–139; A. Hudson, *Creek Paths and Federal Roads*, 91–120; Saunt, *A New Order of Things*, 236–72; Waselkov, *A Conquering Sprit*, 86–95, 98–102, 110–15, 125–42, 144–49, 160–76.

29. Martin, *Sacred Revolt*, 153.

30. Thrower, "Causalities and Consequences of the Creek War," 17–22, quotes from 21–22.

31. Martin, *Sacred Revolt*, 153–54; Thrower, "Causalities and Consequences of the Creek War," 25–26; Collins, "Conspiracy Stories on the 1813 Creek Frontier," 59–62; A. Hudson, *Creek Paths and Federal Roads*, 117; Waselkov, *A Conquering Spirit*, 142–44, 147–49, 161–76, 177–80, 194–95, 211–12.

32. Lumpkin, *The Removal of the Cherokee Indians from Georgia*, 1:9.

33. Ibid., 18.

34. Ibid., 149.

Bibliography

Abbreviations

ASPIA. American State Papers, Indian Affairs. 2 vols.

CILTT. Creek Indian Letters, Talks, and Treaties, 1705–1839. 4 pts. Georgia Archives.

CRG. The Colonial Records of the State of Georgia. Vols. 1–19, 21–26.

DAR. Documents of the American Revolution, 1770–1783. Colonial Office Series. 21 vols.

DEPS. Indian Depredations, 1787–1825. 5 vols. Georgia Archives.

EAID. Early American Indian Documents: Treaties and Laws, 1607–1789. 20 vols.

ETHSP. "Papers from the Spanish Archives Relating to Tennessee and the Old Southwest, 1783–1800." In *The East Tennessee Historical Society's Publications.* Vols. 9–37.

HAR. Hargrett Rare Book and Manuscript Library. University of Georgia Libraries.

HAR DLG. Hargrett Rare Book and Manuscript Library. University of Georgia Libraries. Presented in the Digital Library of Georgia. http://dlg.galileo.usg.edu/.

ITCL. Indian Treaties, Cessions of Land in Georgia, 1705–1837. Georgia Archives.

LP. The Papers of Henry Laurens. 16 vols.

LTB. Unpublished Letters of Timothy Barnard, 1784–1820. Georgia Archives.

Records of the Creek Agency East. Record Group 75, Records of the Bureau of Indian Affairs. Records of the Creek Agency East, 1794–1818. National Archives and Records Service. Microfilm in Georgia Archives.

Records of the Creek Trading House. Record Group 75, Records of the Bureau of

Indian Affairs. Records of the Creek Trading House, Letter Book, 1795–1816. National Archives and Records Service. Microfilm in Georgia Archives.

RRG. The Revolutionary Records of the State of Georgia. 3 vols.

Shoulderbone Journal. Indian Claims (Treaties and Spoilations), Journal of the Treaty of Shoulderbone. Georgia Archives.

Archival Sources

William L. Clements Library, University of Michigan
Henry Clinton Papers, 1736–1850. 304 vols.
Thomas Gage Papers, 1754–1807. American Series. 139 vols.
Thomas Gage Papers, 1754–1807. English Series. 30 vols.
George Sackville Germain Papers, 1683–1785. 22 vols.

Georgia Archives
Creek Indian Letters, Talks, and Treaties, 1705–1839. 4 pts. Edited by Louise F. [Mrs. J. E.] Hays.
File II.
Indian Claims (Treaties and Spoilations).
Indian Claims (Treaties and Spoilations). Journal of the Treaty of Shoulderbone.
Indian Depredations, 1787–1825. 5 vols. Edited by Louise F. [Mrs. J. E.] Hays.
Indian Treaties, Cessions of Land in Georgia, 1705–1837. Edited by Louise F. [Mrs. J. E.] Hays.
Unpublished Letters of Timothy Barnard, 1784–1820. Edited by Louise F. [Mrs. J. E.] Hays.

Hargrett Rare Book and Manuscript Library, University of Georgia
Telamon Cuyler Collection. Presented in the Digital Library of Georgia. http://dlg.galileo.usg.edu/.
Felix Hargrett Papers. Presented in the Digital Library of Georgia.
Historical Maps Database. "A New and Accurate Map of the Province of Georgia in North America, 1779." In *Universal Magazine* 64 (April 1779): 168. London: J. Hinton. http://dlg.galileo.usg.edu/hmap/id:hmap1779n42.
Keith Read Collection. Presented in the Digital Library of Georgia. http://dlg.galileo.usg.edu/.
C. Mildred Thompson Papers. The University of Georgia Libraries.

Library of Congress, Geography and Map Division
A New and Accurate Map of the province of Georgia in North America. [London?: s.n., 1779]. Map. www.loc.gov/item/2008625108/.

Published Primary Sources

Adair, James. *The History of the American Indians.* Edited by Kathryn E. Holland Braund. Tuscaloosa: University of Alabama Press, 2005.

Articles of Confederation. www.ourdocuments.gov.

Bartram, William. *The Travels of William Bartram: Naturalist's Edition.* Edited by Francis Harper. Editorial material copyright, New Haven: Yale University Press, 1958. Athens: University of Georgia Press, 1998.

———. *William Bartram on the Southeastern Indians.* Edited by Gregory A. Waselkov and Kathryn E. Holland Braund. Lincoln: University of Nebraska Press, 1995.

Candler, Allen D., ed. *The Colonial Records of the State of Georgia.* Vols. 1–19, 21–26. Atlanta: Franklin Printing and Publishing Co., 1904–16. New York: AMS Press, 1970 (includes vols. 20–39). Citations refer to the AMS edition.

———. *The Revolutionary Records of the State of Georgia.* 3 vols. Atlanta: Franklin-Turner, 1908.

Caughey, John Walton, ed. *McGillivray of the Creeks.* Norman: University of Oklahoma Press, 1938.

Corbitt, D. C., ed. and trans. "Papers Relating to the Georgia-Florida Frontier, 1784–1800, IV." *Georgia Historical Quarterly* 21, no. 3 (September 1937): 274–93.

———. "Papers Relating to the Georgie-Florida Frontier, 1784–1800, V." *Georgia Historical Quarterly* 21, no. 4 (December 1937): 373–81.

Corbitt, D. C., and Roberta Corbitt, eds. and trans. "Papers from the Spanish Archives Relating to Tennessee and the Old Southwest, 1783–1800." In *The East Tennessee Historical Society's Publications,* vols. 9–37.

Davies, K. G., ed. *Documents of the American Revolution, 1770–1783.* Colonial Office Series. 21 vols. Dublin: Irish University Press, 1975.

Early American Imprints, Series 1, Evans, 1639–1800. Journal of the Congress of the Four Southern Governors, and the Superintendent of that District, with the Five Nations of Indians, at Augusta, 1763. Charles Town, SC: Printed by Peter Timothy, 1764. no. 9706.

Gazette of the United States. New York. 1789-93.

Georgia Gazette. Savannah. 1763–76, 1788–1802.

Hamer, Philip M., George C. Rogers, and David T. Chesnutt, eds. *The Papers of Henry Laurens.* 16 vols. Columbia: University of South Carolina Press, 1968–2003.

Hawes, Lilla M. "Miscellaneous Papers of James Jackson, 1781–1798, pt. 1." *Georgia Historical Quarterly* 37, no. 1 (March 1953): 54–80.

Hawkins, Benjamin. *The Collected Works of Benjamin Hawkins, 1796–1810.* Edited by Thomas Foster. Tuscaloosa: University of Alabama Press, 2003.

Hill, Roscoe R., ed. *Journals of the Continental Congress, 1774–1789.* Vols. 33–34. Washington, DC: U.S. Government Printing Office, 1936.

Thomas Houghton to George Mathews, 20 May 1794. "An Elijah Clarke Document." *Georgia Historical Quarterly* 14, no. 3 (September 1930): 254–55.

Juricek, John T., ed. *Early American Indian Documents: Treaties and Laws, 1607–1789.* Vol. 12, *Georgia and Florida Treaties, 1763–1776.* Bethesda: University Publications of America, 2002.

Kappler, Charles J., ed. *Indian Affairs: Laws and Treaties.* Vol. 2. Washington, DC: U.S. Government Printing Office, 1904.

Lowrie, Walter, and Matthew St. Clair Clarke, eds. *American State Papers, Documents, Legislative and Executive, of the Congress of the United States, from the First Session of the First to the Third Session of the Thirteenth Congress, Inclusive: Commencing March 3, 1789, and Ending March 3, 1815, Indian Affairs.* 2 vols. Washington, DC: Gales and Seaton, 1832.

———. *American State Papers, Documents, Legislative and Executive, of the Congress of the United States, from the First Session of the First to the Second Session of the Twenty-Second Congress, Inclusive: Commencing March 3, 1789, and Ending March 3, 1833, Foreign Affairs.* 6 vols. Washington, DC: Gales and Seaton, 1833.

Lumpkin, Wilson. *The Removal of the Cherokee Indians from Georgia.* Vol. 1. New York: Dodd, Mead, 1907.

M'Call, Hugh. *The History of Georgia: Containing Brief Sketches of the Most Remarkable Events up to the Present Day* (1784). Vol. 2. Savannah: William T. Williams, 1816.

Mereness, Newton D., ed., under the Auspices of the National Society of the Colonial Dames of America. "David Taitt's Journal of a Journey through the Creek Country, 1772." In *Travels in the American Colonies.* New York: Macmillan, 1916.

Milfort, Louis le Clerc. *Memoirs, or a Quick Glance at My Various Travels and My Sojourn in the Creek Nation.* Translated and edited by Ben C. McCary. 1959. Savannah: Beehive, 1972.

The Pennsylvania Packet and Daily Advertiser. Early American Newspapers Series 1, 1690–1876.

Record Group 75. Records of the Bureau of Indian Affairs. Records of the Creek Agency East, 1794–1818. The National Archives and Records Service. Microfilm in Georgia Archives.

Record Group 75. Records of the Bureau of Indian Affairs. Records of the Creek Trading House. Letter Book, 1795–1816. National Archives and Records Service. Microfilm in Georgia Archives.

Return of the Whole Number of Persons within the Several Districts of the United States, According to "An Act Providing for the Enumeration of the inhabitants of the United States," Passed March First, One Thousand Seven Hundred and

Ninety One. Philadelphia Printed. London Reprinted and Sold by J. Phillips, George-Yard, Lombard-Street, 1793.

Royal Proclamation, 7 October 1763. Avalon Project: Documents in Law, History, and Diplomacy. Lillian Goldman Law Library. Yale Law School. http://avalon.law.yale.edu/18th_century/proc1763.asp.

South Carolina Gazette. Charleston, 1732–82.

Stiggins, George. *Creek Indian History: A Historical Narrative of the Genealogy, Traditions and Downfall of the Ispocoga or Creek Indian Tribe of Indians*. Birmingham: University of Alabama Press, 1989.

Swanton, John R. *Creek Religion and Medicine*. Lincoln: University of Nebraska Press, 2000.

———. *Myths and Tales of the Southeastern Indians*. Norman: University of Oklahoma Press, 1995.

———. "Social Organization and Social Usages of the Indians of the Creek Confederacy." In *Forty-Second Annual Report of the Bureau of American Ethnology to the Secretary of the Smithsonian Institution, 1924–1925*. Washington, DC: U.S. Government Printing Office, 1928.

Vaughn, Alden T., series ed. *Early American Indian Documents: Treaties and Laws, 1607–1789*. Vols. 1–9, 11–20. Washington, DC: University Publications of America, 1979–.

Secondary Sources

Anderson, David G. *The Savannah River Chiefdoms: Political Change in the Late Prehistoric Southeast*. Tuscaloosa: University of Alabama Press, 1994.

Aron, Stephen. *American Confluence: The Missouri Frontier from Borderland to Border State*. Bloomington: Indiana University Press, 2006.

Barksdale, Kevin T. *The Lost State of Franklin: America's First Secession*. Lexington: University of Kentucky Press, 2009.

———. "The State of Franklin: Separatism, Competition, and the Legacy of Tennessee's First State, 1783–1789." In *Before the Volunteer State: New Thoughts on Early Tennessee History, 1540–1800*, edited by Kristofer Ray, 155–84. Knoxville: University of Tennessee Press, 2014.

Barr, Juliana. *Peace Came in the Form of a Woman: Indians and Spaniards in the Texas Borderlands*. Chapel Hill: University of North Carolina Press, 2007.

Basso, Keith H. *Wisdom Sits in Places: Landscape and Language among the Western Apache*. Albuquerque: University of New Mexico Press, 1996.

Beck, Robin A., Jr. "Catawba Coalescence and the Shattering of the Carolina Piedmont, 1540–1675." In *Mapping the Mississippian Shatter Zone: The Colonial Indian Slave Trade and Regional Instability in the American South*, edited by Robbie Ethridge and Sheri M. Shuck-Hall, 115–41. Lincoln: University of Nebraska Press, 2009.

——. *Chiefdoms, Collapse, and Coalescence in the Early American South.* Cambridge: Cambridge University Press, 2013.

Blackhorse, Amanda. "Blackhorse: Do You Prefer 'Native American' or 'American Indian'? 6 Prominent Voices Respond." *Indian Country Today Media Network*, May 21, 2015. http://indiancountrytodaymedianetwork.com.

——. "Blackhorse: 'Native American' or 'American Indian'? 5 More Native Voices Respond." *Indian Country Today Media Network*, July 2, 2015. http://indiancountrytodaymedianetwork.com.

Blitz, John H., and Karl G. Lorenz. *The Chattahoochee Chiefdoms.* Tuscaloosa: University of Alabama Press, 2006.

Bossy, Denise. "Indian Slavery in Southeastern Indian and British Societies, 1670–1730." In *Indian Slavery in Colonial America*, edited by Alan Gallay, 210–13. Lincoln: University of Nebraska Press, 2009.

Boulware, Tyler. *Deconstructing the Cherokee Nation: Town, Region, and Nation among Eighteenth-Century Cherokees.* Gainesville: University Press of Florida, 2011.

Bowne, Eric E. *The Westo Indians: Slave Traders of the Early Colonial South.* Tuscaloosa: University of Alabama Press, 2005.

Braund, Kathryn E. Holland. *Deerskins and Duffels: The Creek Indian Trade with Anglo-America, 1685–1815.* 1993. Lincoln: University of Nebraska Press, 2008.

——. "'Like a Stone Wall Never to Be Broke': The British-Indian Boundary Line with Creek Indians, 1763–1773." In *Britain and the American South from Colonialism to Rock and Roll*, edited by Franklin T. Lambert and Joseph P. Ward. Jackson: University Press of Mississippi, 2003.

——. "'Like to Have Made a War among Ourselves': The Creek Indians and the Coming of the War of Revolution." In *Nexus of Empire: Negotiating Loyalty and Identity in the Revolutionary Borderlands, 1760s–1820s*, edited by Gene Allen Smith and Sylvia L. Hilton. Gainesville: University Press of Florida, 2010.

——. "Reflections on 'Shee Coocys' and the Motherless Child: Creek Women in a Time of War." *Alabama Review* 64, no. 4 (October 2011): 255–84.

——, ed. *Tohopeka: Rethinking the Creek War and the War of 1812.* Tuscaloosa: University of Alabama Press, 2012.

Britton, David. "John Montgomery and the Perils of American Identity in the Mero District, 1780–1795." In *Before the Volunteer State: New Thoughts on Early Tennessee, 1540–1800*, edited by Kristofer Ray, 185–200. Knoxville: University of Tennessee Press, 2014.

Brooks, James F. *Captives and Cousins: Slavery, Kinship, and Community in the Southwest Borderlands.* Chapel Hill: University of North Carolina Press, 2002.

Brown, James, and David H. Dye. "Severed Heads and Sacred Scalplocks: Mississippian Iconographic Trophies." In *The Taking and Displaying of Human*

Body Parts as Trophies by Amerindians, edited by Richard J. Chacon and Dye, 278–98. New York: Springer Science+Business Media, 2007.

Calloway, Colin G. *The American Revolution in Indian Country: Crisis and Diversity in Native Americans Communities*. Cambridge: Cambridge University Press, 1995.

———. *The Victory with No Name: The Native American Defeat of the First American Army*. Oxford: Oxford University Press, 2014.

Carson, James Taylor. "Ethnogeography and the Native American Past." *Ethnohistory* 49, no. 4 (Fall 2002): 769–88.

———. "Horses and the Economy and Culture of the Choctaw Indians, 1690–1840." *Ethnohistory* 42, no. 3 (Summer 1995): 495–513.

———. *Searching for the Bright Path: The Mississippi Choctaws from Prehistory to Removal*. Lincoln: University of Nebraska Press, 1999.

Caruso, John Anthony. *The Appalachian Frontier: America's First Surge Westward*. Indianapolis: Bobbs-Merrill, 1959.

Cashin, Edward J. *The King's Ranger: Thomas Brown and the American Revolution on the Southern Frontier*. Athens: University of Georgia Press, 1989.

———. *Lachlan McGillivray, Indian Trader: The Shaping of the Southern Colonial Frontier*. Athens: University of Georgia Press, 1992.

———. *William Bartram and the American Revolution on the Southern Frontier*. Columbia: University of South Carolina Press, 2000.

Cayton, Andrew R. L., and Fredrika J. Teute, eds. *Contact Points: American Frontiers from the Mohawk Valley to the Mississippi, 1750–1830*. Chapel Hill: University of North Carolina Press, 1998.

Chacon, Richard J., and David H. Dye, eds. *The Taking and Displaying of Human Body Parts as Trophies by Amerindians*. New York: Springer Science+Business Media, 2007.

Chappell, Absalom H. *Miscellanies of Georgia, Historical, Biographical, Descriptive, etc.* Atlanta: Meegan, 1874.

Claesson, Henri J. M., and Peter Skalnik, eds. *The Early State*. The Hague: Mouton, 1978.

Claesson, Henri J. M., and Jarich G. Oosten, eds. *Ideology and the Formation of Early States*. Leiden: Brill, 1996.

Cohen, Ronald, and Elman R. Service, eds. *Origins of the State: The Anthropology of Political Evolution*. Philadelphia: Institute for the Study of Human Issues, 1978.

Collins, Robert P. "'A Packet from Canada': Telling Conspiracy Stories on the 1813 Creek Frontier." In *Tohopeka: Rethinking the Creek War and War of 1812*, edited by Kathryn E. Holland Braund, 53–83. Tuscaloosa: University of Alabama Press, 2012.

Cronon, William. *Changes in the Land: Indians, Colonists, and the Ecology of New England*. New York: Hill and Wang, 1983.

Debo, Angie. *The Road to Disappearance: A History of the Creek Indians*. 1941. 5th printing. Norman: University of Oklahoma Press, 1988.

De Vorsey, Louis, Jr. *The Indian Boundary in the Southern Colonies, 1763–1775*. 1961. Chapel Hill: University of North Carolina Press, 1966.

Donnan, Hastings, and Thomas M. Wilson, eds. *Border Approaches: Anthropological Perspectives on Frontiers*. Lanham, MD: University Press of America, 1994.

Dowd, Gregory Evans. *Groundless: Rumors, Legends, and Hoaxes on the Early American Frontier*. Baltimore: Johns Hopkins University Press, 2015.

———. "The Panic of 1751: The Significance of Rumors on the South Carolina-Cherokee Frontier." *William and Mary Quarterly*, 3rd ser., 53, no. 3 (July 1996): 527–60.

Downes, Randolph C. "Creek-American Relations, 1782–1790." *Georgia Historical Quarterly* 21, no. 2 (June 1937): 142–84.

———. "Creek American Relations, 1790–1795." *Journal of Southern History* 8, no. 3 (August 1942): 350–73.

DuVal, Kathleen. *Independence Lost: Lives on the Edge of the American Revolution*. New York: Random House, 2015.

———. *The Native Ground: Indians and Colonists in the Heart of the Continent*. Philadelphia: University of Pennsylvania Press, 2006.

Dye, David H., and Adam King. "Desecrating the Sacred Ancestor Temples: Chiefly Conflict and Violence in the American Southeast." In *North American Indigenous Warfare and Ritual Violence*, edited by Richard J. Chacon and Rubén G. Mendoza, 160–81. Tucson: University of Arizona Press, 2007.

Ellis, Stephen. "Interpreting Violence: Reflections on West African War." In *Violence*, edited by Neil L. Whitehead, 107–24. Santa Fe: School of American Research Press, 2004.

Ethridge, Robbie. *Creek Country: The Creek Indians and Their World*. Chapel Hill: University of North Carolina Press, 2003.

———. *From Chicaza to Chickasaw: The European Invasion and the Transformation of the Mississippian World, 1540–1715*. Chapel Hill: University of North Carolina Press, 2010.

———. "The Making of a Militaristic Slaving Society: The Chickasaws and the Colonial Indian Slave Trade." In *Indian Slavery in Colonial America*, edited by Alan Gallay, 251–76. Lincoln: University of Nebraska Press, 2009.

Ethridge, Robbie, and Sheri M. Shuck-Hall, eds. *Mapping the Mississippian Shatter Zone: The Colonial Indian Slave Trade and Regional Instability in the American South*. Lincoln: University of Nebraska Press, 2009.

Ferguson, R. Brian, and Neil L. Whitehead, eds. *War in the Tribal Zone: Expanding States and Indigenous Warfare*. Santa Fe: School of American Research Press, 2001.

Ford, Lisa. *Settler Sovereignty: Jurisdiction and Indigenous People in America and Australia, 1788–1836*. Cambridge: Harvard University Press, 2010.

Foster, H. Thomas, II. *Archaeology of the Lower Muskogee Creek Indians, 1715–1836*. Tuscaloosa: University of Alabama Press, 2007.

——. "The Yuchi Indians along the Chattahoochee and Flint Rivers (1715–1836): A Synthesis." In *Yuchi Indian Histories before the Removal Era*, edited by Jason Baird Jackson, 101–22. Lincoln: University of Nebraska Press, 2012.

Frank, Andrew. *Creeks and Southerners: Biculturalism on the Early American Frontier*. Lincoln: University of Nebraska Press, 2005.

Gallay, Alan. *The Formation of a Planter Elite: Jonathan Bryan and the Southern Colonial Frontier*. Athens: University of Georgia Press, 1989.

——. *The Indian Slave Trade: The Rise of the English Empire in the American South, 1670–1717*. New Haven: Yale University Press, 2002.

——, ed. *Indian Slavery in Colonial America*. Lincoln: University of Nebraska Press, 2009.

Galloway, Patricia. *Practicing Ethnohistory: Mining Archives, Hearing Testimony, Constructing Narrative*. Lincoln: University of Nebraska Press, 2006.

Gildrie, Richard. "Tennessee in the American Revolution: A Reconsideration." In *Before the Volunteer State: New Thoughts on Early Tennessee History, 1540–1800*, edited by Kristofer Ray, 109–29. Knoxville: University of Tennessee Press, 2014.

Green, Michael D. "Alexander McGillivray." In *American Indian Leaders: Studies in Diversity*, edited by R. David Edmunds, 41–63. Lincoln: University of Nebraska Press, 1980.

——. "The Creek Confederacy in the American Revolution: Cautious Participants." In *Anglo-Spanish Confrontation on the Gulf Coast during the American Revolution*, Proceedings of the Gulf Coast History and Humanities Conference, edited by William S. Coker and Robert Right Rea, 54–75. Pensacola, Fla.: Gulf Coast History and Humanities Conference, 1982.

——. *The Politics of Indian Removal: Creek Government and Society in Crisis*. Lincoln: University of Nebraska Press, 1982.

Grenier, John. *The First Way of War: American War Making on the Frontier, 1607–1814*. Cambridge: Cambridge University Press, 2005.

Haas, Jonathan. *The Evolution of the Prehistoric State*. New York: Columbia University Press, 1982.

Hahn, Steven C. "The Cussita Migration Legend: History, Ideology, and the Politics of Mythmaking." In *Light on the Path: The Anthropology and History of the Southeastern Indians*, edited by Thomas J. Pluckhahn and Robbie Ethridge, 57–93. Tuscaloosa: University of Alabama Press, 2006.

——. *The Invention of the Creek Nation, 1670–1763*. Lincoln: University of Nebraska Press, 2004.

——. "'They Look upon the Yuchis as Their Vassals': An Early History of Yuchi-Creek Political Relations." In *Yuchi Indian Histories before the Removal Era*, edited by Jason Baird Jackson, 123–53. Lincoln: University of Nebraska Press, 2012.

Hall, Joseph M. *Zamumo's Gifts: Indian-European Exchange in the Colonial Southeast*. Philadelphia: University of Pennsylvania Press, 2009.

Hall, Leslie. *Land and Allegiance in Revolutionary Georgia*. Athens: University of Georgia Press, 2001.

Hally, David J. "Mississippian Shell Gorgets in Regional Perspective." In *Southeastern Ceremonial Complex: Chronology, Content, Context*, edited by Adam King. Tuscaloosa: University of Alabama Press, 2007.

Hamer, Friedrich Peter. "Indian Traders, Land and Power: Comparative Study of George Galphin on the Southern Frontier and Three Northern Traders." Master's thesis, University of South Carolina, 1982.

Harrell, Kevin Thomas. "Creek Corridors of Commerce: Converging Empires, Cultural Arbitration, and the Recourse of Gulf Coast Trade." Ph.D. diss., University of Mississippi, 2013.

———. "The Terrain of Factionalism: How Upper Creek Communities Negotiated the Recourse of Gulf Coast Trade, 1763–1780." *Alabama Review* 68, no. 1 (January 2015): 74–113.

Hatley, Thomas M. *The Dividing Paths: Cherokees and South Carolinians through the Era of Revolution*. New York: Oxford University Press, 1993.

Hays, Louise Frederick. *Hero of the Hornet's Nest: A Biography of Elijah Clark, 1733 to 1799*. New York: Stratford House, 1946.

Hilfrich, Fabian. "The Corruption of Civic Virtue by Emotion: Anti-Imperialist Fears in the Debate on the Philippine-American War (1899–1902)." In *Emotions in American History: An International Assessment*, edited by Jessica C. E. Gienow-Hect, 51–65. New York: Berghahn, 2010.

Holland, Kathryn. "The Anglo-Spanish Contest for the Gulf Coast as Viewed from the Townsquare." In *Anglo-Spanish Confrontation on the Gulf Coast during the American Revolution*, Proceedings of the Gulf Coast History and Humanities Conference, edited by William S. Coker and Robert Right Rea, 90–105. Pensacola, Fla.: Gulf Coast History and Humanities Conference, 1982.

Horsman, Reginald. *Expansion and American Indian Policy, 1783–1812*. Lansing: Michigan State University Press, 1967.

Hudson, Angela Pulley. *Creek Paths and Federal Roads: Indians Settlers and Slaves and the Making of the American South*. Chapel Hill: University of North Carolina Press, 2010.

Hudson, Charles. *The Southeastern Indians*. Knoxville: University of Tennessee Press, 1976.

———. *Conversations with the High Priest of Coosa*. Chapel Hill: University of North Carolina Press, 2003.

Inman, Natalie. "Military Families: Kinship in the American Revolution." In *Before the Volunteer State: New Thoughts on Early Tennessee, 1540–1800*, edited by Kristofer Ray, 131–54. Knoxville: University of Tennessee Press, 2014.

Jackson, Jason Baird, ed. *Yuchi Indian Histories before the Removal Era.* Lincoln: University of Nebraska Press, 2012.

Jacobi, Keith P. "Disabling the Dead: Human Trophy Taking in the Prehistoric Southeast." In *The Taking and Displaying of Human Body Parts*, edited by Richard J. Chacon and David H. Dye, 299–338. New York: Springer Science+Business Media, 2007.

Jenkins, Ned J. "Tracing the Origins of the Early Creeks, 1050–1700 CE." In *Mapping the Mississippian Shatter Zone: The Colonial Indian Slave Trade and Regional Instability in the American South*, edited by Robbie Ethridge and Sheri M. Shuck-Hall, 188–249. Lincoln: University of Nebraska Press, 2009

Jennings, Matthew. *New Worlds of Violence: Cultures and Conquests in the Early American Southeast.* Knoxville: University of Tennessee Press, 2011.

Jennison, Watson W. *Cultivating Race: The Expansion of Slavery in Georgia, 1750–1860.* Lexington: University of Kentucky Press, 2012.

Juricek, John T. *Endgame for Empire: British-Creek Relations in Georgia and Vicinity, 1763–1776.* Gainesville, University Press of Florida, 2015.

King, Adam. "Creek Chiefdoms at the Temporal Edge of the Mississippian World." *Southeastern Archaeology* 21, no. 2 (Winter 2002): 221–26.

———. *Etowah: The Political History of a Chiefdom Capital.* Tuscaloosa: University of Alabama Press, 2003.

———. "The Historic Period Transformation of Mississippian Societies." In *Light on the Path: The Anthropology and History of the Southeastern Indians*, edited by Thomas J. Pluckhahn and Robbie Ethridge, 179–95. Tuscaloosa: University of Alabama Press, 2006.

Kevin Kokomoor. "'Let Us Try to Make Each Other Happy, and Not Wretched:' The Creek-Georgian Frontier, 1776–1796." Ph.D. diss., Florida State University, 2013.

Krohn-Hansen, Christian, and Knut G. Nustad, eds. *State Formation: Anthropological Perspectives.* London: Pluto, 2005.

Kwachka, Patricia B., ed. *Perspectives on the Southeast: Linguistics, Archaeology, and Ethnohistory.* Athens: University of Georgia Press, 1994.

Lakomäki, Sami. *Gathering Together: The Shawnee People through Diaspora and Nationhood, 1600–1870.* New Haven: Yale University Press, 2014.

Lee, Wayne E. "Fortify, Fight, or Flee: Tuscarora and Cherokee Defensive Warfare and Military Culture Adaptation." *Journal of Military History* 86 (2004): 713–70.

———. "Peace Chiefs and Blood Revenge: Patterns of Restraint in Native American Warfare, 1500–1800." *Journal of Military History* 71 (July 2007): 701–41.

Loughridge, R. M., and David M. Hodge. *English and Muskokee Dictionary.* St. Louis: Printing House of J. T. Smith, 1890.

Martin, Jack. "Modeling Language Contact in the Prehistory of the Southeastern United States." In *Perspectives on the Southeast: Linguistics, Archaeol-*

ogy, and Ethnohistory, edited by Patricia B. Kwachka. Athens: University of Georgia Press, 1994.

Martin, Jack B., and Margaret McKane Mauldin. *A Dictionary of Creek/Muskogee with Notes on the Florida and Oklahoma Seminole Dialects of Creek*. Lincoln: University of Nebraska Press, 2000.

Martin, Joel W. *Sacred Revolt: The Muskogees' Struggle for a New World*. Boston: Beacon, 1991.

McEwan, Bonnie G. "The Apalachee Indians of Northwest Florida." In *Indians of the Greater Southeast: Historical Archaeology and Ethnohistory*, edited by McEwan, 57–84. Gainesville: University Press of Florida, 2000.

———, ed. *Indians of the Greater Southeast: Historical Archaeology and Ethnohistory*. Gainesville: University Press of Florida, 2000.

Merrell, James H. *The Indians' New World: Catawbas and Their Neighbors from European Contact through the Era of Removal*. Chapel Hill: University of North Carolina Press, 1989.

Miles, Tiya. *Ties That Bind: The Story of an Afro-Cherokee Family in Slavery and Freedom*. 2nd ed. Oakland: University of California Press, 2015.

Milne, George Edward. *Natchez Country: Indians, Colonists, and the Landscapes of Race in French Louisiana*. Athens: University of Georgia Press, 2015.

Nichols, David Andrew. *Red Gentlemen and White Savages: Indians, Federalists, and the Search for Order on the American Frontier*. Charlottesville: University of Virginia Press, 2008.

Nicklas, T. Dale. "Linguistic Provinces of the Southeast at the Time of Columbus." In *Perspectives on the Southeast: Linguistics, Archaeology, and Ethnohistory*, edited by Patricia B. Kwachka. Athens: University of Georgia Press, 1994.

Nooe, Evan. "Common Justice: Vengeance and Retribution in Creek Country." *Ethnohistory* 62, no. 2 (April 2015): 241–61.

O'Brien, Greg. *Choctaws in a Revolutionary Age, 1750–1830*. Lincoln: University of Nebraska Press, 2002.

———. "Protecting Trade through War: Choctaw Elites and the British Occupation of the Floridas." In *Pre-Removal Choctaw History: Exploring New Paths*, edited by O'Brien. Norman: University of Oklahoma Press, 2008.

O'Donnell, J. H. "Alexander McGillivray: Training for Leadership, 1777–1783." *Georgia Historical Quarterly* 49, no. 2 (June 1965): 172–86.

Paulett, Robert. *An Empire of Small Places: Mapping the Southeastern Anglo-Indian Trade, 1732–1795*. Athens: University of Georgia Press, 2012.

Perdue, Theda. *Cherokee Women: Gender and Culture Change, 1700–1835*. Lincoln: University of Nebraska Press, 1998.

Piecuch, Jim. *Three Peoples, One King: Loyalists, Indians, and Slaves in the Revolutionary South, 1775–1782*. Columbia: University of South Carolina Press, 2008.

Piker, Joshua. "Colonists and Creeks: Rethinking the Pre-Revolutionary Southern Backcountry." *Journal of Southern History* 70, no. 3 (August 2004): 503–40.

———. *The Four Deaths of Acorn Whistler: Telling Stories in Colonial America.* Cambridge: Harvard University Press, 2013.

———. "Lying Together: The Imperial Implications of Cross-Cultural Untruths." *American Historical Review* 116, no. 4 (October 2011): 964–86.

———. *Okfuskee: A Creek Indian Town in Colonial America.* Cambridge: Harvard University Press, 2004.

———. "To the Backcountry and Back Again: The Yuchi's Search for Stability in the Eighteenth-Century Southeast." In *Yuchi Indian Histories before the Removal Era*, edited by Jason Baird Jackson, 189–213. Lincoln: University of Nebraska Press, 2012.

———. "'White & Clean' & Contested: Creek Towns and Trading Paths in the Aftermath of the Seven Years' War." *Ethnohistory* 50, no. 2 (Spring 2003): 315–47.

Ray, Kristofer, ed. *Before the Volunteer State: New Thoughts on Early Tennessee History, 1540–1800.* Knoxville: University of Tennessee Press, 2014.

———. *Middle Tennessee, 1775–1825.* Knoxville: University of Tennessee Press, 2007.

Regnier, Amanda L. *Reconstructing Tascalusa's Chiefdom: Pottery Styles and the Social Composition of Late Mississippian Communities along the Alabama River.* Tuscaloosa: University of Alabama Press, 2014.

Reid, John Phillip. *A Law of Blood: The Primitive Law of the Cherokee Nation.* 1970. DeKalb: Northern Illinois University Press, 2006.

Reilly, F. Kent, III. "People of the Earth, People of the Sky: Visualizing the Sacred in Native American Art of the Mississippian Period." In *Hero, Hawk, and Open Hand: American Indian Art of the Ancient Midwest and South*, edited by Richard F. Townsend and Robert V. Sharp, 125–37. Chicago: Art Institute of Chicago, 2004.

Rice, Thaddeus Brokett. *History of Greene County, Georgia, 1786–1886.* Macon, GA: Burke, 1961.

Rindfleisch, Bryan. "'Our Lands Are Our Life and Breath': Coweta, Cusseta, and the Struggle for Creek Territory and Sovereignty during the American Revolution." *Ethnohistory* 60, no. 4 (Fall 2013): 581–603.

———. "The 'Owner of the Town Ground, Who Overrules All When on the Spot': Escotchaby of Coweta and the Politics of Personal Networking in Creek Country, 1740–1780." *Native South* 9 (2016): 54–88.

Roth, Randolph. *American Homicide.* Cambridge: Belknap Press of Harvard University Press, 2009.

Rothman, Adam. *Slave Country: American Expansion and the Origins of the Deep South.* Cambridge: Harvard University Press, 2005.

Saunt, Claudio. "The Native South: An Account of Recent Historiography." *Native South* 1 (2008): 45–60.

———. *A New Order of Things: Property, Power, and the Transformation of the Creek Indians, 1733–1816.* Cambridge: Cambridge University Press, 1999.

———. *West of the Revolution: An Uncommon History of 1776.* New York: Norton, 2014.

Shuck-Hall, Sheri M. "Alabama and Coushatta Diaspora and Coalescence in the Mississippian Shatter Zone." In *Mapping the Mississippian Shatter Zone: The Colonial Indian Slave Trade and Regional Instability in the American South,* edited by Robbie Ethridge and Shuck-Hall, 250–71. Lincoln: University of Nebraska Press, 2009

Silver, Peter. *Our Savage Neighbors: How Indian War Transformed Early America.* New York: Norton, 2008.

Smith, Marvin T. *Coosa: The Rise and Fall of a Southeastern Mississippian Chiefdom.* Gainesville: University of Florida Press, 2000.

Snyder, Christina. *Slavery in Indian Country: The Changing Face of Captivity in Early America.* Cambridge: Harvard University Press, 2010.

Spence, Richard Douglas. "John Donelson and the Opening of the Old Southwest." *Tennessee Historical Quarterly* 50, no. 3 (1991): 157–72.

St. Jean, Wendy. "How the Chickasaws Saved the Cumberland Settlement in the 1790s." *Tennessee Historical Quarterly* 68, no. 1 (2009): 2–19.

Stern, Alexandra Minna. *Eugenic Nation: Faults and Frontiers of Better Breeding in Modern America.* Berkeley: University of California Press, 2005.

Sweet, Julie Anne. *Negotiating for Georgia: British-Creek Relations in the Trustee Era, 1733–1752.* Athens: University of Georgia Press, 2005.

Taylor, Alan. *American Revolutions: A Continental History, 1750–1804.* New York: Norton, 2016.

Thrower, Robert G. "Causalities and Consequences of the Creek War: A Modern Creek Perspective." In *Tohopeka: Rethinking the Creek War and War of 1812,* edited by Kathryn E. Holland Braund, 10–29. Tuscaloosa: University of Alabama Press, 2012.

Usner, Daniel H. *Indians, Settlers and Slaves in a Frontier Exchange Economy: The Lower Mississippi Valley before 1783.* Chapel Hill: University of North Carolina Press, 1992.

Wallerstein, Immanuel. *The Modern World System: Capitalist Agriculture and the Origin of the European World Economy in the Sixteenth Century.* New York: Academic Press, 1974.

Warren, Stephen. *The Worlds the Shawnees Made: Migration and Violence in Early America.* Chapel Hill: University of North Carolina Press, 2014.

Waselkov, Gregory A. *A Conquering Spirit: Fort Mims and the Redstick War of 1813–1814.* Tuscaloosa: University of Alabama Press, 2006.

———. "Fort Jackson and the Aftermath." In *Tohopeka: Rethinking the Creek War and War of 1812,* edited by Kathryn E. Holland Braund, 158–69. Tuscaloosa: University of Alabama Press, 2012.

Waselkov, Gregory A., and Marvin T. Smith. "Upper Creek Archaeology." In *Indi-*

ans of the Greater Southeast: Historical Archaeology and Ethnohistory, edited by Bonnie G. McEwan, 242–64. Gainesville: University Press of Florida, 2000.

Weber, David J. *The Spanish Frontier in North America*. New Haven: Yale University Press, 1992.

Wesson, Cameron. "Creek and Pre-Creek Revisited." In *The Archaeology of Traditions: Agency and History Before and After Columbus*, edited by Timothy Pauketat, 94–106. Gainesville: University Press of Florida, 2001.

———. "Prestige Goods, Symbolic Capital, and Social Power in the Protohistoric Southeast." In *Between Contacts and Colonies: Archaeological Perspectives on the Protohistoric Southeast*, edited by Wesson and Mark A. Rees, 110–25. Tuscaloosa: University of Alabama Press, 2002.

———. *Households and Hegemony: Early Creek Prestige Goods, Symbolic Capital, and Social Power*. Lincoln: University of Nebraska Press, 2008.

———. "When Moral Economies and Capitalism Meet: Creek Factionalism and the Colonial Southeastern Frontier." In *Across a Great Divide: Continuity and Change in Native North American Societies, 1400–1900*, edited by Laura L. Scheiber and Mark D. Mitchell, 61–78. Tucson: University of Arizona Press, 2010.

Wesson, Cameron B., J. A. Wall, and D. W. Chase. "A Spaghetti Style Gorget from the Jere Shine Site (1MT6), Montgomery County, Alabama." *Journal of Alabama Archaeology* 47, no. 2 (2001): 132-152.

White, Richard. *The Middle Ground: Indians, Empires, and Republics in the Great Lakes Region, 1650–1815*. Cambridge: Cambridge University Press, 1991.

Whitehead, Neil L. "On the Poetics of Violence." In *Violence*, edited by Whitehead, 55–78. Santa Fe: School of American Research Press, 2004.

———, ed. *Violence*. Santa Fe: School of American Research Press, 2004.

Wright, J. Leitch, Jr. *Creeks and Seminoles: The Destruction and Regeneration of the Muscogulge People*. Lincoln: University of Nebraska Press, 1986.

———. *William Augustus Bowles, Director General of the Creek Nation*. Athens: University of Georgia Press, 1967.

Wood, Gordon S. *Empire of Liberty: A History of the Early Republic, 1789–1815*. Oxford: Oxford University Press, 2009.

Wood, Peter H. "The Changing Population of the Colonial South: An Overview by Race and Region, 1685–1790." In *Powhatan's Mantle: Indians in the Colonial Southeast*, edited by Gregory A. Waselkov, Wood, and Tom Hatley. 1989. Lincoln: University of Nebraska Press, 2006.

Worth, John E. "Enigmatic Origins: On the Yuchi of the Contact Era." In *Yuchi Indian Histories before the Removal Era*, edited by Jason Baird Jackson, 33–41. Lincoln: University of Nebraska Press, 2012.

———. "The Lower Creeks: Origins and Early History." In *Indians of the Greater Southeast: Historical Archaeology and Ethnohistory*, edited by Bonnie G. McEwan, 265–98. Gainesville: University Press of Florida, 2000.

Index

Treaty of Shoulderbone Creek (1786), 127–8, 246n141; demand Georgians' adherence to treaties, 94, 97, 113, 128, 135, 142–43, 147, 180–81, 202; dominate Lower Towns with Coweta, 21, 41–42; economic interests, 159, 162–63, 172; headmen oppose border patrols, 53, 56–57, 110–12, 114, 123, 163–65, 167, 170–76, 184, 185–87, 202, 235n130, 236n15, 237n16; relations with Spain, 124, 165; relations with Upper Towns, 39, 42, 143; support for border patrols, 47–53, 56–57, 94, 113, 136, 145–46, 181, 198. *See also specific leaders*

Deerskin Trade. *See* Trade
Diplomacy: and American Revolution, 65–71, 79–82, 86–87; Creek color symbolism in, 34, 58, 68–69, 82, 87, 99–100, 111–12, 135–36, 175, 235n130, 236n15; Creek leadership and, 2–6, 11–12; Creek metaphorical language in, 68–69, 86–87, 95–96, 240n103; Creeks demand Georgians' adherence to treaty terms, 90–91, 94–101, 138; and execution, 37–38, 46–59, 61, 73, 172–73; neutrality or play-off diplomacy in, 11, 63–75, 83; reciprocal exchange in, 11, 23, 31–32, 35, 41–43, 54–55, 64–65, 68–70, 72–74, 76–83, 87, 89, 91, 94–95, 97, 99, 103, 111–12, 136, 159, 163, 165, 175–76, 184–85, 187, 189, 195; relations with other Native Americans, 165–67; scholarship, 12–13; and U.S.-Georgia conflict, 182–84. *See also* Crying blood; Government, Creek; Violence; Talwa autonomy; Spain; *specific treaties*

Efau Hadjo (Mad Dog) of Tuckabatchee, 110, 113, 151–52, 167, 176, 183–84, 241n3
Emistisiguo of Little Tallassee: 40–43, 57, 90; acting as national executive, 22, 27–35, 39, 44, 54–55, 107, 166; acting as talwa leader, 53–55, 227n38, 230n126; and American Revolution, 68, 74, 82
Escotchaby of Coweta, 30–31, 39–44, 47, 50, 52, 54, 57, 61, 62, 65, 99, 111, 171

Firearms. *See* guns
Florida, East: 12; under British rule, 11, 29–30, 53, 59, 69–70, 73–74, 82–83; under

Spanish rule, 46, 82–84, 91, 96, 99, 102, 154, 156–57, 159, 162, 167, 174, 180, 204
Florida, West: 12; under British rule, 11, 22–27, 30–33, 36, 40, 42, 53–55, 62, 79, 82; under Spanish rule, 79–81, 84–85, 91, 99, 103, 106, 117–18, 127, 131, 134, 136, 156
Forts: in American Revolution, 70–71, 73, 76–77; Fort Clark, 133; Fort Fidius, 180, 182–84; Fort Mims, 206; Fort Picolata, 29, 69–70; Irwin's Fort, 133, 148; Marbary's Fort, 67, 75; in Oconee valley, 43, 59, 140, 145, 155, 164, 171, 187, 207; in Oconee War, 140, 145, 147–50; Scull Shoals Station, 133, 145, 148. *See also,* Maps, xi, esp. Map 8, 149
Franklin settlements, 85, 106, 122–24, 131, 134, 150, 170
Fusihatchee Micco (White Bird Tail King) acting as national executive, 189–92, 198; of Cussita, 180–81, 255n17
Fusihatchee, 94, 171, 230n126, 235n130, 236–7n15, 246–7n141

Galphin, George: in American Revolution, 65, 69–75, 77–79, 83, 112; as trader, 30–31, 39, 47, 56–57, 65
Galphin, John: and the American Revolution, 65, 79; as border patroller, 113, 166–67, 170–75, 179; as culture broker, 112–13, 118, 135
Generational tension: and American Revolution, 71, 263n2; and communal land ownership, 29–30, 165; customary in Creek society, 2–5, 10–13, 21, 201–4; and diplomacy, 26, 179–80, 188–89, 192–95, 198–99; and Oconee War, 131, 135–36, 139–41; in resistance to land cessions, 90, 97, 100, 110, 115–16, 128, 170–73, 177; and trade, 31, 39–43. *See also* Crying blood, Mad young men, White-Sherrill affair
Georgians: relations with the United States, 2–3, 134, 146–47, 173–76, 178–86, 189–95, 202; trespass in Creek country, 10–12, 14, 22–23, 25–26, 30–31, 33–36, 38, 44–45, 49, 51–52, 62, 75, 77–78, 82–83, 85–86, 90–91, 94–101, 103–5, 117, 120, 122–23, 125–26, 128, 135–39, 144, 148, 152, 155–56, 158, 165–66, 171, 179, 183, 191–95, 197–99, 202. *See also* Theft, Violence
Gifts. *See* Diplomacy, reciprocal exchange in

Leadership. *See* Government, Creek
Little Tallassee: 4, 39–40, 95, 146; and
  Alexander McGillivray, 74, 79, 82, 86,
  90–91, 151–52, 154; and Emistisiguo,
  22, 27–28, 30–31, 39–40, 53, 55, 59, 68,
  82, 227n38, 230n126; and American
  Revolution, 65, 68, 73–74, 79, 82; assent
  to Treaty of Augusta (1773), 39–40;
  assent to Treaty of New York (1790),
  151–52, 156–58, 255n17; assent to Treaty
  of Savannah (1774), 230n126; demand
  Georgians' adherence to treaty terms,
  48; economic interests, 28, 30, 74, 91;
  headmen oppose border patrols, 53, 55,
  59, 227n38; support for border patrols,
  30–31, 73, 83, 110, 127, 134
Livestock, 22, 27, 40, 145, 163, 166–67, 171,
  187, 191, 193, 199, 202–3. *See also* Cattle,
  Horses, Theft
Lower Eufaula, 27, 57, 113
Lower Towns (Lower Creeks), defined,
  11–12, 17, 19–21, 40–41. *See also*
  Apalachicola province; Government,
  Creek; Land; *specific towns*

Mad Turkey, 54, 56, 58–59, 69
Mad young men: Creek, 34, 50–51,
  105–7, 110, 112, 114, 116, 140, 170,
  192, 203; Georgia, 173–74; in the
  American Revolution, 80–81. *See also*
  Generational Tension, Theft, Violence
McGillivray, Alexander: 1–2, 13, 74, 76,
  79–80, 82; envisions a Creek Nation,
  85–86, 90–91, 94, 96–98, 100–104, 107,
  111, 115, 117–18, 124, 127, 131, 137, 152–53,
  156–57, 164–65
Micco, 3–5, 11, 240n103. *See also*
  Generational tension; Government,
  Creek
Miculasa (Mucclassee), 18–9, 230n126
Mississippian Chiefdoms, 3–5, 17–20, 27–
  28, 35, 38, 41, 205
Mississippian culture, 3–5, 7, 10–11, 17, 19–
  20, 28, 35, 94, 139–40
Mobile, 12, 23–28, 32–33, 41, 43, 79, 85, 95,
  118–19, 134, 156, 165. *See also*, Florida,
  West
Mortar of Oakchoy, 34, 42, 55
Muscle Shoals, 144, 149, 184–85
Muskogee language speakers. *See*
  Languages

Nashville. *See* Cumberland River
  settlements
Natchez: Creek talwa, 3, 19, 21, 206; Euro-
  American settlement, 85, 102, 106;
  Mississippian Chiefdom, 19
Nation, Creek: as problematic term, 17, 20–
  21, 29; as envisioned by Creeks, 10, 20–
  21, 27–33, 39, 85–86, 90–91, 94, 96–98,
  100–104, 107, 111, 115, 117–18, 124, 127, 131,
  137, 152–53, 156–57, 164–65, 179, 186–95,
  199; term used by Euro-Americans, 25,
  55–56, 134, 151, 170. *See also*, Government,
  Creek; Land; Sovereignty
Neha Micco of Cussita (Fat King), 86, 94,
  96, 101, 113, 123, 128, 135–36, 142–43, 147,
  188, 236n8, 237nn16, 29, 240n119
New Orleans, 55, 61, 84, 118, 162, 165
New Purchase. *See* Ceded Lands
Niligee (Chewacla Warrior of Coweta,
  Head Warrior of Coweta), 40–44, 52,
  69–70

O'Neill, Arturo, Governor of Spanish West
  Florida, 99, 103, 118–19, 136, 241n3
Oakchoy, 34, 42, 55, 65, 73, 142–43
Ochtullkee, 47–49, 55–57, 59, 173, 226n14
Ocmulgee River, 47, 89, 94, 139, 142, 144,
  164, 172, 176, 180, 194
Ocmulgee town, 52, 56, 116, 230n126,
  240n119
Oconee River valley: defined, 7, 11–14;
  spiritual value, 13–14, 257n44
Oconee town, 56–57, 237n16
Oconee War, 1–2, 12, 130–54
Ogeechee River, 7, 12, 21, 33–37, 43, 47–48,
  73–74, 78, 101, 148
Okfuskee province, defined, 17, 19, 29. *See
  also* Government, Creek; Land; *specific
  towns*; Talwa autonomy
Okfuskee town: and American Revolution,
  65, 69, 72–74, 78, 83; assent to Treaty of
  Colerain (1796), 190–91; assent to Treaty
  of Galphinton (1785), 102, 240n119;
  economic interest, 19, 87, 159, 162, 165–
  66, in diplomacy, 54, 58; reject Treaty
  of Augusta (1773), 42, 47–48; relations
  with Spain, 118; support for border
  patrols, 36; victims of Georgians'
  violence, 170, 176–78
Ooseechee, 38, 52, 110, 116, 118, 159, 162–63,
  165, 171–72, 175–76, 187, 190

135, 137–51, 164–65, 167, 170–71, 174–76,
179, 181, 184, 187–88, 198, 203, 205–6,
226n14, 241n3, 251n111; committed by
Georgians against Creeks, 7, 34, 38, 53–
54, 60, 69–70, 73, 76–78, 80–81, 83, 106,
114–17, 126, 128, 130, 139, 142–43, 152–54,
173–78, 180–82, 185–89, 198, 205, 229n86,
267n118; committed by Georgians
against other Euro-Americans, 74, 76,
78, 80, 103, 153–55; Creek oncepts of,
6–7, 10, 45–47, 56, 57, 60, 106, 113–14, 122,
137, 179, 185, 194, 199; dearth of Creek
violence, 7, 15, 21–23, 38, 63–64, 90,
97–99, 102–3, 105, 110–11, 135, 138, 199;
defines Creek-Georgia relations, 12–13,
21, 157, 188–89, 199; Euro-American
concepts of, 45–46, 59, 60, 182, 192;
exaggerations of Creek violence, 1–3,
6, 10, 14–15, 36–37, 52–53, 60, 63, 112,
119–26, 128, 134, 151, 181, 201–2, 206–7.
See also Captive taking, Crying blood,
Slaves, Scalping, War

War: Border patrols as substitute for, 10,
122, 141, 192; Creek concepts of, 2–6, 7,
14–15, 28, 30, 34, 46, 74, 91, 122–23, 128,
135, 137, 139–41, 192, 202–3; Creek threats
of, 39–40, 97, 100, 107; Euro-American
concepts of, 1–2, 6, 7, 14–15, 122–23, 139,
141, 143, 147, 192; Georgians' attitudes
toward, 59–60, 63, 77, 81, 87–88, 119–24,
134, 141, 174, 176. *See also* Crying blood,
Generational tension, Scalping, Violence
War honors, 2–6, 10, 28, 34, 91, 128, 135, 137,
139, 202–3
White beads. *See* Diplomacy, color
symbolism in
White Lieutenant of Okfuskee (Stochlicta,
Taskina Hutke), 42, 87, 165–66, 176–77
White wings. *See* Diplomacy, color
symbolism in
White, William. *See* White-Sherrill affair
White-Sherrill affair, 45–62, 64, 75, 111
Wind clan. *See* kinship
Women, Creek: and diplomacy, 30–33;
and kinship, 6, 19, 21, 28, 57, 91,
112–13, 174, 205; and trade, 42; and
war, 40, 80, 150–51, 176–77. *See also*
Kinship

Yahola Micco of Coweta (Hallowing King),
73–74, 100, 103, 110, 128, 142–43, 147,
151–52, 165, 188, 193, 240n103
Young men. *See* Generational conflict,
Mad young men
Yuchi language speakers. *See* languages
Yuchi town, 5, 20, 27, 57, 115, 157, 163–64,
185–87, 190, 205–6, 218n43

CPSIA information can be obtained
at www.ICGtesting.com
Printed in the USA
LVHW091956110921
697539LV00036B/548